CAMBRIDGE HISTORICAL SERIES

LATIN AMERICA

THE MACMILLAN COMPANY
NEW YORK · BOSTON · CHICAGO · DALLAS
ATLANTA · SAN FRANCISCO

LATIN AMERICA

A Brief History

BY

F. A. KIRKPATRICK, M.A.

EMERITUS READER IN SPANISH IN
THE UNIVERSITY OF CAMBRIDGE

NEW YORK: THE MACMILLAN COMPANY

CAMBRIDGE, ENGLAND: AT THE UNIVERSITY PRESS

1939

CONTENTS

vi CONTENTS

ILLUSTRATIONS

PLATES

MAPS

PREFACE

To tell in one short volume the history of two empires for three centuries, and of twenty states for a century and a quarter, is not easy. The first typescript of this volume far exceeded possible limits. Much has been reluctantly scrapped, and much condensed. Thus, only a few pages have been allotted, in Chapter IV, to a large subject, the Spanish Empire in America: that subject has been more fully treated by the present writer in *The Cambridge Modern History*, vol. x, chapter 8.

Some dislike the now familiar term 'Latin America', as not accurately descriptive. This objection seems to confuse a name— a convenient and generally accepted label—with a descriptive definition. The terms Amazonas, Costa Rica, Venezuela ('little Venice'), Rio de la Plata, Rio de Janeiro (which is river-less), were originally attempts—unsatisfactory attempts—at description. They remain as convenient names, their signification forgotten. On the other hand confusion has arisen from treating the political term 'Central America' as a geographical description. Political designations, ethnologically or geographically inexact, abound elsewhere; nor have some post-war emendations always proved entirely happy in everyday use. The alternative term 'Hispanic America' is unwelcome—perhaps mistakenly—to Brazilians; nor, if regarded as a descriptive definition, does it include Haiti. 'Eurindia', proposed by some, does not commend itself. Historians native to those lands, when they are writing for Europeans, commonly use the term Latin America. Among themselves Latin-Americans use no epithet: they call themselves *americanos* and their common land America (*América* in Spanish), a word which, to the Peninsula and its daughter lands, denotes what we call Latin America. When occasion makes distinction necessary, they say *Nuestra América*, 'Our America'. In this volume it is impossible to avoid using the word 'American' in a national sense, varied by the unsatisfactory substitutes 'Yankee' or 'North American' in case of ambiguity or awkwardness.

Some lesser verbal questions occur. The Spanish *andino* seems better rendered by 'Andine', used by the Trans-Andine Railway (cf. 'Alpine'), than by 'Andean'. It is perhaps reasonable to write 'Chile'; just as one may prefer 'Zaragoza' to 'Saragossa' or 'Andalucía' to 'Andalusia': but the adjective 'Chilean' is neither English nor Spanish and does not represent *chileno*. One might equally well write 'Brasilean, Panamean, Quitean' for *Brasileño*, *Panameño*, *Quiteño*. The British Museum Catalogue keeps the anglicized forms 'Chili, Chilian'. Sometimes choice must be arbitrary: of the several forms used for *La Habana* by English writers, 'Havana' seems the best.

In personal names the Spanish accentuation has been observed, except in titles of books whose authors omit accents. In geographical names it is often a question. To write México or Perú (properly *el Perú*) would be pedantry. Panamá is a doubtful case. Less common names, such as Córdoba, Cumaná, Tucumán, Yucatán, seem to demand the correct accentuation.

The frequent citations from American historians, to whom this volume owes much, do not imply hesitancy of opinion but discretion in dealing with delicate matters. In these pages there is not the least intention to examine, still less to criticize, the policy or policies of the United States. But the impact of that policy on Latin America and on Latin-American opinion is an essential and unavoidable part of this history.

The estimates of area and population given in the several chapters are taken, with one exception, from the Statesman's Year-book for 1937.

Reviewers, and perhaps some readers, desire lists of books. The word 'bibliography' would be here out of place: a recent 'Tentative Bibliography of the Economic Literature of Latin America', published at Harvard, contains above 12,000 titles. A published bibliography of the Mexican Revolution, 1810–35, contains nearly as many. A volume might be filled by a bibliography of Columbus or of Argentina or of the Monroe Doctrine. Thus it seems best to name only a few useful books and (with rare exceptions) only books printed in English. A list is given here of some works dealing generally with the whole subject. Others concerning the several parts are named at the end of most of the chapters. Asterisks mark the volumes which contain bibliographies. The reader may thus find his way to ample literature on any branch of this history.

GENERAL WORKS: T. C. Dawson, *The South American Republics* (2 vols. New York, 1904); C. E. Akers, *A History of South America, 1854–1904* (London, 1904); H. G. James and P. A. Martin, *The Republics of Latin America** (New York, 1923); A. C. Wilgus, *A History of Hispanic America** (Washington, 1931); W. S. Robertson, *History of the Latin-American Nations** (2nd. edition, enlarged, New York, 1932); T. F. Rippy, *Historical Evolution of Hispanic America** (New York, 1933); F. García Calderón, *Latin America, its rise and progress* (English Translation, London, 1913); C. H. Haring, *South American Progress* (Harvard, 1934); J. Ll. Mecham, *Church and State in Latin America** (Chapel Hill, 1934); A. Coester, *Literary History of Spanish America** (New York, 1916); H. C. Lea, *The Inquisition in the Spanish Dependencies** (New York, 1908); Three works edited by A. C. Wilgus (Washington, 1933, 1934, 1935), i. *Modern Hispanic America*; ii. *The Caribbean Area* (deals with recent conditions in twelve republics); iii. *Argentina, Brazil and Chile since independence*. The quarterly *Hispanic-American Historical Review* (Duke University Press), besides historical articles, gives ample bibliographies and reviews of books. The annual *Handbook of Latin-American Studies* (Harvard) gives recent publications. For those who read Spanish two bibliographies may be named: H. Keniston, *List of Works for the Study of Hispanic-American History* (Hispanic Society of America, New York, 1920); W. W. Pierson, *Hispanic-American History: a Syllabus* (Chapel Hill, 1926).

The *Encyclopaedia Britannica* has good articles, written by historians, on the several republics. *The South American Handbook,* annually published in London, gives much statistical and other information. Descriptive and general matter is found in W. H. Koebel's books on Argentina, Uruguay, Paraguay and Central America; in C. R. Enock's books on Ecuador, Peru, Mexico and Spanish America and in P. F. Martin's volumes on Mexico, Peru and Salvador. Among innumerable travel books may be mentioned Darwin's *Voyage of the 'Beagle'*, Waterton's *Wanderings in South America* and *Tschiffely's Ride*—all obtainable in several editions: also the travel books of three Americans, 'H. J. Mozans' (J. A. Zahm), H. Bingham and I. Bowman.

F. A. KIRKPATRICK

August 1938

Part One

DISCOVERY AND CONQUEST
TO INDEPENDENCE

CHAPTER I

THE LAND

THE NEW WORLD or Western Hemisphere comprises two continents, which curve round more than one-third of the globe, stretching in the main from north to south.[1] The greater part of the northern continent is occupied by two great powers. One of them, the Canadian Federation, a monarchy in constitutional form, covers the northern part of the continent: the other, a republic, the United States, occupies the middle part.

But on crossing the southern frontier of the United States into the Spanish-speaking Republic of Mexico one steps into a totally different world, which is only in part of European complexion. Speech, ancestry, physical appearance, law, customs, diet, government, family life: all these are different. For to the south and south-east of the United States stretch the twenty republics, mainly Iberian in origin, which constitute Latin America. These lands cover an area which is about twice the size of Europe or three times the size of the United States. Their population is probably about one hundred millions. They stretch through almost ninety degrees of latitude or nearly one-fourth part of the circuit of the globe. Thus Latin America, extending through every habitable latitude from the north temperate zone through the tropics to Antarctic seas, possesses every climate and every variety of soil, and accordingly yields, or can be made to yield, all the vegetable and animal products of the whole world. Moreover, most of the republics also severally contain territory of every habitable altitude, so that a man can change his climate from torrid to temperate and thence to frigid simply by walking uphill; and equatorial lands can produce within the range of a few miles all the products of every zone. Most of the republics also furnish an abundance and variety

[1] It should be noted, however, that South America does not lie due south of North America, but far to the east. The longitude of Valparaiso, on the Pacific coast, is east of the longitude of New York on the Atlantic; and Brazil is the nearest American country to the Old World.

of mineral products. To these striking natural features there corresponds a not less striking history. The whole of Hispanic history not only has the imposing secular movement of an epic tale, but also constantly arrests attention by a recurrent element of surprise, of unexpectedness, of sudden crisis or impulse. And this element prevails no less in the New World. The doings of Spaniards and Portuguese beyond the Atlantic—activities which move upon an unaccustomed stage with a bizarre background of indigenous culture or barbarism—resemble nothing done elsewhere. The early phase is like an imaginative romance: much of the later phase too often resembles a lurid melodrama.

Before tracing the history of these lands, it should be briefly told what they are to-day and where their territories lie. Three of them are island countries of the Caribbean Sea. The Republic of Cuba, first of the three, is the largest of the Antilles: the two little Republics of Santo Domingo and Haiti divide between them the next largest: the rich tropical fertility of these West Indian isles has been a proverb for centuries. On the mainland to the west of these islands the vast territory of Mexico and the five republics which constitute the region known as Central America may be regarded as a single region forming a sub-continent, a narrowed continuation of North America sweeping down from the temperate zone into the tropics and looking out to east and west upon Europe and upon Asia across both oceans, Atlantic and Pacific. Through this region a broad and lofty mountain-mass curves from northwest to south-east, so that the products of every climate can flourish at different heights in the same latitude; the torrid coastal strips, typically tropical in character, bordering the shores of both oceans; the beautiful, wholesome and productive country of long upland valleys and level spaces between the mountains; and finally, towering above these, the chilly inhospitable region of the great heights. The long sweep of the country south-eastward through the tropics also provides a wide range of character, from the cattle-rearing plains of northern Mexico to the coffee and banana plantations of Costa Rica.

The small recently created Republic of Panamá completes this northern system of Latin-American countries. Thus, before coming to South America, we count ten republics, three in the Antilles, seven on the mainland.

The other ten republics lie within the continent of South America. That continent, notwithstanding diversity in local detail, possesses certain outstanding features which have determined its history—the immense chain of the Andes; the colossal water-system of the three rivers, Orinoco, Amazon, La Plata; the vast forest of the Amazonian valley measuring 2000 miles from east to west and extending southwards through the basin of the River Paraguay; the wide-stretching plains of the Pampa; and the great Brazilian plateau.

The dominating element is the great backbone, the Cordillera of the Andes, which stretches from the islands of Tierra del Fuego, washed by Antarctic storms, for 4000 miles along the Pacific coast to the northern peninsulas of the Spanish Main and thence throws out a great eastward curve south of the Caribbean Sea. This continuous mountain wall, clinging closely to the Pacific, determines the whole character of the continent: it feeds with rains and snows the multitudinous upper waters of the Orinoco, the Amazon and the western tributaries of the River Plate. On the other hand the western Cordillera opposes to the Pacific, in the southern tropics, a bare dry wall of rock and yellow sand: the rainless desert stretches, a ribbon-like strip, for 1000 miles between the mountains and the sea, producing, by its very barrenness, food for fertility in other lands in the form of guano and nitrate. Far to the south, in the "roaring forties", these conditions are reversed: here moisture-laden winds blow from the Pacific, feeding the dense forests of southern Chile. In these same southern latitudes, to the east of the Andes, the terraced plains of Patagonia, thinly nourished by slight rainfall, feed on their vast extent many millions of sheep. Between these zones of climatic extremes, in the thirties of south latitude, more normal conditions prevail: on one side of the Andes are the rich valleys of central Chile, on the other side the wide plains of the Argentine Pampa, formerly given over to the gaucho (the Argentine cowboy) and to innumerable herds of cattle, now one of the great granaries of the world.

South America, alone of the southern continents, thrusts itself far through the cool regions of the temperate zone. Sydney, Capetown, Buenos Aires and Montevideo lie approximately in the same latitude, about 34° or 35° south. But some of the best parts of Chile and of Argentina stretch far to the south of this latitude.

Yet much the greater part of South America lies within the tropics: it is the most tropical of the continents, and it may seem strange that the first European settlers beyond the seas made their homes—permanent and prosperous homes—in the tropics. This is partly due to the prevalence of the north-east trade winds, partly to the search for a way to the Spice Islands, partly to the accidents of discovery and the finding of mineral wealth. But the lasting prosperity of those tropical homes during three centuries untouched by hygiene is due to the fact that the coasts and uplands of tropical America are in great part habitable in comfort and health by white men. The traveller who has sailed along the east or west coast of tropical Africa finds a contrast on crossing the Atlantic. Along the Brazilian coast he finds a succession of busy ports inhabited largely by Europeans living the normal life of Europe: the sea winds bring coolness and health, and almost everywhere the worker in the ports may make his home upon neighbouring hills. On the west coast tropical conditions south of the Equator are even more striking. Here a soft south wind blows continually from cooler airs, and the Antarctic current flowing northwards refreshes all the coast. At Lima, twelve degrees from the Equator, one may wear European dress at midsummer, and, descending a few miles to the shore, may plunge into a sea almost too cold. Moreover, in these regions the Andine valleys offer every climate, and a short journey from the coast leads one to uplands resembling southern Europe. The broad plateau of Bolivia, though tropical in situation, is a temperate land, lying as it does at a height varying from 9000 to 12,000 ft. or even more. This plateau narrows northwards through Peru and finally contracts into the Ecuadorian 'avenue of volcanoes'. Here, in the central torrid zone, a double line of towering peaks shoot their fires far above plains and slopes of perpetual snow. Thence the Cordillera opens out northwards into the broad triple range of Colombia which encloses wide river valleys of rich fertility and upland savannahs which enjoy perpetual spring.

The great rivers of South America supply natural paths to the vast interior. Upon the Amazon system, Manaos, one of the great ports of Brazil, is 900 miles from the sea: Iquitos, 2300 miles from salt water, is accessible to the smaller class of ocean steamers. Upon the Paraná, 1000 miles from the ocean, stands the port of Asunción, capital of Paraguay, accessible to ocean ships of shallow draught and to large river steamers: stern-wheel steamers can ascend the Paraguay River 1000 miles farther to the remote Brazilian port of Cuyabá. The navigation of both these river systems, the Amazon and the Paraná, is limited or rather interrupted by the Brazilian plateau, 'one of the great uplands of the world, occupying as it does an area of close on a million square miles'[1] at a height varying from 2000 to 3000 ft.

From the north-east shoulder of the Brazilian coast this varied plateau, seamed by many clefts, stretches southward and south-westward in a vast semicircular sweep, dividing the two river-systems. The Paraná and its affluents plunge from the brink of this table-land towards south and west in stupendous waterfalls. The southern tributaries of the Amazon pierce their way north-ward down into the Amazonian valley along defiles, cataracts and rapids sometimes extending scores of miles. The Amazonian affluents are mostly navigable to the foot of these cascades: above the cascades there are reaches of navigable water leading up-stream towards the south. This Brazilian plateau further justifies the description of America as a habitable continent, providing as it does in tropical and sub-tropical latitudes an extensive temperate region suitable for white settlement.

The situation and character of the republics named in this summary will appear in the following chapters.

One point demands explanation. The title 'Central America' is not a descriptive geographical term, for that region is not central in the accepted sense of the word, as in 'Central Asia' or 'Central Europe'. 'Central America' is a political designation adopted upon separation from Mexico in 1823 and does not include Panama, which until 1903 was part of Colombia. On Spanish eighteenth-century maps the Captaincy-General of Guatemala (the

[1] E. W. Shanahan, *South America*, p. 110.

region now known as Central America) rightly appears as part of North America. Despite appearances on the map, there is no passage by land from North America to South America. The two continents are separated by an impassable region of jungle and swamp which forms the real frontier between the Republics of Panamá and Colombia. Even Tschiffely in his famous ride did that bit by sea.

NOTE. This chapter is not meant to be a geographical exposition, but merely an indication of prominent natural features affecting human habitation. The geography of those lands may be studied in E. W. Shanahan's *South America* (London, 1927) and in Stanford's *Compendium of Geography: Central and South America*, 2 vols. 2nd edit. (London, 1909–11). Rippy has a good chapter on 'The Physical Environment'.

CHAPTER II

DISCOVERY

Up to the end of the fifteenth century these lands were unknown to Europe. The story of their discovery opens with a strange adventure. In 1476 a French corsair set fire to a Genoese ship off the Portuguese coast. Among the Genoese who escaped ashore was a young sailor or trader named Christopher Columbus (Christoforo Colombo), a man of scanty education and humble origin, but possessing energy, intelligence and patient self-confidence. This accident led him to settle in Lisbon, where he was caught up into the movement of oceanic discovery which for sixty years past had flowed from Portugal, the country best situated for such a movement and freed for external effort by the conclusion long ago of strife against the Moslem. Year by year the Portuguese were pushing their way along the west coast of Africa to the south. Towards the west they had occupied the distant Azores and had essayed yet more remote Atlantic discoveries. Columbus became convinced that he himself could succeed in leading an expedition to lands beyond the western ocean. In 1483, having petitioned King John II of Portugal in vain for ships, he departed to pursue his quest in Spain.

After eight years of solicitation and repeated disappointments, Columbus at last obtained from Queen Isabel of Castile the grant of all his demands: the office of Viceroy for himself and his heirs in all lands discovered and won by him, with the title of Admiral and large prerogatives and emoluments. Columbus had two objects in view: he hoped by sailing westward to reach civilized and opulent countries of eastern Asia, but he also expected to discover unknown lands. Colonization—the provision of homes oversea for emigrant Spanish families—was not the intention. The objects were to win the profitable trade with rich civilized countries in spices and other oriental commodities and to acquire lands where the discoverer might reign as Viceroy over newly won vassals of the Castilian

Crown and neophytes of the Catholic Church. In modern terms, the objects were commercial, missionary and imperial. But obviously these matters could not be clearly defined until the issue should be known.

On 26 August 1492 three small vessels, manned by about 120 Spaniards, set sail from the port of Palos, in south-west Spain, on a voyage which was to turn the first page of modern history. The little fleet touched at the Canary Isles, and sailed thence westward on 6 September.

For thirty-three days—five weeks of hope and suspense—no land appeared. But at dawn of Friday, 12 October, they anchored off the coast of an unknown island, one of the Bahamas. Columbus rowed ashore; and there displaying the royal banner, while the naked and beardless islanders gathered round, he claimed for Ferdinand and Isabel, the sovereigns of Spain, possession of that land, an island of marvellous woods, climate and foliage. 12 October 1492, the birthday of Latin America, is annually commemorated in every capital of Spanish speech by the Fiesta de la Raza, the festival of the Hispanic race.

Sailing southwards from the Bahamas, Columbus coasted for 300 miles along the northern shore of Cuba, seeking for 'a king and great cities'. He found only naked dwellers in huts: but, persuading himself that these were Asiatic shores, he called the people 'Indians', a name which has stuck; and the transatlantic dependencies of the Spanish crown were thenceforth known as *Las Indias*, 'The Indies'. Sailing thence eastward, he discovered the beautiful and fertile island of Haiti, which he named La (Isla) Española—a name corrupted on English lips into 'Hispaniola'. He found the docile inhabitants friendly, and collected specimens of gold. Having lost his flagship, he left thirty-nine men in a rude fort when he sailed for home in January 1493, bringing news of 'the great victory which Our Lord has given me...not only for Spain; all Christians shall find here refreshment and gain'.

In order to obviate possible Portuguese claims, the Spanish sovereigns now obtained Papal authority for western conquest, with the proviso that the inhabitants should be brought to the Catholic faith. To remove ambiguities in the Papal Bulls—for there were several Bulls—the Spanish and Portuguese Crowns finally agreed by the famous Treaty of Tordesillas in 1494 that a line drawn from north to south 370 leagues west of the Cape Verde Islands should divide the western discoveries and conquests of the Spaniards from those of the Portuguese to the east. This agreement had a result unforeseen by the Spaniards, for the dividing line gave eastern Brazil to the Portuguese.

But already, in September 1493, the Admiral had sailed westward with a great fleet, carrying some 1500 men with seeds, ploughs and spades; also animals unknown to the New World, cattle, swine and (above all) horses, the monstrous creatures which were to terrify the gentiles and everywhere win victory for the Christians. This voyage revealed the lovely chain of tropical islands which fringe the Caribbean Sea: but the fort in Española had perished with all its occupants, a fate brought on by outrages committed on the Indians. Columbus repaired this disaster by tracing the rectangular plan of a city which he named Isabela,[1] nominating town councillors (*regidores*) and two magistrates (*alcaldes*), thus establishing the first permanent European settlement in the New World and inaugurating, after the ancient Spanish model, the municipal system which was to be the basis of Spanish dominion in the West. But the early years of the Spanish Empire were darkened by scarcity, discontent, indiscipline, sickness and a serious Indian revolt, which was crushed by slaughter and by the terror of horses, muskets and savage dogs; famine followed, the beginning of the rapid disappearance of these unfortunate islanders.

In a third voyage (1498) the Admiral discovered the island of Trinidad and the adjoining mainland which, seeing the great volume of water flowing from the Orinoco, he rightly judged to be a great continent. His discovery of the Pearl Coast, where the naked inhabitants wore great ropes of gems and his men got pearls by the pound, encouraged the wildest hopes. But his attempt to govern Española was a tragic failure, and after two years a magistrate, despatched from Spain to remedy these ills, sent the Admiral

---

[1] This city, afterwards removed to a healthier site on the south coast and renamed Santo Domingo, was for half a century the chief seat of government for the Spanish Indies.

home in chains. The Crown was taking over the administration of the new lands, and a Colonial Office, predecessor of the famous Council of the Indies, was taking shape. Yet Columbus was the first legislator of the Spanish Indies, the first founder of a city in the New World, and also—by the assignment (*repartimiento*) of a group or tribe of Indians to every settler—the initiator of a less admirable institution, the *encomienda*, to be mentioned later.

Meantime, other explorers, mostly Columbus' former companions, were at work. In 1499–1500 five Spanish expeditions ranged along 3000 miles of coast, some sailing south-east far beyond the mouths of the gigantic Amazon to latitude 7° south and coasting Brazilian shores; others sailing westward from Trinidad to the Isthmus of Panamá. At last in 1502 Columbus himself, in his last voyage, explored the coasts of Honduras, Nicaragua and Costa Rica (to use the modern terms) as far as the Isthmus, suffering much hardship in stormy uncharted seas and savage lands.

When Columbus died in 1506, the way had been prepared for future wide dominion at the cost of untold losses by shipwreck, sickness and accident. The institution in 1503 of the Casa de Contratación or Board of Trade at Seville, to regulate intercourse between Spain and the new lands, proves that such intercourse was now frequent and increasing; but no settlement had yet been made beyond the island of Española.

THE PORTUGUESE IN BRAZIL

The Portuguese movement of discovery, mentioned on p. 9, continued to flow from Lisbon, mainly to the shores of Africa and India; but it also struck out a path across the Atlantic. In September 1499 the great Portuguese navigator Vasco da Gama sailed into the harbour of Lisbon with rich cargoes of spices, returning from the first European voyage to India. Six months later a fleet, commanded by Pedro Alvarez Cabral, set out from the Tagus upon the second voyage round the Cape to India. Steering far to the west, Cabral sighted land on Easter Day 1500. It was the southern part of the present State of Bahia, lying considerably to the south of the shore coasted by Vicente Yáñez Pinzón and by the Spaniard Lepe a few months earlier. Cabral named the country

'Island of the Holy Cross', despatched a vessel to Lisbon with the news and sailed away for the Cape and the shores of India, leaving two criminals ashore to serve, if they should survive, as interpreters to later Portuguese arrivals.

King Manoel of Portugal at once announced this discovery to his parents-in-law, the Catholic sovereigns of Spain, and claimed the land for Portugal. During the following years the whole coast of Brazil was explored by Portuguese navigators; but for a full generation little was done towards the occupation of the land. Brazil—destined to achieve later an astonishing expansion—was still in its infancy when the Spanish Empire in both American Continents had grown into solid form. Accordingly, in order to avoid a narrative in fragments, the conquest and organization of the Spanish Empire will first be told and then the origins of Brazil.

It was, till recently, generally believed that Cabral in 1500 accidentally discovered an unknown coast. But there is evidence of an earlier Portuguese voyage thither, kept secret for diplomatic reasons. Portuguese historians believe that the Portuguese negotiators at Tordesillas knew of the Brazilian coast. But investigators differ about dates. Mr Yule Oldham in the *Geographical Journal* (March 1895) and Professor E. E. Nowell in the *Hispanic American Historical Review* (August 1936) put the earlier voyage before 1448. Professor P. A. Martin in the same *Review* (May 1937) puts the first Brazilian voyage in 1498 and finds 'the evidence of pre-Columbian voyages by the Portuguese to the New World both shadowy and fragmentary'.

NOTE. The much-discussed early biography of Columbus is here irrelevant; so also the immense literature of discovery. Columbus' four voyages—which are the main point—are well known and are narrated by all the biographers. The Hakluyt Society has published the original narratives, Spanish and English on opposite pages. R. B. Merriman, *The Rise of the Spanish Empire* (New York, 1918), gives an excellent summary in vol. II, ch. XVII. The three large volumes of T. A. Thacher's *Columbus* (New York, 1903–4) tell the full story. The Portuguese voyages are summarized by Professor Prestage, *The Portuguese Pioneers* (London, 1933), and the Spanish voyages by F. A. Kirkpatrick, *The Spanish Conquistadores* (London, 1934).

CHAPTER III

EXPANSION AND CONQUEST

Plus ultra

THE YEAR 1508 marks a double movement of expansion, to the islands and to the mainland. The Spaniards established themselves on the islands of Puerto Rico, Jamaica and Cuba, with some fighting and much hardship, but with comparatively little difficulty, everywhere setting up 'cities', which, although at first mere groups of huts, had all the character of civic communities claiming jurisdiction over wide areas, every city having its body of councillors (*regidores*) and its two alcaldes. Advance on the mainland was more difficult: two expeditions, together numbering more than 1000 men, under gallant and experienced leaders, Ojeda and Nicuesa, attempted settlement, one on the north coast of the present Colombia, the other on the shore of the Isthmian region. After a few months less than 100 survived shipwreck, starvation, fever, hardship and poisoned arrows shot from ambush by the untamable Indians of the Spanish Main. The remnant, reinforced by newcomers from Española, were led to ultimate success by the energy and sagacity of Balboa, a gay adventurer, who escaped from his creditors in Española as a stowaway hidden in an empty cask. Thrusting aside superior officials, he founded the city of Darien— the first step towards the occupation of two continents. He won ascendancy over the neighbouring tribes by a combination of force, terror and amicable diplomacy. Hearing of another sea to the south and of lands richer in gold, he led his men southward through the Isthmian jungle until from the dividing height he looked down on another ocean. The date, September 1513, is the second great landmark in the story of the conquest. A few days later, wading, sword in hand, into the waters of the Gulf of San Miguel, he raised the banner of Castile and claimed aloud for his sovereigns that sea and all its adjacent lands. That sea was the Pacific Ocean.

Balboa was preparing to embark upon that sea for southern enterprise, when he was arrested and beheaded on an absurd charge of treason by Pedrarias, an arrogant Governor sent from Spain. Pedrarias, in turn, pushed on the work, committing and permitting brutal outrages upon the Indians. In 1519, he founded the city of Panamá, to be for over two centuries the gateway of the Pacific. In the following years several adventurers pushed north-westward, fighting, killing and robbing, through Costa Rica and Nicaragua until they met the men despatched from the north to Honduras and Guatemala by Hernán Cortés, who sought to add these provinces to the dominions won for Spain by the conquest of Mexico.

The Conquest of New Spain, 1519–23

That conquest has been narrated for all time in the classic work of Prescott. Here a few lines must suffice. Two expeditions, coasting the shore of the Mexican Gulf, brought news to Cuba of people wearing dyed cotton, living in solidly built cities, skilful artificers in gold and carved stone, but addicted to human sacrifices and cannibal feasts. Velásquez, Governor of Cuba, appointed as com-mander of a third expedition Hernán Cortés, a spirited adventurer, noted for his gallant audacity. Warned of this, Velásquez withdrew the appointment. Cortés disobeyed recall and sailed, a defiant rebel, for the coast of Yucatán with about 600 men, 16 horses, 15 muskets and 7 small cannon shooting stone balls. Fighting at need, but offering peace and proclaiming the Christian faith, he followed the coast to the spot where he founded the city of Vera Cruz, appointing municipal authorities, who in turn nominated him Governor of 'New Spain'.

After winning over the coastal tribes, proclaiming Christianity and overthrowing idols, he set out on his 200-mile march west-ward over the mountains. Negotiating and fighting by turns, after three months he led his men, with a host of Indian auxiliaries, along the broad causeway which crossed a lake to the island city of Mexico, where the 'great Montezuma' reigned in more than Oriental state. Cortés seized the royal person, gathered much hoarded gold and silver and had apparently finished the conquest, when news came that a force double his own had landed at Vera Cruz, sent by Velásquez to arrest him. Cortés hurried to the coast, fell upon the rival force by night and added the whole of it to his own troops. Thence he hastened back to the capital, whose inhabitants, under great provocation, had risen against the little Spanish garrison.

Cortés entered the city unresisted, but afterwards was forced by ceaseless attacks from furious crowds to abandon the city. Retreating by night over the causeway and assailed from all sides, half his men perished in the ghastly confusion of the 'sorrowful night', slain or drowned or captured for sacrifice to the Mexican war-god. Cortés, with the survivors, fought his way to safety.

Six months later he came back with stronger forces and launched a war fleet upon the lake. In three months' siege he destroyed the city of Mexico and thus subdued all the provinces tributary to it. He then sent out his captains south-eastward to fresh conquests in Guatemala and Honduras. Two streams of conquest joined when these captains met those despatched by Pedrarias from Darien. Thus the inhabitants of many provinces, mostly dwellers in towns and cities, became subjects to the Crown of Castile.

Cortés founded on the island site of Mexico a stately Spanish city, and, as holders of the land, other lesser cities, each with full municipal organization, granting to every settler a building site in the city and land for cultivation outside. He was also obliged to satisfy his companions by assigning to every conqueror who became a householder (*vecino*) a group or tribe of Indians in *encomienda*. But his political authority was diminished by the appointment of a Royal Audiencia (at once a Supreme Court and a Governing Council) in the city of Mexico in 1527, and was ended when the first Viceroy, Antonio de Mendoza, entered the capital in 1535, the first of a long list of Viceroys who ruled down to 1821.

The empire thus won by Cortés in North America expanded for three centuries northwards, until it stretched beyond San Francisco; and a vast region, now forming the southern part of the United States, passed under the dominion of the Spanish King.

MAGELLAN

Simultaneous with the first great advance of the Spaniards by land through the conquest of New Spain was their greatest advance by sea in the voyage which first circled the globe (1519–22). Magellan (Magalhaens in Portuguese, Magallanes in Spanish), a Portuguese captain in the Spanish service, having sailed with five ships from the Guadalquivir, coasted the Atlantic shore of South America and solved the problem of the sea-route to the Indies by discovering the strait, 'Magellan's Strait', which links the two oceans in the far south. Having passed through the strait, he spent ninety-eight days—days of suspense, famine and sickness—in traversing the unknown expanse of the Pacific Ocean, 'so vast that the human mind can scarcely grasp it', to the discovery of the Philippine Islands, where Magellan fell in an obscure skirmish with a native chief. The command passed to a Basque navigator, Sebastián del Cano, who sailed southward to the Moluccas ('the Spice Islands'), continued his voyage later round the Cape of Good Hope and, three years after the first setting out, sailed into the Guadalquivir with seventeen companions and one ship laden with cloves—a cargo which paid all the expenses of the five ships and the three years' voyage. This stupendous achievement, which added to the map the widest of the oceans and in some sort revealed the globe to its inhabitants, has place in Latin-American history, since it did much to teach the Spaniards the form and extent of their newly found lands and prepared the conquest of the Philippines fifty years later. Moreover, the quest for the spice trade was one of the main currents in the movement of discovery and was repeatedly resumed during the following half-century.

THE CONQUEST OF PERU, 1530–50

A wider dominion than the conquests of Cortés in North America was won in yet stranger fashion in South America by the illegitimate and illiterate soldier of fortune, Pizarro, who conquered the vast and elaborately organized Inca Empire, stretching more than 2000 miles along the Andes and the Pacific coast. Pizarro and his associate Almagro spent four years (1524–8) in three preliminary expeditions, sailing southwards from Panamá, which apparently led only to suffering, mortality and disaster, but finally brought back evidence of the wealth abounding in the Inca Empire. At last in December 1528, Pizarro set sail from Panamá with 180 men and 27 horses to the conquest of a great empire. Such were the obstacles of sea, desert, mountain and hostile tribes that nearly two more years passed before he marched inland with 108 infantry and 62 horsemen from the city of San Miguel (now Piura) which, after regular Spanish custom, he founded near the coast to be his base, endowing the householders with allotments (*repartimientos* or *encomiendas*) of Indian serfs. Prescott tells the story; the passage of the western Cordillera to the lofty Andine plateau, the meeting, outwardly amiable, with Atahualpa, the Inca sovereign; the massacre of his unarmed followers and the seizure of his royal person, to be the mouthpiece of the conqueror's authority; the huge ransom of the Inca; his death at the hands of the Spaniards and the division of the spoil, the march to Cuzco, the Inca capital, which yielded another rich treasure, and the establishment there of a Spanish municipality; the foundation of Lima, the 'City of the Kings', in January 1535 as a purely Spanish capital: an event which ought to have completed the conquest, if the victors had not first provoked by greed and violence a perilous native insurrection and then fallen out with one another about the limits of their territories and destroyed one another in internecine strife. The last stage of the conquest was the suppression by royal authority of the dictatorship set up by the *pronunciamiento* of Gonzalo Pizarro, brother of the murdered conqueror.

All this medley of strife did not undo the work of conquest and of municipal organization already accomplished. Besides, Pizarro had sent out his captains north and south to win new provinces. In 1534 one of these, Belalcázar, conquered the kingdom of Quito (now Ecuador) by hard fighting, and in the following years pushed northwards into the southern part of the present republic of Colombia. In 1540 Valdivia, a veteran of Italian wars, marched southward far into the temperate zone to the conquest of Chile, there to meet the unconquerable Araucanian Indians of the far south and to die thirteen years later at their hands, but not before he had founded six cities and won a kingdom which was thenceforth held for the Spanish Crown, although for more than two centuries there was intermittent but unending warfare with the unconquered Indians of the far south.

Most of the regions thus won by the Spaniards to north and south yielded much hoarded treasure; and after the conquest the mining of gold and silver by forced Indian labour was vigorously pushed forward, particularly in the Province of Charcas (now Bolivia). The famous silver mines of Potosí, accidentally discovered in 1545 by an Indian labourer, became a proverb for magnificent opulence.

THE SPANISH MAIN

The lands won by Cortés, Pizarro and their captains were inhabited for the most part by sedentary peoples, tilling the soil, who became tax-paying subjects of the Spanish Crown. But the north coast of South America, inhabited not by a docile peasantry but by bellicose and barbarous tribes using poisoned arrows, many of them cannibals, was at first the scene of pearl-fishing, gold-hunting and slave-raiding, rather than regular settlement. So late as 1528 there were but two widely separated groups of Spaniards on 1300 miles of coast, at Cumaná and at Santa Marta. But in that year the German banking house of Welser undertook, by licence from Charles V, to subdue the country about Lake Maracaibo. Their explorations, although not very fruitful at the time, prepared the way for later Spanish occupation. Moreover, from that time other 'cities', starting-points for later penetration inland, were founded on the coast.

NEW GRANADA

There remained one remote country, rich in gold and possessing a settled polity, known only by vague rumour. In April 1536 a lawyer, Jiménez de Quesada, the peer of Cortés and Pizarro, set out from Santa Marta to find this 'Kingdom of Bogotá' by way of the River Magdalena. Out of 900 men who started, some by land and some by sea and river, 166 survivors with 62 horses crossed the River Suárez eight months later to enter the fertile Andine valleys and upland savannahs, the country of the Chibchas. Their powder was all spoilt; but the possession of horses enabled them to win great booty in gold and emeralds and to found the city of Santa Fe de Bogotá to be the capital of the Kingdom of New Granada, another rich realm won for the Crown of Spain. A strange episode, illustrating the abundant and audacious enterprise of the conquistadores, was the meeting of three expeditions on the plateau of Bogotá in 1539, Belalcázar coming from the south-east and the German Federmann from the east, to find Quesada already in successful possession. Thenceforward royal Governors were regularly sent out to Santa Fe, and the establishment of an Audiencia in 1549 marks that city as the capital of an organized kingdom. But the Kingdom of New Granada did not attain the dimensions of the present Republic of Colombia until long afterwards. The penetration of the three mountain ranges and intervening lowlands of that strangely difficult and diversified country, partly from the Atlantic port of Cartagena, partly from the Pacific port of Buenaventura, was the gradual work of several generations.

THE RIVER PLATE

Meantime, a country of comparatively easy access from Europe, now the richest part of South America, marked out by climate and fertility to be the seat of a civilization of European type, drew tardy attention, partly because it yielded no treasure. In 1516, Solís, Chief Pilot of the Crown of Spain, discovered the huge estuary of the River Plate, but was killed by the cannibals of the northern coast. In the following decade Sebastián Cabot, who had left England to take service in Spain, spent three years exploring that great river system; and at last in 1535, a rich captain, Pedro de Mendoza, leading a great expedition from Seville, founded a city which he called Santa María de Buenos Aires. This settlement, isolated by the hostility of savage tribes, perished from starvation rather than from armed attack. But some of the men made their way nearly 1000 miles up the river and set up in 1536–7 the city of Asunción among more docile Guaraní Indians, to be a base for recovery and the capital of a vast country. In 1580 sixty men (mostly Creoles, Spaniards born in America), came down the river from Asunción to found a second and enduring Buenos Aires. Men descending from the Peruvian plateau or crossing the Andes from Chile founded the interior Argentine cities—a strange inversion of natural and expected ways.

The tragedy and the romance of the many expeditions which

plunged into the wilds of both continents, seeking new conquests or drawn by the lure of fabulous kingdoms, cannot here be narrated. Two may be mentioned, the brilliant expedition of 600 men led westward from Florida by de Soto, the discoverer of the Mississippi, who perished with half his company; and the exploit of Orellana, who was detached from Gonzalo Pizarro's expedition into the Montaña and sailed down the River Amazon to the Atlantic Ocean.

It would be austere pedantry to narrate the discovery and conquest of tropical America otherwise than by tracing the activities of the men who accomplished these things, for it was in the main a work of individual effort driven forward by vehement personal impulses and motives. Thus the main thread of the story is essentially biographical. But these activities of Spain should also be viewed as a whole, as a movement of immeasurable scope, economic, political and social, a movement which added to the map of the world two continents and the widest of the oceans, made the world known to itself and brought into contact two streams of human life which so far had flowed parallel and unseen by one another. It shifted westward the activities of the Old World; it was the beginning of the immense movement of European colonization beyond the sea, and was the biggest step in that Europeanization of the world, which was thenceforth perhaps the most significant trend of general history down to the close of the nineteenth century.

NOTE. Prescott's *Conquest of Mexico* and *Conquest of Peru* demand first mention; then A. P. Maudslay, *Bernal Díaz del Castillo* (London, 1930); Arthur Helps, *The Spanish Conquest in America*, 4 vols. (London, 1855–61; 2nd edit. 1904); F. H. H. Guillemard, *Magellan* (London, 1890); P. A. Means, *The Fall of the Inca Empire** (New York, 1928); R. B. Merriman,* vol. III, chs. XXVII–XXIX; F. A. Kirkpatrick, *The Spanish Conquistadores*, summarizes the whole story; R. B. Cunninghame Graham, *The Conquest of New Granada* (1922), *Pedro de Valdivia* (1926), *The Conquest of the River Plate* (1924); F. A. MacNutt, *Letters of Cortés*, 2 vols. (New York, 1908), *Fernando Cortés and the Conquest of Mexico* (New York, 1909).

CHAPTER IV

THE SPANISH EMPIRE

FROM the beginning of Spanish dominion in the American continents to its final extinction, 331 years passed (1493–1824).[1] But for Napoleon's aggression upon Spain, it would have doubled the duration of British dominion in the Thirteen Colonies. The vast extent of that Empire, the wealth and dignity which it brought to Spain, the international animosities and conflicts which it aroused or aggravated, the hispanicization or partial hispanicization of so many lands: all these things together make the Spanish Empire in America one of the great things of history. Portuguese dominion in Brazil lasted nearly as long and eventually made good its claims to political possession of half the South American Continent: an achievement of outstanding historical magnitude.

Within sixty years of Columbus' first voyage the spaces of an empire nearly twice the size of Europe had been staked out, an empire extending through the tropics and far into both temperate zones. Most of the existing capitals had been founded, and the framework of administration had been set up. The foundation of Buenos Aires in 1580, a work of colonization rather than conquest, marks the conclusion of a second phase of expansion and (approximately) the date when a system of government had been elaborated, a system which stood, with modifications, for two centuries (1580–1780) and survived, with considerable reforms, for a generation longer.

That system can be best understood by tracing its origin.

From the beginning in 1493 every advance was secured by the foundation of cities, the jurisdiction of every city extending in theory—and also in reality so far as the occupation of the land permitted—for many leagues to the limits of its neighbouring cities on all sides, and thus in many cases covering an extensive region. The official Geographer of the Indies, Juan López de

---

[1] Spanish dominion in the islands of Cuba and Puerto Rico lasted seventy-four years longer, until 1898.

Velasco, drew up in 1574 a 'General Description' giving statistics of 200 cities and towns (*ciudades y villas*): a network of civic communities covering the whole Empire. In the early days before viceregal government was established, the town councils (*cabildos*) of these cities exercised, each over a wide area, administrative and even, in some degree, legislative authority. The first councillors (*regidores*) were nominated by the founder of the city, but in important places, where a seat in the cabildo was valuable, the King soon began (as in Spain itself) to sell these posts to 'proprietary councillors' for life, often with the right of transference to others. Sale for benefit of the royal treasury became general before 1600 and in 1620 it was ordered that all these posts should be sold by auction. Where no buyers appeared, the cabildo was usually allowed to choose its successors at the end of every year, subject to confirmation by the Governor. This oligarchical body, apparently lacking popular vitality, was valuable as enabling Creoles to exercise civic functions and attain profitable posts. Moreover, the cabildo annually elected two alcaldes from the prominent townsmen (not from their own body) and in the larger towns they appointed other officials. Although not, in the modern sense, representative, the regidores regarded themselves as representing the city. They were viewed with consideration and surrounded with etiquette.

The cabildos had the right of sending deputies to Spain to represent their interests before the King and the Council of the Indies, and in case of emergency they could summon, with the Governor's consent, the civil and ecclesiastical officials and the principal vecinos to a meeting called *cabildo abierto* or ' open cabildo ' to discuss an urgent matter such as defence against Indian attack. Upon the death of a Governor in a province possessing no audiencia, the cabildo, unless royal provision had been made for a substitute, sometimes assumed the Government or named an acting Governor. Asunción affords an extreme example. A royal decree of 1537 empowered the River Plate settlers to name their Governor in case of vacancy; as conquest merged into settlement, the cabildo of Asunción claimed this power and pushed it far beyond the royal intention, declaring vacancies without warrant and appointing

Governors of Paraguay in disregard of Viceroy and of King; so late as 1732 Asunción is like a city state alternating between anarchy, oligarchy, and elective monarchy and was only reduced to order by troops sent from Buenos Aires.

But in general the theory of government was supreme royal authority. The provinces of the Spanish Indies were not colonies nor were they dependencies of Spain or of the Spanish people. They were kingdoms belonging to the Crown of Castile. Legislation consisted in *cédulas reales*, royal decrees issued in the King's name by the Council of the Indies, which had authority over all civil matters and scarcely limited authority over ecclesiastical matters; for by Papal Bull the entire patronage of the Indies was vested in the King; and the Pope was precluded from communicating directly with the Church in America, no Bull passing thither unless approved by the Council; even the tithes were granted to the King on condition of supporting the Church and teaching the Indians. The activity of the Council was all-pervading; a perpetual stream of *cédulas* was showered upon the Governor of every kingdom in the Indies, treating with almost ludicrous minuteness the greatest and smallest matters of state, justice, religion, trade, finance, social conduct, etiquette, precedence, and private morality.

There were two Viceroyalties. The Viceroy of New Spain, holding a stately Court in Mexico, nominally controlled all the Spanish dominions in North America and the Philippine Islands. But the Philippines, the Kingdom of Guatemala (comprising the five modern states of Central America) and the Province of Yucatán were ruled by Captains-General or Governors nominated by the King and almost independent of the Viceroy. The northern frontier provinces were also ruled by Governors of military experience and high official rank. Three audiencias, at once administrative Councils and Courts of Appeal, sat in the cities of Mexico, Guatemala and Guadalajara. The country was divided into districts, each ruled by an Alcalde Mayor or Corregidor appointed for three or five years by King or Viceroy. Every Indian village had its Indian councillors and officers and also an Indian cacique, sometimes hereditary, sometimes nominated for life by the Viceroy.

The Viceroy of Peru, holding a more magnificent Court in Lima, ruled nominally over dominions extending 3500 miles along the Pacific coast, from Panamá to Valdivia, and 3000 miles overland from Lima to Buenos Aires. Except Venezuela, which was dependent on the Audiencia of Santo Domingo and financially supported by the Mexican treasury, the whole of Spanish South America was nominally under his control. But the kingdoms of Chile, Quito (now Ecuador), New Granada (now Colombia) and Tierra Firme (Panamá and the Isthmus) and the three River Plate provinces of Paraguay, Tucumán and Buenos Aires, formed seven distinct Governments.[1] The magistrates over lesser districts were known as *corregidores* in South America. The system of Indian villages resembled that of New Spain, but owing to the vast distances and the great mountain ranges control was more difficult and obedience to authority was more doubtful; and, as in the case of gold diggings at other times and places, the rich silver mines of Potosí and Puna attracted a crowd of turbulent fortune-hunters whose sanguinary faction fights sometimes almost amounted to local civil wars. Audiencias were set up in Lima, Panamá, Bogotá, Quito, Santiago de Chile and the city of Chuquisaca or La Plata (now Sucre). The Audiencia, consisting of experienced Spanish lawyers, varying in number from four to twelve according to the importance of the place, was both a Court of Appeal and also an administrative council exercising authority, almost amounting sometimes to legislative authority, over a wide region. The Viceroy or Governor had the right of presiding in the Audiencia and usually did so when it sat as a Council. But to some extent they were rival powers. In case of vacancy, unless provision had been made for an acting successor, the Audiencia acted as interim Viceroy or Governor.

There was no rigid uniformity in the system, which was often modified by local conditions. Important places on the coasts were under military governors. That royal authority might be maintained, all tenure of office was brief; and every official, from the Viceroy

---

[1] These divisions have been the origin of six present-day republics; not seven, because Tucumán and Buenos Aires are now parts of one Republic. Chile was ruled by a Captain-General, the highest rank after that of Viceroy; the other six regions by magistrates differing in rank and title.

downwards, submitted, on retiring from office, to a public judicial
enquiry into his past conduct. The Inquisition, introduced into
Lima and Mexico in 1570, was a powerful organ of government
among the Spaniards; the native Indians were not subject to its
jurisdiction.

Corruption and abuse were rife. A corregidor, holding brief and
ill-paid office, retired with a fortune. Impossibility of control over
vast regions so far from Europe favoured lax conduct. Magistrates
were unable to execute or reconcile the multitudinous *cédulas*,
which were often ambiguous or unworkable owing to changed
conditions. The Viceroys exercised a dispensing or suspending
power: subordinate governors were no less independent: a royal
cédula was kissed and placed on the head with the words: 'I obey,
but I do not execute', and in turn the white settlers rendered what
obedience they chose. Quarrels between authorities were frequent,
and also popular seditions against authority accompanied by the
cry *Viva el rey y muera el mal gobierno*; in fact movements as serious
as many, which in the nineteenth century have been dignified with
the title of revolution, were scarcely abnormal. Prominent and
lucrative posts were held, with rare exceptions, by European
Spaniards, and there was much animosity between Creoles and
Peninsulares.

The whole Empire was divided into archbishoprics, bishoprics
and parishes. But the licence of the civil administration also pervaded the Church and most of the Religious Orders. There were,
however, large exceptions. The Missions required and found
excellent and self-sacrificing priests; and the Jesuits observed
admirable conduct, labouring at education, study and the ministrations of religion or charity.

In a large sense, despite irregularities, the Latin heritage of
organized life was preserved. The Universities of Mexico and of
Lima, founded in the middle of the sixteenth century, had all the
privileges of Salamanca, and the printing-press was at work in
both those capitals from about the same time. Elsewhere printing-
presses were few and only permitted by superior authority. Twelve
or more minor universities were founded during the colonial
period.

During the formative period there was considerable freedom of emigration, but after the first half-century emigration was controlled, and no Europeans except Spaniards were allowed to reside in the Indies. During the first half of the sixteenth century, in order to protect merchant ships from attack, a strict system of trade was evolved, whereby gold, silver, pearls, emeralds, cacao, tobacco, indigo, cochineal, hides and other products of the Indies were exchanged for European goods. Two fleets sailed from the Guadalquivir every year according to legal theory; in fact less often. One fleet, generally called the *flota*, made for Vera Cruz, where European goods were exchanged for those of New Spain in the fair of Jalapa. The other, usually called the galleons, being convoyed by warships, sailed to Cartagena, where the merchants of New Granada dealt with those of Seville. Meantime the silver bars from Potosí, packed in hides, had been carried by llamas to the port of Arica, and thence by sea to Panamá. From Panamá the silver was carried by mules northward to Portobello. On the arrival of the galleons from Cartagena, this pestilential village became for six weeks one of the great centres of the world's trade. The agents of the Seville and Lima merchants first met to fix prices, and then the silver bars were exchanged for bales of silk and cloth; but during the fair many died, and if war or accident detained the galleons for the winter, pestilence swept away the crews and soldiers.

Trade from Europe to the viceroyalty of Peru was confined to these fairs; European goods reaching Buenos Aires by this strangely circuitous route, including a land journey of 1000 leagues from Lima, were worth six times their original cost; but from 1620 a strictly limited trade by the Atlantic was permitted to the port of Buenos Aires.

This strict regulation of trade, though needlessly rigid and absurdly uneconomic, achieved its main object, the protection of the ships: only three times in the course of its long history was the homeward-bound fleet prevented by enemies from reaching port, although single ships were often cut off by corsairs and losses by shipwreck were frequent. The arrival of the fleet at Seville was an event of national and even international concern, and was awaited with intense anxiety by the merchants of Seville, who held the monopoly of this transatlantic trade, and also by the royal treasury; for the fleets conveyed home not only the silver and other goods consigned to merchants, but also, in the form of silver bars, the revenue received by the King from his dominions in the Indies.

New Spain had a lucrative trade with China through the Philippines. Every year a galleon, usually accompanied by a smaller vessel, sailed from Acapulco across the Pacific to Manila carrying priests for the Philippine missions and silver (*plata y frailes*), to return laden with Chinese goods, notably silk and muslin, which were eagerly bought for the clothing or adornment of both sexes, to the huge profit of merchants.

Most of the revenue raised by the Spanish Crown in America was spent, with much waste and loss by the way, on the costly civil and ecclesiastical establishments in the Indies. Some of the provinces brought no profit but only expense and were supported by the treasuries of the mining regions in New Spain and Peru: thus the surplus which reached the royal exchequer in Spain was but a small part of the proceeds of taxes and royal dues in the Indies.

The chief problem for the Crown and the royal magistrates was the government and treatment of the native population: or rather there were many problems owing to the wide differences between the settled peoples of New Spain or Peru and tribes descending through lower grades to ferocious savagery. Relations with the Spaniards varied from allegiance or submission to independence and intermittent warfare. But the first concern was with the people living under law in the more settled kingdoms. The care, defence and conversion of the Indians were entrusted at first to the encomenderos, the Spanish feudal lords whom they served. The result was such abuse and oppression that the Crown, after a vain attempt to abolish the encomiendas, deprived the encomenderos of all authority by enactments dating from 1552, forbade them to live among their Indians, restricted their rights to the receipt of the poll-tax and transferred their other functions to the corregidores. Official Protectors of the Indians were appointed everywhere. But the existence of the widely separated Spanish communities depended on Indian labour, unobtainable except under compulsion.

Hence a system was established, known as *mita* in Peru and *tanda* in New Spain, whereby the able-bodied men took turns, under protective regulations, to furnish limited hours of paid labour. Grievous abuse and oppression followed, especially in the Peruvian mining districts; indeed, the *mita* of Potosí depopulated an extensive country.

The humane decrees of the Crown are proved to be inoperative by their constant reiteration and are inconsistent with the ceaseless demands from Spain for increased revenue. But in regions remote from the mines the Indians seem to have been fairly content, and those who became servants or retainers to Spanish households were well treated. But the indigenous population rapidly decreased owing to unaccustomed conditions, mere contact with European intruders and, still more, the abuse of alcohol and recurrent plagues of small-pox and measles. Yet to-day throughout the tropics of Spanish America there is a large population of pure Indians speaking native tongues. Moreover, as the natives decreased, the mestizos, of mixed blood, increased until they formed a large part of the population, and very many of those who passed as white had some Indian ancestry.

The Creoles, mestizos and sometimes the Indian caciques were oppressors no less, indeed perhaps more, than the Peninsular Spaniards. Oppression provoked various Indian disturbances, particularly on the eastern frontier of Peru, where in the eighteenth century the tributary Indians sometimes made common cause with invading gentiles. The great Indian revolt of 1780-3 in southern Peru, led by an Indian noble who took the Inca name of Tupac Amaru, shook the whole fabric of state, but was finally suppressed, after great loss of life, by troops consisting mainly of loyal Indians. This revolt was not a prologue of independence: its aim was not to emancipate the Spanish settlements but to destroy them.

There was a further native question, the defence of frontiers exposed to the attacks of unsubdued tribes. The south of Chile, bordering the lands of the indomitable Araucanians, was protected by a permanent military force; and the long frontier of New Spain, gradually though intermittently advancing northward, was held by a line of small widely separated garrisons. But upon the interior frontier of South America, measuring some 7000 miles, there was no military establishment except the militia maintained in theory by the towns but in fact much neglected. The pacification, defence and advance of the frontier was in reality the work of Christian missionaries, notably the Jesuits, who with great devotion, often meeting death by the way, pushed forward through forest and wilderness the work of evangelizing the gentiles. The best known missions were those of La Guaira, on the Upper Paraná River, where the Crown forbade all entry of white men except the few Jesuit fathers who gathered their neophytes into thirty organized villages.[1] But industrious and orderly communities were also formed among the Mojos and Chiquitos to the east of the Andes, and in the Orinoco region, also in California and the other northern provinces of New Spain. Here the miner, farmer and soldier were preceded by the missionary, foremost and most humane of pioneers of empire. The missions had their defects: in the Orinoco region the fathers sometimes led their native converts to attack their savage neighbours and gather neophytes by force. But in general the missions strove to maintain and extend the Pax Hispanica which was the leading note of Spanish Empire in America.

That Empire also successfully resisted the attacks of European rivals, envious of the treasures of the Indies, not only during the many wars which troubled Spain, but also during nominal peace. The raids of corsairs, French, Dutch and English, in the sixteenth century—Drake, Candish and others—left no permanent impression except the Dutch settlement in Guiana. More serious were the attacks of the buccaneers or Brethren of the Coast, French at first but afterwards rascally adventurers of all nations, who established themselves as inhabitants in the western part of Española and in some of the smaller West Indian islands in the following century: many of the islands were picked up by French, Dutch and English. In 1656 the English captured Jamaica, and soon afterwards the French established themselves on the Guiana coast. The eighteenth century brought a series of four wars with Great Britain between 1700 and 1783, which were largely concerned with

[1] The population of these thirty 'reductions' never exceeded 140,000 and was usually much less.

imperial and commercial designs upon the Spanish Indies. In 1715 Spain granted to the English the *asiento de negros* or contract for supplying negro slaves to Spanish America for thirty years; a monopoly which was for a time the vehicle of a great system of contraband trade. But the Spanish Empire emerged from these wars not only intact,[1] but growing in extent, wealth, population and international consideration.

The Bourbon kings after 1700 loosened the shackles upon trade. In 1740 the Portobello Fair, long since moribund, was discontinued, and thenceforth trade from Cadiz (which had replaced Seville) passed round Cape Horn to Chile and Peru. From 1760 further relaxations followed, and in 1778 all the chief ports of Spain and also those of the Spanish Indies (with some exceptions, afterwards removed) were opened, and the kingdoms of the Indies were permitted to trade with one another. Political administration was also improved. Two new Viceroyalties, that of Santa Fe or New Granada from 1749 and that of Buenos Aires (comprising all the River Plate region and Upper Peru) from 1786 relieved the unwieldy Viceroyalty of Peru, and audiencias were set up in Caracas and Buenos Aires.

But the paternal despotism of Charles III (1759–88) brought less welcome reforms: tightening of authority, greater efficiency in tax-collection and the division of most of the Empire into large provinces ruled by *intendentes*, whose first duty was care of the royal revenue. This meant increased officialdom, encroachment on ancient municipal rights and supervision of matters hitherto conveniently neglected. The long-standing animosity between Creoles and Peninsular Spaniards grew, the Creoles resenting the superior airs assumed by the Spaniards and their own exclusion from the more profitable posts.

But the greatest blow to royal authority came from the Crown itself, through the banishment in 1768 of the Jesuits, the ablest, most industrious and most orderly subjects of the King; on the frontiers the best protectors of the natives and the firmest pillars of the monarchy. The main causes of this expulsion were European,

[1] The British acquisition of a small settlement in Honduras is an insignificant exception. Havana was in British hands for thirteen months in 1762–3, and Florida for the following twenty years. Both were restored to Spain.

but one potent motive was a fantastic accusation that the Jesuits aimed at erecting their Indian villages on the Paraná into an independent empire. In California and New Spain their place was taken by Regulars of other Orders, notably Franciscans: but in South America most of the lands won by them relapsed into barbarism.

In 1780–3 the Spanish King offered a strange example to his transatlantic subjects by aiding with arms the revolt of the Thirteen British Colonies. Their achievement of independence impressed thoughtful observers, rather than the general population, in Spanish America. Liberal ideas and the theories of Rousseau were already evading censorship and finding voice in academic lecture-rooms and conversational gatherings when the rapid crashes of the French Revolution and the fall of the French throne reverberated throughout the world. The wars with Great Britain (1796–1801 and 1804–8) brought financial burdens and the interruption of communications with Spain, leading to trade with neutrals and even with the enemy.

It is tempting to regard as preludes to independence a futile conspiracy organized by two Frenchmen in Chile in 1780, a serious armed revolt against increased taxation in New Granada in the same year and a conspiracy organized in Caracas in 1797 by two Spaniards who had been deported to La Guaira on account of revolutionary activities in Spain. There is obviously some truth in this view; but more serious revolts of Spaniards had menaced Spanish authority in the sixteenth century. Control from Spain of those vast and remote dominions had always been difficult and had suffered frequent shocks. During the eighteenth century there had been several conspiracies, but they had not taken hold of the general population nor of the Creole aristocracy, nor—most important of all—had they found support in the cabildos. Conspiracy in Latin America is a daily occupation now and governments seldom command cordial adhesion. In the eighteenth century no distinct idea of separation from Spain had taken root. The atmosphere of these settlements, mostly tropical, where widely separated communities of European origin formed an indolent and well-fed aristocracy surrounded by a subject peasantry and (in the coastal districts) by negro slaves, was not revolutionary. Such a society is usually conservative and acquiescent; and in Spanish America the 'service of both Majesties', God and the King, was still a potent watchword. It is true that, with the increase of education and of contact with the outer world there was a growing dissatisfaction among the white or quasi-white population over many grievances. But to translate these sentiments into action an impulse was needed from without.

Strict chronological sequence would here compel divergence from the main course to an intricate and tenebrous insular bypath (1790–1803): the repercussions of the French Revolution on the French Antillean colony of Saint Domingue, the negro revolt and the emergence of a black 'Emperor' ruling over Haiti, the first tropical American country to become independent. But since that is a separate story which would confuse the main narrative, it is left for treatment in a later chapter.

NOTE. E. G. Bourne, *Spain in America** (New York, 1906); *Cambridge Modern History,** vol. x, ch. VIII; R. B. Merriman,* vol. III, ch. XXX; vol. IV, ch. XXXIII; C. H. Haring, *The Buccaneers in the West Indies in the Seventeenth Century** (London, 1910); *Trade and Navigation between Spain and the Indies under the Hapsburgs** (Harvard, 1918); F. Depons, *Travels in South America*, 2 vols. (London, 1807, English trans.); W. B. Stevenson, *Twenty Years' Residence in South America*, vol. I (London, 1825); W. Robertson, *History of America*, Book VII (Edinburgh, 1796 and many reprints); H. J. Priestley, *The Coming of the White Man* (New York, 1929); C. H. Lea, *The Inquisition in the Spanish Dependencies* (New York, 1928); H. H. Bancroft, *History of Mexico*, vols. I–III; *History of Central America*, vols. I and II (San Francisco, 1882–90); T. Gage, *The English-American...a new survey of the West Indies* (London, 1648; reprint edited by P. A. Newton, 1929); A. von Humboldt, *Travels to the Equinoctial Regions of the New Continent*, 5 vols. (London, 1814–21) and Bohn's reprint in 3 vols. (1852); *Political Essay on the Kingdom of New Spain*, 4 vols. (London, 1810–11); A. de Alcedo, *Geographical and Historical Dictionary of America and the West Indies*, translated with additions by G. A. Thompson, 5 vols. and atlas (London, 1812–15), is a valuable work of reference. *17545*

CHAPTER V

PORTUGUESE BRAZIL

FOR thirty years after Cabral's voyage in 1500, the Brazilian coast, although reserved for Portugal by the Treaty of Tordesillas, was almost a no-man's-land, except for the forcible landing of a few pairs of criminals and the temporary settlement of a precarious group. 'The whole history of Brazil in the sixteenth century may be contained in a few words', says the Brazilian historian Oliveira Lima. Accordingly, greater brevity in treating the early history of Brazil is not due to any designed inequality, but to a certain sameness in a story which narrates not conquests among remote mountain kingdoms and the administration of subject empires, but the gradual occupation of a fertile coast offering no extraordinary obstacles and accessible to navigation from Europe. Moreover, there was another reason for difference in action and movement: the external energies of the small Portuguese nation were bent upon the development of their great and opulent Empire on both coasts of Africa, in India, Ceylon and the East Indies. Their business was with Rajahs of Hindustan, Sinhalese potentates, Sultans of the Moluccas and of Malaya, and Chinese Mandarins. Their treasure fleets were laden not with gold and silver from the Western Hemisphere, but with pepper and cloves, muslins and silks from the Orient. They were pushing forward imperial expansion in three continents at once; and at the time South America was the least tempting of the three. No precious metals were found, as yet, in Brazil; and the indigenous inhabitants were scanty tribes of barbarians, many of them cannibals, always warring with one another. Indeed, the early part of Southey's *History of Brazil* is largely concerned with the manners of these tribes and with the Robinson-Crusoe-like adventures of a few white men, such as Caramasu ('Electric Eel'), who—having saved himself from the cooking-pot by his dexterous usefulness to his captors and by an exhibition with his musket—'from a slave became a king' and patriarch of a dusky brood; a useful ally, like others of his kind, to his more prosaic countrymen who followed; pleasant episodes which could be paralleled, if space admitted, from the history of Spanish America.

But the visits of French traders gathering cargoes of dye-wood— the Brazil wood ('flame-wood') which gave its name to the country —roused apprehensions in Portugal; and in 1531 a fleet was despatched from Lisbon under a notable commander, Martin Afonso de Souza, who set up in January 1532 the first substantial Portuguese settlement at São Vicente, near the present port of Santos. This event, the real birth of Brazil, is commemorated by a monument which stands to-day on the spot where the founder set foot upon the shore.

But a single settlement on 2000 miles of coast was not enough. The Portuguese Crown resolved to fill its vacant dominion by a system of feudal sovereignties which had been adopted in Madeira and the Azores. The Brazilian coast was divided into fifteen captaincies, each measuring fifty leagues along the shore, with hinterland only limited by the shadowy and movable western line stipulated at Tordesillas. These captaincies were granted about 1534 to Donatories who received almost unlimited powers of government and administration, including the right of enslaving the natives and sending a limited number annually to Lisbon for sale; also the right of founding cities and appointing magistrates. Two of these captaincies, at Olinda in the northern province of Pernambuco and at São Vicente in the south, grew and prospered through the cultivation of the sugar-cane, introduced from Madeira. But in general this scheme of empire was no more than an unsubstantial outline. Some captaincies were never occupied; others languished or withered, little isolated plantations widely separated from one another. Accordingly in 1549 King John III withdrew the extraordinary powers granted to the Captains (who, however, retained possession of their grants) and appointed as Governor of the whole country Tomas de Souza, a soldier already distinguished in India, to rule (so far as he could reach them) the small and scattered settlements from his residence at Bahia, thenceforth for two centuries the capital of Brazil. Thus from the mid-sixteenth century Brazil made real progress, a progress due in part to the self-sacrificing labours of the Jesuits in persuading dangerous tribes to make peace, in evangelizing the natives and in striving to protect them from enslavement and oppression.

The most famous names in early Brazilian history are those of Father Nobrega, who came out with the first Governor, and the younger Jesuit priest Anchieta, who obtained an extraordinary influence over the natives. When Indian assaults threatened all the southern settlements with extermination, Anchieta went to the Indian camps and persuaded the chiefs to accept a truce, himself remaining among them for three years as a hostage for its faithful observance. Both these priests favoured conquest. 'Conversion', says Anchieta, 'must be the work of fear rather than love.'

The infant settlements, already harassed by the attacks of native tribes and by revolts of the Indian slaves on the sugar plantations, were menaced by a French attempt to establish a Huguenot colony in an unoccupied region on the great Bay of Rio de Janeiro. French navigators had traded here with the natives, who hated the Portuguese: and in 1556 an adventurer known (by an assumed name) as Villegagnon, having won the support of Coligny, set up a fort, with eighty companions, on an island which still bears his name: 400 fervent Huguenots (who were also vigorous pirates) arrived from France; but finding Villegagnon to be a capricious tyrant and no true Protestant, most of them returned home: and four years later an expedition from Bahia destroyed the French settlement. Some Frenchmen, escaping to the mainland, roused the Indians against the Portuguese, but these in 1567 secured their hold on the south by founding the city of São Sebastião (Rio de Janeiro), to-day a great capital almost unrivalled in the magnificence of its setting. The new city was a starting-point for coastal settlement and later for penetration of the interior.

French attempts on Maranhão and on other points of the coast during the following half-century failed; and the dreams of an 'Antarctic France' ended in nothing more than the colony of Cayenne (French Guiana) founded in the second half of the seventeenth century.

The coastal settlements, with their sugar fields and factories, had expanded when in 1581 Philip II of Spain assumed the Crown of Portugal. For sixty years Brazil was ruled by Spanish kings. The country was not, however, annexed to Spain, as is evident from the fact that immigration, previously permitted to all Catholics, was from 1592 restricted to Portuguese, the Spanish subjects of the King being debarred as foreigners; just as in legal theory, though not always in fact, Portuguese were excluded from the Spanish Indies.

Yet the union of the Spanish and Portuguese Crowns exposed Brazil to attacks by the enemies of Spain, tempted by the dye-woods and rich sugar-harvests. Brief mention suffices for raids and pillage by English corsairs (1586–94). More formidable was the Dutch attempt to establish a Protestant empire in Brazil and thence to attack the Spanish dominions. In 1624 the Dutch West India Company sent an expedition which took Bahia and held it for a troubled year, constantly assailed by the militant Bishop of Bahia at the head of his flock. A Spanish-Portuguese armada, the greatest armament which had yet crossed the Equator, expelled the intruders.

A second expedition from Holland took the city of Olinda and the neighbouring port of Recife, which remained in Dutch hands for twenty-four years (1630–54) in spite of two great armaments sent out from the Peninsula and a constant 'war of ambuscades' carried on by the Portuguese of Brazil, with aid from regular forces. Recife, the Dutch capital, was at war with Bahia, both sides receiving reinforcements from Europe and help from Indian and negro auxiliaries under bold captains of red or African hue.

For seven years (1637–44) the princely statesman and soldier, Count Maurice of Nassau, was Governor of Dutch Brazil. Although he failed to take Bahia and effected little by sending an expedition against Chile, he extended Dutch dominion almost from the Amazon to the São Francisco, over an area equal to that ruled by the Portuguese and richer in population and resources. He granted to his Portuguese subjects religious toleration (afterwards modified in deference to Dutch sentiment); and, with a liberality unparalleled in that age, he opened the port to all foreign trade. He added to Recife a new quarter, which shows to-day the marks of its Dutch origin. His ships, crossing the Atlantic to Africa, captured the Portuguese ports in Angola, the source of the Brazilian slave-supply. 'The Brazilians', says Southey, 'were... dismayed at this unexpected stroke...so completely were they dependent upon the labour of this unhappy race that their ruin appeared inevitable now that the supply was in the hands of the Dutch.' They were dismayed at the 'quantity of Maurice's artillery, his strong fortresses, his ships so numerous, so abundantly stored and so perfectly equipped; and the weapons of the Dutch soldiers, so clean, so polished, so bright that they looked more like silver than iron beside those of the Portuguese'.

The Portuguese revolt in 1640 and the Portuguese-Dutch alliance against Spain did not check the Brazilian conflict and the spread of Dutch dominion. But resistance was growing in the north, when Maurice resigned his post in 1644. The Dutch company, bent on profits, grudged the expense of maintaining their conquest, which fell from them piecemeal. The hero of this recovery—honoured to-day as the creator of Brazilian nationality— was João Fernandez Vieira, a Portuguese of humble origin, who by industry had become a wealthy planter, noted for generous charity and hospitality, and had been a friend and councillor of Count Maurice. But to him the Dutch were heretic intruders, and for ten years he sacrificed everything to the struggle. His few companions multiplied: he entangled the Dutch in ambuscades and forest skirmishes; the slaves deserted the Dutch as rats abandon a doomed ship. Two victories in 1648–9 presaged the end, but it was not until 1654 that Recife, the last Dutch stronghold, fell, no aid coming from Holland on account of the war with Cromwell. After long dispute, the States-General in 1661 withdrew their claims to Brazil and Angola in return for a money payment. The Portuguese retained or recovered their possessions in America and Africa, although they lost most of their East Indian Empire—a loss which left them more free to expand their Brazilian domain.

Notwithstanding the set-back caused by the Dutch war and by the appearance of yellow fever in 1680—to be a scourge for more than 200 years—the seventeenth century was a time of progress and expansion, which received a great impetus from the discovery in 1694 of rich gold mines, whence the State of Minas Gerães derives its name. First came the familiar story of the rush to the mines; men and women; old and young; black, white and coloured; struggling along the forest paths towards a deceptive goal, which many never reached. Ships from Portugal were crowded with fortune-hunters: new mines were opened; more adventurers flocked to fresh discoveries, and the exodus from the plantations caused lasting injury to the sugar industry. Then came more regular working of the mines, the addition of great weight of gold to the diminished cargoes of sugar and dye-woods in the homeward-bound fleets, a great increase of revenue from the royal dues and a keen royal interest in so productive a dominion. The gold-fields were open to prospectors and mine-owners, but the diamond deposits, found some thirty years later, were, after various experiments, fenced off as the property of the Crown. But diamonds were found outside the fence and the royal dues on gold and gems were largely evaded. The mining camps were the scene of much lawlessness, disorder and licentiousness. But it was in great part due to the miners and mine-hunters that the eighteenth century was a time of growth and expanding occupation, thin and sporadic but nevertheless staking out a vast region as the Portuguese domain. 'The mere area of Brazil, with its 3700 miles of Atlantic sea-board and inland depth of some 2500 miles, was enormous; it was rich in fertile territory, in gold, and diamonds; and it possessed in the River Amazon and its tributaries the most magnificent navigable river system in the world. That so small a people had been able to occupy and administer successfully this vast dependency...is one of the wonders of history.' So writes G. Edmundson in the *Cambridge Modern History* (vol. x, ch. x).

This wonder is partly, but only partly, explained by three considerations: (1) the importation of negro slaves; (2) possession of the Amazon mouth and exclusive navigation of the whole river; and (3) the armed invasions and attacks on unsubdued tribes by the half-caste Paulistas, expert slave-hunters and slave-traders.

(1) The Portuguese possessed in Angola the source of the slave-trade; and Brazil was colonized from Africa, by forcible immigration, more than from Europe by voluntary immigration. The

whole structure of society rested upon abundant slave labour. The average annual importation of slaves in the seventeenth century is estimated at 44,000 and in the eighteenth at 55,000. On the eve of independence the negro slaves in Brazil outnumbered the white and quasi-white population; and the coloured population, including mulattoes and free negroes, largely outnumbered the whites. The Portuguese historian, Oliveira Martins, even speaks of the 'colonists, infinitely few, in face of the masses of black slaves'.

(2) The Portuguese, possessing the mouth of the Amazon, were masters of the only gate to a vast interior. An immense vacant estate, fenced in for them by nature and unapproachable by others, awaited their leisure and capacity to occupy it. The wonder is, not that the Portuguese pushed their dominion here so far westward, but that the Spaniards, starting from Quito and surmounting the eastern Cordillera, succeeded in establishing their claim so far to the east, to the present limits of Peru and Colombia. In 1609 the Portuguese founded the city of Belem (Pará) near the mouth of the river. Communication between these northern conquests and the south was so difficult that Philip IV instituted a separate northern government, independent of Bahia, under the name of Maranhão in 1624; a division which subsisted down to 1763.

From about 1630 the intricate waterways of the Amazon were explored, and in 1669 the city of Manáos, 900 miles from the sea, was founded. Forty years later the French claimed that their colony of Cayenne extended to the north bank of the river. British negotiators at Utrecht in 1713–14, in alliance with Portugal, frustrated that claim. The French then sought the right to navigate the Amazon; a concession which might have endangered Portuguese possession of the interior. This second French claim was also defeated by British diplomacy, which thus secured to the Portuguese the only road to an immense region. But the occupation of that region was in great part the work of the nineteenth century and even to-day is by no means complete.

(3) The third point is that, whereas armed incursions upon unsubdued tribes were forbidden by law to the Spaniards from the beginning of the seventeenth century and although the same law was in theory imposed upon his Portuguese subjects by Phillip III

of Spain, nevertheless from about that same time the Portuguese dominion was pushed forward by the frequent raids of the Paulistas. The city of São Paulo and its neighbourhood, remote from the coastal towns and from government control, became the refuge of adventurers and runaways, who by union with the native women produced a vigorous half-caste race known as Mamelucos, intrepid and ruthless slave-hunters. A struggle with the Jesuits for pre-eminence in São Paulo ended in complete victory for the Mamelucos, who became semi-independent, ignoring the civil Government and defying the Church. When the capture of Angola by the Dutch cut off the supply of negro slaves, these Paulistas made a business of supplying the coastal towns of Brazil with Indian slaves. In 1629–31 they fell upon the Spanish Jesuit Missions of La Guaira, burning, killing, destroying and carrying off 2500 Christian neophytes to be sold in Rio and São Vicente; many of these victims perished by the way. With complete impartiality the Mamelucos raided also the Portuguese Jesuit Missions. Aided by Indian followers, who were always ready to fight and destroy rival tribes, these *bandeiras*, marauding bands, ranged far afield, killing, enslaving and preparing the way for Portuguese dominion. Sometimes the *bandeirantes*, with wives and children, spent years upon the march, like a nomad tribe, halting in case of need to sow and reap a crop of maize or mandioca. In 1660 and 1679 these valiant backwoodsmen and pioneers, traversing an unknown wilderness from São Paulo, reached the upper waters of the River Tocantins. But the most notable of these journeys was the discovery by a Paulista in 1714 of the gold mines of Cuyabá on an affluent of the Upper Paraguay in the very centre of the continent.

This outpost at Cuyabá, hundreds of miles from the nearest Portuguese settlements, established a claim not only to all the intervening region (mostly thick forest, *Matto Grosso*) but also to an extensive country farther west. Thenceforth an annual expedition of sixty or seventy armed canoes traversed the country of many warlike tribes from São Paulo to Cuyabá, navigating a succession of six rivers, with many portages—a perilous journey of some two months, including a long halt half-way.

Territorial rivalry between Portuguese and Spaniards dates from the discovery of America and continued long after the achievement of independence. In 1678 the Portuguese strove to push their boundary southward to the River Plate estuary by setting up the fortified post of Colonia del Sacramento on the northern shore, opposite to Buenos Aires, on a spot 1000 miles to the south of the nearest Portuguese settlement and regarded by the Buenosaireans as their cattle pasture. Colonia was promptly destroyed by the Spaniards, but rebuilt by the Portuguese. It flourished by a lucrative smuggling trade, in which English traders had a share, with the Spaniards of Buenos Aires and Paraguay. Repeatedly taken by the Spaniards in war and repeatedly restored to the Portuguese in peace, Colonia finally fell to the Spaniards in 1776. The permanent possession of this place and of Montevideo, founded in 1726, secured to Spain the Banda Oriental, now the Spanish-speaking Republic of Uruguay. With this exception the Portuguese, acting from an inner base, were generally successful, particularly in the diplomatic skill of their negotiators. The imminent Spanish conquest of the southern projection of Brazil (Santa Catharina and Rio Grande do Sul) was averted in 1776 by peace preliminaries. The negotiations of 1750, of 1777–8, of 1801 cannot here be detailed: the result may be seen in the present-day map of Brazil.

The Portuguese system of government and trade, dealing with simpler conditions, was less elaborate than the Spanish system. But Brazil was still in the making when Philip II became King of Portugal, and the chief law-givers of Brazil were the Hapsburg monarchs. After the formative and experimental period there was a general resemblance between the Spanish and Portuguese systems: the all-embracing and all-powerful authority of the King, acting through a Governor-General or Viceroy and through subordinate magistrates in provinces, districts and cities; the tenure of all prominent posts in State and Church by European Portuguese; the vigour of the municipalities, which, especially during the Hapsburg period and afterwards, had privileges resembling those of the Spanish cabildos; the exclusion of foreign immigrants, not always rigidly enforced; the annual sugar-fleet convoyed to and from Lisbon, and the restriction of trade to the mother-country; the prohibition of all manufactures except that of sugar; monopolies more numerous and more irritating than in the Spanish Indies; heavy taxation, grievously wasted by maladministration and corruption. Indeed, corruption and personal interest pervaded the tribunals and the public offices. There was bitter animosity between Creoles and European Portuguese, an animosity which blazed out in 1710 into a little local civil war when Recife, the home of Portuguese traders, received full civic privileges and was attacked by the Creole inhabitants of Olinda, the historic capital of the Province of Pernambuco. There was no university in Brazil and no printing-press.

The treatment of the natives, tribes living in varying degrees of barbarism or savagery, was a less complicated question than in the Spanish Indies, and consisted mainly in a conflict between the Jesuits, protectors of the Indians, and the settlers, their enslavers and exploiters; the Crown (after the initial period) in general favouring the Jesuits and attempting to protect the natives, but without much consistency or determination. The Portuguese historian Oliveira Martins puts the case briefly: 'The adaptation of the Portuguese race to the South American climate brought the extermination of the Indian tribes...from 1531 began the extermination of the aboriginal races.' In 1575 the chivalrous young King Sebastian forbade the capture of Indians as slaves 'except in just war': this provoked such indignant protests that the order was modified and in fact meant little: indeed, the frequency of such orders proves their futility. In 1680 a royal order decreed that the Indians, even those captured in war, were free men and should receive grants of land. This command, coupled with an attempt to institute a monopoly of the slave trade and to limit the import of slaves, provoked a revolt in Maranhão, where a Junta took charge, deposed the Governor and expelled the Jesuits. But the tumult was suppressed by force. In the seventeenth century the efforts of the Jesuit Vieira, a truly great man and the founder of a chain of missions in Maranhão, secured some protection for the natives in the north, where to-day there is a considerable survival of Indian blood; although this is probably due to climate and conditions of labour more than to the work of the Jesuits. In the southern provinces the Indian admixture is hardly discernible, though the African mixture is strong.

The famous Portuguese minister Pombal (1750–77) decreed sweeping measures of reform. He declared, too late, that the Indians were free men and were to receive gifts of lands. He banished the Jesuits, abolished the Inquisition, introduced settlers from the Azores, corrected abuses in finance and administration, extinguished the remaining feudal captaincies, moved the capital to Rio de Janeiro and united the Government in the Viceroy's hands, abolishing the division between north and south. He abolished the annual organized fleets, opening all Brazilian ports to trade with Portugal, but not with other countries: he encouraged education and agriculture and employed native Brazilians in important civil and military posts. But the reforming zeal of 'enlightened despotism' also drew tighter the bonds of authority, exercised an unaccustomed stringency in the collection of taxes and created new imposts. The convenient laxity of earlier days gave place to an unwelcome vigour, often hasty and indiscreet in the details of its action.

Throughout the colonial period the administration seems to have been less rigid than in the Spanish Indies, possibly because rules of trade were more difficult to enforce upon coasts so easily accessible from Europe. Yet 'the traditional policy, which held that Colonies existed solely for the benefit of the home country... continued up to 1807 to govern the relations between Portugal and Brazil'.[1] But the Brazilians, among whom were many men of Jewish ancestry, were excellent business men and most efficient smugglers. Moreover, as in the Spanish Indies, there were many exceptions to the rigid rules of trade. From 1650 foreigners were allowed to trade with Brazil through the agency of Portuguese merchants: a privilege used to the utmost by English traders. For a time after 1660 both English and Dutch had some limited rights of direct trade with Brazil. About the middle of the eighteenth century four Englishmen were allowed to reside in each of the leading Brazilian cities with the same rights as Portuguese subjects.

[1] Edmundson in *Cambridge Modern History*, vol. X, p. 311.

Such privileges always go a good deal farther than their strict intention.

Many Brazilians in the interior regions of São Paulo, Goyaz and Matto Grosso lived remote from all authority. The sturdy cattle-farmers (*sertanejos*) who inhabited the *Sertão*, the uplands stretching inland from the coast of Pernambuco and Bahia, people who, notwithstanding some mixture of blood, preserved the primitive vigour of the Portuguese peasant, knew no laws but their own patriarchal customs; and even in the coastal towns the effective range of authority was limited. There is no evidence of profound or general disquietude; but the conspiracy of 1788 in Minas Gerães demands mention because its leader, a cavalry officer named Silva Xavier and nicknamed Tiradentes ('tooth-drawer') is honoured in Brazil as Precursor of Independence. A group of Brazilian youths studying in France and Portugal, hearing of the achievement of independence by the Thirteen British Colonies, became fired with revolutionary projects and French political theories. One of them, returning to Brazil, found sympathizers in Minas, largely owing to a rumour that the authorities were about to exact payment of huge arrears of the royal dues on gold. The plot was revealed. Tiradentes was hanged; the penalties inflicted on the other conspirators were afterwards mitigated. Four years afterwards a conspiracy in Bahia was suppressed without difficulty. It was an impulse from without, from Portugal itself, which pre-pared the way, a generation later, to the independence of Brazil.

NOTE. R. Southey, *History of Brazil*, 3 vols. (London, 1810–19); R. G. Watson, *Spanish and Portuguese America*, 2 vols. (London, 1884).

CHAPTER VI

THE MOVEMENT OF INDEPENDENCE

THE chief precursors of independence were Nariño, a prominent citizen of Bogotá, who suffered long imprisonment (varied by strange escapes) for printing and distributing a Spanish translation of the French revolutionary *Declaration of the Rights of Man*; and the Venezuelan Francisco Miranda, a versatile and persuasive political adventurer, whose life was an almost incredible romance. As a Spanish infantry officer he saw some service against the British in the war which liberated the Thirteen Colonies. In 1784 or earlier, he was planning the emancipation of Spanish America. During fifteen years (1790–1804) he urged in turn upon the United States, France and Great Britain an expedition to arouse and aid revolt in the Indies. Pitt's cabinet, upon the outbreak of war with Spain in 1804, planned such an expedition but abandoned the project. Miranda then determined to act alone. In 1806 he sailed from New York with 200 deluded volunteers, many of whom were captured by a Spanish warship. Some were executed, others were put to hard labour in tropical heat. But Miranda was still hopeful: he recruited a few more men in the British West Indies and landed at Coro in Venezuela, expecting a general uprising of the inhabitants. Nobody joined him and he sailed away. There was no public opinion among the general population, mostly illiterate people of mixed blood. The landowning Creole aristocracy, the only class which counted in a political sense, desired no revolution.

In the same year another filibustering adventure in the far south aimed not at emancipation, but at conquest. Sir Home Popham, a captain in the British Navy, who had known Pitt's designs (since abandoned) upon South America, finding himself in command of a squadron anchored idly in Table Bay in the midst of the world-wide Napoleonic War, sailed from Capetown without orders against the River Plate carrying 1600 troops under Beresford, who in June 1806 marched unresisted into Buenos Aires. The Viceroy fled to

Córdoba, thereby in some sort abdicating Spanish authority in the capital. Beresford named himself Governor under the British Crown. But in six weeks he was compelled to surrender by an uprising of all the townspeople, aided by a small relief force which had been organized in the Banda Oriental (now Uruguay) by a naval officer named Liniers, acting in concert with the Cabildo of Buenos Aires.

Political action followed this victory of the people. The Cabildo summoned about 100 notables to a 'general congress' (a novel and significant term) to prepare future defence. This assembly named Liniers Commander-in-chief in place of the absent Viceroy.[1] Subscriptions were raised, recruits enlisted, and all men of military age were called up. Nearly 10,000 troops were raised and equipped, and a prominent Creole, Cornelio Saavedra, took command of the Creole battalions.

These measures were needed. In February 1807 an expedition from England took the fortified city of Montevideo. More British troops came, and in July General Whitelocke, having crossed the estuary with some 8000 men, attacked Buenos Aires. The attack failed: the British troops, entering the city with unloaded muskets in thirteen separate columns along thirteen parallel streets, were assailed from all sides and suffered heavy loss. Whitelocke signed a capitulation, that all prisoners should be restored, that the British should re-embark and that Montevideo should be evacuated.

Buenos Aires, unprotected by the Spanish Crown, had twice repelled invasion, had deposed the King's representative, and had raised a citizen army, not disbanded after victory: novelties which made a deep impression throughout Spanish America. Admission of foreign trade to Montevideo during British occupation was a revelation. Yet, except a few men secretly nursing separatist ideas, the people maintained sincere allegiance to the Spanish throne.

The fall of that throne in 1808 initiated long conflicts on both sides of the Atlantic. Events in Spain, leading to transatlantic independence, must first be summarized.

---

[1] Six months later a similar Junta deposed the Viceroy and shipped him, under arrest, for Spain. The Crown sanctioned this proceeding by appointing Liniers to be *interim* Viceroy.

In 1807-8 Napoleon laid hands on Spain. In March 1808 Charles IV abdicated and his son was proclaimed as Ferdinand VII: a month later both father and son, decoyed into Napoleon's power at Bayonne, renounced the throne, and in July 1808 Joseph Bonaparte entered Madrid as King. Within twenty days he fled before Spanish armies: all Spain was in revolt, and local Juntas sprang up everywhere. In September a 'Central Junta' met near the capital, but in two months fled southward to Seville, while Napoleon entered Madrid and restored Joseph. During 1809 the Central Junta sat in Seville; but in January 1810 escaped before French advance to the island city of Cadiz, protected by the British fleet. There the Junta dissolved, after arranging for Cortes to represent Spain and America. The Governor and cabildo of every American capital were to choose a deputy; but pending their arrival, *americanos*, happening to be in Cadiz, took their seats. The Cortes met in September 1810, appointed a Regency of three and drew up the radical 'Constitution of 1812'. But in 1814 the restored Ferdinand dismissed the Cortes and established his stupid and bungling tyranny (1814-20). It was ended by an event decisive for American independence, for in 1820 the army destined for the reconquest of America revolted at Cadiz and aided a radical revolution which restored the 1812 Constitution. The radical *trienio* ended in 1823, when an invading French army restored Ferdinand's absolutism. During these vicissitudes Spanish America was separated from Spain.

On the abdication of Charles IV in 1808, Ferdinand VII was proclaimed King in every American capital with universal applause. But French emissaries brought letters from the Council of the Indies announcing the abdication of Ferdinand and the confirmation of all actual Governors and officials by King Joseph. The news was everywhere received with fierce anger at this French insult to the nation. The next news—the national uprising against the French —was greeted with enthusiasm. Contributions poured in and were remitted to Spain. Thus the first disobedience to the Council of the Indies was a revolt not against Spain but against the French usurpers. In the course of three years it was gradually turned into a revolt against Spanish authority by the force of circumstances, by the agitation of a few separatists and by the hostility of Colonial Governors and the Cadiz Regency.

In August 1809 the Audiencia of Chuquisaca, in Upper Peru, deposed an unsatisfactory Governor and assumed his functions. This act of European magistracy had many precedents and was hardly unconstitutional; but in existing conditions it pointed to revolution, and the neighbouring city of La Paz, catching the infection, proclaimed autonomy. About the same time some citizens of Quito deposed the Governor and assumed authority as a 'Sovereign Junta', alleging 'the example of our Spanish brothers, the unsettled state of Spain, the annihilation of the lawfully constituted authorities', and the danger of passing under French dominion. In the general tension these movements, suppressed with impolitic truculence, caused a stir beyond their intrinsic importance.

Spanish news came that the French had overrun Andalucia and that in February 1810 the Central Junta had dispersed. Already theorists had been arguing that, since the monarchy was the only constitutional link between Spain and America, all Spanish authority was ended by the fall of the throne. They now urged 'Spain is lost; there is no more Spain'. Between April and July 1810 many cabildos formed Juntas—sometimes under the presidency of royal governors, soon to be displaced—'to preserve the authority of Ferdinand VII'. But only in Buenos Aires was the movement uninterrupted. Therefore that movement may be traced first, though not earliest in its inception.

At news of Charles IV's abdication, Ferdinand was proclaimed in Buenos Aires amid loud indignation at Napoleon's pretensions. But Elío, the ultra-royalist Governor of Montevideo, disavowed the 'Frenchman' Liniers, knocked down an officer sent to supersede him and summoned a royalist Junta in Montevideo. Thus, by a strange inversion, an extreme absolutist was the first rebel against constituted authority.

Amidst these confusions, a small group was quietly working for independence, led by Manuel Belgrano, a lawyer of high character educated in Europe; and when Admiral Cisneros arrived in July 1809 as Viceroy appointed by the Central Junta, he found that in the viceroyalty, as in Spain, power was passing from officials to semi-municipal, semi-popular bodies. Indeed, Cisneros himself, driven by financial needs, acted as head of an autonomous state in admitting British trade. In these changes the small party having the most definite and logical aim held strong ground. The commander of the Creole battalions, approached by them, promised to declare for independence upon the capture of Seville by the French. On 13 May 1810 an English ship brought news that Seville had fallen four months earlier and that the Central Junta had fled to Cadiz and dissolved. The moment for action had come. A week later Cisneros assented perforce to the summoning of a *cabildo abierto*. This body decided after an animated debate that Cisneros should be deposed and that the Cabildo should appoint a Junta to rule until the election of a Congress. The Cabildo hesitated, but under pressure from a clamorous crowd and from the Creole battalions, a Junta of nine persons was sworn in to 'preserve this part of America for our August Sovereign Ferdinand VII'. The date, 25 May, is annually observed as the birthday of the Argentine Republic. The Viceroy and the Oidores were afterwards deported. 'A bloodless Revolution', remarks the contemporary historian Funes, 'produced by the very course of events.' The remark is equally true of the movements in Chile, New Granada and Venezuela in their early stages. These movements followed traditional Spanish methods which were hardly unconstitutional in order to meet an extraordinary emergency— the collapse of royal government. But obviously the creation of a provisional committee was only the first step in the construction of a new polity embracing the whole country.

The Junta at the first opportunity sent an emissary to England. He reached London on 6 August 1810; and next day news of the Buenos Aires revolution appeared in *The Times*.

Most of the interior cities, although later adhesion or submission to Buenos Aires was doubtful, accepted the lead of the capital in this first step. Liniers, the hero of the reconquest, attempting a 'reactionary' movement in Córdoba, was captured and shot by an expedition of 1150 mounted men, which was despatched from Buenos Aires to Córdoba and to the far north-west, 'to carry the commands of the people on the points of their bayonets', says Mitre. But the attempt to unite the whole of the unwieldy Viceroyalty failed. Belgrano was sent with a small force to offer to the people of Paraguay independence and union. Paraguay declined union, or rather declined submission to Buenos Aires, but accepted independence without having to fight for it; or rather she allowed the Argentines to fight her War of Independence without offering any aid; for the defeat of the Argentines would have exposed Paraguay to royalist attack, whereas Argentine victory meant security for Paraguay; since Paraguay, isolated and self-contained in the interior of the continent, was only accessible by way of the River Paraná, flowing through Argentine territory.

Notwithstanding professed loyalty to Ferdinand VII, the leaders in Buenos Aires saw that their revolution meant war—war in two regions, against the royalist stronghold of Montevideo and also against the Peruvian Viceroy. After four years of fighting on land and water, the nearer war was ended through a great effort by the capture of Montevideo: a victory which deprived the Spaniards of a base in the River Plate, brought a store of munitions, removed the danger of invasion from Spain and also checked invasion from the Viceroyalty of Peru.

For during those same years the Argentines were fighting with hastily raised troops under self-taught commanders among the mountains of Upper Peru, remote from their native plains. They claimed that province as part of the Viceroyalty of Buenos Aires: but in fact they were invading an alien land, a country of lofty plateau and mountain-masses inhabited by an Indian peasantry, a recruiting ground for the royalists and held by the forces of the Viceroy of Peru. The first advance up these heights led to a delusive victory (Suipacha, November 1810) and a triumphant entry into Potosí. Then came crushing defeat and retreat to Tucumán. The royalists under a Creole commander pushed southwards to Tucumán, but were in turn defeated and were forced to capitulate by a second defeat at Salta (February 1813).

Belgrano, victorious at Tucumán and Salta, led a second invasion of Upper Peru, was twice defeated and retired to Tucumán. The royalist commander was advancing southwards towards that place in 1814 when he heard of the fall of Montevideo and turned back; for unless he could win through to Montevideo, advance meant isolation. Moreover, the country had risen behind him under the inspiring guerrillero leader Arenales. A third invasion of Upper Peru in 1815 repeats the story: initial success, advance northwards, defeat and demoralized retreat. Armies on either side in these battles varied from 2000 to 5000 men. The population of the Argentine Provinces, excluding Paraguay and the Banda Oriental, was probably about half a million. The final issue of this 'northern war' was that each side failed in attack and succeeded in defence. The Argentines never effectively penetrated Upper Peru: the Peruvians never got beyond Tucumán and failed to hold anything south of the plateau. Thenceforth the frontier was defended by the gauchos of Salta under the chieftain Güemes, who organized all the inhabitants for guerrilla war. The invasions of Upper Peru, although repelled, had not wholly failed, for in that country many local revolts flamed out. Out of 102 insurgent leaders only nine survived the war; the rest perished in fight or on the scaffold.

The fact that this 'northern war' was an indecisive frontier war was grasped by the Argentine soldier San Martín, who formed another secret plan for securing Argentine independence by crossing the Andes into Chile and thence invading Peru by sea. The grave, cautious and reserved Lieutenant-Colonel San Martín, now aged thirty-three, son of a Spanish magistrate in Misiones, had served twenty years in the Spanish army, when in March 1812 he landed in Buenos Aires to fight for the Argentines. After two years of signal service against the royalists, he established himself as Governor of the sub-Andine Province of Cuyo, there to spend another two years in preparation. During those two years the Argentine war was a stationary one of successful defence; and notwithstanding political disorder and civil strife, the country maintained its independence. Already in 1813 both the substance and the symbols of the Spanish system had been swept away; and at last in July 1816, six years after the real winning of independence, the United Provinces of the River Plate (comprising most of the existing Argentine provinces) published a

PLATE I

SAN MARTÍN

solemn Declaration of Independence in a Congress which met at Tucumán.

At that time Ferdinand VII appeared to have regained all his other American possessions. The nascent Republic of Chile, after three years of stormy life, had succumbed before invasion from Peru, which was securely held by the Viceroy, barring all contact between the northern and southern 'patriots'. Revolt in Mexico had been checked; and the republican movement in Venezuela and New Granada, after many vicissitudes, had apparently collapsed. These things now demand narration.

For books see notes on Chapters VII and XIV.

CHAPTER VII

INDEPENDENCE IN SOUTH AMERICA

The capital of Venezuela has been the principal forge of the American insurrection. TORRENTE.

When in July 1808 news reached Caracas of the royal abdications, the Captain-General himself proposed to the Cabildo the formation of a Junta, but afterwards withdrew his proposal and even arrested its supporters, thus foolishly provoking revolt. The Creole aristocracy, who had been hostile or indifferent to Miranda's attempts, felt that their supremacy, linked with traditional loyalty to the throne, depended on themselves now that the throne had fallen. On 17 April 1810 news came of the fall of Seville, the flight to Cadiz and the dissolution of the Central Junta. Two days later the Cabildo, having assembled for the usual ceremonial meeting on Holy Thursday, effected a facile revolution. The boldness of a few men who thrust their way into the Cabildo, and the skilfully directed clamours of a crowd in the Plaza, forced the Captain-General to resign: a 'Supreme Junta' of twenty-two members 'to preserve the rights of Ferdinand VII' sprang into being. The Audiencia was swept aside; the authority of the Cadiz Regency was expressly renounced; the ports were opened to the trade of all nations: a manifesto was sent to all the Venezuelan Cabildos inviting the election of deputies to a Congress; and commissioners were despatched to Washington and to London to solicit support. Among the latter was Simón Bolívar, the youthful head of a wealthy family of Creole aristocrats, descendant of a Simón Bolívar who in 1595 had gone to Madrid as Procurador of the city of Caracas.

Coro, the oldest city in western Venezuela and once the capital, moved by jealousy of Caracas rather than by loyalty, gave a defiant answer and rejoiced that the Cadiz Regency had decreed a blockade of the coasts of Caracas and had issued letters of marque to privateers:[1] a blunder which stamped the Caraqueños as rebels and pushed them to independence. Maracaibo in the far west necessarily followed the lead of Coro, and the Province of Guayana in the south-east, that is to say the city of Angostura (now Ciudad Bolívar), was equally defiant. An expedition from Caracas against Coro was repulsed: the beginning of civil war.

In March 1811 a Congress representing seven provinces met at Caracas; and three months later, on 5 July, this Congress issued a Declaration of Independence, thus setting the first example to the Kingdoms of Spanish America. A protesting crowd of Isleños (Canary Islanders) was dispersed, and sixteen were executed. But an anti-republican revolt in Valencia cost a month of bloodshed before it was suppressed by Miranda; who had returned, after forty years' absence, to his native country, had sat in the Congress and now commanded the troops.

In December 1811 the Congress promulgated a republican Constitution, modelled on that of the United States. Not understanding that federation was a means of uniting separate political bodies, they adopted the federal system, erecting insignificant districts into autonomous States and authorizing that disruptive regionalism which has been the chief obstacle to national organization in Spanish America. Yet Venezuela appeared to have leapt at once into full nationhood. The delusion was brief: in February 1812 a Spanish naval officer named Monteverde led a party of some 300 men eastwards from Coro. Quadrupling his numbers by recruiting on the way and by desertions from the republican cause, he pushed on, gathering booty, munitions and recruits from the sack of towns. He was already threatened by counter-movements in his rear, when an appalling catastrophe opened the way to him. On Holy Thursday, 1812, the first anniversary (in the Ecclesiastical Calendar) of the Declaration of Independence, an earthquake destroyed half the city of Caracas, buried in the ruined churches the crowded worshippers and killed 10,000 people in Caracas and La Guaira, besides 4000 in other 'patriot' cities, sparing the royalist cities. The clergy preached Divine judgment to a terrified people;

---

[1] The insurgents responded by issuing letters of marque in their turn. This was the beginning of the piratical activity and violent disorder in the Caribbean region, depicted in Michael Scott's romance *Tom Cringle's Log*.

on 3 May Monteverde entered Valencia amid popular acclamations; an insurrection of slaves, incited by the royalists, threatened the capital.

To meet these disasters the veteran Miranda was appointed *generalísimo* with dictatorial powers: his troops, 4000 in number, largely exceeded those of Monteverde. Bold promptitude was needed. But the sexagenarian commander, strange to the country, disliked by the Creole aristocracy and distrusting his own troops, preferred to consult, to organize, to discipline. Sporadic skirmishes brought no success. Miranda was still deliberating, when in July 1812 a despatch from Simón Bolívar, commander of the fortified port of Puerto Cabello, announced the loss of that place with all the stores and munitions of the 'patriots'. 'Venezuela is stricken to the heart', exclaimed Miranda. Despairing of success or disillusioned about the whole movement, he proposed an armistice: Monteverde demanded capitulation: Miranda agreed: he surrendered everything on condition of general amnesty and of free departure to all who chose to emigrate. He chose departure; but Bolívar and other officers arrested him in his bed on the night before his intended embarkation at La Guaira and left him in prison, to fall into Monteverde's hands and to die four years later in a Spanish dungeon. Bolívar received a safe-conduct and journeyed by sea to serve the republicans of New Granada.

Monteverde now ruled in the capital and his satellites elsewhere with capricious cruelty. Despite the stipulated amnesty 1500 persons were crowded into unwholesome dungeons where many perished.

But Bolívar, a refugee in Cartagena, was planning recovery, and henceforth devoted life and fortune to the cause of independence. He was a childless widower of twenty-nine, educated in Europe, where he had imbibed revolutionary ideas. Small in frame and stature, anxious and melancholy in countenance, possessing little military experience, a true urban Creole in candid vanity and unashamed sensuality; repeatedly beaten and apparently abandoning his associates, but always renewing the struggle; he came to be recognized as the chief inspiration of the movement and ultimately as the Liberator of five extensive republics.

Cartagena, the strongest fortress in Spanish America, encircled by massive walls of medieval aspect, possessing a permanent garrison (largely coloured troops) and a well-stored arsenal, had formed a Junta and deposed the Governor in June 1810. A month later Bogotá, the capital, on its remote and lofty savannah, whither news travelled slowly, formed its Junta and soon afterwards expelled the Viceroy, proclaiming allegiance to the King but not to the Cadiz Regency, and attempting to unite the country under its own leadership. But in that country of valleys and mountains Juntas sprang up everywhere, even in insignificant villages. Nariño, the Precursor, anxious for a strong centralized government, commanded the militia of Bogotá in an intermittent civil war against a garrulous 'federal' congress, sitting now in one city, now in another. Popayán, in the south, waged a long civil war against the stubborn royalists of Pasto, who thwarted every republican attack upon themselves and upon the kingdom of Quito, which was ruled by Spanish magistrates down to 1821.

In November 1811 Cartagena issued an ill-judged Declaration of Independence, claiming to be a detached sovereign city-state. Cartagena was at war with the older and rival city of Santa Marta, which naturally remained royalist, receiving support from the Spanish Antilles and from Panamá, which was the residence of the titular Viceroy of New Granada since the revolution of Bogotá.

Bolívar and other Venezuelan refugees were welcomed in Cartagena (November 1812) which was menaced by land and sea and cut off from the interior by royalist posts. Bolívar disobeyed his instructions to hold a small post on the River Magdalena, advanced southward with 200 men and dislodged by rapid movement several royalist garrisons on the river and on the adjoining mountains, recruiting as he went and opening the way to the capital. Victory won pardon; his next success was to persuade the Congress of New Granada (in session at Tunja) and the authorities of Cartagena that the reconquest of Venezuela was essential to the independence of New Granada. In April 1813 he set out from Cartagena with 500 men; augmenting his numbers as he went; welcomed in some places; defeating royalist detachments in six combats; proclaiming 'War to the death...no quarter to Spaniards, pardon

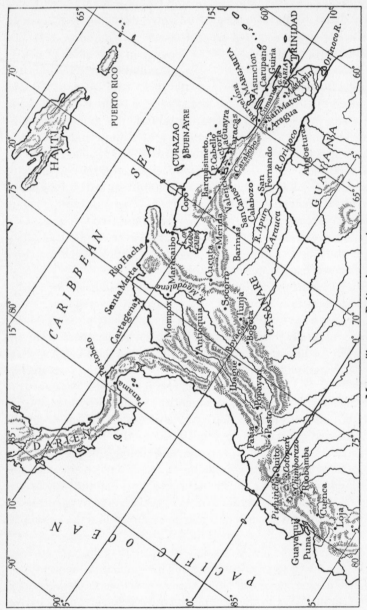

Map to illustrate Bolívar's campaigns

to Americanos' (June 1813); crossing two mountain ranges, seven formidable rivers, extensive forests and plains; evading hostile bodies, setting up patriot administrations in the places which he passed; capturing guns and munitions; he accomplished his march of some 800 miles to Caracas in a campaign of ninety-three days. At his approach Monteverde retired to Puerto Cabello, followed by a miserable exodus from the capital of those who feared re-publican vengeance. On 6 August 1813 Bolívar entered the city, greeted as 'Liberator' by an acclaiming crowd.

This success in western Venezuela was only made possible by victories of others in the east. In January 1813 a group of forty-five Venezuelan refugees—among them Sucre, of later fame—possessing five muskets among them, landed from Trinidad on the neigh-bouring coast, overpowered a small Spanish post, gained adherents owing to general disgust at royalist excesses, inflicted a severe defeat on Monteverde and, after a six months' campaign, entered Cumaná two days before Bolívar's entry into Caracas. Mariño, their leader, was dictator on the eastern coast, as Bolívar in the west.

But these rapid successes, although necessary in order to win renown and gain adherents, did not mean the winning of the country. The population in general cared nothing for independence and wanted peace: the royalist forces were strong and were enlisting recruits. One Boves, a Spanish sergeant who had been dismissed from the army for misconduct but had contrived to re-enter the service, gained ascendancy over the half-savage mounted herdsmen of the southern plains by ferocity and skilful daring and by promises of booty and debauchery. Crouching almost invisible by their horses' necks and charging with the lance, these irresistible barbarians, of mixed Indian and negro blood, spread panic every-where. To Boves and his men the slaughter of prisoners and of non-combatants was an amusing diversion. He was outdone in fiendish cruelty by his second-in-command Morales, who later succeeded him.

Bolívar, finding his position in the capital precarious, ordered the 880 prisoners in Caracas and La Guaira to be killed (February 1814). Three months later he suffered severe defeat and in July abandoned the capital to the ferocious vengeance of Boves, retiring to Barcelona, whither he was followed, in his twenty days' march through torrential rain, by crowded fugitives, men, women and children, many of whom perished by the way. Further disaster followed; and although the republicans held the island of Margarita and a few still fought on the mainland, Bolívar desisted from the struggle and embarked for Cartagena, to serve the Congress of New Granada in reducing its unruly cities to obedience.

Having compelled Bogotá to submit to the Congress, he was prevented from attacking Santa Marta by a miserable quarrel, amounting to civil war, with the Governor of Cartagena; and, to avoid disaster, he resigned command and withdrew to Jamaica in May 1815.

A month earlier, sixty Spanish transports, convoyed by warships, carrying a siege-train and 10,000 Spanish troops, commanded by General Morillo, a stout soldier who had fought his way up from the ranks in the Peninsular War, had reached the Spanish Main, despatched by Ferdinand VII to reconquer his American kingdoms: the fall of Montevideo in 1814, leaving the royalists no base in the River Plate, had diverted this formidable armament from its intended destination. Morillo easily reduced the island of Margarita, the only remaining republican territory: he was received in Caracas with an ovation resembling that accorded to Bolívar two years earlier. Unresisted in Venezuela, he moved westward to the conquest of New Granada with 9000 troops, many of them native Venezuelans. The siege of Cartagena cost him 3000 men; and when after three months he entered the evacuated city (December 1815) the few remaining inhabitants were dying of hunger. The other republican cities of New Granada, weakened by divisions and by war against royalist Pasto, were conquered with less difficulty. Bogotá was occupied in May 1816, and in the following months many prominent citizens were executed as traitors. A Spanish Viceroy was once more installed at Bogotá to rule over all New Granada and Quito.

Thus in the year 1816 only the Rio-Platense provinces remained independent; for the energy of the septuagenarian Peruvian Viceroy Abascal had not only held Peru, but had also recovered Chile.

Except in the River Plate, the revolution after five years of effort appeared to be crushed and its leaders dead or in exile: a collapse due perhaps less to external attack than to divisions among the insurgents and to defects in the new governments.

Yet that same year initiated a double movement of recovery. In the south, from the security of achieved independence, military skill and political foresight were preparing a decisive counter-move. Even in the north ruin was not complete. Starting from points 6000 miles apart, two distinct movements of recovery from south and north, the Argentino-Chilian movement led by San Martín and Cochrane and the Colombian movement led by Bolívar, deprived Spain of half a continent. The former movement comprised the lands south of the tropics, drove the Spanish navy from the Pacific, and initiated the revolution of Peru. The northern movement covered the whole tropical region and finally included Peru and Upper Peru, taking up the struggle against these central royalist strongholds where San Martín laid it down.

These separate movements, which finally met and in some degree merged together, need separate narration. But they were simultaneous and complementary to one another: communications passed between the leaders, and the earlier successes of San Martín encouraged the critical struggle in the north and facilitated its ultimate success.

It has been told how San Martín became Governor of Cuyo, having determined to attack Peru by way of Chile. The project met with a serious check at the outset: the fall of the Chilian Republic before invasion from Peru. Fugitive soldiery streamed over the Andine passes into Cuyo under two rival leaders, the loyal, upright, impulsive O'Higgins, and the profligate, self-seeking radical aristocrat Carrera. San Martín's first task was now to reconquer Chile. Treating O'Higgins as a colleague, he suppressed Carrera's turbulence. Uncontrolled by the Buenos Aires authorities, he spent two years in assembling and training his army of Argentine recruits and Chilian refugees. In January 1817 he led 5000 men over two passes 12,000 ft. high, defeated the royalists at Chacabuco and entered Santiago, the capital of Chile. Leaving O'Higgins in command, San Martín travelled to Buenos Aires to solicit naval aid in the Pacific. But the royalists were strong in southern Chile, and during his absence of several months—for the Andes are impassable in winter—there were serious reverses. San Martín himself after his return to Chile suffered defeat at Cancha Rayada (19 March 1818) but brought off his army intact except for 500 desertions— the normal result of defeat in these volunteer forces. The capital, filled with consternation, was saved by the victory of Maipú (5 April 1818), where a royal army of 5500 was defeated by Argentino-Chilian troops slightly less in number. Maipú secured Chilian independence.

In the same year an improvised Chilian squadron captured a Spanish frigate and several transports, depriving Spain of the command of the Pacific. The sea-road to Peru lay open, and the greatest living sailor, Cochrane, notable for sensational successes as a British officer in the war against France, took command of a much-increased Chilian fleet which in three years was to sweep the Spanish flag from the Pacific. His first serious effort, an attack upon Callao, failed; but in January 1820 the fortress of Valdivia, deemed impregnable, was captured by an extraordinary assault.

Yet invasion of Peru was delayed for two years by faction in Chile, by Argentine plans for ending the war by diplomacy and by disorder and alarm in the River Plate provinces. In 1819 the Buenos Aires Government, distracted by anarchy and menaced by an army of 20,000 men assembled at Cadiz for the reconquest of America, summoned San Martin and his army to their aid. He disobeyed, supported by his officers. He judged rightly, for in January 1820 the mutinous army of Cadiz refused to embark. Thenceforth no reinforcements, except a few warships, reached the royalist combatants in America. It was everywhere the turning-point of the struggle.

In 1820, the 'Terrible Year', when Argentine national life seemed to have disappeared at home, it survived in the camp: for in August–September the Argentino-Chilian 'Liberating Army of Peru', nearly 5000 strong, was convoyed in ten transports by Cochrane's armed vessels from Valparaiso to Pisco, south of Lima. Soon afterwards Cochrane achieved the astonishing feat of carrying off the Spanish frigate *Esmeralda*, anchored under the guns of

Callao; and the Numantia regiment, the finest battalion in the royal service, which had been sent southward by Morillo to aid the defence of Peru, deserted to San Martín, 650 strong. Negotiations, opened by the royalist leaders by command of the recently installed radical Government of Spain, led to nothing: for independence was the only possible basis of peace. Two successful expeditions to the north under Arenales, and one to the south under Miller, Cochrane's commander of marines, pointed to victory: but San Martín, hoping for bloodless revolution and hampered by illness, by the use of drugs and by a devastating epidemic in his army, remained almost inactive. In July 1821 the royalists evacuated Lima: San Martín peacefully entered the city, proclaimed the independence of Peru and assumed the government as 'Protector of Peru'—an unwise step which enhanced the suspicious dislike with which the viceregal city regarded this foreign intruder. Callao surrendered to the republicans in September 1821. But the possession of the capital and its port did not win the country. The Spanish Viceroy and his officers still held the southern heights, recruiting at their ease; and although cut off from all the world and divided among themselves (the European officers favouring the existing radical government of Spain, while the Creoles swore by an absolute King) they fought on with Quixotic pertinacity for a mother country unable to aid them.

Meantime Bolívar and Sucre had conquered Quito. The two movements of emancipation were converging from north and south. In July 1822 the chiefs, Bolívar and San Martin, met in a secret interview at Guayaquil. Two months later San Martín, having assembled a Constituent Congress at Lima, resigned command and retired into private life, leaving to Bolívar the task of completing his work, a task which cost two more years of effort.

VENEZUELA

The story of the northern movement must be resumed at the critical epoch of 1816. In that year the republics of New Granada and Venezuela were reduced to a few patriot guerrillas precariously struggling among a population largely royalist. In the plains of the River Apure, José Antonio Páez, an almost illiterate peasant, gathered a party of horsemen, which he increased by small successes and also by the unusual method of sparing the lives of his royalist prisoners, many of whom, formerly followers of Boves, now joined Páez, who told them that *La Patria* was the thing to fight for. Without hospital or commissariat, clothed and shod (if at all) by stripping fallen enemies, living on beef and water without bread or salt, picking up remounts anywhere, expert swimmers in a land of annual floods and many rivers, disappearing upon any reverse to attack rapidly elsewhere, bound not by rigid discipline but by the law of comradeship and by devoted admiration of their leader— who was prompt to impose obedience at the point of his own lance —these mobile horsemen, indomitable on their own plains, wore out the royalists by continual annoyance.

Meantime Bolívar was at work in exile. Petion, the negro dictator of Haiti, aided him to equip an expedition. Luis Brion, a wealthy Dutch merchant of Curazao, provided transport; and in May 1816 Bolívar reached the island of Margarita with 250 companions but with munitions for 6000. Crossing to the mainland, he was accepted by the patriot leaders in north-eastern Venezuela as 'Supreme Chief of the Republic'. He now announced the cessation of 'War to the Death', provided that the royalists should follow suit. The reply of the Spanish Captain-General of Venezuela, Moxo by name, was to set 10,000 pesos on Bolívar's head.

In the campaign of 1816–17 Bolívar strove in vain to win the coastal towns. It was the mulatto general, Piar (afterwards executed for conspiracy against Bolívar), who saw that the first need was the possession of Guayana, a country undevastated by war, rich in cattle and open to supplies from the sea by way of the great River Orinoco, which was also a means of inland communication with Páez and with New Granada and served as a defensive line in emergency. A campaign by Piar, backed up by the vessels of Brion, 'Admiral of Venezuela', on the Lower Orinoco, led to the capture in July 1817 of the river port of Angostura (now Ciudad Bolívar) and to the possession of all Guayana, abandoned by the royalists.

This recrudescence of war in Venezuela had brought back Morillo and his best troops from New Granada; and for nearly two years an indecisive conflict dragged on between Morillo, who held most of the north, and Bolívar, who, hoping to win the northern cities and encouraged by some initial successes, approached the capital; but in a disastrous campaign (May–July 1818) was driven back with heavy loss to the River Apure, where the republicans still held out. Fresh disasters followed in the northeast; but 'help was coming from beyond the sea'.[1] Money and munitions came from England, and also troops, many of them disbanded veterans of the Peninsula and of Flanders, now enlisted in England and Ireland for Venezuelan service by lavish promises. In 1817–18 came officers, sergeants and a few private soldiers, forming three skeleton regiments (one had perished by shipwreck), to train Bolívar's men; then in 1819 came troops, probably numbering about 4600, some of them (particularly the 'Irish legion') an unruly lot, who had been duped into enlisting by unscrupulous 'officers' and hated the whole affair. But a 'British Legion', containing some Germans, took shape, to stiffen Bolívar's irregular levies and to form infantry battalions into which native recruits could be drafted. For the llaneros, indomitable in their own country, were useless in the mountains, averse from distant campaigns and from service on foot, and recognized no leader but their comrade Páez. These foreigners did much for the training of newly raised native troops: for example, five years later, the 'Rifle Battalion' consisted of 1200 Indians with ten British officers.

Most of the British Legion perished in the war. They joined an army of almost naked men, destitute of baggage, tents, commissariat and ambulance, fighting in a tropical country of indescribable difficulty; where capture meant probable death, and victory was usually followed by a general slaughter of prisoners; where the path of war led across plains which turned from desert to swamp with the change of season, through a labyrinth of deep rivers infested by crocodiles, mosquitoes and *caribes* (man-eating fish) and over a vast mass of frozen mountains.

In November 1818, when his cause seemed to be almost sunk in disaster, Bolívar, hearing of proposed European intervention, issued from his capital at Angostura a proud manifesto of indepen-

---

[1] Hasbrouck, *Foreign Legionaries...*, p. 29.

dence and of equality with Spain, and to the Argentine Provinces wrote confidently of 'an American pact, uniting all our republics in one political body, in a single society with the watchword of Unity in South America'.

His work was interrupted by a hurried journey to the Apure, where Páez had allowed himself to be acclaimed as Captain-General. A stern message from Angostura checked the sedition; Bolívar now tempered his rebuke by a conciliatory visit, haranguing Páez' troops and granting promotion to Páez himself.

The events of 1819 justified his confidence. In February 1819 he delivered to the 'Congress of the Venezuelan Republic', assembled in Angostura, a memorable address, the work of a thinker, an orator and a master of expressive Spanish prose. Making briefest mention of the war, he assumes the firm existence of the Venezuelan Republic, urges the need of a stable central government (rejecting the inapt federal form), recommends the study of the British constitution as combining liberty and stability, and urges the need of an educational authority.

New Granada and Venezuela, 1819–21

But it remained to justify in action this nation-making on paper. Leaving his proposals to the Congress, Bolívar set out upon an apparently foolhardy enterprise which was to prove a triumph of military and political strategy. In June 1819 he led 2500 men, among them a British contingent, south-westward from the Apure. The campaign had been carefully planned: the Granadan Santander held command in the plains of Casanare, to join Bolívar on the way: Páez with his cavalry was to screen his rear: other commanders were to divert Morillo's attention by attacks in the east. Bolívar's little army traversed a flooded plain under torrents of seasonal rain which sent Morillo into 'winter quarters'. Thence they crossed the icy Andine heights, where all the horses and many men died of cold, among them one-fourth of the British contingent. A hard-fought combat at Vargas (20 July), although apparently inconclusive in a narrowly tactical sense, in fact decided the campaign, breaking the enemy's morale and not checking Bolívar's advance to the victory of Boyacá (7 August) which swept away the

royalist resistance. The Viceroy Sámano, whose tyranny had prepared the way for the patriots, fled to Cartagena, and Bolívar
entered the capital, acclaimed as 'Liberator of New Granada'.

Having sent detachments to occupy the outlying provinces and
having installed Santander as Vice-President of New Granada
with a provisional Government, Bolívar hastened back to Angostura, where his presence appeased factious disputes. The Congress
during his absence had promulgated a Venezuelan Constitution,
obviously a provisional system, notable in rejecting (as Bolívar
wished) the federal form, but also rejecting Bolívar's plan of a
hereditary senate. And now with grandiose optimism the Congress,
at Bolívar's instance, decreed the union of Venezuela, New
Granada and even of Quito, still possessed by the royalists, into
one Republic to be entitled Colombia[1] (December 1819). This
meant the union of an immense region, roadless and indescribably
difficult of transit, where a deputy to the capital at Bogotá from the
southern limit at Loja or from the eastern limit at Angostura had
to spend weeks of travel through scorching heat and piercing cold
at the risk of health and even of life.[2] Since Quito had been subject
to the Viceroy of Santa Fe, it was assumed that Quito, whatever its
inhabitants might think, must join New Granada. In the movement of independence it was generally agreed that the limits of the
new States should follow the *uti possidetis* of 1810, that is to say
the limits of the Spanish 'Viceroyalties, Captaincies-General or
Presidencies'. But the Quiteños might argue that the 'Kingdom
of Quito' was a 'Presidency', ruled by a President and Audiencia
of its own, with merely a remote dependence on Santa Fe.

The year 1820 opened a new phase in the struggle. In March–
April came news of the mutiny at Cadiz and of a radical Government in Spain. By order of that Government Morillo opened
negotiations with Bolívar: the two chiefs met amicably and on

---

[1] Spanish-American historians give the name *Gran Colombia* ('Great Colombia') to this short-lived State decreed by Bolívar, in order to distinguish it from
the present Republic of Colombia, which was formerly called New Granada.

[2] O'Leary, on an urgent mission from Bolívar in 1826, spent a month in
travelling from Guayaquil to Bogotá, first a week at sea and then three weeks by
horse and mule: he reached Bogotá 'more dead than alive, from hunger, rain,
weariness and a whole catalogue of pains and fatigues'. His journey from Bogotá
to Valencia took three weeks.

27 November signed an armistice for six months and an agreement which 'regularized' the war; thenceforth to be conducted after the customs of civilized nations. In this document Bolívar is described as 'President of the Republic of Colombia'. A few days later Morillo departed for Spain, leaving to his second-in-command, La Torre, the impossible task of restoring Spanish authority, without fresh troops from Spain, amid the confusion of ideas dividing royalists owing to the Spanish revolution.

Within two months the armistice was broken by a republican movement on Maracaibo. On 28 April 1821 the armistice was formally declared to be ended. On 24 June 1821 La Torre with an army of about 5500 men was defeated on the plain of Carabobo by Bolívar with 6500 men and fled to Puerto Cabello. The brunt of the fight and more than half the casualties were borne by the British Legion. Carabobo is remembered in Venezuela as Maipú in Chile. It is true that Venezuelan independence was not completely secured until a republican flotilla, by a victory on Lake Maracaibo two years later (July 1823), deprived the Spaniards of supremacy at sea and led to the fall of the royalist strongholds at Maracaibo and Puerto Cabello. The definite conclusion of the war was the capture of Puerto Cabello by Páez in November 1823. But the victory of Carabobo, by making royalist reconquest impossible in Venezuela and New Granada, set Bolívar free to extirpate royalism from the continent by victory in Quito and in Peru.

Yet not entirely free; for in the midst of war, the creation of a new polity was urgent. A week after Carabobo there met at Cúcuta, near the Venezuelan-Granadan border, a Constituent Congress of fifty-seven members, all that could be mustered out of ninety-five deputies to be chosen: in the Province of Caracas election was impossible, and it was assumed that Quito, still in royalist hands, must accept all decisions. After four months (August 1821) the Congress promulgated a Constitution, centralized or unitary (as Bolívar insisted), with Bogotá as capital and one bicameral elected Parliament for the whole of a Colombia as yet unmade. One clause, supplemented by decrees, in effect granted autocracy to the executive in emergencies. Gil Fortoul notes the 'contradictions between constitutional theory and the necessity of dictatorship, the only possible government at that time for the Spanish-American peoples'. The city of Caracas, unrepresented in the Congress, protested against some clauses. This wartime Constitution, obviously not definitive, was declared to be unalterable for ten years: an order later broken by Bolívar himself.

The Congress chose Bolívar President and Santander Vice-President. Bolívar protested that he was a soldier, averse from civil office, but accepted on condition of being allowed to pursue the campaign, 'leaving the entire government to the Vice-President'. Yet before his departure he nominated Cabinet Ministers, and also, with supreme faith in the future, sent an envoy to Peru, Buenos Aires and Chile, inviting those republics to send deputies to a Congress to be held on the Isthmus of Panamá.

QUITO AND PERU, 1822–24

In December 1821 Bolívar set out from Bogotá for the south to co-operate with Sucre, best and noblest of his officers, who for seven months past had been supporting independence in Guayaquil, aided by 1100 troops sent from Peru by San Martín. The two movements from north and south were meeting. Campaigning in extremely difficult country (January–March 1822) Bolívar lost one-third of his 3000 men by disease and exhaustion and one-fourth of the rest in battle against the stubborn royalists of Pasto and Patia. But the combined campaign was successful; and the battle of Pichincha (25 May 1822) fought by Sucre on the slope of the volcano overlooking the capital, won for the republicans both the city and the whole kingdom of Quito.

Here a pacific episode interrupts the narrative of war. The Spanish Bishop of Popayán, Jiménez de Enciso, had devoted the resources of his diocese to the royalist cause, and when the 'patriots' entered Popayán, he withdrew to Pasto, excommunicating any of his flock who should aid the republicans. Thereupon Vice-President Santander (acting much as Belgrano, San Martín and O'Higgins did in similar cases) decreed the banishment of Enciso and, later, of any who should aid him to communicate with his diocese. But Bolívar wrote to Enciso in January 1822, pointing out the anti-religious character of the radical Spanish Government, promising protection to the Church and commending the example of three bishops who had joined the independent cause 'on seeing the cursed torrent of crime...desolating...the Spanish Church'. The Bishop did not reply, but on the fall of Pasto, he wrote to Bolívar asking for a passport to Spain. Bolívar in reply reasons, in deferential but convincing words, that the Bishop is not fulfilling his sacred duties if for political reasons he abandons his flock: the letter ends with a hint that such negative conduct endangered the unity of the Roman Church.

Bolívar followed up his letter by a visit to the Bishop, who was completely won over, promised obedience to the Republic and returned to his diocese, which he ruled until his death in 1841.[1] His conduct in doing so was approved by the Vatican. Father Leturia, S.J., who traces the story from the Vatican archives, remarks how it was due to Bolívar's management and tact that, in Colombia alone, a Spanish-born bishop, appointed under the Real Patronato, became 'Father and Patriarch of the new national Episcopate'. He adds that Bolívar, after the armistice and the regularization of the war, worked sincerely to conciliate royalists and European Spaniards and to effect the 'social and religious consolidation of the infant Republic'.

But that Republic was incomplete until the people of Guayaquil, who were talking of a separate republic or of union with Peru, were coerced or persuaded by Bolívar into joining Colombia. Thus the Kingdom of Quito became, for eight years, the third member of the Republic of Colombia.

At last in July 1822, the two chiefs, the Protector of Peru and the Liberator of Colombia, met in a private interview at Guayaquil. San Martín offered to serve under Bolívar, but real co-operation was impossible; and two months later San Martín resigned his authority into the hands of a Peruvian Congress in Lima and left the country, announcing that Colombian troops were coming to aid Peru.

A year passed before Bolívar arrived in Lima, a year of confusion in the council-chamber and disaster in the field for Peru. His

[1] J. P. Hamilton (vol. II, pp. 39–46) gives an entertaining account of a visit to the genial and hospitable Bishop Enciso.

PLATE II

BOLÍVAR

arrival in September 1823 put new life into the struggle. 'There was a charm in the name of Bolívar', says General Miller, a person not given to rhetoric, who had served under Cochrane and under San Martín. By force and diplomacy combined, civil strife was first suppressed. Then Bolívar, himself supervising every detail, was assembling his troops in the north when he heard that a mutiny of unpaid Argentine soldiers had yielded Callao and Lima to the royalists. The Peruvian Congress, amid general demoralization and frequent desertions, granted to Bolívar dictatorial powers and then dissolved, 'closing its existence by an act of unquestionable wisdom', says Miller.

Although almost prostrated by illness, Bolívar pushed forward preparations. Reinforcements came from Colombia, his own devoted soldiers: the army of Peru joined him from the south. All had to traverse deserts and snowy mountains. Horses dragged up precipitous tracks to alpine heights, whole battalions prostrate with mountain sickness, an entire division of 3000 men groping helpless for a day from snow-blindness: these were some of the incidents. At last in July 1824 Bolívar was able to review 7700 troops, besides 1500 guerrilleros, at Cerro de Pasco in northern Peru, 12,000 ft. above sea-level.

Meantime Canterac, the royalist commander, French by birth, was moving northward. The first clash was a cavalry combat at Junín (7 August 1824). The fight was over in forty-five minutes: not a shot was fired; but 360 royalists fell by lance and sabre, and that night most of the wounded died of cold. Two months later Bolívar, leaving Sucre in command, departed for Lima, to raise recruits, to provide pay for the troops, to organize reinforcements expected from Colombia, and to invigorate a distracted administration terrorized by the royalist garrison in Callao and by marauding bands calling themselves royalist troops. The decisive stroke was delivered on 9 December 1824, when Sucre at Ayacucho with 6000 republican troops defeated 9000 royalists, of whom only 500 were Spaniards. Canterac signed a capitulation which included the 23,000 royal troops remaining in Peru; and La Serna, the last Spanish Viceroy, became a prisoner.

Ayacucho sealed the independence of Peru and of South

America. When the victory was known in Buenos Aires six weeks later—for communication was slow across the disturbed Argentine Provinces—salvoes of cannon and pealing of church bells greeted the news and riotous jubilation was prolonged for a month.

Two months before the battle of Ayacucho, Bolívar—on his way to Lima to organize victory—was informed, in a letter from Santander, that the Colombian Congress had taken from him the command of the Colombian troops and the extraordinary powers granted to him in the theatre of war. Bolívar, though deeply mortified at this blow from Santander—for such it was—obeyed, declining the request of his officers that he should retain the command or forward a petition from them to the Colombian Congress. He was still Dictator of Peru and (strange to say) President of Colombia, and, owing to the unselfish generosity of Sucre, who still regarded Bolívar as his chief, this formal deprivation made no difference in the conduct of the war. After the triumph of Ayacucho, the Peruvian Congress voted a million dollars to the liberating army and another million to the Liberator himself, the true author of victory. Bolívar declined the personal gift, but, under pressure, accepted it not for himself but for his native city of Caracas, ruined by earthquake and civil war.

Sucre, begging in vain relief from command, still had the task of occupying Upper Peru, where the stubborn Creole royalist, Olañeta, repudiated the capitulation. As Sucre moved southward, the royalist garrisons in succession joined him. Olañeta, retreating and losing men by desertion, fell at last in fight against his own officers, who passed over to the patriots. On 3 April 1825 Sucre from his quarters at Potosí declared the war to be ended.

Thus ended after seventeen years (1808–25) the movement of independence in South America. Rodil, the Spanish Governor of Callao, declaring that he took his orders only from the King, still held out, but was reduced by starvation in January 1826. A month later the island of Chiloe in southern Chile, the last royalist stronghold in South America, surrendered to the Chilians. Thenceforth the Spanish cause, though favoured by some in the towns, was only upheld in the field by bands of guerrilleros and brigands in Chile and in Venezuela, who were finally suppressed about 1830.

The war-time rhetoric with which revolutionary leaders claimed to be redressing the wrongs of the conquest, avenging Atahualpa and restoring oppressed peoples, did not deceive the Indians. The Revolution was rather a completion than a reversal of the conquest, since it placed the conquered countries in the power of the Creole or semi-white descendants of Spanish conquerors and settlers.

NOTE. W. S. Robertson, *Life of Miranda,** 2 vols. (Chapel Hill, 1929); *Rise of the Spanish-American Republics** (New York, 1918); W. Pilling, *The Emancipation of South America*, a condensed translation of Mitre's *History of San Martín* (London, 1893); E. L. Petre, *Simón Bolívar** (London, 1909); A. Hasbrouck, *Foreign Legionaries in the Liberation of Spanish South America** (New York, 1928); *Cambridge Modern History**, vol. x, ch. ix; J. P. Hamilton, *Travels through . . . Colombia*, 2 vols. (London, 1827); C. S. Cochrane, *Journal of a residence in Colombia in 1823–4*, 2 vols. (London, 1825); W. B. Stevenson, *Twenty years' residence in South America*, 3 vols. (Liverpool, 1825); J. Miller, *Memoirs of General W. Miller in the Service of Peru*, 2 vols. (London, 1828; 2nd edit., 1829); Earl of Dundonald (Lord Cochrane), *Narrative of Services in Chile, Peru and Brazil*, 2 vols. (London, 1859).

CHAPTER VIII

INDEPENDENCE IN NORTH AMERICA

THE Viceroyalty of New Spain, with its rich silver mines (which had become far more productive than those of Peru), its busy mint, its stately capital and university, was in the early nineteenth century the most wealthy, populous, orderly and cultured of the American kingdoms, apparently the most apt for the tranquil evolution of decent government. Owing to the large trade with Spain in peace time, there were about 70,000 resident Spaniards. But the Creoles and mestizos together exceeded two million; and the troops, about 9000 regulars and 22,000 militia, were almost all Creole. The bulk of the population were Indian peasants and labourers. Humboldt in 1803 estimated that, in a total population of about six millions, there were only 6000 negro slaves.

The first move towards autonomy came nearly two years earlier than the movements in Caracas and Buenos Aires, and emanated more distinctly from constituted authority. In June and July 1808 Mexico heard of the royal abdications, the French aggression and the uprising of the people in Spain. The Cabildo of the capital, a body mainly Creole, represented to the Viceroy that, the throne having fallen, sovereignty now resided in the local authorities, pending restoration of royal command. The Viceroy, against the advice of the Audiencia, summoned a meeting of all officials (including two Indian magistrates) and the chief vecinos, eighty-two persons in all (9 August 1808). Francisco Verdad, spokesman of the Cabildo in this Junta, argued that sovereignty had devolved on the people, who should organize provisional government. The European party denounced this doctrine as seditious, urging recognition of any authority representing the King in the Peninsula: not a very definite proposal. One point only was settled by acclamation, the oath of allegiance to Ferdinand VII. During the following month the Junta met thrice, without concluding anything; but the Viceroy took the remarkable step of inviting all the cities of New

Spain to send deputies to a General Congress. This Congress never met: for a group of the European party, seeing that the Viceroy, whether designedly or not, was working for independence, arrested and deposed him, with the acquiescence of the Audiencia, which nominated his successor. Seven Creole leaders were imprisoned, and Verdad died in prison, the first martyr of independence. Thus the first round between the Creole regidores and the Spanish oidores brought victory for the Spaniards. But this was not the end. The action of the Audiencia itself had been and continued to be independent and almost revolutionary. The rapid changes of authority in Spain and also in New Spain, where viceregal authority changed hands four times in two years (1808–10), forbade any standing still.

But all prospect of a general move for independence starting from the capital and supported by reputable authority—as in Caracas and Buenos Aires—was swept away by the outbreak of a hasty local insurrection, mainly an Indian revolt. On 14 September 1810 the Viceroy Venegas, appointed by the Central Junta of Spain, made his state entry into the capital. Two days later in the village of Dolores, some fifty miles north-west of Querétaro, resounded the call to revolt, the Grito de Dolores. The date is annually celebrated as the birthday of the Mexican Republic. It was in sober fact the beginning of a confused conflict, which devastated the country for eleven years, a conflict between colours and races—with many cross-currents, personal impulses, mutinies and desertions—rather than a war between *rey* and *patria*. A brief summary of this indeterminate struggle must suffice.

In the mining town of Querétaro, under cover of a literary society in which the corregidor of the place and his wife took part, a small group of Creole conspirators in nocturnal meetings were plotting revolt and independence early in 1810 or possibly sooner. Among them were Ignacio Allende, captain in a mounted militia regiment and two brother officers: but the moving spirit, though seldom present at the meetings, was the sexagenarian Miguel Hidalgo, parish priest of the village of Dolores, who had been twice accused before the Inquisition (but not convicted) of heretical opinions and was noted for his efforts to promote the industry and prosperity of his Indian parishioners. Revolt was planned for December 1810; but on the night of 15 September Hidalgo was awakened by Allende, who had ridden twenty miles from San Miguel with the news that all was discovered.

Hidalgo acted at once. Before dawn he gathered a few men, opened the gaol and added the convicts. When the bell rang for Mass—for it was Sunday—he called on his Indian parishioners to follow him and led out a promiscuous rudely armed crowd, taking with him as captives the principal Spaniards in the place. A banner bearing the image of the Virgin of Guadalupe, picked up at a wayside chapel, was raised upon a lance to the cry *Viva la Virgen de Guadalupe. Viva Fernando VII; muera el mal gobierno!* 'That battle-cry', says Priestley, 'invoking the Virgin of Guadalupe, patroness of the Indian population, unfortunately made its appeal to the worst spirit of racial hatred.... Through it Hidalgo rapidly gathered about him a rabble of some 4000 Indians.' He told them they were fighting for King and Church against the wicked Spaniards who were delivering the country to the French. But the Indian war-cry was a simpler one, *Viva la Virgen de Guadalupe y mueran los gachupines!* (Perish the Spaniards!) At San Miguel the militia regiment of Creole dragoons joined them: Allende became a general and the sergeants became officers: the gaol was opened: the Spaniards were arrested, to follow the march as captives: their houses were pillaged and their goods destroyed. The town of Celaya surrendered upon Hidalgo's threat that, if resisted, he would kill his seventy-eight Spanish captives. A week later (28 September) Hidalgo summoned the rich mining town of Guanajuato, announcing 'no quarter' in case of resistance and declaring that his aim was the independence and liberty of the nation: a point to be emphasized, for he led the Indians to battle in the name of King and Church.

Despite a stout resistance offered in a strong fortress-like block of buildings by a handful of troops under the Governor (Intendent) of the Province, who fell in the defence, an undisciplined crowd of some 20,000 Indians, infuriated by their own losses, swept at last through the place to sack and slaughter. A military chest was provided by seizing public treasure and private property, and some attempt was made to organize government in the city. Fresh successes followed, and at the end of October 1810 Hidalgo approached the capital with a host estimated at 80,000 men, a few having muskets, but most of them armed with lances, clubs, pikes and slings—the last a formidable weapon in expert hands. Allende urged advance on the city; but Hidalgo, menaced in front and rear by regular troops, preferred cautious retreat.

The revolt spread. Insurgent leaders appeared in various places. The peasant-priest Torres raised a band and occupied Guadalajara, the capital of the north. Here Hidalgo set up an independent administration by appointing 'patriot' magistrates and oidores. He also decreed the liberation of negro slaves and the grant or restitution of lands to the Indians. This last point deserves emphasis; for this attempt to give a salutary aim to the Indian revolt is Hidalgo's best title to statesmanship; a title difficult to sustain. Priestley—an authority to be heard with respect—gives him credit for a 'constructive program'. But Justin H. Smith finds no statesmanship in Hidalgo. Bancroft, an enthusiastic admirer of Hidalgo, nevertheless writes: 'There appears to have been no political or military plan adopted.' W. S. Robertson notes his failure 'to formulate a plan of action'. J. F. Rippy writes: 'Hidalgo seemed to have struck somewhat blindly. He seems to have had few notions of statecraft.' Señor Navarro y Lamarca, a fair and sympathetic historian, compares the hordes of Hidalgo to those of Tupac Amaru and to those who followed the Soudanese Mahdi in 1883. In his manifesto of December 1810 Hidalgo writes: 'Let us consider as strangers and as enemies of our prerogatives all persons who are not Mexicans.' (A singularly illiberal and short-sighted proposal.) 'Let us establish a congress of representatives of all the cities, towns and villages....Our lawmakers will rule us with the tenderness of parents. They will treat us like brothers; they will banish poverty; they will check the devastation of the kingdom and the exportation of its money; they will encourage the arts and cause industry to revive...in the course of a few years, the Mexicans will enjoy all the delights which the Sovereign Author of Nature has bestowed upon this vast continent.' These prophecies, uttered after the shocking scenes of Guanajuato by one who signed himself

'Captain-General of America', these imaginings of a golden age, to be created by a Spanish-American congress, are hardly the words of a constructive statesman. Yet none question his courage, fine qualities and zealous intentions. To the Mexican people he is at once a semi-legendary and a very real figure, the patriarchal hero of independence.

Hidalgo had not the country behind him. 'The Creoles beheld with alarm their fate depending on an ignorant and infuriated body of Indians, and were compelled to rally round the existing authorities as the only means of personal safety'; so wrote a contemporary American observer, W. D. Robinson, an ardent friend of Mexican independence. 'The loyal army,' says Priestley, 'was largely composed of mestizos officered by Creoles.' The slightest reverse bewildered Hidalgo's ignorant and predatory horde, and four months after the Grito de Dolores, it was routed by an army of 6000 disciplined troops under the royalist General Calleja (17 January 1811) who earned an evil name by the sanguinary cruelty of his reprisals and repression during the following years.

This defeat was fatal. Two months later Hidalgo and Allende, hoping for support in the United States, fled northward, carrying what treasure they could. They were captured through the treachery of a former comrade.[1] Both were executed as traitors and also some thirty of their followers.

But the revolt continued, shifting from the northern region to the country south of the capital. The successor of Hidalgo, after an interval, was the mestizo Morelos, a sturdy peasant-priest of great physical strength and stubborn determination, far more skilful than Hidalgo as a military leader and better endowed with practical common sense in policy. For nearly four years (1811–15) he held his ground in the southern provinces of the *tierra caliente* against much superior forces. He took the Pacific port of Acapulco, established a republican government of limited range, and issued in November 1813 through a makeshift Congress a Constitution which definitely claimed independence; for Morelos, overruling his colleagues, abandoned the fiction of loyalty to Ferdinand VII

[1] They could not have escaped in any case. The Province of Texas, which lay upon their route, had reverted to royalism, owing to the tyranny of a local 'patriot' dictator.

to which Hidalgo had clung. He anticipated more distinctly than Hidalgo the agrarian movement of to-day by declaring that the Indian villagers should be owners of their lands: and he swept away all distinctions of colour or race, so that all born in the country should rank equally as *Americanos*. But before long the Congress was a fragmentary and itinerant body; Morelos' followers fell away before Calleja's activities; and in December 1815 Morelos suffered the same fate as Hidalgo.

There still remained about 9000 insurgents in the field, divided into six or seven detached bodies under leaders most of whom were jealous of one another and cared little for any independence but their own. Some were outrageous tyrants, notably the priest Torres, an intrepid fighter but a monster of cruelty, rapacity and debauchery, who from his mountain fastness at Los Remedios terrorized a wide region in the Province of Guanajuato. Most of the insurgent leaders were gradually reduced by the discreet policy of the Viceroy Apodaca, a sensible and moderate man, who assumed office in August 1816. He combined vigorous action against the resisting chieftains with a promise of pardon to all who should submit, a promise which was faithfully kept.

One episode demands mention, the headstrong venture of the young Navarrese warrior Mina, who in 1808 had fought the French invaders in his native Pyrenees, and six years later had risen in Navarre against the despot Ferdinand VII. In April 1816 he landed from the United States at Soto la Marina, a small port on the Gulf of Mexico, marched inland with 300 men, gained some successes and adherents, vainly attempted active co-operation with Torres and finally was captured and executed in October 1817. Two months later (1 January 1818) Torres, who had been besieged for four months and had no ammunition left, attempted to evacuate by night the fortress of Los Remedios. The royalists observed the movement and fell upon the escaping crowd. Torres himself got away with a few men, his path marked by the bodies of his followers, slain by the pursuing assailants. Some months later Torres, a wandering fugitive, was killed in a quarrel with one of his own captains.

In 1819, though bands of brigands calling themselves patriots were still at large, only one considerable leader, Guerrero, held his ground in the south-east. But a word is due to one valiant irreconcilable, who exchanged his commonplace name Fernández for the defiant pseudonym Guadalupe Victoria. With a price upon his head, he wandered among caves and thickets for more than two years, friendless, naked, alone and often starving. Such was the school of those who were to guide the first tentative steps of independent Mexico, Victoria as the first republican President, Guerrero as the second.

The defeat of the revolt which had been started by Hidalgo actually favoured the cause of independence: for many of the Creoles, who had helped to suppress the revolt, had been fighting not against independence but against disorder and anarchy. Now plans for independence were being discussed in conversational gatherings (the characteristic Spanish *tertulia*) and in Masonic meetings, when the movement received an unexpected impulse. The Spanish revolution of 1820, the subjection of the King to a radical Government, the inroads upon the property of the Church and upon the privileges of the clergy; all these measures in Spain, soon to be applied to New Spain, alarmed the higher clergy and the conservatives, including many Spaniards, and drove them into separatism in strange alliance with freemasons and radicals, in order to save traditional New Spain from radical Spain. A military leader was found in a handsome, persuasive and vigorous Creole officer in the prime of life, Agustín de Iturbide, who had been active and inexorable in the earlier campaigns against the insurgents, but, being accused of financial irregularities, had withdrawn to private life. So early as 1814, while besieging an insurgent stronghold, he had confided to a colleague his desire for independence, adding the words: 'but first we must finish with these people.'

Iturbide, short of funds from dissipation, threw himself into this new phase of the separatist movement, obtained from Apodaca a command and led out 2500 men, ostensibly against Guerrero; but, after some useless bloodshed, he persuaded Guerrero to support him in publishing at the village of Iguala in February 1821 the 'Plan of Iguala', which, like most incidents in Mexican history, resembles nothing done elsewhere. Iturbide himself summarized its twenty-three articles into three main provisions, 'The Three Guarantees': (1) Maintenance of the Roman Catholic religion, none other to be tolerated; (2) independence and a limited monarchy, the throne to be offered to Ferdinand VII and, in case of non-acceptance, to another prince of the reigning house; (3) equality of all inhabitants, white, African or Indian; all being qualified for public office. The plan was astute, being designed to attract men of all opinions.

Iturbide was now in command of a revolutionary army. One after another the chief cities and the royalist commanders accepted the Plan of Iguala. Among these was a spirited young officer in the King's army named Santa Anna. He was sent out by his chief from Vera Cruz against the insurgents, fought them and then suddenly went over to them, entering Iturbide's army as a full colonel at the age of twenty-seven. It was a characteristic entry on a sensational career which for thirty-five years was to be almost identical with the history of Mexico.

The Viceroy Apodaca, suspected of lukewarmness in combating this new insurrection, was deposed by an *émeute* of Spanish troops in the capital on 5 July. Iturbide was approaching the city, when he heard that General Juan O'Donojú had landed at Vera Cruz on 30 July as Captain-General of New Spain. Iturbide turned aside and at Córdoba met O'Donojú, who, powerless to resist, signed the 'Treaty of Córdoba', accepting the Plan of Iguala, with the further significant proviso that, if the Bourbon princes declined the Mexican throne, then the Mexican Cortes should elect a sovereign. By O'Donojú's order the Spanish troops evacuated the capital, soon to embark for Spain; and Iturbide led his troops into the city on 27 September 1821. Mexico was independent: only the island-castle of San Juan de Ulúa, opposite to Vera Cruz, remained in Spanish hands until 1825, garrisoned by European troops: a troublesome threat rather than a real danger to Mexican independence.

A Regency was formed. The death of O'Donojú ten days later cleared the way. The Spanish Cortes repudiated the Treaty of Córdoba, thereby wiping out the Bourbonist proposal; and the

Mexican Constituent Congress, meeting in February 1822, were free to elect a monarch. One night in May a sergeant, followed by a few soldiers, rushed from the barracks, shouting *Viva Agustín Primero!* A mob outside Iturbide's house took up the cry. A truncated Congress was coerced into agreement, not unanimous; and on 25 July Iturbide was crowned Emperor with the stately ceremonial traditional in old-world hereditary monarchies.

Iturbide, as monarch, quietly shelved the Plan of Iguala. Nominally a constitutional sovereign, he soon ripened into a capricious and irresponsible dictator. His reign was brief. The guerrilleros who had fought against Ferdinand VII now rose against the Creole monarch. The first to turn against him was Santa Anna, now Governor of Vera Cruz, who at the head of his troops proclaimed the Republic. Province after province joined the republican movement: Iturbide's troops deserted him; and after nine months he abdicated (February 1823) and the Republic of Mexico entered on its stormy career.

The Congress decreed that Iturbide should live in Italy and assigned to him, from their bankrupt treasury, a liberal pension. He remained three months in Italy. In April 1824 the Congress received a message dated from London, announcing his intended return to Mexico in order (as he said) to serve his country against Spanish designs. The Congress thereupon proscribed him as an outlaw if he should enter Mexican territory. Knowing nothing of this decree, Iturbide landed in July 1824 at Soto la Marina. The State Congress of Tamaulipas, which was in session, ordered his immediate execution. It was an evil precedent.

CENTRAL AMERICA

With some disturbances and local revolts between 1810 and 1814, the Kingdom or Captaincy-General of Guatemala, inhabited by a small minority of white men among a mass of subject Indians, continued to be ruled until 1821 by Spanish Governors, with the powerful support of the clergy and the acquiescence of the principal Creoles. But, as elsewhere, the Spanish revolution of 1820 upset this equilibrium. The clergy in Guatemala dreaded and hated the radical Spanish Government. The example of New Spain and the action of Iturbide were infectious. And when elections were held of Guatemalan deputies to sit in the Spanish Cortes, a local authority emerged which forced the aged and inert Captain-General Urrutia to hand over his authority to a soldier named Gainza. This locally appointed Spanish Captain-General convoked an Assembly which proclaimed independence in September 1821. The question then arose concerning future status: Gainza favoured union with Mexico; and for a time Iturbide, who sent troops to enforce his authority, appeared to have extended his empire to the Isthmus of Panamá. But distance, the unwelcome financial decrees of Iturbide and the regional tendency characteristic of all Iberian history precluded union; the fall of Iturbide broke a precarious tie; and finally—with the exception of the Province of Chiapas, which adhered to Mexico—the Captaincy-General of Guatemala broke off in 1823 to form, under the novel and not very appropriate title of 'The United Provinces of the Centre of America', later simplified to 'Central America', a Federal Republic of five provinces, soon to fly apart tumultuously into five separate and discordant sovereign States.

NOTE. H. I. Priestley, *The Mexican Nation, a History** (New York, 1923), chs. XI–XIV; 'Book II' of H. G. Ward, *Mexico in 1827*, 2 vols. (London, 1828); F. Robinson, *Memoirs of the Mexican Revolution*, 2 vols. (London, 1821); Brantz Mayer, *Mexico*, 2 vols. (Hartford, 1853); W. S. Robertson, *Rise of the Spanish-American Republics*, ch. III; Bancroft, *Mexico**, vol. IV, *Central America**, vol. III.

CHAPTER IX

INDEPENDENCE OF BRAZIL

THE bizarre character which pervades Latin-American history marks the winning of Brazilian independence: for that movement had its root in the migration of an ancient royal court and dynasty from Europe to America. Queen Maria of Portugal being insane, her son John ruled that country in most critical and troublous times, an excellent and well-intentioned man, but timid, hesitating and indolent: qualities which were reflected in his obese frame and heavy countenance. The Regent anxiously strove to keep out of the struggle between Great Britain and Napoleon. The hope was vain: in October 1807 Napoleon signed an agreement with Spain for the conquest and partition of Portugal. Already Junot with a French army had traversed Spain and entered Portugal, when Prince John yielded to the insistence of Sir Sidney Smith, who commanded a British fleet in the Tagus, and of the British Ambassador, Lord Strangford. On 29 November 1807 the Regent, accompanied by his mother, his wife (the Spanish princess Carlota), his two sons and six daughters, with a numerous following of nobles and functionaries—some 10,000 in all—and the treasures of the kingdom, set sail in crowded confusion from the Tagus for Brazil in a fleet convoyed by a few British warships. Next day Junot's vanguard marched into Lisbon.

The ships, overcrowded, insufficiently provisioned, unfurnished with the commonest necessities and tossed by storms, reached Bahia on 22 January 1808, and for the first time a European reigning prince set foot on American soil, welcomed with loud acclaim by the people of Bahia, both black and white.

It was the beginning of independence.

Resisting their desire that their city should be the royal residence and capital, the Prince-Regent, after due repose, continued his voyage to Rio, where he arrived on 8 March.

Already a week after landing at Bahia, the Prince-Regent had decreed the opening of all Brazilian ports to the trade of all friendly nations, thus releasing Brazil at once from the shackles of economic dependence on Portugal. As in the case of Cisneros' decree in Buenos Aires (see p. 50), it was a large step towards complete political independence. Fresh reforms followed; industries were freed from all restriction: immigrants from all nations were admitted and even introduced at Government expense; 'they came in crowds to fix their residence on the shores of the modern El Dorado': new tribunals were created, also a Junta of Commerce, a Military Academy, a Medical School and a National Bank; a printing-press was introduced: the royal library of 60,000 volumes was opened to the public, and after the fall of Napoleon a National Institute was set up which invited, chiefly from France, artists, scholars and men of letters. In December 1815 the Regent raised Brazil to full equality with Portugal, unifying his dominions under the title 'United Kingdom of Brazil, Portugal and the Algarves'. Three months later, the demented Queen having died, he was formally proclaimed as John VI, King of Portugal and Brazil.

But the presence of the Court was not an unmixed blessing. The wasteful prodigality of the royal establishment was a heavy burden, the Portuguese nobles and functionaries expected support at the expense of the Brazilians, whose hospitality they abused: a crowd of needy Portuguese adventurers were also seeking an easy and idle life. There was a growing animosity between the Creoles and these arrogant intruders, an animosity only in part allayed by the lavish distribution and sale of titles, stars, crosses and knighthoods among the Brazilians.

In 1817 a republican revolt broke out in Pernambuco: but the capital, remaining loyal, contributed money and volunteers: the uprising was suppressed and many of the leaders executed. Two external adventures also demand mention, a brief occupation of French Guiana and a much more notable attempt to achieve the long-standing ambition of Portuguese expansion to the River Plate, which, although a Spanish province stood in the way, seemed to be the natural geographical frontier of Brazil. In 1812 Portuguese troops, taking advantage of the troubles following Argentine independence, entered the Banda Oriental, but were stayed by an armistice concluded with Buenos Aires. However, in 1816, on the pretext of the anarchy prevailing in a province contiguous to

Brazil, Portuguese troops again invaded the Banda Oriental, and early in 1817 occupied Montevideo, thus apparently accomplishing their territorial design: a delusive achievement, as will appear later.

Events in Europe precipitated independence. In 1820 a revolutionary movement in Portugal overthrew a despotic Regency in Lisbon: Cortes met and adopted the radical Spanish Constitution of 1812. After long hesitation King John decided that, in order to guide events and save his dynasty, he must return to Lisbon. He appointed his son Pedro as Regent of Brazil, and in April 1821 embarked for Lisbon accompanied by 3000 Portuguese. The subsequent proceedings of the Cortes at Lisbon drove Brazil into independence, an independence which sooner or later was bound to come. The Cortes, radical and revolutionary in Portugal but absolutist and reactionary towards America, attempted to reduce Brazil to the former condition of complete dependence on the mother-country. They declared the ills of Portugal to be due to the King's residence in Brazil and to the opening of the Brazilian ports; and they undermined the Regent's authority by inviting the Brazilian provinces to detach themselves from Rio and communicate directly with Lisbon. They abolished the Brazilian institutions founded by the King, thereby turning a crowd of dispossessed officials into 'patriots'. Meantime the Portuguese troops in Rio exasperated both Prince and people by dictating to the Regent, assuming a praetorian authority which in fact meant military rebellion. The culminating point was an insolent decree of the Cortes (September 1821) commanding the Prince to return to Europe.

Dom Pedro, an impulsive, romantic and active Prince, twenty-two years of age, became the popular liberating hero. He was besought to remain by urgent petitions from Rio and from São Paulo, the latter drawn up by Jose Bonifacio Andrada, a man of outstanding ability and character, scholar and man of science, matured by travel and study in Europe, who, as chief Minister of the Regent, guided the movement. In January 1822 the Prince replied *Fico*, 'I remain', to a municipal deputation from Rio. Five months later he convoked a Constituent Assembly. Then, on 7 September 1822, in response to a provocative decree of the Portuguese Cortes, the Regent himself raised the cry of 'Independence or Death'. A month later in presence of a vast concourse he was proclaimed Constitutional Emperor of Brazil.

The assumption of sovereignty by the Regent was an act of continuity rather than of revolution. The object was to save Brazil from disintegration and preserve the institutions established by royal authority. So far as there was revolution, it had been already effected peaceably by King John VI himself.

The movement was not to be entirely bloodless; for an attack by Brazilian volunteers failed to dislodge a Portuguese garrison in Bahia. But Cochrane now passed from his Chilian service in the Pacific to serve Brazil in the Atlantic, bringing with him some British officers and a few seamen. He contrived to enlist in Brazil more British and American seamen. One ship was commanded by a Frenchman, Beaupaire, and manned by Frenchmen. Finally Bahia, attacked on land by the Brazilians and assailed by Cochrane's tiny squadron, was evacuated by the Portuguese, whose huge escaping fleet was pursued and much damaged by Cochrane's ships. Two bloodless victories followed; first at Maranhão, where Cochrane with a single ship, by a combination of ruse and audacity, cleared the Portuguese out of the town; and then at Pará, where Grenfell by Cochrane's orders did the same. The Brazilians themselves expelled the Portuguese garrison from Montevideo, and by the end of 1823 the independence of Brazil was secure. In the following year the unity of the country was also saved, when a separatist republican movement at Pernambuco was suppressed by Cochrane.

Thanks to the wisdom of Dom Pedro's advisers and his own discretion (in this matter at least) authority was supported and guided by the forces of liberalism. In consequence Brazil, although she was to pass through troublous times, was saved from the chaos into which the Spanish-American states were plunged, and enjoyed a comparatively continuous political and economic development; and, although slow to deliver herself from the evils of slavery, she was saved for seventy years from the evils of military autocracy and *pronunciamientos*.

NOTE. J. Armitage, *History of Brazil* 1808–1831, 2 vols. (London, 1836); J. Fortescue, *Dundonald* (London, 1895); P. A. Martin in *Argentina, Brazil and Chile*.

CHAPTER X

RECOGNITION

England is the political godmother of Latin America....England's support
assumed a material shape: it...consisted in diplomatic and financial and even
military and naval facilities.   OLIVEIRA LIMA

INDEPENDENCE, even when won by force of arms, was not complete
nor secure from external shocks until the new States should be
received into the comity of nations through recognition by great
powers. In 1821 the Court of Portugal, then resident at Rio,
formally recognized the independence of Buenos Aires: indeed for
a decade previously communications had passed between Rio and
Buenos Aires as between the capitals of nations; and in negotiating
an armistice in 1812 the Portuguese Foreign Office spoke of 'the
amity which should exist between neighbouring nations', thus
implicitly recognizing an independence which had not yet been
claimed! The recognition granted in 1821 by Portugal was naturally
continued by Brazil when that monarchy became independent a
few months later. But the essential matter was the action of the
United States and of Great Britain. The Argentine historian
Ricardo Levene remarks that the main external object of the new
Argentine Government was to obtain British support and the same
object frequently recurs in Bolívar's correspondence; and in 1822,
the year in which the United States recognized the new republics,
a United States envoy to South America reported thus: 'There
exists with all the governments of Spanish America a great desire
to conciliate Great Britain; and although the people everywhere
are more attached to us, the governments seek uniformly and
anxiously to establish diplomatic relations and to connect themselves with that of Great Britain.' This was inevitable, for Great
Britain was then the strongest power in the world and particularly
strong at sea. The historical and economic contacts of the new
States were mainly European, and their need was to end the conflict
with Spain and set themselves right with Rome and with Europe.

The Junta of Caracas in April 1810 sent commissioners to

Washington and to London. The former had a friendly interview, necessarily unofficial and non-committal, with Smith, the Secretary of State, who expressed a desire for friendship and commercial intercourse, and soon afterwards appointed a commercial agent to the Venezuelan ports. Towards the end of the year an able and active emissary, Joel Poinsett, was despatched to Buenos Aires and Chile. He spent about two years in Chile, entitled Consul, afterwards Consul-General, by the State Department; but he does not appear to have solicited or received an *exequatur*; nor did he confine himself to consular functions, for he took a prominent part in the activities of the radical leader Carrera and even commanded troops against the royalists. He left Chile in April 1814, just before Spanish reconquest.

The Venezuelan Commissioners for England reached London in July 1810, namely, Simón Bolívar, Luis López Méndez, who remained in London as Venezuelan agent and (as auxiliary) Andrés Bello, afterwards distinguished in the literary, educational and juridical life of South America. The Marquess Wellesley, the Foreign Minister, received them in a cordial unofficial interview, after which they assured him in writing that the 'Sovereign Junta' was hostile to the French invader, and owed allegiance to Ferdinand VII but not to the Cadiz Regency. They solicited British mediation with the Regency and the support of British naval commanders and West Indian Governors, particularly in respect of trade with Venezuela. Wellesley sent a written reply to the Commissioners and also to the Spanish Ambassador in London, urging an accommodation between the Regency and the Venezuelan Junta, suggesting that Venezuelan complaints of treatment by the Regency were not so much a ground for separation as matter for 'urgent representations' to the Regency and possibly the 'good offices of their allies'.

A month after the arrival of the Venezuelan Commissioners, an emissary from Buenos Aires arrived in London. With regard to these two revolutions at opposite ends of South America Lord Wellesley's policy appears to have been the same; that Great Britain should protect the new governments from any French aggression and should attempt mediation with Spain.

In 1812, Castlereagh being then Foreign Minister, a British mission was sent to Cadiz in hopes of effecting some arrangement between the Regency and the insurgent colonies. But the Regency was uncompromising, even demanding armed aid from Great Britain against the insurgents; and nothing was done. During the following decade, Great Britain showed herself ready, whenever occasion offered, to act as common friend in any movement towards an agreement between her ally Spain and the new Spanish-American Governments; and, as long as there seemed any chance of agreement, was anxious for the maintenance of the Spanish Empire on the basis of equality among all its inhabitants and the opening of all its ports to trade with all nations. Yet British offers of mediation were felt to give some moral support to the insurgents; and British ships, unhampered by their Government, traded with all the ports held by the insurgents, ignoring the pretended blockade of the Spanish Main. This was not strange, seeing that the Spanish Viceroy Cisneros had opened Buenos Aires to British trade in 1809.

In 1814 Great Britain by treaty with her ally Spain undertook to prevent her subjects from furnishing arms and munitions to the insurgents: yet British subjects predominated among the European officers who joined the insurgents on the conclusion of the Napoleonic wars. British naval commanders in the Pacific, who, owing to the abnormal conditions, held a quasi-diplomatic position, maintaining amicable relations with both contending parties, generally sympathized with the insurgents. In 1817–19 the Spanish Government not unnaturally complained of the attitude of an allied power: for agents from the revolutionary Governments raised loans and enlisted soldiers in London undisturbed: whole regiments were formed in Great Britain, the officers wearing Venezuelan uniform in public; ships, chartered for the Spanish Main, were openly loaded with military stores and artillery. Then the ablest of British sailors, accompanied by many British officers and seamen, led a fleet against the Spaniards. The mercantile interest generally favoured the insurgents, as also did the anxious and growing body of subscribers to the loans raised in London by revolutionary authorities. Not until 1819 was a tardy and ineffective measure passed after much debate to prevent enlistment for alien service.

In May 1817 Ferdinand, supported by Russia, suggested to the allied powers that they should aid him in reducing the insurgents. For nearly a year communications passed on the proposal. But the attitude of Great Britain, together with the difficulties of arranging terms of intervention, led to its abandonment. Great Britain was, however, bound by alliance with the powers and with Spain; and when in February 1819 the United States, naturally sympathetic towards the young republics, communicated to Great Britain their intention of receiving a Consul from Buenos Aires and expressed a hope for the recognition of the new States by Great Britain and the European powers, Castlereagh replied that the hope of peace on the basis of Spanish supremacy with improved administration was still entertained by the European Alliance.

In 1817–18 the United States sent Commissioners and soon afterwards Consuls to Spanish America, thus according full commercial recognition. Popular sympathy with the revolution and the popular desire to add diplomatic recognition were increasing and were eloquently voiced in Congress. Nor was neutrality strictly observed; for from the beginning of the revolution privateers, receiving letters of marque from the insurgent Governments, regularly sailed from the port of Baltimore to attack Spanish shipping, returning thither to refit. But Adams, the great Secretary of State, had reasons for delay. He was anxious not to endanger, by offence to Spain, the ratification of the Treaty of 1819 by which Spain ceded Florida to the United States. Being in charge of all the foreign relations of his country, he could not be indifferent to the attitude of the European powers; and he also desired evidence of more decided revolutionary success in South America. As to this point three discordant reports from the Commissioners in Buenos Aires were not reassuring: they had reached Buenos Aires early in 1818 and had witnessed the breakdown of the National Government amidst increasing anarchy. But in 1821 the Florida treaty was ratified by Spain; the battle of Carabobo presaged the delivery of Venezuela; the Congress of Cúcuta gave a Constitution to Colombia; and Bolívar set out on his southern campaign. The time had come; and in 1822 the United States recognized the independence first of Colombia and then of Mexico, of the United Provinces of the River Plate and of Chile.

Meantime, as Spanish success became more hopeless, particularly after 1820, Great Britain found her half-way attitude unsatisfactory and was drifting away from the policy of the European Alliance. For a generation past, and even since the early eighteenth century, trade had been the chief motive of British policy concerning Spanish America; and now the British trade, which had recently sprung up, suffered much from the confusion of authority and from the West Indian pirates, who, calling themselves royalist or patriot privateers, attacked unarmed ships of all nations.

In June 1822 Castlereagh took a notable step towards commercial recognition by admitting the ships of the revolted Spanish dependencies to all the ports of the British Empire, thus granting a national character to the republican flags which in Spanish eyes were piratical symbols. Furthermore, at the Congress of Verona, which met in the autumn of that year, the British envoy, Wellington, announced in a written memorandum that Great Britain had been obliged to recognize the existence *de facto* of new Governments so far as to treat with them, that pirates could only be extirpated by co-operation with the actual authorities on the coasts, and that such co-operation must lead to further recognition.[1] To this suggestion the French envoy returned an ambiguous but not favourable answer; the other powers rejected any suggestion of recognition so long as Spain should maintain her claims. When the Congress, after contemplating joint intervention in Spain, authorized the French monarchy to suppress by force the radical Spanish Government and to restore Ferdinand to his absolute throne, Wellington protested and withdrew (November 1822).

Canning, who had succeeded Castlereagh as Foreign Minister in August 1822, took a further step. The pirates who infested the Spanish island of Cuba were increasingly active in their attacks on British shipping. Spain was unable to repress them and refused all compensation to British merchants. So Canning decided to apply

---

[1] Instructions, drawn up by Castlereagh before his death in August 1822, were approved by the Cabinet and transmitted to Wellington.

'a local remedy' by policing the West Indies with a British squadron. In December 1822 he informed the French Government that this squadron 'had orders, if the consent of the Spanish Governor was refused, to land in Cuba and attack the pirates in their hiding-places'. He added: 'a solemn...disclaimer by England that, though she meant to land in Cuba, she had no aggressive designs.' A month later he suspended these West Indian operations, because the Spaniards were in difficulties with France and now offered full compensation to Great Britain.

Great Britain, now detached from the European Alliance, was threatened with the danger of French supremacy not only in Spain, but also in the Indies, a danger similar to that which she had opposed by arms in 1702–13 and in 1808–14. In March 1823, just before the French invasion of Spain, Canning intimated to France that Great Britain considered the separation of the Colonies from Spain as decided, that formal recognition was a question of time and circumstances, that Great Britain intended no territorial acquisition in Spanish America and was satisfied that France had no such design. In August the French army, having traversed Spain, was besieging Cadiz; and in view of a proposed Conference[1] of the Allies to settle Spanish-American affairs, Canning sought the co-operation of the United States in a policy which, while leaving the ground open for amicable settlement between Spain and the Colonies, should oppose the acquisition of any part of Spanish America by any other power. The United States Minister in London undertook to pledge his Government to this co-operation if Great Britain would promptly recognize the independence of the new States. Canning found himself unable to grant immediate recognition; and accordingly the two Governments, having generally similar aims but differing in their attitude both towards Spanish America and towards the European Continent, proceeded to take separate action.

In October 1823 Canning, in his historic interview with Polignac, the French Ambassador, declared that Great Britain would recognize the new States if France should employ force against them,

[1] This proposed Conference never met, being frustrated by the action of Great Britain.

and clearly signified uncompromising opposition to any such action.[1] In December President Monroe addressed his famous message to Congress. That message enunciated four principles or rules: (1) American abstention from purely European affairs;[2] (2) respect 'for the existing colonies or dependencies of any European power'; (3) 'a principle...that the American continents...are henceforth not to be considered as subjects for future colonization by any European powers'; (4) an announcement that 'with the Governments...whose independence...we have acknowledged, we could not view any interposition for the purpose of oppressing them, or controlling their destiny by any European Power in any other light than as a manifestation of an unfriendly disposition towards the United States'. It is the last of these four announcements which chiefly concerns the present topic.

In the autumn of 1823 Canning sent Commissioners to Colombia and Mexico to report on conditions; and he also appointed Consuls in the principal Spanish-American ports, thereby according full commercial, but not yet diplomatic recognition to the republican governments.

Early in 1824 Spain opened Spanish-American trade to all European nations. Since Spain now possessed few American harbours, this tardy concession was purely hypothetical. Yet it moved Canning to a last effort to procure from Spain recognition of her revolted dependencies. The effort was vain. British recognition could not now be delayed. In June 1824 the London merchants petitioned for such recognition; and in July the Cabinet decided that Woodbine Parish, the British Consul-General in

---

[1] In March 1824 Canning published the Memorandum of this interview. The international aspects of Canning's policy are here briefly considered because they obviously concern the history of Latin America. The more purely British interests served by that policy and his difficulties with his colleagues and with King George IV do not concern that history and need not be considered here. They can be studied in Temperley, *The Foreign Policy of Canning* (pp. 103–53). This gives the reasons which hindered the grant of recognition in 1823.

[2] Some writers minimize this first statement: but Professor Perkins has shown that the 'Doctrine of the Two Spheres' pervades the history of the Monroe Doctrine. Monroe's third or non-colonization principle was mainly concerned with Russian advance in Alaska but obviously has a general application. There is some ground for thinking that there was little or no danger to Spanish America from France or the Holy Alliance and that both Monroe's warning and Canning's were not necessary for that immediate object. It does not follow that these two statements of policy were unwise or impolitic.

Buenos Aires, should be instructed to negotiate a commercial Treaty, the conclusion of which would mean full recognition. But Parish was instructed first to assure himself of the 'power of the Government of Buenos Aires to bind by its stipulations all the... United States of the Rio de la Plata'. Such power did not exist; so Parish informed the Buenos Aires Government that the 'erection of a National Government was the one thing necessary to secure recognition'. Accordingly the Buenos Aires Government reported to the Constituent Congress then sitting in Buenos Aires: 'Great Britain, unfettered by the engagement of the (European) allies, has adopted with respect to the States of America a conduct noble and worthy of a nation the most civilized, the most independent and certainly the most powerful of Europe....This important event (recognition) with respect to the Provinces of the River Plate, depends principally on their appearing as a national body.' Acting on this hint, the Congress obtained the consent of all the provinces to a Fundamental Law, providing that the Government of Buenos Aires should act as a provisional National Government in charge of Foreign Affairs until a Constitution should be framed to be submitted to the provinces. Thus the preliminary condition was fulfilled. On 24 January 1825 Parish despatched to Canning a copy of this Law; and a week later the Treaty with Great Britain was signed in Buenos Aires amid popular rejoicing.

This Treaty gave priority of recognition to Buenos Aires: but already on the last day of 1824 Canning had sent a despatch to Madrid, announcing his intention to recognize Colombia, Mexico and Buenos Aires. He added that owing to the continuance of the struggle in Peru 'a just consideration for the rights of Spain and for the chance, whatever it may be, of the practical assertion of them, forbids any interference on the part of His Majesty's Government' and that information concerning conditions in Chile was insufficient. But recognition of all the independent Governments was not long delayed.

The solution which Canning had earnestly desired for the Spanish-American Republics, recognition of independence by the mother-country, was facilitated in the case of Brazil by the fact that Braganza monarchs ruled both in Lisbon and in Rio, and by

UNITED STATES OF MEXICO

CENTRAL AMERICA

COLOMBIA

PERU

BRAZIL

BOLIVIA

PARAGUAY

ARGENTINE

URUGUAY

PROVINCES

CHILE

INDIAN FRONTIER

LATIN AMERICA
AFTER THE
WARS OF INDEPENDENCE
❖ 1825 ❖

the long-standing British influence in Portugal, an influence now effectively exercised. After long negotiation and natural reluctance, King John of Portugal in May 1825 consented. In August 1825 a treaty—negotiated by Sir Charles Stuart in the strange character of Portuguese envoy—was signed in Rio, whereby 'His most Faithful Majesty recognizes Brazil as an Empire independent and separate from Portugal'. During the following two years most European States recognized Brazilian independence. But here too the United States can claim priority. In April 1824 one José Rebello came to Washington sent by Pedro I as Chargé d'Affaires. A month later he was officially received by President Monroe, who thus recognized the independent Brazilian monarchy.

The action of the United States and of Great Britain fixed the status of the Spanish-American Republics. Although Spain long kept up the fiction of continuing the war, the British recognition was decisive in Europe; and in 1830 the liberal monarchy of Louis Philippe accorded recognition.

A word should be added about diplomatic recognition by the Vatican. Here relations were complicated by the fact that the Pope was not only spiritual Head of the Church but also a reigning sovereign with temporal power over his dominions. Thus purely spiritual and ecclesiastical relations with existing authorities in America, including such matters as the acceptance of names proposed for bishoprics by those authorities, did not imply political or diplomatic recognition of the new governments. Nevertheless, these measures for ministering to the spiritual needs of those lands evoked vigorous protests from the Spanish representatives at the Vatican, as encroaching on the rights of His Catholic Majesty and the royal patronage. It is related in Chapter XI how in 1827 clerics, proposed by the Government of Colombia for consecration as Proprietary Bishops, were accepted by the Pope. Four years later this was done in other parts of Spanish America; a concession which was made by the Pope as Head of the Church and not as a reigning sovereign, but which was a step towards diplomatic recognition. The Vatican in its political character was obviously obliged to await the action of the great powers. Finally, in 1835, all prospect of Spanish reconquest having vanished and the international position of the new governments being secure, the Vatican gave full diplomatic recognition by receiving Ministers from them and sending to them Nuncios, who had the character of diplomatic envoys from a reigning sovereign.

Long-delayed recognition by Spain was granted to most of the republics in the course of the sixty years following achievement of independence. The several dates are not profoundly important. Mexico received Spanish recognition in 1836, Venezuela in 1845, Argentina in 1859, New Granada in 1881, Honduras not till 1894. But long before formal recognition ships under republican flags were admitted in Spanish ports and Spanish ships in republican ports: consuls were appointed on both sides, and Spanish immigrants were welcomed. In many cases recognition was delayed by questions concerning liability for public debts contracted during the time of Spanish dominion.

NOTE. F. L. Paxson, *Independence of the South American Republics* (Philadelphia, 1903); W. S. Robertson, *Hispanic-American Relations with the United States** (New York, 1923); D. Perkins, *The Monroe Doctrine 1823–1826* (Harvard, 1927); J. B. Lockey, *Pan-Americanism; its beginnings* (New York, 1920); W. F. Reddaway, *The Monroe Doctrine* (Cambridge, 1898); C. K. Webster, *The Foreign Policy of Castlereagh*, 1815–1822 (London, 1925); H. Temperley, *The Foreign Policy of Canning* (London, 1925); A. Alvarez, *The Monroe Doctrine* (New York, 1924); R. Rush, *A Residence at the Court of London*, 1819–25, 2 vols. (London, 1833–45); W. R. Manning, *Diplomatic Correspondence of the United States concerning the Independence of the Latin-American Nations*, 3 vols. (New York, 1925).

CHAPTER XI

BOLÍVAR AND THE TROPICAL COUNTRIES

UPPER PERU, 1825

AFTER Ayacucho two courses seemed open to Bolívar, to continue his work in the south or to return to Colombia (where his presence was urgently needed if his political work was to endure), leaving to others the settlement of Peru and Upper Peru. Bent on following up his southern triumphs, he left Colombia in Santander's charge. An immediate question was the future status of Upper Peru; a point which demands exposition in order to explain the origin of a State which was later involved in two territorial wars.

Since 1776 Upper Peru, by an arrangement which seemed to defy both geographical and ethnological convenience, had belonged to the Viceroyalty of Buenos Aires: but upon the revolt of Buenos Aires in 1810 the Viceroy of Peru had taken over the country and had foiled all Argentine attempts to reconquer it. Thus there were seemingly three alternatives, union with the 'United Provinces of the River Plate', union with Peru, or complete independence. A fortnight after Ayacucho Sucre wrote to Bolívar at Lima, asking 'what political course' he was to follow: he received no instructions. A fortnight later he wrote again from Cuzco indicating the reasonable solution, 'the country desires no master but itself', and begging for instructions, which never came. But he had reason to believe, from earlier communications, that Bolívar wished the question to be settled by a representative assembly of Upper Peru. Accordingly, having crossed the frontier from Cuzco into Upper Peru, Sucre sent out from La Paz on 9 February 1825 letters to the cities, convoking an assembly, after writing to tell Bolívar of his intention to do so.

Upon receiving this despatch, Bolívar, who had ignored Sucre's requests for instructions, sent him (in the course of a friendly letter, dated 21 February 1825) a reprimand for this 'act of sovereignty' encroaching on the rights of the River Plate Provinces and violating the principle that the limits of the new republics should be those of the former Spanish 'Viceroyalties, Captaincies-General or Presidencies', that is to say the *uti possidetis* of 1810.

Bolívar adds (with truth, as appeared later) that Sucre's action was a dangerous precedent for Quito. Sucre in his reply (4 April) pleaded want of instructions and argued that the River Plate Provinces were in a state of dissolution[1] and that Upper Peru was infected by their example, every cabildo regarding itself as sovereign. Sucre had judged the situation rightly: for on 8 February, the eve of his decree, the Buenos Aires Government had sent orders to Arenales, Governor of the Argentine Province of Salta, that the Provinces of Upper Peru 'should have complete liberty to decide what suits their interests and government'. On 16 May Bolívar, having been informed of the decision of the Buenos Aires Government, issued a decree from Arequipa (on his way to Upper Peru) convoking an Assembly of Upper Peru.

The Assembly met on 6 July 1825 and in a three months' session declared the country—under the name of 'Republic of Bolívar', afterwards simplified into 'Bolivia'—to be 'independent of all the nations both of the Old World and the New', solicited the protection of Bolívar, granted him dictatorial powers during his residence in the country and requested him to draw up a constitution for them.

In April 1825 Bolívar set out southward from Lima on a five months' triumphal progress to the frontier, attempting to reform the administration wherever he halted. Approaching Arequipa, he was presented with a horse caparisoned with solid gold. At Cuzco he received a similar gift and also a golden civic crown set with gems and the keys of the city in gold: he distributed the gold and jewels among his companions, and gave the golden keys to his aide-de-camp, O'Leary. Those who feel distaste at these adulatory incidents should remember that, in giving a touch of histrionic colour to his career, Bolívar knew his public.

[1] Sucre did not know that an Argentine Constituent Congress had met at Buenos Aires two months earlier and had entrusted the management of Foreign Affairs to the Provincial Government of Buenos Aires. See p. 95. It may be added that on 9 May 1825 the Buenos Aires Government promulgated a law which mentioned Sucre's decree of 9 February without comment or complaint and granted to the Provinces of Upper Peru 'complete liberty to dispose of their destiny'. O'Leary, Bolívar's aide-de-camp and affectionate admirer, approves Sucre's action: and General Heres, a loyal subordinate of the Liberator, suggests that Bolívar's vexation was partly due to pique at being deprived of the sole 'glory' of convoking the Assembly in Upper Peru.

In September 1825 Bolívar crossed the frontier into Upper Peru, everywhere received in triumph. He spent five months in Bolivia, labouring at the improvement of administration and of finance in this, the last of the countries liberated by him, disposing the opening of a port at Cobija on the strip of Pacific coast assigned to Bolivia, drafting the Bolivian Constitution, receiving a congratulatory mission from Buenos Aires, discussing with them a possible alliance against Brazil (a proposal which came to nothing) and considering grandiose plans of action concerning every part of the South-American continent.

DESIGNS ON CUBA

Although his health and vigour were already impaired by the exhausting labours of fifteen years, by wearing anxieties, by his restless activity even in the intervals between toil and by the eager zest of his social and amorous recreations—he was an enthusiastic dancer and a noted Don Juan—Bolívar in 1825 was at the apogee of his career, dictator and legislator of Peru and of Bolivia and President of the Republic of Colombia, which was now recognized as such by Great Britain, that *señora de las naciones*, as Bolivar wrote on hearing of the recognition. But the war, in his view, was not concluded until Spain should be deprived of her last American possessions and should make peace by recognizing independence: and his next design—an obvious strategical move—was an expedition, possibly in conjunction with Mexico, against the Spaniards in Cuba and Puerto Rico, with the expected aid of the negroes of those islands. The arsenal of Havana had been a base of operations against Venezuela and was still a menace to the Spanish Main and yet more to independent Mexico. There was another motive: to provide distant employment for ambitious leaders, particularly Páez, and for the victorious Colombian armies, mostly mulattoes, Indians and half-castes; who, whether disbanded or kept on foot, were now a danger to the state.

Colombia could not afford costly adventures, the entire revenue being insufficient to pay interest on a recent London loan of six million pounds. If this difficulty could have been overcome and Spanish warships evaded, as perhaps might have happened in view of the wealth of Cuba and the prizes constantly captured by Colombian privateers, an attack on the Spanish Antilles had a chance of success.[1] But the United States Government made objections and the plan was dropped. The disapproval of the United States was well-founded. Colombian or Mexican-Colombian victory in the islands would have brought a hopeless political tangle. Cuba and Puerto Rico could not have stood alone. Colombia and Mexico (already suspicious of Colombia) would have fallen out over the prey. Neither of the two, in the absence of domestic order and of a strong navy, could have managed transmarine provinces. And the United States would have been inevitably drawn into a many-sided conflict.

CONGRESS OF PANAMÁ, 1826

Two days before Ayacucho, Bolívar, confident of victory, had sent a circular to all the Spanish-American republican Governments, renewing his invitation to a Congress at Panamá; and at last, after long delay, representatives from Colombia, Peru, Mexico and Central America, that is to say four of the seven then existing Spanish-American Republics, met in assembly at Panamá in July 1826. The Republic of Bolivia, not yet recognized by Peru, was unable to send representatives in time. The men in power in Chile and in Buenos Aires, suspicious of Bolívar's supposed ambition, made a show of adhesion, but sent no delegates. Paraguay was isolated, under the sombre despotism of Francia. The Emperor of Brazil, invited later (not by Bolívar), accepted but, being at war with Buenos Aires, sent no one. Great Britain and Holland were invited and also, though not at Bolívar's instance or desire, the United States. A Dutch delegate came, but without credentials, Holland not having officially recognized Spanish-American independence. The United States, after some debate, named two delegates: one died on the way and the other arrived when the Assembly had separated. The British representative, Dawkins, duly arrived, having been instructed by Canning: he did not attend the sessions, but had much conversation with the members,

[1] Bolívar's suggestions of expeditions, after Cuban victory, to the Canaries, to the Philippines, to Spain itself, need not be seriously considered.

urging particularly an accommodation with Spain even at the cost of some pecuniary sacrifice. In the course of three weeks (July–August 1826) ten sessions were held, and it was agreed that a permanent confederation of Hispanic republics should be formed, with a central authority meeting every two years: this authority was to have armed forces provided by the members but not controlled by them, was to protect the integrity of all the component States and settle all disputes by arbitration.

Owing to the unhealthy climate of Panamá and the insistence of the Mexican delegates, the Congress adjourned to Tacubaya, a village near the Mexican capital; but it never reassembled there or elsewhere. The agreement was impracticable and came to nothing. Bolívar, who was not present at Panamá, compared the Congress to the madman who, seated on a rock, believed that he was directing the movements of the ships in the surrounding ocean. Yet the amicable meeting of delegates from four extensive Republics, discussing a scheme of union, was in itself worth something. These four States covered the whole of tropical Spanish America, a vast region now divided between twelve Republics.

PERU AND COLOMBIA

Bolívar himself had his hands full elsewhere. Sucre having reluctantly consented to take charge of Bolivia until the Bolivian Congress should meet in August 1827, Bolívar in January 1826 left Bolivia for Lima, where he was received as dictator with almost delirious adulation and brought peace by his authoritative presence. He recommended to the Peruvian Congress his 'Bolivian Constitution', which, except in name, was a limited monarchy without the trappings of hereditary royalty; for under this Constitution the President was to hold office with limited powers for life, and was to name (with some insignificant limitations) a Vice-President who should succeed him. The moral authority was provided by a Board of Censors appointed for life.

To Bolívar's luxurious and almost Caesarian retreat in a country house near Lima (January–September 1826), the centre of political observation and of flattering attention, there soon came disquieting news of disorders in Colombia. To remedy these ills and to prevent the recurrence of similar ills in Peru, Bolívar proposed a Federation 'closer than that of the United States', between Bolivia, Peru and Colombia, each member of the Federation to adopt the Bolivian Constitution ('my youngest child, the ark to save us from shipwreck'), which was also to be the Constitution of the central federal authority: there was to be 'one flag, one army, one nation'. The Liberator himself, as 'Supreme Chief', was to visit annually every part of this vast territory. The scheme seems to mean three federated constitutional monarchies (or 'monocracies', to use Mitre's word) with an itinerant Emperor to inspect and guide them.

But Colombia alone, his first creation, demanded all the Liberator's cares. In February 1826 a messenger from Páez arrived at Lima, offering him a crown. The Liberator refused, as he later refused similar offers from others. Páez' offer was a bribe, to secure Bolívar's acquiescence in sedition. Páez held the anomalous position of military chief in one of the three Venezuelan Departments and at the same time Commander in the war against the royalists. In November 1823 he had ended that war by taking Puerto Cabello, a fine feat of arms. Thenceforth, dissatisfied with the mere command in one department and regarding Venezuela alone as his *patria*, Páez was a danger to the Colombian State. Nine months later he was flouting the authority of the Vice-President Santander; who, hating Páez, was tactless and provocative in handling the situation. In April 1826 a 'revolution' broke out in Venezuela, the beginning of civil war. To restore peace in his native country, Bolívar, although all the authorities in Lima besought him to remain, embarked at Callao for the north in September 1826, abandoning Peru to twenty years of confusion. Two months later he was in Bogotá, and in December 1826 he led a few troops into Venezuela. Páez meant to fight Bolívar, but his *pronunciamiento* collapsed at the Liberator's approach. Bolívar, not realizing his own strength, condoned all the past and declared Páez to be the 'Saviour of his Country'. They met amicably, but it was a patched-up and hollow accommodation.

The successive steps in the dissolution of Colombia, the tragedy of the last four years (1827–30) of Bolívar's brief life, can only be indicated; his laborious efforts at administrative and financial reform in Venezuela, in New Granada, in Quito, then again in New Granada; his alternate refusal and acceptance of supreme power; the intrigues of Santander, a Granadan by birth, against Bolívar the Venezuelan, who was regarded as a foreigner in New Granada and lost ground during his long absences from Bogotá; for during half of 1827 he was in Venezuela, and spent the whole of 1829 in an expedition to Quito and Guayaquil. The years 1828–9 brought an accumulation of disasters; invasions of Guayaquil and of Bolivia by Peruvian troops, invasions which, although they were repelled, were fatal to the dream of unity; in Bogotá a nocturnal conspiracy (September 1828) of 150 persons against the life of Bolívar, who, aided by his mistress, escaped through a window;[1] a revolt in Pasto, repressed with unspeakable savagery by the barbarous soldiery of Colombia; two serious military *pronunciamientos* or mutinies in New Granada; the futile 'Convention of Ocaña' which was to reform the Constitution, but owing to the irreparable split between 'Santanderistas' and 'Bolivianos' dissolved without a quorum.

In January 1830 came the definite separation of Venezuela under Páez. Four months later the Kingdom or Presidency of Quito broke off to form a separate Republic, under the fanciful but now familiar name of Ecuador. In March Bolívar, grievously ill, resigned power for the last time; two months later he left Bogotá for Cartagena, hoping to find passage for Europe. Once the owner of enormous wealth, he was now obliged, after years of supreme power, to sell his plate and furniture to provide a retreat for his last days. On 10 December 1830 he dictated a message exhorting Colombians to union. A week later he died, at the age of forty-seven, in the house of a hospitable Spaniard near Santa Marta, bitterly lamenting the failure of his efforts at political reconstruction. 'I fear peace more than war', had been his utterance on the eve of his triumph at Carabobo in 1821; and on his death-bed he exclaimed, 'I blush to say it, we have achieved nothing but independence at

[1] Santander, though not an active conspirator, was privy to the conspiracy, apparently not desiring the murder of Bolívar, although he must have known that murder was intended. He was condemned to death but allowed to go into exile. After Bolívar's death he returned, to become President of the Republic of New Granada.

the cost of all other things': but he added, 'independence is a gate through which we may recover those things'. This latter remark is not out-of-date to-day.

With regard to Bolívar's attempt to implant in those war-shaken and half-desert lands the imported exotic of representative parliamentary forms, Gil Fortoul in his *Constitutional History of Venezuela* and the Venezuelan Blanco-Fombona both declare that dictatorship was the only possible government. But Bolívar is his own best critic. In a letter addressed to Páez in September 1826 'which seems to be dictated by the spirit of prophecy', says Blanco-Fombona, Bolívar writes: 'The executive...has sought a premature perfection, plunging us into an ocean of laws and institutions excellent but at present unnecessary...the provinces have developed in the midst of chaos; each province draws authority to itself; each wishes to be a national centre...every department desires to be sovereign; every hand desires to grasp the staff of command, every turbulent self-seeker to wear the magistrate's robe...it is needful to maintain a strong authority and use force in calming passions and repressing abuses, by the printing-press, the pulpit, the bayonet....In tranquil times theory is excellent; but amid general agitation, theory is like an attempt to rule our passions by the ordinances of Heaven, which, although perfect, are inapplicable.' And in September 1829, fifteen months before his death, he wrote to O'Leary that the existing Government of Colombia was unworkable owing to the vast distances and difficulty of transit, that local magistrates in assuming supreme authority were usually justified by necessity, and that the only alternative to the separation (imminent at the time) of New Granada and Venezuela was the creation of a strong (personal) government for life.

But to say that Bolívar ought to have established autocracy is much like saying that he ought to have lived twenty years longer: for virtuous autocrats, proof against demoralization by power, are hard to find. Nor was his political work fruitless: he held together his Great Colombia until fighting was over and independence won. The tripartite division of that unwieldy creation was not destruction: for every one of the three republics owed much to him; and the successors, who divided his inheritance, were his men:

Santander, who undertook a difficult task in New Granada; Páez, who for seventeen years maintained comparative peace in Venezuela; Flores, Venezuelan by birth, who ruled Ecuador for fifteen years. Even Bolívar's few months of political work in Peru and Bolivia bore some fruit. When the five republics which call him Liberator joined recently in honouring his memory, they were honouring him as statesman as well as soldier.

Bolívar's utterance of disillusionment was echoed twelve years later by his rival or colleague San Martín, who wrote in 1842 from his retirement in Europe to a friend in Chile: 'The labour and the blood given for the independence of America have been, if not wasted, at any rate unfortunately spent in most of the new States, except in your country.' These remarks by the two great leaders of the movement in South America might almost seem to justify turning down the page of history which follows emancipation: but rather they demand that the historian should examine that initial failure (so far as it was a failure) in the light of later events and later progress.

The year 1830, which brought the tripartite division of 'Great' Colombia, is a notable landmark. To 1830 belong the Constitution of independent Uruguay and the accession of the Brazilian Emperor Pedro II. About the same time the experimental period in the south was ended, in Argentina by Rosas' dictatorship and in Chile by the establishment of the oligarchical system. In 1830 French recognition, prelude to recognition by Rome, strengthened the international position of the new republics; and after the failure of the Spanish expedition to Mexico in the previous year, the theoretical pretensions of Spain were no longer serious. Accordingly, at this point, it seems well to offer in the next chapter some general remarks on the early course of these republics.

NOTE. Petre, *Simón Bolívar*; W. S. Robertson, *Rise of the Spanish-American Republics* (New York, 1919); J. B. Lockey, *Pan-Americanism: its Beginnings* (New York, 1920) gives a good account of the Panamá Congress. *Colombia: a geographical, statistical and political account*, 2 vols. (London, 1822) is a remarkable work published in the English language by the Colombian Government.

CHAPTER XII

REVOLUTION AND RECONSTRUCTION

DURING the wars of independence and also after victory the leaders had an unprecedented task—to construct a new polity from the fragments of the old. Those wars were not the uprising of a united people against alien domination: they were bitterly contested and destructive civil wars, which blurred all order and confused any existing political experience. The movement for independence and the accompanying revolution were not democratic. This is clear in the case of Mexico, where popular outbreaks were crushed by the privileged classes who afterwards brought about independence. As to the tropical republics of South America, the Venezuelan historian Blanco-Fombona, a searching interpreter of Bolívar's work, declares that Bolívar liberated peoples against the wish of the majority. In the Buenos Aires revolution *el pueblo*, 'the people', had their part, but Argentine historians have lately proved that the popular demonstration was in great part arranged by the battalion commanders and by a group of enthusiasts; and indeed it can hardly be that democracy uprose for a day, then to disappear for an indefinite time. In any case the people whose voice was heard were only those of the capital: their wishes were conveyed 'on the points of bayonets' to the provinces: and none but 'patriot vecinos'—men belonging to the privileged class of householders and known to hold acceptable opinions—were allowed to vote for deputies to the Constituent Congress of 1813. Woodbine Parish, a friendly observer, who was in Argentina from 1824 to 1832, writes thus of the Province of Salta: 'The form of government in this province, as in all the rest, is based upon that of Buenos Aires, consisting of a popular assembly, which has the power of electing the Governor. But, though democratic in theory, it is far otherwise in practice: the lower orders have not the smallest notion of the real meaning of representative government and bow with submission to the dictates of a patriarchal coterie of influential families, which, alternately electing and elected, arrange the Government among themselves very much as suits their own convenience and interests.' Lord Bryce (*Modern Democracies*, vol. I, p. 212) puts it briefly: 'The people did not rule because they could not rule.'

It is true that some of the leaders, inspired by North American and French example and theory, hoped to create democracy, or used, often sincerely, liberal phrases which seemed to further the independent cause but did not represent anything tangible. Yet the masses played their part in the new States, not as supporters of liberal republicanism but more often as servants of disorder or autocracy; for the half-barbarous illiterate population of the frontiers, the mountains and the prairies, people with little civic sense, had been organized in the wars; and also *montoneros*, irregular soldiery no better than brigands. Here was fiery material ready for any ambitious politician or rude chieftain who might win them by his personal prowess and his promises; and in the tropical regions the docile Indians could be swept into the armies of aspirants for power or into those of uneasy potentates.

Everywhere public finance and the cost of war were a bewildering difficulty. Most of the new governments borrowed on most onerous terms in London: the beginning of a disastrous financial history for some of the tropical states. Extravagant waste and peculation dissipated both revenue and loans. Belgrano, Moreno, O'Higgins, Bolívar, Sucre and other leaders were men of disinterested integrity: but the crowd of new officials, heirs of the corrupt Spanish tradition, were hard to control.

The centrifugal and localist tendencies, thoroughly Spanish in character, which often marred the first efforts at independence and pervade the story of reconstruction, were commonly styled Federalism, the word being used in a sense almost opposite to its usual meaning, and implying an effort not at union but at separation. These self-styled 'Federalists', with hazy notions of the United States Constitution, believed that, by division and subdivision, they were imitating its merits. When royal authority disappeared, the cabildos remained, almost the only civic base for reconstruction. These bodies, already possessing a prescriptive power of self-modification to meet emergencies, generally faced their new and strange responsibilities with vigour and discretion in the early stages of the Revolution, acting as a constitutional channel for setting up provisional governments. But, as in the case of the mother-country, the very success of Spanish local institutions told against national unity. Every city felt itself to be the capital of its own district rather than a member in a community of cities. When the Spanish Governor of a province disappeared, the province often broke up into city-states, jealous of one another. Thus the local patriotism and limited outlook of the municipalities were a hindrance to the building-up of strong states. Bolívar in 1828-9 abolished all the cabildos in New Granada: and soon afterwards Páez, having first used the Venezuelan cabildos to effect separation from New Granada, abolished them also.[1]

But there was one institution, stable, comprehensive and unifying in character, which almost all the revolutionary leaders wished to support and in turn to win its support for their political work, namely the Catholic Church, which had been closely united with the State in the Spanish Indies. With some this was a matter not merely of policy, but also of principle. Belgrano daily knelt to recite the Rosary among his soldiers and named La Virgen de la Merced Commander-in-Chief. At a portable altar in San Martín's camp, his army chaplains said Mass on Sundays and festivals. On the other hand, Bolívar's desire for episcopal support and for the favour of the Vatican was probably a matter chiefly of public policy. Whatever his own opinions, he valued highly the spiritual, moral and educational work of the Church; work which, if it could harmonize with the new polity, would help to make orderly citizens as well as good Christians.

Although many of the lower clergy, especially in the River Plate, supported the revolution, as did also a few dignitaries, notably Dean Funes of Córdoba and two bishops, those of Caracas and Cuzco (both of them deported by the royal authorities in conse-

---

[1] There is one instance of voluntary union. In 1821 the Province of Panamá quietly assumed independence, the Bishop being foremost in the movement. The leaders, having debated the question of union with Mexico or with Colombia, decided for the latter. Thus Panamá became a province of Great Colombia, and later of the Republic of New Granada, now known as Colombia.

quence), the clergy on the whole naturally favoured the monarchy: and the bishops, most of them Spaniards and all nominees of the Crown, were royalists not merely as a matter of policy but also as a religious duty.

Accordingly the leaders had two difficult tasks: to ensure continuity of ecclesiastical order and ministrations by procuring the consecration of bishops for vacant sees; and to win the support of the existing bishops and their successors. The first of these tasks was complicated by the fact that all the new Governments claimed to have inherited from the displaced King the royal patronage (*patronato real*), that is to say the right of designating to the Pope persons to be consecrated as bishops. The Vatican has never recognized this claim; and (quite apart from the theoretical question of the *patronato*) the Pope was unable to accept names proposed by the new Governments so long as Ferdinand VII had any authority or prospect of regaining authority in America. During the years 1814–19, when Ferdinand VII had recovered dominion over most of his American kingdoms, several bishops were consecrated to American sees on the King's nomination, all naturally royalists. And in an encyclical of January 1816 Pius VII urged the bishops of America to suppress sedition by 'exposing the grave evils and dangers of defection' and by 'expounding the noble and exceptional qualities and virtues of our dear son and your King, Ferdinand, Catholic King of Spain, to whom nothing is more important than religion and the happiness of his subjects'.

Moreover, with the exception of Bolívar, insurgent leaders, even those most loyal to the Church, usually expelled royalist bishops: Belgrano did so in Salta,[1] O'Higgins in Chile and San Martín in Peru. Many bishops, after republican victory, left their sees and retired to Spain. In 1819 there were no bishops in Chile or in the River Plate: and elsewhere sees falling vacant remained unfilled, since the authority of the King (who had the sole right of presentation) had disappeared or was disappearing.

---

[1] Thus from 1812 there was no bishop in charge of a diocese in the United Provinces of the River Plate, and, upon the death of the Bishop of Salta in 1819, there was no bishop at all in those Provinces. The Bishop of Santiago, after four years' exile at Mendoza, was allowed to return to Chile, but only as a private citizen. In 1825 he was banished to Spain.

But the Spanish Revolution of 1820 brought a change within the Church in America. It has been seen that the higher clergy in New Spain, loyal to the King, refused loyalty to the radical, anti-clerical and almost anti-monarchical Spanish Government; which in effect held the Catholic King a prisoner, was at variance with the Vatican and was attacking ecclesiastical institutions and abolishing clerical emoluments and privileges. This Spanish Revolution also gave Bolívar his opportunity. The diocese of Maracaibo, which spread far over mountain and coast, was held by a Creole, bearing the historic surname of Lasso de la Vega, an excellent prelate of solid rather than brilliant qualities. Having been nominated for his see by Ferdinand VII and residing in the royalist city of Maracaibo, he naturally favoured that cause: but he was shocked at the radical revolution in Spain, and when Maracaibo declared for the patriots[1] in January 1821 and the Bishop was placed under arrest in his own house, he declared that, although he could not declare himself a republican, he did not oppose the movement of the city, offered his ministrations equally to all, and asked permission to present himself before the Congress at Cúcuta. On the way thither he met Bolívar at Trujillo.[2] The Bishop, with due regard for the dignity of his office, received the Liberator not at the entrance to the town but at the church door, robed in his vestments. Here Bolívar 'edified the whole town', says the Bishop, by kneeling to kiss the episcopal cross, and then knelt at the sanctuary steps during prayers and Benediction. A cordial interview followed, Bolívar promising protection and the Bishop promising adhesion. Finally the Bishop entered the Constituent Congress of Cúcuta as republican deputy for Maracaibo and afterwards was a Senator in the regular Congress,[3] a champion of Church rights but also a supporter of the Republic. The Bishop differed from Bolívar, and still more from Santander, about State claims to the *patronato* and the tithes: but they worked harmoniously together for Church and State. The Cúcuta Congress, which

[1] Maracaibo was afterwards retaken by the royalists and it was not till 1823 that it was finally captured by the republicans.

[2] Bolívar was on his way to the campaign which led to the victory of Carabobo, 24 June 1821.

[3] C. S. Cochrane gives an amusing description of Bishop Lasso as a Senator, *Residence and Travel in Colombia*, vol. II, p. 65.

abolished the Inquisition, established or restored episcopal tribunals with spiritual authority over all Catholics and with power to impose penalties.

By agreement with Bolívar, Bishop Lasso de la Vega wrote in October 1821 to Pius VII reporting the needs of the Church in Colombia, begging that a successor might be appointed in case of his own death, and defending the Republic in the significant words: 'When the King swore to the Constitution (in May 1820) the supreme Majesty returned to the source from which it had sprung, that is to say the will and consent of the citizens. It has returned to the Spaniards: why not to our people also?'[1] The letter took nearly a year to reach its destination. The Pope sent a sympathetic reply (September 1822), the first communication from the Vatican to a republican bishop, avoiding political matters, expressing his desire to provide for the spiritual needs of the faithful in America and asking for information about the vacant sees. He concludes with the Apostolic Benediction for the bishop and his flock. The letter was received with joy in Bogotá: the Vice-President Santander publicly kissed the Papal signature: the document was printed and circulated throughout Colombia and even beyond the frontier. The Apostolic Blessing of a republican bishop and his flock meant a change in the attitude of the Vatican since the encyclical of 1816, a change due to the fact that the *Patronato Real* in America was now an impossibility.

Bolívar's dealings with the Bishop of Popayán have been already told. A letter to Bishop Lasso de la Vega from the newly elected Pope Leo XII, dated November 1823, which contained the words, 'that American nation', whereas Chile in the same letter is styled 'that region of Chile', roused enthusiasm in Bogotá, although obviously the words quoted were not intended to convey the meaning read into them by the recipients. But it is true that in Colombia particularly the efforts of Bolívar, Santander and Lasso

---

[1] The bishop, in a speech to the Congress of Cúcuta, argued that obedience was due to the King only, not to the Spanish people. By his oath to the Constitution the King had surrendered his sovereignty to the Spanish people, thereby releasing America from all obligations to him. The argument, though not identical, resembles that put forward some years earlier by lawyers, that the Crown was the only link between Spain and the Kingdoms of the Indies and that the fall of the Spanish throne in 1808 had broken that one link.

de la Vega succeeded in winning episcopal support for the new order.

In July 1824 the Colombian Congress, in Bolívar's absence, passed a law[1] that 'the Republic of Colombia shall continue to exercise the right of patronage, which the kings of Spain possessed ...in this part of America'. This claim was not meant as a blow to the Church. On the contrary, the legislators desired to provide for the spiritual needs of the people and to conclude a Concordat with the Vatican. But in September 1824, Ferdinand VII having been restored by French arms to his absolute throne in the previous year, Leo XII issued an encyclical to the bishops of America urging them to support the cause of 'our very dear son Ferdinand VII, Catholic King of Spain, whose sublime and solid virtues cause him to prefer the lustre of religion and the happiness of his subjects to the splendour of his greatness'. It was a set-back to the efforts of Bolívar. Those efforts only reached final success when Great Colombia was near disruption. In 1826 the Pope appointed an auxiliary bishop for the see of Maracaibo; and in the following year (May 1827) six clerics, proposed by the Government of Colombia on the recommendation of Bishop Lasso, were accepted by the Pope for consecration as proprietary bishops[2] of Colombian sees. Herein the Vatican and the Colombian Government both worked discreetly for the good of Church and State, without prejudice to the views held by each concerning the *patronato*. The Government, in proposing the names, did not assert the right of presentation; and the Pope, in accepting the names, did not concede that right. With the exception of Bolivia, no other republic received proprietary bishops until 1831. Father Leturia remarks that no other republic possessed a bishop equal to Lasso in zeal, patriotism and influence, or a Government so comprehensive and

[1] This law is still in force in Venezuela to-day.
[2] It was due to the patience and discretion of Tejada, Colombian emissary in Rome, that these were proprietary bishops and not merely apostolic vicars with titular bishoprics. Vásquez, emissary in Rome from Mexico at the same time, failed to obtain this privilege, because by instruction from his Government he claimed to be received as a diplomatic envoy, a claim which the Vatican could not admit. Tejada contented himself with the character of ecclesiastical agent. It is another example of the conciliatory moderation of the Colombian Government.

conciliatory (*flexible*), and these, he adds, were the 'fruit and continuation of Bolívar's personal action'.

The relations of the Government with the Church took a very different course in Chile and Argentina, although the Chilian State desired to work with the Church and was the first republican Government to approach the Holy See in a direct and worthy manner. The dictator O'Higgins, having expelled in 1818 the royalist Bishop of Santiago, was advised by the cleric in charge of the diocese, Cienfuegos, a fervent republican, to send a mission to Rome. Cienfuegos himself, with a staff of five persons, led the mission, sailing from Valparaiso in January 1822: his instructions were to signify 'filial obedience to the Holy See...to ask for an Apostolic Nuncio...to solicit the concession to the Chilian nation of the *patronato* possessed by the Crown of Spain, the establishment of five bishoprics and of a metropolitan see in the capital; to beg that Chile might at least be succoured by two titular bishops to supply provisionally the indispensable need of proprietary bishops'. Cienfuegos reached Rome in August 1822 and was cordially received by the Cardinal Secretary of State, Consalvi, as a person come 'to expound the spiritual needs of those peoples', but not as a political or diplomatic envoy. He also had an audience with the Pope, which, says Leturia, 'had a certain official air'. Although his credentials as an ambassador had not been accepted, he assumed ambassadorial state by hiring a palace and a carriage with two liveried servants and taking an Italian priest into his service, probably as an interpreter. His first petition—the *patronato* and the rest—was at once rejected. His second request—an Apostolic Vicar with full powers—was granted by the Pope after careful consideration by a committee of Cardinals. A priest of diplomatic experience named Muzi was chosen and was consecrated with the title of Archbishop of Philippos.

In October 1823 Muzi embarked with Cienfuegos at Genoa, accompanied by Canon Conti Mastai, the future Pius IX. Muzi was empowered to consecrate three titular bishops in Chile and to regulate the affairs of the Church. The Vatican, having been informed that La Plata had greater need than Chile, extended his mission to include that region, and, upon the receipt by the Pope of the letter from Lasso de la Vega mentioned on p. 113, his mission was extended to the whole of America. When Muzi arrived at Buenos Aires, he had an enthusiastic popular reception: but Rivadavia, the real power in the Government, would have nothing to do with him and finally ordered him to leave the country.

In Chile he was received with enthusiasm by the people and with ceremonious veneration by Freire, O'Higgins' successor as dictator; to whom he delivered an autograph letter from the recently elected Pope, Leo XII, the first communication from the Vatican to the Government of a Spanish-American Republic. But Muzi was soon faced with a deadlock. Cienfuegos had sent from Rome a misleading account of Muzi's mission, stating that the Chilian Government was to nominate three Bishops for consecration by Muzi, as a provisional arrangement until independence should be recognized and a Concordat should be established placing all nominations in the hands of Chilians. 'I am persuaded,' he adds, 'that the Holy Father cordially desires our independence.' Relying on this wildly imaginative letter, Freire claimed the right of presenting names for consecration. Muzi's instructions forbade that claim.[1] Nothing could be done: Muzi sailed from Valparaiso for Europe on 30 April 1824, six weeks after his arrival in Chile.

The general acceptance of the *uti possidetis* of 1810 as a guide for delimitation of frontiers saved much dispute, even though this rule sometimes admitted varied interpretation: but the fixing of frontiers did not bring about the consolidation of each area into a compact community. In 1826 the Spanish-speaking Republics (excluding the Antilles) numbered, nominally at least, eight: to-day they are sixteen. Comparison with the United States misleads; for Spanish America possessed no parliamentary system; moreover New Granada alone is equal to the Thirteen British Colonies in mere extent, with immensely greater difficulties of communication. As to union of all South American republics, Caracas and Buenos Aires could communicate with Europe almost more easily than with one another.

[1] Cardinal Consalvi had assured the Spanish Government that nothing would be done to prejudice the rights of the King in case he should ever recover dominion over Chile.

An improvised congress, made possible by the cabildos and not bearing close scrutiny concerning its source, was everywhere the obvious means of supporting the proclamation of independence and the authority of the early executives: indeed the occasional assembly of deputies from cities for a particular purpose was not unknown under the Spanish Government. But the continuance of a parliamentary system, an imported and ill-understood machine, was in most parts a hollow form. 'Congresses and legislative Assemblies', wrote Woodbine Parish, 'were everywhere convoked; but generally aiming at more than was practicable or compatible with their circumstances, they in most cases failed and by their failure rather confirmed the absolute power of the military chiefs.' The last two words are significant. During the fighting, military autocracy was necessary, as an emergency Government, in those provinces which were the scene of war. But after independence, unless autocracy at once took charge (as in Paraguay) confusion followed. The succession of quasi-republican experiments, the strife between parties, persons and principles, the rapid vicissitudes and recurrence of anarchy led everywhere, except in Chile, to despotism, usually under a soldier ruling by force.

Although the early revolutionary governments failed to establish the political order indispensable to a prosperous civilization, they deserve full credit for completing the work of independence by legislative and executive measures, which varied little in the different republics and, to avoid repetition, may be summarized here: abolition of the Inquisition and of judicial torture; opening of ports to ships of all nations; liberty of the press (not always maintained); encouragement of immigration; attempts to improve education and open schools; establishment of native tribunals; abolition of the slave-trade and in parts some initial steps towards the gradual extinction of slavery. Either by definite enactment or by implication the forced labour of Indians was abolished (legally, that is to say, but not always in fact) and also the poll-tax known as *tributo*: not always a benefit to the Indian, who, by being legally raised to the status of a citizen, sometimes became liable to imposts exceeding that single tax.

But among these liberal reforms complete religious toleration found no place. Almost all the constitutions and fundamental enactments declared the Roman Catholic religion to be that of the State and forbade any other public worship.[1] In each country it was assumed, quite reasonably, that all the natives were Catholics. Moreover, these constitutions and enactments, by abolishing the Inquisition, by using the word 'public' and sometimes by express statement, recognized liberty of conscience and of private worship: this was a liberal innovation and a degree of toleration never admitted under the former Spanish Government. It should be added that the exclusive privileges granted to the Roman Church were everywhere accompanied by measures of ecclesiastical reform, dealing with laxity of conduct among the secular clergy, with abuses in the Religious Orders and with the excessive number (as was thought) of small religious communities.

Bolívar, almost alone among the prominent leaders, desired complete religious toleration, but, seeing its impossibility, took care, as he said himself, 'that nothing should be said (in the Colombian Constitution of 1821) about religion, so that foreigners could adore God as they pleased, since there was no clause prescribing the form of worship.' The words are inaccurate, for the preamble of that Constitution declares: 'These laws should conform to the dogmas of the Roman Catholic Apostolic Religion...its ministers alone enjoy the free exercise of their religion.' But in the English translation of the Constitution, published in London by the Colombian Government in 1822, these words are omitted, evidently for reasons of policy; and Bolívar may have held that this was the proper version. The later Colombian Constitution of 1830 declares that it was the duty of the Government to forbid the public exercise of any other religion; and the first Constitution of the separate Republic of New Granada in 1831 contains the same declaration.

In the Bolivian Constitution Bolívar urged the omission of all mention of religion, without success: the Bolivian Assembly added

---

[1] There were two exceptions: the Uruguayan Constitution of 1830 and the Central American Constitution of 1832 granted full religious toleration. In the latter it was a theoretical liberal gesture, for Central America had no Protestants. Carrera, in his brief Chilian dictatorship, promulgated an ephemeral constitution which declared the 'Catholic Apostolic Religion' to be that of Chile. The omission of the word 'Roman', due to the influence of the American Poinsett, caused scandal.

the words: 'The Roman Catholic Apostolic religion is the religion of the Republic, to the exclusion of all other public worship.'

One clause in the Treaty of February 1825 between the United Provinces of the River Plate and Great Britain (a clause only accepted after much opposition) granted to British subjects complete religious toleration in the United Provinces, with the right of building churches and of burial in their own cemeteries. Thus toleration (still not quite complete) found its way into Buenos Aires as it were accidentally, not by legislation but through a diplomatic incident. But although the Treaty was signed on behalf of the United Provinces, freedom of public worship was forbidden (with one doubtful exception) in the other provinces; and it was not until the Constitution of 1853 that complete religious toleration became the law of the Argentine Confederation after warm discussion. In practice the Treaty of 1825 was duly observed, since only in Buenos Aires was there a 'British Colony' large enough to need churches and a cemetery. Indeed, owing to the paucity of foreigners throughout Latin America except in the great capitals, the whole thing mattered less than might appear.

Thus both in ecclesiastical and in purely civil matters legislation swept away restrictions and inhibitions, and gave greater freedom to normal human activities, even though for a generation or more it failed to establish a settled polity. In recording that failure, the solid benefits achieved by independence, even in the early days, should also be recorded: two examples may be given from opposite ends of the Spanish-American world. In 1822 Captain Basil Hall near the Mexican port of San Blas talked with a 'tall, copper-coloured semi-barbarous native of the forest', who on being asked his opinion of the open trade, replied: 'Formerly I paid nine dollars for the stuff of which this shirt is made; I now pay two: that forms my opinion of the open trade.' Woodbine Parish writes: 'Education, the press, a daily intercourse with the rest of the world and experience, not the less valuable because dearly bought, are all tending gradually to enlighten the inhabitants of these new countries and to prepare them for their future destinies; and although their advancement may appear slow...they have made immense progress compared with their old condition under the yoke of Spain.'

Concerning the Province of Salta he writes: 'the establishment of a printing-press, from which occasionally a newspaper is produced, and of schools, in which reading, writing and the first rules of arithmetic are taught, are great steps compared with things under the old régime. The clergy, too...are daily becoming more tolerant; and opinions, which in old times it would have been heresy to think of, are now as freely discussed as at Buenos Aires, where religious toleration has become the law of the land.'

NOTE. These matters are best studied in the general works named in the Preface. The part concerning the Church is based on Mecham, *State and Church in Latin America*; and on P. Pedro Leturia, S.J., *La acción diplomática de Bolívar ante Pío VII* (Madrid, 1925).

Part Two

THE INDEPENDENT STATES OF
LATIN AMERICA

CHAPTER XIII

SOME DEFINITIONS

NATIONALITY, REVOLUTION, CONSTITUTION, DEMOCRACY

"What's in a name?" SHAKESPEARE

SINCE the origin of the Spanish-American republics has no parallel elsewhere, and since their history is always treated as something exceptional, some explanations are necessary; for the European student finds his vocabulary at fault. Although the republics differ widely from one another in political development and political aptitude; and although there are ethnological differences due to the greater or less admixture of African or Indian blood and, more recently, to European immigration; still 'Nationality' cannot have quite its usual meaning in a group of States whose origin, language, customs and sentiments are generally similar, so that the Americano is a recognizable type from Mexico to Chile. It is true that if one wants to hear damaging things about a Latin-American republic, one should visit the neighbouring republics. But the jealousies between these neighbours are like the coolness which sometimes— owing to questions of property or precedence—divides branches of a large family. Latin-Americans, withal, feel themselves to be a community of peoples *sui generis*.

The word *Revolución*, as there used, is not equivalent to the English 'Revolution'. Usually *revolución* does not mean constitutional change or alteration in form of government: it need not mean even change in methods of administration, but merely an attempt, whether successful or not, to replace rulers. Thus any seditious movement from a sanguinary civil war to the *pronunciamiento* of a battalion is called *revolución*. A bloodless *coup d'état* leading to the resignation of a president and the installation of a provisional successor is so styled. Thus the reputation of Latin America for chronic 'revolutions' is partly due to mistranslation or misuse of terms. When one reads that Venezuela during seventy years 'had fifty-two revolutions, of which twelve were successful,' this means that the Government has been forcibly displaced a dozen times (not necessarily with a complete revolutionary turn of the administrative wheel and probably with little change) and that forty uprisings have collapsed or been suppressed. Even so, the record is far from smooth and is one of many examples that, owing to the fragility of paper constitutions, the flexibility of the suffrage and the hollowness of the parliamentary structure, throughout most of the history of tropical America and in part also that of the south temperate zone an unsatisfactory administration could only be unseated by force or the menace of force, which thus took the place of a general election in the more humdrum parliamentary atmosphere of other lands.

It should, however, be added that many of these *coups d'état*, which displaced or tried to displace one head of the State and his friends by another head and his friends, were not popular movements, but merely contests, in which the 'outs', raising a cry of 'Liberty and Reform', attempted to expel the 'ins', not always unconcerned for the public weal, but usually stirred in the main by appetite for place, power and profit.

The many successive constitutions enacted by most of the states have also been adduced as proving political instability. Of this instability no proof was needed; but the many new constitutions prove little: for a small modification, such as an extension of the franchise or a change in methods of election—changes which elsewhere are effected by an act of legislation—in Latin America usually involves the convocation of a Constituent Assembly and the ceremonious promulgation of a fresh fundamental document, which is not in reality a new constitution, but merely a slightly altered fair copy of the existing one.[1] In Argentina and in Chile this tiresome process has been avoided: the Argentine Constitution of 1853 is still valid, thrice amended: the Chilian Constitution of 1833, several times amended, was maintained until 1925, when a new Constitution, new in reality, was promulgated.

The constitutional history of twenty States cannot here find

---

[1] Measured by this rule, Great Britain might be credited with a dozen new constitutions since 1832. Since there is no constitutional finality in Great Britain, it would be unreasonable to demand it of Latin-American republics.

place: but the general character of their constitution-making may be indicated. Upon the achievement of independence, the separation into many States and (in tropical South America) the abandonment of the Bolivian experiment, all the republics, with trifling exceptions,[1] adopted the framework of the United States Constitution; that is to say a President elected for a fixed term and two Chambers, both elected for a fixed term and sitting annually for a fixed number of days. But there was much variety in the suffrage and in the modes of election, direct or indirect. In several States the Senate had a continuous life, being renewed by fractions at fixed intervals as in the United States. In some, including Uruguay[2] and Argentina, the House of Deputies was never dissolved, the membership being renewed in the same way, so that there were frequent partial elections but never a general election. In some republics a Council of State (not the same thing as the Cabinet of Ministers) was instituted to aid and control the president. In others there was a permanent Parliamentary Commission, to protect the Constitution and the laws during the interval between sessions. Both these arrangements were copied from the Cadiz Constitution of 1812. But these checks on the power of the president amounted to very little except in Chile, which adopted both institutions, Council of State and Parliamentary Commission. The Constitution of Cadiz also prescribes ministerial responsibility to Parliament, a custom or arrangement which is possible in a constitutional monarchy or in a republic where the president is above party, but difficult to work in a country where the president is his own Prime Minister. The system came partly into use in Chile owing to special conditions in that country, but has not been effectively maintained even there.

[1] Ecuador in 1830 adopted a single Chamber, but soon changed over to the bicameral system. Later it was enacted that the Ecuadorian Congress should meet only in alternate years, avowedly for the sake of economy but obviously also for the convenience of the President. Finally the Congress, as elsewhere, met annually. Four of the five Central-American republics have a single Chamber, Nicaragua alone being bicameral. In those small states, where Congress is usually dominated by the executive, this single-chamber system has no profound historical significance.

[2] Uruguay abandoned this arrangement in 1917, instituting complete periodical general elections. Under the Constitution of 1934 President, Senate and House of Deputies are all elected at the same time for four years.

Everywhere the constitution conferred large powers on the president, including the power (subject to certain ineffective checks) of declaring a state of siege and suspending constitutional guarantees (that is to say individual liberty) in case of foreign war or of *internal disorder*. Accordingly the president, being sole judge of the need, has power to suspend the constitution and supersede tribunals, arresting or (more usually) banishing men suspected of disaffection to his authority: Mirkine-Guetzévitch hardly exaggerates in saying that (many) Latin-American constitutions contain a clause of legal dictatorship. Most of the constitutions forbid immediate re-election of a president. Accordingly a president commonly hopes to continue his rule either by some exceptional legislation or by securing the election of a successor acceptable to himself. From all this it is evident that the word 'Constitution' does not mean the fundamental rule and principle of political life, but rather a frame or form, not indeed entirely empty and inefficacious but usually adapted, controlled or expanded by personal action. Yet, even though executive authority often strains or overrides constitutions, thereby provoking unconstitutional methods of opposition, this does not mean that constitutions are nugatory. Even if the rule be sometimes broken and seldom observed with precision, it is essential that the rule should exist. The Argentine Constitution of 1853 filled a disastrous blank and its subsequent amendments were indispensable. The Colombian Constitution of 1886, the Mexican Constitution of 1917 and the Uruguayan Constitution of 1917—to take a few examples—are notable historical landmarks.

Judges are appointed in various ways in different republics and in some only for a term of years. The independence of the judiciary is not always what it might be; and in remote parts of the more extensive republics the action or inaction of the tribunals will hardly bear scrutiny.

The word 'Democracy', constantly acclaimed by Latin-American politicians, has a certain negative meaning, the absence of any recognized hereditary element in government, of titles, and (in theory at least) of permanent personal or oligarchical authority. But obviously, although representative forms exist, the word has not, in any practical or positive sense, its usual meaning. 'The deadly readiness of men of Spanish blood to confound the fine word with the substantial fact' is a familiar matter. Lord Bryce adds an observation about many of these republics: 'It is one of the oddest instances of the power of a word that the less educated and even many of the more educated persons among the free nations have continued, especially in the United States, to believe them to be, because called "Republics", entitled to a confidence and sympathy which would not be given to a military tyranny under any other name.' Yet American historians are outspoken on the matter: in 1932 Professor Cleven wrote of Latin America generally: 'There is a class to which the government of the country belongs as of right. This right is regarded with a tenacity remarkable in the extreme.' And Professor Wilgus in the same volume (*Modern Hispanic America*) is still more emphatic. Some Latin-American historians also are quite candid about these matters.

Thus the word Democracy seems often to be little more than a political label. But in everyday use Democracy, though not with strict etymological accuracy, denotes other things which may have little to do with politics: a reasonable degree of social equality, room for individual action for those who keep clear of politics, a fair chance for an intelligent and industrious man to improve his condition. Although in some parts there is a wide gap between the 'haves' and the 'have nots', a gap symbolized by minute attention to masculine toilette among the *gente decente* or *gente distinguida* and by aversion from anything remotely resembling manual labour, these opportunities generally exist. In Spain and in Spanish literature the *indiano* is a familiar figure, who went from Spain to the 'Indies' as a penniless boy and returns home in advanced years to live on his savings in his native village. And the thrifty Italian, who saves money and buys land or returns home with a competence, is almost a proverb in those lands. And here one must forget for a moment the unfortunate Indian aborigines in some republics. Under the despotism of Porfirio Díaz, which was the very negation of political democracy and oppressively unjust to the native Indians, the poor Spaniard from Galicia or Asturias found an open opportunity. Socially, Spain, touched by the East, is the most democratic country in Europe; and, notwithstanding the wide gap between the very rich and the poor in some parts, Hispanic America is still fundamentally Spanish.

To save repetition, it may here be mentioned that in the depression years, 1929–31, only two of the ten South American Republics, Colombia and Venezuela, escaped *coups d'état* and the overthrow of governments, and even in Venezuela there were revolts, crushed by force. Economic trouble and the consequent discontent among both wage-earners and business people contributed to these political upheavals, but the cause is also to be found in defects and errors of governments. The following pages will show that some of these political strokes were not merely personal or ambitious ventures but had a backing of principle or of a desire to improve matters.

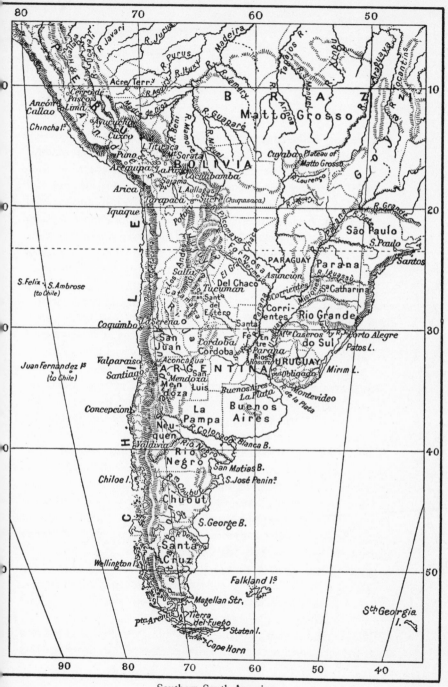

Southern South America

CHAPTER XIV

THE ARGENTINE REPUBLIC

THE territory of the Argentine Confederation, about nine times that of the British Isles, with about twelve million inhabitants, extends from the tropics to Antarctic Seas. It rises westward to the Andine peaks: in the north are extensive forests, with many swamps and streams; in the north-west a country of wooded hills and valleys; between the Andes and the mountains of Córdoba a strange parched region of broken heights and hollows, where irrigating streams feed oases of vineyards and gardens; to the south the bleak terraces of Patagonia. But the typical Argentina, the main theatre and sustenance of national life, is the vast plain of the Pampa, stoneless and treeless, level to the eye but sloping up imperceptibly from the Atlantic westward; the plain where the gaucho cowboys, having ousted their Indian forerunners and rivals, followed a rude pastoral industry until they in turn reluctantly yielded before the locomotive and the plough.

Argentina comprises fourteen autonomous provinces and ten outlying territories (*gobernaciones*) administered by the Federal Government. These territories, with a fraction of the population, cover half the national area. For seventy years (1810–80) the nation passed through agitated vicissitudes; not sterile, but preparatory for later remarkable growth and also concerned with international questions—the relations of South American countries with one another and with Europe. Those years may be approximately divided into three twenty-year spaces and an intervening decade:

(1) 1810–29. Inconclusive experiments; recurrent civil strife; disruption thrice, in 1815, 1820, 1829.

(2) 1829–52. Dictatorship of Rosas.

(3) 1853–62. A decade of constitutional problems and disputes.

(4) 1862–80. Settlement of questions and conclusion of constitutional arrangement.

The 'United Provinces of the River Plate' (the official name down to 1830) seemed to have every initial advantage, a country marked by climate and fertility to be the seat of a great civilization of European type; a flourishing capital more European in character than any other Spanish-American city; a Creole army in existence, victorious over the British invaders; independence tranquilly won and never interrupted; the disappearance, without a blow struck, of Spanish authority except in Montevideo. No Spanish troops ever approached within 800 miles of the capital; and after the capture of Montevideo in 1814 no royalist enemy trod Argentine soil except for abortive incursions into Salta in the far north-west. The five years' attempt to win Upper Peru diverted the national vigour, but the abandonment of the attempt in 1815 lightened that difficulty.

These hopes were disappointed, partly owing to two exceptional dangers. The Argentines, alone among Spanish-American peoples, while they were defending their territory against Spanish attempts at reconquest, had to contend at the same time against the aggression of the Portuguese Court established at Rio and afterwards of the Brazilian monarchy. And the savage Indian tribes of the Pampa were a perpetual menace upon the frontier barely 200 miles south of Buenos Aires; at any sign of weakness or division among the Christians, they galloped in destructive raids against the pastoral homesteads, driving off cattle, killing men and carrying off women into hideous bondage.

But the main obstacles to peace and union were internal: divisions among the people themselves. The centrifugal and regional forces which pervade Iberian history found here a wide field. The capital, since the establishment of the Viceroyalty and the opening of the port in 1776–8, had far outstripped the other cities. The city of Buenos Aires, with the territory which from 1814 formed the Province of Buenos Aires, had one-third of the population and at least half the wealth of the whole country. The city, having the only profitable custom-house and the only gateway of commercial and diplomatic intercourse with the outside world, was indispensable to the rest of the country. But, standing on the very edge of the country, the capital, in those days of slow and dangerous communication, was ill placed to become a social and political centre of attraction to dwellers elsewhere. 'To have the capital at twenty days' distance', wrote Alberdi in 1852, 'is like having it in Spain.'

These difficulties could only have been overcome by conciliatory and magnanimous statesmanship in the capital, meeting with some common sentiment in the provinces: but, so far from this, the word *porteño* (the man of the port, the Buenosairean) became elsewhere almost a proverb for pretentious pride; and when the bond of the Spanish monarchy was broken, the other cities, separated from one another by vast stretches of pastoral or desert land often infested by hostile Indians, drew apart; and every cabildo finally claimed, with success, to be the capital of an autonomous province. The needs of war held together the provinces in some degree: but the slackening of that need brought segregation in 1814–15. Before 1817 the three Spanish Intendencies of Buenos Aires, Tucumán and Salta had split into thirteen provinces; and the final number was fourteen.

It is fair to add that Buenos Aires had a difficult task in dealing with the caudillos who dominated the ignorant and scanty population of some of the remote provinces. These matters are complicated by the fact that the conflict between the supporters of provincial autonomy and the supporters of centralized government, between Federals and Unitarios (to use later terms) was not identical with the difference between Liberals and Conservatives. In legislation Rivadavia was an advanced liberal reformer; yet the Radicals of to-day, who regard the 'Federals' as their political ancestors, abhor Rivadavia as a reactionary die-hard, an enemy of local government. The great landowners in every province were Federals, hating the concentration of power in Buenos Aires; but in local matters they were conservative, desiring power for themselves and not for the masses. 'It is a strange contradiction', says O. R. Amadeo, 'that the conservative Rosas had the populace on his side, while Rivadavia, a man of the Left, was only supported by a group of aristocrats of the Right.' In every province, including that of Buenos Aires, the gauchos hated and despised all urban ways; they also hated and dreaded all government, law, tribunals and police. Living in the saddle; expert with the lasso, the boleadora and the lance; they fought for any provincial Governor or any

Provinces and Territories of Argentina (Territories are underlined)

adventurous caudillo who won their loyalty. 'What other troops in the world', exclaims Darwin, 'are so independent? With the sun for their guide, mare's flesh for food, their saddle-cloths for beds; as long as there is a little water, these men would penetrate to the end of the world.'

The Provisional Junta appointed in May 1810 soon lost its two ablest members. Belgrano, who had guided the preliminaries of independence and had wished quietly to replace the fallen absolutist monarchy of Ferdinand VII by an independent constitutional monarchy, departed for distant campaigns. The fervent young democrat Mariano Moreno, Secretary and at first guiding spirit of the Junta—a man beloved of the Argentine people for his uncompromising zeal, his impulsive human utterances and his tragic fate—resigned his post after seven months owing to differences with his more cautious colleagues, accepted a mission to England and died at sea. In September 1811 the Junta, divided in itself and discredited by defeat in Upper Peru, gave way to a triumvirate of periodically changing membership, an executive most unfit for the triple task of thwarting Portuguese aggression, waging war against royalists on two fronts and constructing a national polity. The Junta first and then the Triumvirate, though local in origin, claimed authority over all the former Viceroyalty, provoking segregation by high-handed attempts at authoritative union. Moreover, through an error in the mode of summoning deputies, these Porteño authorities blundered into a quarrel with Córdoba and the other cities. After a year the Triumvirs, clinging to power and evading the convocation of an Assembly, were evicted by a *coup d'état*[1] headed by two soldiers, San Martín and Alvear, and were replaced by three designated persons who at last summoned an Assembly, hardly representative in the modern sense, but notable for what it accomplished.

Already the Triumvirate, guided by their Secretary Rivadavia—afterwards himself a triumvir—had reversed the Spanish system by a series of liberal measures: the Press freed, the slave-trade for-

[1] The five minor *coups d'état* which punctuate the history of the Junta and Triumvirate cannot here find place.

bidden, the customs reformed, native tribunals established. And now the Assembly of 1813 implicitly assumed independence as 'deputies of the nation', obliterating the remains of the royal fabric, but avoiding the two decisive measures, Declaration of Independence and promulgation of a Constitution.

Deputies from the Banda Oriental, instructed by the gaucho chieftain Artigas to demand a Declaration of Independence and a federal system of a peculiar kind, were, by the wayward and indiscreet influence of Alvear, excluded from the Assembly as not duly elected: Artigas, already a doubtful friend, became an enemy, the champion of secession in the Banda Oriental.

The ephemeral experiments of 1810–14 taught the need of a personal Head of the Nation. But the Supreme Director was chosen, through Alvear's ambitious intrigues, on personal grounds. After sixteen months' rule and a brief attempt at military autocracy by Alvear, the National Government collapsed (May 1815); Alvear fled and the caudillos of the three Littoral Provinces, Santa Fe, Corrientes and Entre Ríos, broke away from the Union, forming a loose federation of half-barbarous leaders commanding irregular gaucho cavalry under the headship of Artigas and proclaiming a 'federation' which meant disruption and local despotisms.

An effort at recovery and a tardy concession to the provinces took form in the meeting at Tucumán of a Constituent Congress, without deputies from the Banda Oriental or the Littoral Provinces. This Congress proclaimed Independence and chose as Supreme Director Pueyrredón, a Porteño, but a man of proved capacity.

Pueyrredón kept his seat for three years and supported San Martín in his invasion of Chile and design upon Peru. But the Director's position crumbled owing to the contemptuous opposition of the provinces, his impotence in face of the Portuguese aggressors who occupied Montevideo in 1816, and the discredit caused by his schemes to end disorder by establishing a Bourbon monarchy. In 1819 the Congress, which had sat for three years in Buenos Aires (earning the odium of the provinces by migrating thither from Tucumán) promulgated a unitary and centralized constitution—an abortive measure which was the signal for disruption. Pueyrredón resigned. His successor, Rondeau, like himself the son of a French-

man and also concerned in monarchical designs, was swept away
by the invading gaucho hordes of Santa Fe and Entre Ríos
(February 1820). Directorate, Congress, National Government
collapsed; and a hastily constructed Provincial Government of
Buenos Aires was compelled by Ramírez, the fighting chieftain of
Entre Ríos, to consent by the Treaty of Pilar (23 February 1820)
that the United Provinces should have a Federal Government to
be arranged by a Congress; a short-lived agreement which fore-
shadowed the settlement of forty years later. But settlement was
remote: in the 'terrible year' 1820 all union disappeared: every
province had its own government, usually a dictatorship; and in
the Province of Buenos Aires a hurried procession of some thirty
'Provisional Governments' passed with bewildering rapidity. By
one of those strange contradictions which recur in Iberian history,
in that year Peru was invaded by the Argentine General San
Martín.

From 1820 to 1824 there was no National Government. But
from the confused experiments of 1820 there emerged in the
Province of Buenos Aires—under Rodríguez, one of the *próceres* of
the Revolution, as Provincial Governor—a four years' period of
peace and beneficent legislation, chiefly due to Rivadavia, Minister
under Rodríguez: and the Province adopted a bicameral parliamentary constitution. During those years, Artigas having disappeared
and Ramírez having fallen in battle, the provinces were at peace
with one another: and in several provinces constitutions were
framed, resembling that of Buenos Aires. At last in December 1824
a Constituent Congress met in Buenos Aires and authorized the
Provincial Government to act as 'Provisional National Government in charge of Foreign Affairs': an indispensable measure; for
three national questions were pressing, the future status of Upper
Peru, the imminence of war with Brazil, and the relations of the
young nation with Europe.

As to this last point, the rejoicings over the news of Ayacucho,
which reached Buenos Aires on 21 January 1825, were renewed by
fresh rejoicings at the formal recognition of independence by Great
Britain through the signature of a Treaty in Buenos Aires on
2 February 1825.

In that year Argentina seemed to be approaching national consolidation, thanks to internal peace. The Swiss physician Rengger,
revisiting Buenos Aires after six years in 1825, hardly recognized
the place, with its animated commerce, many schools, a forest of
masts on the river, 6000 French residents. Rivadavia, he says, had
established order, justice and religious toleration. In 1819, the
era of Artigas, Rengger had seen the city of Corrientes wretched
and ruined: he found it peaceful and prosperous in 1825, and a
similar happy change in the Province of Entre Ríos. This hopeful
promise was dashed by a fresh outbreak of strife, partly due to
discord between Buenos Aires and her neighbours, partly to an
external conflict which embittered that discord.

For in that same year 1825 the long rivalry between Spaniards
and Portuguese for the possession of the Banda Oriental broke out
in war, a war imminent for a dozen years past and now precipitated
by the Uruguayan revolt against Brazil, to be narrated in the next
chapter. The Province of Buenos Aires, with little aid from the
other provinces, but possessing in the custom-house the chief
source of national revenue, fought the Empire of Brazil for nearly
three years (1825–8), winning victory by sea and land; but inconclusive victory owing to the disruption of the 'United Provinces'
and the civil wars of provincial caudillos. Through British diplomacy, which was powerful in Rio and esteemed in Buenos Aires,
the two belligerents agreed in 1828 that both should drop the bone
of contention by recognizing the independence of the Banda
Oriental, which thus became the Republic of Uruguay, a buffer
State between two powerful neighbours.[1] Since the Convention
satisfied neither belligerent, it was probably a fairly just *via media*.
It proved entirely satisfactory to the Uruguayans themselves.

In February 1826 the Constituent Congress, being at war with
Brazil, appointed Rivadavia President of the United Provinces, by a
stretch of authority perhaps justified by the emergency but keenly
resented by the provinces. Rivadavia, eager for a strong executive,

---

[1] This 'Preliminary Convention' was not embodied in a formal treaty until
1859, when Uruguay was a party to it. But the Convention was accepted from
1828 by both belligerents, although neither strictly observed it.

attempted to settle the 'capital question' by the summary method of abolishing the Provincial Legislature in order that Buenos Aires should be the seat of one Government only, that of the nation. He thus assumed, as President of the nation, personal control over the territory of the defunct Province of Buenos Aires, the richest part of the country. This arrangement pleased no one; nor was Rivadavia's zeal for reform, particularly in ecclesiastical matters, generally acceptable.

At last, in December 1826, the Congress promulgated a unitary and centralized constitution. It was rejected by all the provincial caudillos, and in July 1827 Rivadavia, a townsman who did not know the provinces and had provoked a fall by his dictatorial measures, abandoned a hopeless task by resignation. A month later the Congress dissolved. The nation fell to pieces in the midst of a foreign war.

As before, the Province of Buenos Aires, coming back to life on the fall of its destroyer, undertook the work of the nation under a 'federalist' Governor, Dorrego, a genial person, once a gay soldier but now matured by experience. Dorrego accepted the Convention with Brazil, strove for internal peace and aimed at an understanding with the provinces. The endeavour was brief. Upon the return of the disappointed and resentful troops from Brazil, Lavalle, an officer popular with the soldiers, was acclaimed as Governor by an irregular street gathering. Dorrego fled, was overtaken and shot by Lavalle.

This homicide let anarchy loose. Civil war flamed out everywhere. After a disordered year Rosas, a wealthy Porteño landowner, ablest and strongest of the caudillos, who during the Brazilian War had held a bloodless command in the south and had there organized a mounted militia of gauchos and Indians devoted to his person, was chosen in 1829, at the age of thirty-six, Governor of the Province of Buenos Aires for three years with unlimited powers. An educated man of aristocratic connexions, a successful business man and a great landowner, he was supported by the conservative classes. Handsome, gallant in bearing, a consummate horseman, expert in the craft of the Pampa and the rodeo, he was also the comrade and captain of cowboys and Indian chieftains, a man who represented the Creole tradition and was popular with the masses.

Lavalle's proceedings are variously judged to-day in Argentina by followers of the unitary and the federal traditions. Woodbine Parish, British chargé d'affaires in Buenos Aires at the time, simply says: 'the army mutinied against the Governor and set up a military despotism.' In his view the shooting of Dorrego was a 'brutal act' and through Rosas' victory 'the cause of order was everywhere triumphant'.

ROSAS, 1829–52

A three years' interval (1832–5), filled by stop-gap governments, during which Rosas increased his wealth and reputation by a campaign against the southern Indians, hardly interrupted his long dictatorship. A league of unitary provinces, headed by Córdoba, was broken up with sanguinary thoroughness; and Rosas, repeatedly re-elected by a nominated Provincial Legislature, was Governor of the Province of Buenos Aires, entrusted by the allied autocrats of the other Provinces with the National Executive and conduct of Foreign Affairs of the 'Argentine Confederation', the name which he ordered to be used: but it was a Confederation 'without a Congress, without a President, without federal tribunals'. Rosas was the chief of fourteen despotic caudillos ruling fourteen provinces and suppressing by blood and terror any disturbances within their respective dominions.

In spite of arrests, summary executions and the pitiless persecution of unitarios, many of whom fled to Montevideo, this rigid autocracy, energetic, efficient and financially honest, found general acceptance in Buenos Aires as a remedy for twenty years of disorder and ephemeral expedients; but a remedy with harsh ingredients: the press silenced, the University disendowed owing to the cost of war, everywhere a sombre and silent dread in contrast with the scarlet 'federal' badge worn perforce on every breast. The dictator's portrait was displayed over the altars, engraved on domestic crockery and even on women's gloves; every printed paper bore the heading 'death to the foul savage Unitarios'.

In 1837–41 Rosas thwarted a succession of shocks: a brief war with the Bolivian dictator Santa Cruz; a French blockade of the coast provoked by the stubbornness of Rosas over some diplomatic questions; a declaration of war by Uruguay and an invasion of Buenos Aires by Argentine exiles; a conspiracy in the capital among his own supporters; a gaucho revolt in the south; the defection for a time of the three Littoral Provinces and afterwards of five northern provinces. The strain of these dangers twice provoked an orgy of violence and murder in Buenos Aires: assaults on houses, floggings, shootings, nocturnal throat-cuttings by the Mazorca, a band of authorized bullies and assassins. Although this extreme savagery was checked in 1842 at a word from Rosas, the terror endured ten years longer.

During those ten years Rosas strove to conquer Uruguay. The declaration of war by Uruguay in 1839, and the civil strife of Uruguayans opened the way to him. Rivera, first President of Uruguay (1835–9), a shifty and self-seeking gaucho caudillo, leader or founder of the colorado party (which may be described, by a stretch of words, as the comparatively liberal party), had to fight for his throne and afterwards stuck to that throne, driving out his successor Oribe (chieftain of the blancos, the party of order and comparatively conservative), who fled to Buenos Aires and took service under Rosas. The Dictator gave him troops, and Oribe, claiming to be President of Uruguay but in fact a Rosista general, besieged Montevideo, 'the Modern Troy', for nine years. In 1841 the Uruguayan Government offered to Great Britain commercial privileges in return for protection. The British Government declined the offer, but proposed to the French Government a joint intervention to secure 'Uruguay from further violation...and lead...to permanent peace.'

Rosas successfully defied three Anglo-French interventions, continued (through Oribe) the siege of Montevideo and achieved a triumph in the withdrawal of the British forces in 1849 and of the French in 1850. But although the European interventions failed to impose peace, Montevideo, weakened by dissensions and desertions, would certainly have fallen but for this maritime support and the organization of a foreign legion of French and Italians, the sole defenders of the city in the later months of the siege. Throughout these long disputes with France and Great Britain, consular and diplomatic agents from the United States attempted to strengthen Rosas' hands, but received no support from the Government at Washington; which, fully occupied with Texas and Mexico, kept aloof from affairs in the Southern Hemisphere.

The aggressive ambition of Rosas and his stubborn avoidance of the duty of national organization were his undoing. His power depended on the adhesion of the caudillos ruling the other provinces, which were all jealous of Porteño predominance. The Littoral Provinces, repeatedly shaky in their allegiance, had suffered much from French and Anglo-French blockade. In 1851 Urquiza, Governor of Entre Ríos, a despot more autocratic in his own country than Rosas himself and fully his equal in capacity and vigour, revoked the powers granted to Rosas and concluded an alliance with Paraguay (which was threatened by Rosas' territorial ambition) and with Brazil, justly alarmed at Argentine encroachment northward. In October 1851 Urquiza invaded Uruguay, defeated Oribe and raised the siege of Montevideo. A Brazilian fleet then enabled him to cross the Paraná into the Province of Santa Fe, which joined the revolution; and Urquiza led towards the capital 24,000 men, the largest force yet assembled in South America, of whom 3000 were Brazilians and 2000 Uruguayans. In February 1852 Rosas, deserted by half his troops, fled from the battle-field of Monte Caseros. He spent the remaining twenty-five years of his long life farming near Southampton. Once the richest landowner in the province, he left the country a poor man.

Urquiza promptly undertook the work of national organization. An assembly of provincial autocrats, the only existing authority, ordered that a Constituent Congress should meet, and that meantime Urquiza should be Provisional Director of the Confederation in charge of Foreign Affairs and in command of all the provincial troops, now to form a national army; Urquiza was empowered to check hostilities between provinces and to suppress risings within any province.

The Porteños vehemently rejected this arrangement, and Buenos Aires, by the bloodless revolution of 11 September 1852, seceded from the Confederation, assuming independent sovereignty. For seven years there were two distinct Governments, that of Buenos Aires and that of the Confederation of thirteen provinces, with its capital at Paraná in Entre Ríos. The Constituent Congress duly met at Santa Fe (but without deputies from Buenos Aires) and promulgated in 1853 a Federal Constitution, which with some modifications is that of Argentina to-day, resembling in the main that of the United States but containing one provision which authorizes the President to intervene in any province under certain conditions by sending an 'interventor' to supersede the provincial Government and instal a more satisfactory one. This elastic authority has been freely used and gives much power to the Federal Executive. The Constituent Congress also passed a law that the city of Buenos Aires should form a Federal District under national control. The Legislature of Buenos Aires rejected the Constitution and also this law.

At the same time (1853) Urquiza concluded identical treaties with France, the United States and Great Britain, opening all interior Argentine waters 'to the merchant ships of all nations'; and thus deprived the dissident province of control over the river for ever.

But the truncated Federation could not long exist, for two reasons. The legal experience necessary for a Federal Tribunal was only to be found in Buenos Aires, and that city possessed most of the trade and therefore most of the customs. The result was first a tariff war between the up-river ports and Buenos Aires, and then armed conflict. Buenos Aires, defeated in the first clash (at Cepeda, October 1859), accepted the Constitution of 1853 with some amendments and was reincorporated in the nation. But peace was not yet. The Porteño leader Mitre, soldier, scholar and historian, who was to be for half a century a prominent figure in the national life, was victorious in a second fight (at Pavón, September 1861), assumed national authority and imposed order on the provinces.

In May 1862 a Federal Congress met in Buenos Aires and agreed, after hot debate, that the city of Buenos Aires, while remaining capital of the Province, was to admit the 'coexistence' of the Federal Government within its precincts. Five months later, Mitre, duly elected, initiated his six years' term as first

Constitutional President of undivided Argentina. The nation had taken form, and thenceforward strengthened that form through the economic progress of the country, a progress which was checked but not seriously impeded by the costly effort of the Paraguayan War (1865–70), to be narrated later.

For eighteen years (1862–80), the space of three presidential terms, two Parliamentary Governments resided in Buenos Aires, that of the nation and also that of the province, which constantly encroached on national affairs. The provinces, most of them now dominated by landowning oligarchies who filled all official posts and nominated the provincial legislatures by controlling the elections, hated Porteño influence and formed a League of Provinces, centred in Córdoba, to win control of the National Government. An epidemic of cholera, which swept through Buenos Aires and left the city half-deserted, helped them to a victory in the presidential election of 1868, whereby a native of San Juan became President, the 'schoolmaster President' Sarmiento, a self-made man of robust energy, wielder of a powerful pen and subservient to no party. A clearer victory was the election in 1874 of the Tucumano, Avellaneda. Mitre, the defeated candidate, led an armed revolt, alleging fraudulent election but in fact fighting for Porteño domination and for his own hand, knowing that no electioneering campaign, not even his own, would bear scrutiny. He was beaten in the field and retrieved this blot on an otherwise estimable career by working thenceforth for peace.

Avellaneda, a man of vigorous determination, surrounded by able ministers, cured the age-long sore of the Indian menace. The ineffective system of defensive lines was abandoned; and General Roca, a soldier distinguished in several campaigns, thrust the Indians beyond the Río Negro by a sweeping military operation in 1878–9, opened up to white settlement an extensive region, and by giving security to the already settled lands greatly increased their value. This Conquest of the Desert roused a wave of wild speculation, townsmen buying and selling unknown lands and remote wastes.

Avellaneda also settled the 'capital question' by drastic action which was forced upon him. A dispute concerning the newly conquered lands increased the tension between the Porteños and the provinces. The Porteños prepared for the presidential election of 1880 by rifle practice and drill. Accordingly Avellaneda withdrew the National Government from an armed and hostile city to Belgrano, four miles distant; and decreed the 'intervention' of the Province of Buenos Aires. Hard fighting followed between the National troops and the Porteño militia, with 3000 casualties. The National Government prevailed; and it was settled, ostensibly by decent Parliamentary forms but in fact by presidential authority, that the city of Buenos Aires with its neighbourhood should form a Federal District controlled by the nation. The Provincial Government found a home two years later in the city of La Plata, thenceforward capital of the Province of Buenos Aires. The long conflict thus finally settled is summed up by the Argentine writer Amadeo in an epigram: 'For seventy years the Argentines fought one another for the custom-house.'

Notwithstanding revolutionary outbreaks in the provinces and two radical revolts in the capital (in 1890 and 1905) the settlement of 1880, in a large sense, initiated half a century of peace, of political and also of economic advance. The country had always enjoyed a certain rude plenty. Woodbine Parish wrote in 1832: 'beef is dear at a penny a pound; good fish can be had as cheap; and partridges as big as pheasants may be had for little more than the trouble of catching them.'

But a more distinct economic progress can be traced from the middle of the century. Advance was rapid from 1870 (the year when the first great railway was opened, from Rosario to Córdoba) and leapt forward from 1880, when the export of grain began,[1] which has since made Argentina one of the great granaries of the world. The first exports of meat followed, to become later a great industry. The national union, achieved in the council chamber by the settlements of 1862 and 1880, was only achieved in fact by the railways, mostly constructed by Italian labour and British capital. They peopled the Pampa and brought tillage, as improved transport and the use of machinery in agriculture made export profitable.

[1] The first shipment, 4500 tons, was in 1878. Avellaneda used to declare that this was the proudest event of his presidency.

Wherever rails were laid, they multiplied the value of land, some-times tenfold or more, making revolution too costly. The use of wire-fencing, first introduced about 1850 and becoming general in the 'seventies and 'eighties, was nothing less than a peaceful revolution, turning the rude methods of the gaucho herdsmen into scientific stockfarming, making tillage possible and impeding the activities of the caudillo and the galloping of gaucho hordes over the plain.

This economic progress was furthered by a succession of able presidents, who borrowed largely (chiefly in London) for public works. The later construction of state railways extended to out-lying regions the great network of lines radiating from the capital and from the grain ports of Rosario and Bahia Blanca, railways now measuring some 26,000 miles, half the mileage of all the railways of South America. The capital, with above two million inhabitants, is the greatest city in the Southern Hemisphere and one of the great ports of the world. Nearly five million persons entered the country by sea between 1857 and 1913, of whom 3,371,000 re-mained and made their homes in the country—most of them from Italy and Spain, people easily assimilated. The number of settlers would have been much greater but for difficulty in acquiring land: for although many Italians and Basques saved money and bought land, and although some Italian or Swiss 'colonies' were founded, these were occasional matters. The great landowners clung to their *latifundia*. Public lands were sold or granted in large blocks. The legislatures, both Federal and Provincial, were until recently con-trolled by landowning oligarchies; and the Republic has had no system enabling immigrants to acquire moderate-sized farms. But the growth of the country, the spread of agriculture and the increase of wealth have been astonishing. Sheep-farming extends through Patagonia and into Tierra del Fuego. Sugar is grown in the north-west, tobacco and some cotton in the north. The sub-tropical forests yield timber and quebracho extract, rich in tannin; and the cattle industry has penetrated the Chaco.

While prosperity thus favoured tranquillity, the menace of external conflict was averted by the peaceful settlement of frontier disputes with Chile. In 1881 Roca settled a long-standing question

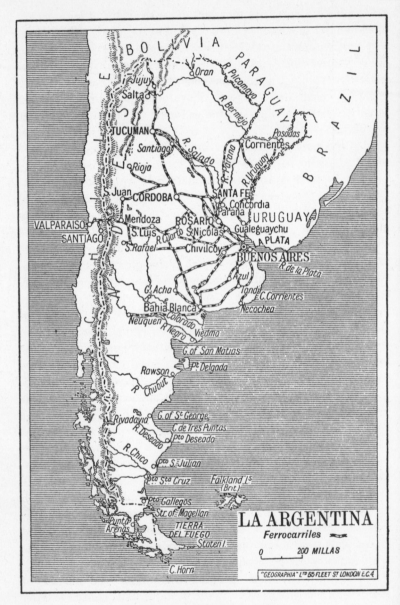

Chief Towns and Railways in 1914

by a Treaty recognizing Chilian possession of both shores of Magellan Straits. The same Treaty declared that from 52° northwards the boundary should 'pass along the highest crests of the Cordillera which divide the Andes'. Since the watershed was found not to coincide with the highest peaks, war over conflicting interpretations seemed imminent in 1895. Three years later a dispute over the boundary in the plateau of Atacama was submitted to an arbitral tribunal consisting of a Chilian, an Argentine and Buchanan, the United States Minister in Buenos Aires. Buchanan solved the difficulty by dividing the disputed line into sections and ensuring a majority on each section by his own vote. Through the moderation of Roca (President a second time in 1892–8) and of the Chilian President Errazuriz, the main question, concerning the Andes, was submitted to the arbitration of the Sovereign of Great Britain. A Commission, consisting of four officers of the Royal Engineers, travelled through the mountains to examine the question on the spot; and the award, given in 1902, was peaceably accepted. A frontier question with Brazil was also settled by arbitration.

Political and economic progress was not uninterrupted. In 1890 the reactionary and almost absolutist Government of Roca's successor Celman—coupled with financial scandals, over-borrowing, extravagance, grants and sales of concessions—provoked a revolt in the capital, organized by the founder of the radical party, Leandro Alem, a striking figure with his tall lean frame, his patriarchal beard and harsh passionate utterance. Though the revolt collapsed, Celman resigned. But the radicals wished to sweep away the whole oligarchical machinery which nullified representative institutions. They held that, since constitutional methods were denied to them, force was justifiable. In 1893 Alem again attempted revolt. After his death by suicide in 1895 his nephew Hipólito Irigoyen took up his task and in 1905 headed another unsuccessful revolt; a misguided attempt, for electoral reform was in the air and was favoured by many prominent men. Serious labour troubles, sometimes marked by violence, were largely due to immigrants from Europe and hardly affected the political situation. In 1912 President Roque Sáenz Peña, a courageous and romantic figure, who had fought in the Peruvian army against Chile, passed through Congress the law of secret, universal and compulsory male vote. This law effected a peaceful revolution or rather added a necessary chapter to the Revolution of May 1810. In 1916 Argentine citizens for the first time freely chose electors who should nominate the President: the radical leader Irigoyen was elected by a narrow majority and was carried shoulder high to Government House.

Irigoyen was the most powerful ruler since Rosas and the most autocratic. By frequent interventions and by other customary methods he contrived that his own supporters should hold sway in the provinces and in the municipalities. But although he initiated no sweeping social changes and suppressed with bloodshed a dock strike which paralysed the business of the port, he befriended the working-man by legislation concerning wages, hours, pensions, sanitation, industrial arbitration. His discreet handling of the problems of the Great War is described in Chapter XXXII.

Since the Constitution forbids presidential re-election, a moderate radical, Marcelo Alvear, a genial and cultivated person, of fine presence and firm character, was elected President in 1922. He continued the social legislation of Irigoyen, so far as a recalcitrant Congress permitted; and by agreement with the railway companies did something for the much-needed settlement of working farmers on moderately sized holdings. But the refusal of Alvear to be merely a shadowy locum tenens of Irigoyen angered the Irigoyen-istas or Personalistas, who regarded themselves as the only true radicals.

In 1928 Irigoyen—who appeared as a candidate a week before the election, made no speeches and wrote no address—was elected by a great majority, expected by his followers to initiate a period of constructive liberalism. But the President was old and ill. Although more autocratic than ever and leaving no initiative to any Minister, he was unequal to the routine business of his office. Salaries fell in arrear for want of the President's signature; posts were unfilled, debts unpaid. And the on-coming of the world-wide economic depression brought perplexing problems. Irigoyen, a man of upright integrity, failed to check the rapacious parasites of his party. In September 1930 he fell before a *coup d'état* headed by

General José Uriburu; not a mere barrack rising, but a spontaneous movement of the people of the capital.

For over a year Uriburu was dictator, but in November 1931 he permitted a controlled presidential election. General Justo, a moderate man who had served in Alvear's cabinet, was the only candidate, ostensibly supported by a coalition (*la concordancia*) but in reality mainly by conservatives and adherents of the former oligarchical *régimen*. In fact the *coup d'état* of 1930, although a popular rather than a party movement, brought a conservative reaction: inevitably so, for the radicals, new to public life, had wasted their opportunity and provoked a fall by the arrogant, extravagant and finally inefficient autocracy of their leader, by their personalism, their failure to use the reformed Parliament for which they had agitated during forty years and their needless dissensions, which still frustrate their activities. Democracy cannot work as long as personalism outweighs a political creed. A radical outbreak at the end of 1933 was put down: sixty persons were sent to a Patagonian penal settlement and some leaders were banished for a time to Europe. The episode, perhaps justly, was hardly noticed abroad.

Although Argentine radicals, the majority of the nation, are denied the Government which they desire, the country—aware of general prosperity and sound public credit—accepts a Government which is tolerable, which appoints moderate Ministers of different affiliations, favours 'social services' (the special province of the radicals) and has learnt by experience that government by decree will not do; since public opinion, the excellent newspaper press and Congress all have influence, constituting 'a strong undercurrent of democracy'.[1] Whether democracy, as a political system, is merely in abeyance or whether there is a substantial return—complete return is impossible—to pre-Irigoyen ways, cannot yet be told. The new authorities have abandoned Irigoyen's attitude of aloofness from the League of Nations and of suspicious reserve towards the United States.

The Revolution of 1930 left untouched the public credit of Argentina, the normal activities of her citizens and the fundamental

[1] *The Times*, 31 December 1936.

basis of her well-being, the working of her rich soil for her own benefit and for that of the Old World. Although Argentina, an exporter of pastoral and agricultural products, suffered much from the world depression of recent years, that basis of her national life is sound.

The presidential election of September 1937 brought much disorder, several fatal casualties and some violation by officials of the law prescribing secret votes. The radical candidate, ex-President Alvear, was defeated, as every one foresaw, by the official candidate recommended by President Justo and supported by the *concordancia*, Dr Ortiz, who had been Finance Minister in Justo's Cabinet and, like Justo himself, had served in Alvear's radical Cabinet (1922-8). Dr Ortiz announced his intention to continue existing arrangements.

NOTE. R. Levene, *History of Argentina*, translated by W. S. Robertson (Chapel Hill, North Carolina, 1937); F. A. Kirkpatrick, *A History of the Argentine Republic* (Cambridge, 1931); A. C. Wilgus (editor), *Argentina* (by J. F. Rippy), *Brazil and Chile since Independence* (Washington, 1934); G. Ross, *Argentina and Uruguay* (London, 1917); Woodbine Parish, *Buenos Ayres and the River Plate* (London, 1838; 2nd edit. enlarged 1852); J. A. King, *Twenty-four years in the Argentine* (London, 1846). For travel and description: F. B. Head, *A ride across the Pampas* (London, 1825, several re-issues); W. Latham, *The States of the River Plate* (London, 1886); A. S. Pennington, *The Argentine Republic* (London, 1910); W. A. Hirst, *Argentina* (London, 1910); W. H. Hudson, *A Naturalist in La Plata* (1892); *Idle days in Patagonia* (1893); *El Ombú* (1902).

CHAPTER XV

URUGUAY

The history of the South American republics may be reduced to the biographies of their representative men.   GARCÍA CALDERÓN

LA REPÚBLICA ORIENTAL DEL URUGUAY—still usually called La Banda Oriental in the River Plate, and its people calling themselves Orientales—smallest in area (considerably less than England and Scotland together), least in population (about two millions) of the South American republics with the exception of Paraguay, and for nearly a century one of the most turbulent, nevertheless fills much space in all writings about Latin America. This is due partly to the international questions which have gathered about this buffer state, partly to the excellent commercial position and wholesome climate of Montevideo, partly also to the intellectual activity of her citizens, her decided action in foreign relations and her recent striking social and constitutional experiments. The people are mainly European in origin, Spanish, Italian and Basque. The country is mostly a grassy prairie of rolling undulations where the flanks of the ridges (*cuchillas*, many miles long) slope into wide intervening hollows, along which streams move slowly; a treeless land except where scrub and low trees fringe the more considerable streams. Though agriculture has increased, the land, excellent sheep pasture, is still mainly pastoral; not long ago the home of gaucho life and often traversed by troops of riders under some caudillo, killing the cattle for food, taking the horses for remounts and—in the name of liberty and reform—forcing the men to mount and ride on with them.

In Spanish days the Banda Oriental, though included in the Viceroyalty of Buenos Aires, had a military Governor appointed by the Crown. Thus the fortified and garrisoned city of Montevideo repudiated the Buenos Aires revolution of 1810 and was held for the King until 1814. Already in 1810 two leaders—rather surprisingly (if anything Iberian surprises) a Brazilian and a Spaniard —gathered insurgent bands in the open country. But the national hero of Uruguay is José Gervasio Artigas. In his youth an expert smuggler and (according to repute) cattle-lifter from Brazilian estancias, skilful in the gaucho craft of the plains, Artigas at the age of twenty-three (1797) became an officer of Spanish mounted police. Furious at a rebuke from his commander, he left that service in February 1811 and offered himself to the Junta in Buenos Aires. Commissioned by the Junta as Commander of Militia, he recrossed the river in April with 150 companions, united the parties already out, added recruits and after a month led 1000 horsemen to victory over a larger royalist force at Las Piedras, twelve miles from the capital (May 1811). But the Porteño Junta, bent on the war in Upper Peru, concluded an armistice with Elío, leaving him in possession of Montevideo. Artigas repudiated the armistice and led his troops on a two-months' journey across the prairie, together with the population of the villages and plains, fleeing from Portuguese soldiery, gaucho bandits and 'patriot' deserters. He crossed the River Uruguay into Entre Ríos, where 4,300 fugitives, besides the troops, lived for months encamped like a nomad tribe, men, women and children being fed on beef and water and huddled under makeshift shelters. What this strange migration endured and how many perished, cannot be known.

The armistice was soon broken; and an Argentine army, together with Artigas' men, took the field early in 1813. The Banda Oriental having been invited to send deputies to the Assembly in Buenos Aires, Artigas summoned to his quarters a dozen men as a Representative Congress of the Banda Oriental. At his behest this body sent five deputies to Buenos Aires, instructed to demand a Declaration of Independence and a federal system with a capital outside Buenos Aires: so far a reasonable proposal, though possibly premature. Indeed the Argentine historian Ravignani—to be quoted with respect—regards Artigas as the prophetic exponent of the system which was to solve Argentine political problems. But Artigas also demanded religious toleration (which might have wrecked the Assembly) and also a most anti-federal degree of independence for the Banda Oriental. The document imparts terms dictated by a potentate, not instructions from electors to their representatives. The Assembly evaded the difficulty by excluding the five Oriental deputies as not duly elected.

In January 1814 Artigas, angered at this affront and dissatisfied with his treatment in the campaign, withdrew his troops by night from the lines besieging Montevideo, endangering the whole operation. The Buenos Aires Government thereupon declared him a traitor and set a price on his head.[1] When after long effort Argentine forces delivered Montevideo from Spanish domination, the Uruguayan hero was not among the deliverers.

Artigas and his allied chieftains, notably the redoubtable gaucho Rivera (afterwards first President of Uruguay) now made war on the Argentine masters of Montevideo. The distracted Porteño Government, at war with Peru, was unable to hold the place and in February 1815 Artigas' men entered Montevideo. He now called himself 'Protector of the Free Peoples'; for the chieftains of the three Littoral Provinces accepted him as the head of a loose federation opposed to Buenos Aires. The lands controlled by him had an unhappy time. Rengger, who traversed them in 1819, describes Artigas' life as a 'tissue of horrors', ascribing the worst of these horrors not to Artigas himself but to his lieutenants, since 'his standard was the rallying point for the dregs of the human race, brigands, assassins, pirates, robbers, deserters...Indians'. Robertson, joint author of *Letters on Paraguay*, visited Artigas in his quarters in 1815, and found the Protector of Free Peoples seated on an ox-skull on the mud floor of a hut drinking rum[2] from a cow's horn and eating beef from a roast spitted on the floor, surrounded by officers chattering, eating and drinking. The floor was strewn with envelopes, and Artigas was dictating to two secretaries, while couriers constantly galloped up or rode away bearing despatches. The chieftain handed to his visitor a slice of the roast, passed to him the cow's horn and surprised him by his courteous manners.

Artigas' hold on the Banda Oriental was brief. In 1816 Portuguese troops from the north invaded the country. Artigas, de-

---

[1] The ban was removed in the following year: and the cabildo of Buenos Aires even invited Artigas to overthrow Alvear, who was acting as a capricious military dictator in the capital. Artigas readily consented.

[2] Robertson says gin, but it must have been *caña*, white rum.

clining proffered aid from Buenos Aires, attempted to resist. But in the long run his irregular levies were unavailing against regular troops. In January 1817 Lecor, the Portuguese commander, approached Montevideo. The Oriental garrison evacuated the place to join Artigas in the open country. Next day a truncated cabildo surrendered the city on condition of preserving their legitimate customs. Lecor entered the place in January 1817, and for twelve years the Banda Oriental was incorporated with Brazil.

For some months Rivera blockaded Lecor in Montevideo; and for three years Artigas fought the Portuguese in the open plains, twice carrying the war into the enemy's country by invading Brazil: fruitless efforts, which brought devastation, not deliverance, the Oriental troops (at one time estimated at nearly 10,000) living on the country and consuming the cattle. Artigas, stubbornly refusing Argentine aid and from 1817 at war with Buenos Aires as well as with the Portuguese, was attempting impossibilities. At last in January 1820 he led his gaucho troops across the river Uruguay into Entre Ríos, abandoning Uruguay to the Portuguese. Rivera, the only Oriental leader still under arms, was obliged to yield and took service under the conquerors.

Though he never re-entered his native country, Artigas still attempted with his gaucho followers to dominate the Littoral Provinces and to treat as his subordinates Estanislao López, who for thirty years (1818–48) ruled Santa Fe, and Ramírez, the gaucho chieftain of Entre Ríos. These two men, incited by Artigas himself, were preparing to overthrow the Congress and the Directorate. In February 1820 Ramírez, victorious in the field, compelled the Buenos Aires Government to agree, by the Treaty of Pilar, that the United Provinces should have a Federal Government to be settled by a Congress. Artigas rebuked Ramírez for making this Treaty without his authority. Thereupon Ramírez turned against the 'Protector of Free Peoples', who, fighting against heavy odds, was beaten and fled to Paraguay, where the dictator Francia granted him a dwelling and a pension. There he lived for thirty years and died at the age of eighty. To most Argentines he is a monster: to Uruguayans a magnificent hero.

The comparatively peaceful period of Portuguese-Brazilian domination need not be described, nor the Revolution of 1821–2 (of little concern to the general population) whereby the country passed from Portuguese dominion to that of the Brazilian Emperor. The alien Government was on the whole tolerant, respected the Spanish character of the inhabitants and employed Orientales in the public service: indeed Artigas' comrade Rivera became Commander of the rural districts.

But Oriental exiles in Buenos Aires were planning revolt. After preparing the ground through emissaries, the 'Immortal Thirty-three', under the notable guerrillero Lavalleja, crossed the estuary in April 1825. The country rose at their call. Rivera, deserting the Brazilians, joined them with his troops. An improvised Oriental Congress met at Florida, seventy miles from the capital, and declared for incorporation with the United Provinces. The Constituent Congress, then sitting at Buenos Aires, accepted the invitation. The resulting three years' war with Brazil and the Peace of 1828, which left the Banda Oriental independent, have been already related.

Thus in 1828 the 'Oriental Republic of Uruguay' started life with about 60,000 inhabitants. A Constituent Assembly met, and in July 1830 a Constitution was promulgated: three months later Rivera was elected President. But already stormy scenes, due to the rivalry of Lavalleja, presaged eighty years of strife. Revolt, executions, fresh revolts, fill Rivera's four years' term. In turn Rivera, with some provocation, revolted against his successor Oribe. The aggression of Rosas, the foreign intervention in favour of Uruguay, the siege and defence of Montevideo, have been already told. Only after Monte Caseros in 1853 was the Republic able to enter upon its national life, and even then not with entire freedom, for exiles or 'outs' were always able to plot and arm on Argentine or Brazilian soil.

Although the fall of Rosas seemed to remove the cause of strife, yet strife continued between two parties, or rather between their chiefs, the Blancos (Whites), Oribe's men, allied with Urquiza, who were supposed to stand for order and tradition; and the Colorados (Reds), Rivera's followers, favoured by Mitre and by the Porteños and claiming to represent Liberalism and progress.

But in fact principles distinguishing them are hard to find. The Blancos, when in power, were perhaps more imperious in deporting opponents and slaying prisoners: but the Colorados, in their years of success, turned their backs on democracy and were perhaps more unscrupulous in exploiting the State. As time passed, men were born into either party and so remained. But, as everywhere in Spanish America, opprobrium always gathered round the party in power, and the 'outs' gained corresponding favour. The countrymen who rode after an insurgent standard were moved by the prowess and promises of a cavalry caudillo and by hatred of all existing authority rather than by political faith. Yet the disorders after 1853—intrinsically not profoundly momentous—demand attention as the ostensible cause of the Paraguayan War which involved four countries: the greatest tragedy of South American history.

The brief presidencies, resignations, revolts, acting governments left the Blancos generally in power during the decade 1853–63, although menaced by the growing number of angry exiles in Buenos Aires. An incursion by some of these was castigated by a slaughter of prisoners ('the Martyrs of Quinteros') so savage and revolting as to provoke in April 1863 a determined invasion by Venancio Flores, successor to Rivera as chieftain of the Colorados. For eighteen months Flores ranged the plains with 2000 horsemen, unable to oust the Blanco President, Berro, from Montevideo but never decisively beaten. Foreign intervention ended this impasse. The Brazilian Government, which had long complained to Montevideo of injury to Brazilians through frontier disorder, now became insistent. The bewildered Blanco President begged the Paraguayan dictator López for protection against the Brazilian menace. López, after much wrangling, consented, and in August 1864 notified the Government at Rio that any Brazilian violation of Uruguayan soil would be a *casus belli* for Paraguay. A few days later that violation took place: Brazil sent aid to Flores. Thus the Uruguayan civil war became a duel between Paraguay as protector of the Blanco President and Brazil as protector of the gaucho chieftain. López did nothing for his protegé, whereas the Brazilians effectively backed their man. President Berro was forced to yield; and the intruder Flores, supported by a Brazilian fleet, entered the capital as dictator, thus initiating the period of Colorado dominance which nominally endured to our time.

Flores owed his elevation to Brazil and had to pay the price. On 1 May 1865 Uruguay signed the secret Treaty of the Triple Alliance against Paraguay. Thus by a strange reversal the country, on whose behalf López had ostensibly gone to war, now joined his enemies, and Uruguay was drawn 'into a foreign war in a quarrel not her own'.[1]

For three years Flores was dictator, naming a delegate during his sixteen months' absence in command of the Uruguayan contingent in Paraguay. Once seated in power, he ruled with prudent moderation. In April 1867 he ceremoniously cut the first sod of the Central Uruguay Railway, which has done so much for Uruguayan progress.[2] Except during the ruinous period of the Guerra Grande (1839–52) and of the civil war waged by Flores himself (1863–5), the country suffered less than might have been expected from the chronic disturbances, in great part local and engaging small bodies of fighters. This fact is proved by the influx of immigrants. In the 'thirties the population rapidly increased, and the defenders of Montevideo in the later stages of the siege by Oribe were French and Italian.[3]

In February 1868 Flores surrendered his office, to offer himself for the post of Constitutional President. Before election day he was stabbed in the street. That same evening ex-President Berro, suspected of complicity, was murdered by Colorado avengers. Tumults, brief administrations, economic disasters, with a short interval of peace in 1872, fill seven years. At last in January 1875 (the 'terrible year') Colonel Latorre, a rude soldier of humble origin but of masterful personality, commander of the battalion which garrisoned the city, ended sanguinary election riots by marching his men into the plaza. Thrusting into the presidential

---

[1] Pelham H. Box, *The Origins of the Paraguayan War* (Illinois, 1927), p. 227.
[2] The railway was opened to Durazno in 1874 and reached Rivera, on the Brazilian frontier, in 1892.
[3] In 1862 the population was estimated to be 281,500, in 1883 to be 450,000, of whom four out of ten were foreign-born, the children of foreigners being counted as natives. In 1883 there were 5372 foreigners owning property in the Department of Montevideo and only 2904 native proprietors.

chair a man of straw for a few months, he initiated six years of dictatorship. In 1879 he had himself elected 'Constitutional President' and made some attempt to justify the title. But a year later he resigned, declaring the country to be ungovernable, and became manager of an estancia in Argentina. Although unscrupulous in method, muzzling the Press and dealing summarily with his enemies, he gave peace to Uruguay and, without troubling the law-courts, suppressed the brigandage which was the legacy of civil wars, thus facilitating the progress of the pastoral industry by which the country lived.

Santos, a soldier of a baser type than Latorre, ruled from 1880 to 1886, first as the power behind a puppet President and then as head of the State. He ruled like a sultan from his garish palace, sending to the custom-house when he wanted money. He had a gunboat built at the artillery barracks a mile or two from the port and then dragged down to the water in triumphal procession through beflagged streets. A cage of 'tigers' (jaguars), which he kept in his garden, gave rise to a fearsome legend concerning the quiet disappearance of his political enemies. An attempt at assassination which broke his jaw, a revolt gathering in the north and the resignation of his Ministers compelled Santos to retire. Tajes, the soldier who succeeded him, an honest and moderate man, served his country well. He disbanded or reformed regiments whose commanders were given to politics, dismissed useless officers and imposed an internal peace which favoured economic progress. In 1890, after sixteen years of autocracy under three dictators, Congress freely chose as President Herrera y Obes, an able lawyer and ex-Minister. But constitutional presidents brought no sound government. The administration of Herrera (1890–4) and of his successor Idiarte Borda was (but for the early months of Borda's term) a time of overborrowing, waste, corruption, shameless personal interest, excessive taxation and methods hardly less autocratic than those of the military dictators.

The return of all the President's nominees in the farcical parliamentary election of November 1896 provoked a revolt of Blancos, calling themselves 'Nationalists' with some reason; for the Blancos, excluded from office since 1863, had become the more popular party. From the Brazilian frontier 300 men rode under Aparicio Saravia, a leader of the old gaucho type. Troops of a more regular kind came from the Argentine frontier under Lamas, an officer trained in the Argentine army. Soon 3000 insurgents were in the field. Within five months the Government, whose press-gang swept the streets of the capital every night, had 10,000 men under arms. No end was in sight, when on 25 August 1897 the President, as he left the Cathedral after the *Te Deum* in celebration of Independence Day, was shot dead by a bystander. Cuestas, Chairman of the Senate, now acting President, made terms with the insurgents, consenting that in six of the nineteen Departments the Jefe Político, chief Magistrate and in effect Governor, should be a member of the Nationalist or Blanco party. The ovation to the revolutionary chiefs in the capital shows that their action was regarded not as a partisan rising but as a popular revolt against scandalous misrule. But handing over one-third of the country to the control of the half-gaucho, half-Brazilian Saravia meant an unstable armistice; and the conflict revived when Battle y Ordónez became President (1903–7), ex-Senator and ex-Governor of a Department; an outstanding figure in recent South-American history; founder at the age of twenty (in 1880) of an influential newspaper preaching social justice and now urging that public ills were due to excessive presidential power and patronage and to the temptations which they offered. President Battle spent two years fighting the insurgents to a finish—to the defeat and death of Saravia. He left the country at peace, passed four years in Europe studying forms of government; and in his second Presidency (1911–15) pushed through, against much opposition, his scheme for rule by a Council, not a President. The new Constitution, promulgated in 1917, divided executive authority between the President and a National Administrative Council—nine men, renewable by thirds every two years—which appointed and controlled four Ministers; the other three Ministers being appointed by the President. Proportional representation and the ballot ensured minority representation, and the largest minority group had seats in the Administrative Council.

Church and State were separated, the Church retaining its

property with liberty of teaching and worship. But the calendar was purged of Church festivals: 25 December became 'Family Day': to block observance of Holy Thursday and Good Friday, Holy Week became an official seven days' festive holiday, called 'Creole Week', afterwards amended to 'Tourist Week'. A costly programme of social measures was partly carried out, and a scheme of employment by magnificent public works. But this profusion, favoured by the war-time and post-war booms, afterwards brought financial confusion and social unrest.

The elaborate machinery for eliminating personal influence involved the paradox that only a strong and determined man could make it work. Such was Baltasar Brum, who as Foreign Minister had handled the problems of the Great War and now as President (1919–23) managed the new Constitution. For a decade or more Uruguayan constitutional tranquillity seemed to be 'an example for Latin America of political wisdom and democratic spirit'. When a French historian printed these words in 1932, collapse was imminent. The cumbrous slowness of the system had long been a trouble. In 1927, at the inaugural date of a new presidency, the result of the voting three months earlier had not been declared; and the Senate, by a common-sense breach of the Constitution, pronounced that the favourite had won. It was also increasingly difficult to get the constantly shifting little groups under rival leaders to work together. Some decisive authority was evidently wanting.

Dr Terra, an able and vigorous man who became President (his opponents alleging unfair election) in March 1931 amid world-wide depression, won much support in an oratorical campaign for constitutional reform. But—faced by four anti-reformist 'parties'—he failed to unite the five irreconcilable reformist groups, of which one was collecting arms. An autocratic stroke cut the knot: in March 1933 he dismissed both Administrative Council and Congress, nominating a Junta and an Assembly. He then secured a plebiscite for reform and convoked an elected Constituent Assembly. He told this Assembly that national bankruptcy and civil war had been imminent, economies and suspension of debt amortization were urgent, revenue was falling, uncontrolled expenses mounting and

—amid poverty and unemployment—paid posts increasing; no one was responsible. 'No one governs, so dilute is administrative action.' The fallen Constitution, he concluded, had been anti-democratic and he had 'opened the closed channels of national democracy'.

A new Constitution, accepted by a plebiscite in April 1934, abolished the Administrative Council, restoring the presidential system. It did homage to Battle's memory by providing that three of the nine Ministers, appointed by the President, should come from the largest minority party and justified the Uruguayan reputation for advanced experiment by establishing the principle of ministerial responsibility to Parliament. Elections are simplified, administrative expenses reduced, and an Accounting Board controls expenditure.

An attempt at revolt in January 1935, organized on the Brazilian frontier and favoured by sympathizers within the country, was quelled without much difficulty and the leaders were treated with clemency. By a peaceable election the author of the *coup d'état* became, as always in such cases, President (1936–9). Terra had welcomed with genial tact and dignity the seventh Pan-American Congress which met in Montevideo in 1933 in an atmosphere not at all revolutionary. In 1935 he produced a surplus and at the end of that year permitted the return home of the men whom he had banished after the custom of these republics in such times. Uruguay, still a pioneer, had produced a revolution even less martial and violent than those of Argentina and Chile.

The new Constitution is already under revision. Critics argue that the largest minority group, supplying three Ministers, may be a small fraction of Congress; also that ministerial responsibility means a Ministry drawn from the majority. But the real bane of public life is the rivalry of personalist groups, not true political parties.

The sight of two former provinces of the Buenos Aires Viceroyalty, Paraguay and Bolivia, shedding their blood for three years in a sanguinary territorial conflict may raise regrets concerning the dismemberment of that Viceroyalty. But the vigorous life and intellectual activity of Uruguay suggest that there is something to be said for the sovereignty of small states, as against top-heavy concentration in the capital of many provinces. Montevideo, having the character and atmosphere of a national capital, commands a life far different from that which would be hers if she were sending deputies to a Federal Congress in Buenos Aires, submitting her disputes to Federal Tribunals and accepting 'Interventors' at the will of a Federal President. There is constant intimate intercourse with Argentines, and much intermarriage. Indeed the Uruguayan Florencio Sánchez, the most notable dramatist of the River Plate, puts the scene of his dramas in Argentina. Yet Uruguay sturdily and almost jealously goes her own way. Whereas Argentina has generally been content with amicable rather than markedly cordial relations with the United States and has shown little enthusiasm for plans of inter-American union, Uruguay has been forward in the Pan-American movement, almost going ahead of the United States in some proposals. Argentina maintained neutrality in the Great War, whereas Uruguay took every possible anti-German step short of a declaration of war; had it been possible, Germany would have been justified in treating Uruguay as a belligerent. There is an amusing instance of this assertive Uruguayan spirit. In Argentina it is almost a point of honour to exalt San Martín by belittling Bolívar, who was not at his best in dealing with Argentines and in his lifetime did not win their unstinted admiration: but the Uruguayan Rodó, whom many regard as the foremost prose writer of Latin America, published an eloquent and convincing eulogy of Bolívar. He wrote with full sincerity, but also perhaps with a touch of harmless malice in setting right the people across the river.

NOTE. See the books named on p. 150; also Haring ch. IV, and an article by P. A. Martin in *The Hispanic-American Historical Review*, vol. VIII. An article in the same periodical, vol. XVI, by E. G. Collado and S. G. Hanson on 'Old Age Pensions in Uruguay', gives more information than the title suggests. W. H. Hudson's romance, *The Purple Land that England lost*, depicts former conditions.

CHAPTER XVI

PARAGUAY

THE Paraguayan Creoles—distinguished even under Spain by a national spirit, proud of their country's history and of their ancestors, who founded the first Rio-Platense settlement—were nevertheless content to pass their lives in ignorance and idleness. They inhabited a beautiful, varied and fertile land, easily producing the necessaries of life and favouring, by its genial climate, gentle indolence and siestas in a swinging hammock—bedsteads were an unknown superfluity—with endless matés and cigars, the constant solace of men, women and children. The term Creole (*criollo*), denoting pure European ancestry, needs qualification. The early settlers married native wives and all the older Paraguayan families had Indian ancestors: but they forgot this and looked down on those recently intermarried with people not reputed white. Indian peasants were the bulk of the population.

Paraguay, behind broad river boundaries, had a distinct character and also its own language. Spanish, the official tongue and spoken by the leading Creole families among themselves, was understood by few of the populace: the vernacular was and still is Guaraní.

When Belgrano, at the head of 1000 men, offered to the Paraguayans independence from Spain and union with Buenos Aires, they forcibly declined subjection to the Porteños (March 1811). Two months later a gathering of leading citizens of Asunción quietly deposed the royal Governor Velasco and installed a triumvirate. Thus Paraguay, independent without striking a blow, had the singular blessing of immunity from the devastating wars of independence.

The leading triumvir was the secretary, Rodríguez de Franza—amended to Francia, to conceal Portuguese origin and pretend French ancestry—son of a royal official, graduate of Córdoba University, teacher of theology in the College of Asunción, then —having lost his post owing to supposed irregular opinions—an advocate noted for austere integrity, Senior Alcalde in the Asunción Cabildo in 1808 at the age of forty-two. Slighted by his colleagues, Francia resigned his post after eight months; but was found indispensable and reappointed. Businesslike, indefatigable, astute and incorruptible, he discerned that the preventive of disorder was autocracy. In 1813 he contrived that a Congress, nominated for the purpose, should appoint two Consuls, himself and another. Thrusting aside his incompetent colleague, he became omnipotent. A year later (October 1814) 1000 persons, largely illiterate villagers, were ordered to meet in Congress and to appoint Francia dictator for three years. Before the triennium ended, another ephemeral Assembly obediently named him dictator for life. To complete his autocracy, he declared himself Head of the Church, ignoring the Vatican: a step facilitated by the mental collapse of the bishop under the indignities inflicted on him. Marriages contracted without the dictator's permission were declared to be null.

His tyranny grew. At first he shed no blood; but an imprudent word or gesture, a suspicion or whim, might mean a heavy fine or imprisonment in chains or banishment to some remote malarial spot. Spies were everywhere: men dreaded their neighbours, their servants, their own family: they hardly dared to whisper the word *El Supremo*, by which he chose to be known. Even before the conspiracy of 1820 there were summary executions, on two occasions for an imprudent word, carried by an informer to the palace. The physician, Rengger, who, living in Paraguay from 1819 to 1825, knew Francia well and does full justice to his merits, declares that his recurrent seasons of hypochondria amounted to insanity, a diagnosis explanatory of his strange caprices and impulses. This dreaded autocrat, tall, gaunt, celibate, of severe and even ascetic aspect, inhabited a gloomy palace in sombre contemptuous solitude, simple in life, frugal in diet, spending little on himself,[1] friendless, without advisers—for his ministers were but obsequious clerks— exact and capable in public finance, substituting his own word for law but strict in punishing crime, the enemy of all injustice and

[1] On the other hand Francia was the Exchequer. He collected and allocated the revenue without published accounts, as did also his two dictatorial successors. The Republic of Paraguay had no budget down to 1870.

oppression except that inflicted by himself and his armed guards.

In 1820 a plot was discovered to overthrow the Government with the help of Ramírez, chieftain of Entre Ríos. The terror now reached its height: arrests, swift executions, evidence extorted by 100 or 200 lashes with a whip of leather thongs in the 'Chamber of Justice'. Men were shot and bayoneted under the Dictator's window and before his eyes. Political prisoners suffered solitary confinement, heavily shackled, in underground cells.

After 1820, Artigas being a refugee in Paraguay, Ramírez killed in fight and Buenos Aires at peace with Santa Fe, Francia dreaded the tranquillity of the neighbouring provinces, which might leave them free for aggression, more than he had dreaded their previous anarchy. A decree, issued in revolutionary fervour and afterwards disused, which forbade Spaniards to marry white women, was now revived and extended to natives of Santa Fe, Entre Ríos and Buenos Aires; the decree sorely hurt the Paraguayan women and encouraged irregular unions: 300 Spaniards were imprisoned and some were kept for nineteen months until they secured release by a huge fine: the venerable and estimable Velasco, once royal Governor, died in prison. A cargo of arms consigned to Francia having been seized by the Cabildo of Santa Fe, Francia imprisoned all the Santafecinos in Paraguay and shot one of them, brother to a town-councillor of Santa Fe. Only Francia's death released the survivors. These vicarious penalties were not merely vindictive; they were to prevent recurrence of the offence. As the Supremo rode daily from his palace to the barrack, his head sunk upon his breast, his guards struck with the flat of their swords any bystander or loiterer: finally the chief rode through his capital as through a desert.

His commercial policy seems to have been at first capricious and experimental rather than calculated. So early as 1815 he would suddenly close the port of Asunción and as suddenly open it, to be closed again without notice, so that ships loaded for departure were unloaded and left idle, to the destruction of goods and loss to merchants. For some years the country was not wholly secluded. Many from the neighbouring provinces fled into peaceful Paraguay from the devastation of their homes; and when a horde of Artigas' Indian followers under the Irish gaucho Campbell seized and pillaged the city of Corrientes in 1818, a crowd of Correntinos crossed the Paraná into Paraguay.

But finally the dictator isolated Paraguay from contact with the outside world. Yerba (Paraguayan tea) and timber, which were State monopolies, were exported in limited quantities (under strict precautions against contaminating intercourse) at a small down-river port and sold at great profit in order to obtain munitions and army clothing, the only imports which the dictator valued. There was also a limited trade with Brazil through a small port on the Upper Paraná. The Post Office was abolished. Entrance into the country was not totally forbidden, but no one might pass out, apparently lest they should act as guides to Francia's enemies. The river guards were watchful, and to escape through the Chaco meant almost certain death. Francia neither sent out nor received consuls or diplomatists, with one brief exception. The Court of Brazil, with which Francia maintained friendly relations, sent a Consul to Asunción in 1824, and raised him to the rank of Minister two years later. But when Brazil sought Paraguayan aid in the war of 1825–8 against Argentina, Francia 'courteously secured the removal of the Brazilian Minister'.

To maintain isolation, the dictator made the country self-supporting. The peasants, content with the lazy planting of yuca, were now made to cultivate unaccustomed crops: maize, wheat and vegetables; and also cotton, that the material for their simple clothing need no longer be imported from Corrientes. The crops over a wide district having been devoured by locusts towards the end of 1819[1] (the early summer), Francia commanded the farmers to sow their land again; and to their astonishment the second crop was abundant. Throughout Francia's reign agriculture improved, and the land yielded more than ever before; but the increase of industry among the cultivators either has been exaggerated (which is probable) or else was not very lasting, as the quotation on p. 169 shows. The country being rich in cattle, hides were abundant for leather-work. Under stern compulsion workmen were turned into

[1] The date is variously given.

skilled artisans. Population increased: the peasantry, needing little, prospered; and whereas in parts of Spanish America independence was little or no boon to the native Indians, to the Paraguayan Indian it brought some consideration. Their freedom, it is true, was limited: the labour of men and beasts might be requisitioned at any time, and the workers on the State farms were at the mercy, not tender, of the overseers: the same is probably true of those who cut timber or gathered and cured yerba in the woods at Francia's command. To protect his person, support his authority and defend the country against the savage northern Indians and against possible danger from the south, Francia increased and improved his troops. The greater revenue (as compared with Spanish times) needed for their maintenance was supplied by fines for small offences or for none, by State monopolies, confiscations and the *droit d'aubaines* rigorously applied. By commanding all landowners to produce their titles, he took for the State extensive lands, where cattle-farms were worked for the benefit of the Treasury. Moreover all property and persons, and the forced labour of men and beasts, were at the disposal of the State. On the other hand the taxes paid by the peasantry were reduced.

The extreme terror of 1820–1 was mitigated in 1824, and in the following two years several people were allowed to leave the country; but the tyranny lasted until Francia's death in 1840 at the age of seventy-four.

The best defence of Francia is Rengger's remark that if he had not seized power, Paraguay would have suffered the same fate as the Banda Oriental and Entre Ríos. For nearly thirty years Francia maintained internal peace, a peace unknown in any other part of Spanish America; and by his system of defence and isolation he saved his country from the anarchy of the neighbouring provinces. The sufferings inflicted by Francia, mostly on the well-to-do classes and not on the peasantry, were as nothing compared with the misery which swept over the adjoining provinces under Artigas and his satellites.

Francia, like other dictators, failed to provide for future government. Crushing thought and action, suppressing into timorous servility such elements of culture and public spirit as existed, he left his country without a council or a legislature or ministers or magistrates trained in public affairs, with a scanty and debased clergy. On the other hand he left no national debt, no criminals, no destitution except among the children of his victims, a peasantry having all they needed in the way of food, shelter and clothing, a treasury crammed with accumulated silver dollars and with silver plate confiscated from the well-to-do families and the clergy. To the illiterate peasantry he had taught industry by command and had improved their condition. But the one political lesson which he inculcated was blind obedience: a fatal lesson, as it proved.

Francia's despotism seems hardly to merit such full exposition. But this, the earliest and one of the longest and most efficient of tyrannies after independence, has significance as setting a pattern for others. Rosas owed something to Francia's example. One cannot assert that later autocrats learnt from Francia and from Rosas the value of terrorism as part of their stock-in-trade. But to Francia belongs the dubious distinction of priority.

On Francia's death a group of officers took charge. It speaks well for army discipline and for the influence of the late dictator that, without much disturbance, a Junta was formed, then a Congress of the usual manufactured kind, which nominated two Consuls, namely Alonso, commander of Francia's escort, and Carlos Antonio López, a lawyer of unwieldy corpulence, unprepossessing in countenance and manner, but possessing both astuteness and legal ability, which he had wisely concealed in rural retirement during Francia's reign. López soon unseated his colleague with the brief command *ándate, bárbaro* ('Get out, you dolt') and became President-dictator in 1844; but in fact he ruled from 1841, continuing, with mitigation, the despotism of Francia, espionage, occasional imprisonments, but not many unjust executions.

López' internal administration was beneficent, except for a nepotism which allowed extortion to his five children. The first step was taken towards gradual abolition of negro slavery; for Francia had done nothing for slaves. Confiscation and torture were abolished by decree, the only form of legislation. But the flogging of delinquents or suspects having any trace of negro blood, and the incarceration of white men in heavy chains, were continued. George Thompson, who was in Paraguay during López' last five years, writes: 'Probably in no country in the world has life and property been so secure as all over Paraguay during his reign. Crime was almost unknown and, when committed, immediately detected and punished. The mass of the people was perhaps the happiest in existence. They had hardly to do any work to gain a livelihood. Each family had its house or hut in its own ground. They planted, in a few days, enough tobacco, maize and mandioca for their own consumption, and the crop hardly wanted looking at till it was ready to be gathered. Having at every hut a grove of oranges...and also a few cows, they were almost throughout the year under little necessity of working....Everybody was liable at any moment to have himself and his property pressed into the public service, without payment, at the call of any justice of the peace; but this power was not generally abused....The only revenue was from the yerba, a monopoly of the Government, which bought it from the manufacturers at one shilling for 25 lb. and sold it at 25 to 32 shillings.' Thompson omits the ills of primitive life, infant mortality and prevalent disease untended. But his picture is a striking contrast to the wretched condition of the Indians in Bolivia and Peru.

In 1842 the independence of Paraguay, which had been assumed in 1811, was formally proclaimed and was recognized in 1844 by Brazil,[1] by the Argentine Confederation under Urquiza in 1852, and a year later by the United States and European powers. Argentina, clinging to the fiction that Paraguay was merely an Argentine province, delayed recognition till 1859. López ended the system of isolation, although it was not till 1845 that the country was declared open to foreigners for trade and residence, with some troublesome restrictions. López was no fighting man; but, with meddling self-assertion, he unwisely abandoned Francia's system of political aloofness. He affronted Rosas by alliance with the dissident Province of Corrientes. Rosas in reply closed the river

[1] The appointment of a Brazilian Minister in Asunción in 1824, noted on p. 166, had already implied recognition. Apparently this previous recognition had been forgotten or conveniently overlooked. It is one of the many diplomatic anomalies of Latin-American history.

which was the only road into Paraguay. López also provoked Brazil, claiming the River Paraguay as interior waters and petulantly attempting to prevent Brazilian ships from using that only possible route to the Brazilian Province of Matto Grosso. He had to give way; but he constructed the fortress of Humaitá to form a southern river-gate to his territory, increased his army and accumulated munitions; and at his death in 1862 bequeathed to his son the most formidable army in South America and complete autocratic command of the property, persons and lives of all his subjects.

López II, a corpulent voluptuary, flattered from childhood, had returned from a European mission full of self-conceit and military ambition and although (to quote the Paraguayan historian Cecilio Báez) he was 'a fatuous ruler, incapable as a commander and monstrous as a despot', he determined 'to make his voice heard' in the affairs of the River Plate from his sham court surrounded by guards, obsequious Ministers and ready executioners and presided over by his mistress, the notorious Madam Lynch.

Paraguay had a frontier question with Brazil in the north and two with Argentina, in the Chaco and in the Missions east of the Paraná. But López' position was strong; for Argentina also had a frontier question with Brazil; and in 1863 President Mitre proposed to López a joint commission to examine frontier questions, co-operation in territorial disputes with Brazil and non-intervention in the Uruguayan civil war. López declined this overture and provoked a conflict by his challenge to Brazil about Uruguay. When Brazil intervened there, López did nothing to support the Montevideo Government, being unable to do so without violating Argentine territory. His provocative blunder recoiled upon himself. His friends in Uruguay were driven out; a pro-Brazilian Government seized power in Montevideo and Uruguay joined his foes.

But López was able to attack Brazil elsewhere. In October 1864 he seized, in the River Paraguay, without declaration of war, a Brazilian ship which was conveying a new Governor to Matto Grosso. He then sent a force up the river which invaded Matto Grosso, sacked several places and occupied much of the province, carrying off cattle and munitions. A month passed before the invasion of the province was known in Rio. War had begun, but only with Brazil: the beginning of a tremendous and pitiful five years' tragedy.

In February 1865 Mitre rightly refused López' request that his troops might cross Corrientes to invade the Brazilian province of Rio Grande. Two months later five Paraguayan warships appeared off Corrientes, seized two Argentine gunboats and landed a force which occupied the city. This insolent aggression meant war with Argentina; and in May 1865 Brazil, Argentina and Uruguay signed the treaty whereby they undertook to overthrow López, never to negotiate separately, to respect the independence of Paraguay, to disarm that country and exact the expenses of the war. Argentina and Brazil were to obtain the desired boundaries.

The odds were not so unequal as might appear; for the whole resources and population of Paraguay were organized for war; every man, on pain of torture and death, blindly obeyed the dictator's inflexible will; and the difficult entrance to the country was fortified, and held by a strong army. López had 80,000 troops. The Argentine regular army numbered 6000 men, scattered through the provinces. The war-fleet was Brazilian. Mitre[1] commanded the troops, whose first task was to expel the invaders from Corrientes. In seven months, before December 1865, they had been driven back into Paraguay. López also had thrown away 12,000 men in an unsupported invasion of Rio Grande: he had lost several of his wooden ships in an attack on the Brazilian ironclads anchored near Corrientes (through his own blundering commands, according to Thompson); and the army of 6000 which had successfully invaded Matto Grosso was lost for the real conduct of the war. Most of his remaining troops died during the war from cholera or from diseases caused by unwholesome quarters and bad food.

In April 1866, a year after the Paraguayan attack on Corrientes, the allies crossed the Paraná into a region of jungle and swamp where transport and supply were difficult. For the war, which was to have been a triumph of imperial conquest, had become a struggle for defence by the diminishing forces of a small country against the

---

[1] Mitre on three later occasions was obliged to relinquish or depute the command owing to his presidential duties in Argentina. After 1867 the command and also the main burden of the war passed to the Brazilians.

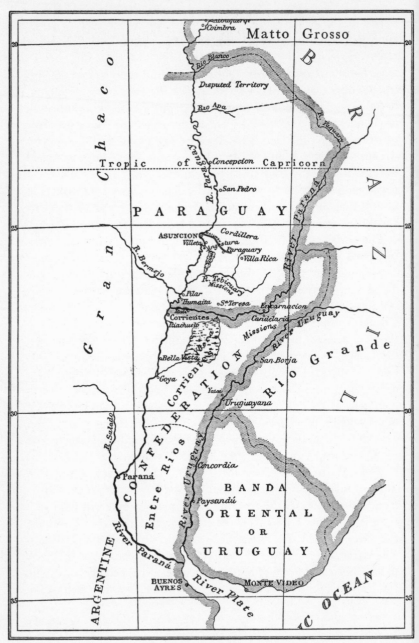

The Seat of War

gathering forces of powerful opponents. The ground favoured defence; but López himself, keeping beyond reach of any possible danger, wasted the endurance and valour of his men by repeated onslaughts which merely checked the allied advance without winning decided victory. In May 1866 the main Paraguayan army, attacking instead of awaiting attack, was routed, losing 11,000 killed and severely wounded. The allies, who also lost heavily, failed to advance and gave López time to assemble 20,000 troops, half of them boys, old men, negro slaves and men who had been wounded: and in September the allies, attacking a fort on the River Paraguay, were in their turn repulsed with heavy loss. Fourteen months of inaction followed, while cholera swept both camps. In November 1867 the Paraguayans surprised and stormed the allied camp, but dispersing to pillage (owing to an imbecile order from López) fell an easy prey to allied reinforcements. In February 1868 the Brazilian fleet steamed past the fortress of Humaitá, losing one ironclad ship, captured by Indian canoes. Thereupon López sent thirty canoes, covered with foliage to resemble floating islands, to attack the Brazilian fleet. The canoe-men boarded one Brazilian warship, driving the crew and marines below. But they were swept away by fire from the shore, and cannon-shot sank the canoes. The heroes of the Paraguayan War were not the victorious invaders.

In August 1868 the starving garrison of Humaitá surrendered. It was the beginning of the end. Yet the war dragged on for nineteen months longer, López being determined to fight or rather to make his people fight for him as long as any men or boys were left, although abdication would have secured peace and saved the remnant of his people. Accompanied by Madam Lynch in a comfortable equipage, he retired from post to post, driving before him or leaving to perish by the way the starving remnant of his people, aged men, women and children; forcing children of ten or twelve to bear arms; torturing and killing many men for alleged treason or conspiracy, flogging to death or shooting his best officers and nearest companions, including his own brother and the bishop; flogging his mother and his sisters; confiscating property, apparently in some vain hope of final escape. Hunted down at last, he fled on horseback, but was caught in a quagmire and fell by a lance-thrust, refusing to surrender. Execrated at that time by all his countrymen, López has since been exalted by popular sentiment into a national hero.

His death ended the war. A provisional Paraguayan Government concluded peace, yielding to Brazil the disputed territory and to Argentina the Missions east of the Paraná; after long negotiation the River Pilcomayo was fixed as the boundary in the Chaco by the arbitration of President Hayes in 1878. In the five years' war all the able-bodied men had perished and more than half of the women. Some say one-third of the pre-war population remained; some say one-sixth.

Misery pursued these—the land untilled and the cattle killed or scattered: but the women turned to work the land, raising yuca and maize. A new generation grew, unfortunately accustomed to leave labour to women. Fugitives returned from exile. Men from Argentina and from Europe came to work cattle-ranches and to extract tannin from the hard quebracho ('hatchet-breaker'). After fifty years the population approached its pre-war level: in 1932 it was estimated to be 870,200, mainly mestizos, for the Indians had been almost exterminated. But most of the people speak Guaraní and live in primitive villages after the Indian fashion.

After the war Paraguay had few educated citizens and no political tradition except autocracy and (among the peasants) acquiescence in any power which emerged. Hence prosperity has been impeded by political unrest and by a rapid succession of revolutions or *coups d'état* as rival politicians strove for power and profit. In the decade 1906–16 eight presidents held office, six of them being styled provisional. But national danger united rivals in support of President Ayala, elected in 1932.

For another storm was rising about dominion of the Chaco, the forest region west of the River Paraguay, rich in quebracho wood and cattle pasture. President Hayes' arbitration in 1878 fixed the River Pilcomayo as boundary between Argentina and Paraguay, thus assigning the southern part to Argentina: the northern part, the least valuable, is undisputed Bolivian territory: the intervening part, from the Pilcomayo northwards, Paraguay regarded as hers by virtue of early exploration, undisturbed settlement and the

Hayes arbitration. But Bolivia claimed that the *uti possidetis* of 1810 made the country hers, maintaining that the Charcas Audiencia had jurisdiction eastward to the river. Bolivia made no protest at the Hayes arbitration, but soon afterwards asserted her claim, pushing it more decidedly when at the Peace of Ancón in 1883 she lost her Pacific outlet and therefore desired access to the Atlantic by the Paraguay. The finding of petroleum in Bolivia east of the Andes intensified that desire. Negotiations were fruitless and from 1927 friction grew about small posts and movements of patrols on either side. In 1929 a Paraguayan advance caused a clash. For three years tension increased until in 1932 the seizure of a Paraguayan post by Bolivians precipitated war[1], for which Bolivia, with thrice the wealth and population of Paraguay, had long been preparing by training an army under a German general and by accumulating munitions, especially aeroplanes; for owing to the distance of the disputed territory from the Bolivian bases, war in the Chaco was impossible without air transport. But the Paraguayans had the advantage of nearness to their base. Their men were more at home in the Chaco jungle, flooded in summer and dusty in the rainless winter, than the Bolivians, mostly mountaineers who suffered horribly in the strange and cruel lowland forest. Moreover the Paraguayans were national troops intimate with their officers, and eager to repel what they regarded as an invasion of their country; whereas the Bolivian soldiery were mostly Indians, without sense of Bolivian citizenship, dragged from their mountain villages to serve their white masters (not beloved masters) in the invasion of what seemed to them to be a hateful, remote and alien land. Thus in any difficulty they were ready to surrender.

Fighting in the Chaco meant a soldier's war, where large bodies of men could not act together and much depended on the woodcraft and self-reliance of small groups and even of single men. The Bolivian aeroplanes, indispensable for transport, were almost useless for combat in the concealing jungle; and artillery, difficult to move, could hardly find a target. The Paraguayans, creeping unseen

---

[1] A year later (August 1933) the Bolivian President admitted that a Bolivian force had 'occupied a Paraguayan post...contrary to our will and the instructions of our Government'.

behind the Bolivian lines, cut their communications, compelled whole brigades to choose between starvation and surrender, and got weapons and bullets from the enemy. Their loss in killed and wounded was great, but far less than that of the Bolivians by disease, hardship and combat. Indeed the Paraguayan Commander-in-Chief, Colonel Estigarribia, outwitted the Prussian, General Kündt, commanding the Bolivian army.

But as the war moved westward from the forest and farther from the Paraguayan base towards the higher ground, conditions changed. Ballivián, one of the two key-fortresses of inhabited Bolivia, was taken: much stores were captured and prisoners said to number 10,000: the rest of the defenders fled northward or into Argentina. But the other fortress, Villa Montes, situated on high ground and well furnished with artillery, resisted the assaults of the diminished and exhausted Paraguayan troops. Three years of fighting led to a stalemate. The Bolivians could do nothing in the Chaco, which was the object of the war. The Paraguayans held the Chaco but could not impose a victorious peace. In June 1935 both governments agreed to preliminaries of peace and accepted a Commission of Mediation representing the United States and the Republics adjacent to the belligerents, namely Argentina, Brazil, Chile and Peru. Bolivia held 2300 Paraguayan prisoners: Paraguay held 28,000 Bolivian prisoners, besides 10,000 civilians made prisoners on Bolivian soil occupied by the Paraguayan troops; in all above one per cent. of the total population of Bolivia. The losses in men, proportionate to the population, had been equal to that suffered by the European belligerents in the Great War.

This conflict has international import as bearing on possible methods of adjusting disputes between American nations. The Conference on Conciliation and Arbitration which happened to be assembled at Washington in 1929 (see Chapter XXXIII) probably postponed the outbreak for three years; but a Commission appointed by the Pan-American Union in 1929 failed to reconcile the disputants. Offers of mediation by neighbouring republics and a joint offer by the four powers contiguous to the belligerents were equally ineffective. Intervention by the League of Nations was withdrawn when settlement on the spot looked promising. It is probable that, but for United States action, neighbourly mediation would have failed owing to jealousies between Argentina and Brazil and also between Argentina and Chile concerning any forward move by any one of the three.

The peace terms—now in course of detailed settlement—give most of the disputed area to Paraguay, establish a demilitarized frontier zone and grant to Bolivia part of a Paraguayan river port, with access to the same through the Paraguayan Chaco.

Victory did not bring domestic peace. In February 1936 Colonel Franco, a war hero and President of the ex-combatants' Society, was exiled on the charge of communist activities—a bugbear to all South America. A fortnight later two colonels led most of the garrison of Asunción into revolt. President Ayala, with Estigarribia, took refuge on a gunboat, resigned and was arrested. Ministers and friends of the fallen Government fled to foreign legations. Colonel Franco, arriving by air from Buenos Aires, received a popular ovation as Provisional President. On 11 March he proclaimed, in the workers' interest, a Totalitarian or Fascist State. Decrees followed announcing supervision of prices, nationalization of industries, a Government monopoly of exports and State control of all social, industrial and political activities, including newspapers. Political parties were forbidden for a year, 'unless emanating from the State'.

The movement was no mere barrack revolt or personal *coup d'état*. Peasants and workers returning from the war were bitterly discontented, angry with politicians and landowners. A quotation from the Overseas Report of 1934 provides a commentary: 'Hookworm is the most common disease in all parts of the country, and will remain so until the standard of living is so high that the wearing of shoes is the rule rather than the exception. Infantile mortality is high. It is calculated that 75 per cent. of the population is beyond the reach of adequate medical attention.' To improve the lot of these brave, kindly and patient people, Franco decreed in May 1936 the expropriation of four million acres of unused land, with compensation to the owners, to be distributed in lots to 70,000 peasants.

In August 1937 Franco, who had tried to carry out a provision of the peace agreement with Bolivia which offended the patriotic pride of the army, was forced by a group of officers to resign the presidency. The military leader of this decisive stroke then handed the presidency to Dr Paiva, a professor of law, who in 1920–1 had been a Cabinet Minister and, for a few months, Vice-President of the Republic. Three weeks later an armed attempt at counter-revolution in the capital was suppressed after several hours of firing and a score of killed and wounded. Colonel Franco, who had been summoned from Buenos Aires by his friends to head this counter-movement, was carried back into exile by the same aeroplane which had brought him to Asunción.

NOTE. There is no comprehensive history of Paraguay in English. The following are valuable: J. R. Rengger and Longchamp, *The Reign of Francia* (London, 1827, a translation from the French translation of the German original); J. P. and W. P. Robertson, *Letters on Paraguay*, 2 vols. (London, 1839); G. F. Masterman, *Seven eventful years in Paraguay* (London, 1869); G. Thompson, *The War in Paraguay* (London, 1869); C. A. Washburn, *History of Paraguay*, 2 vols. (Boston, 1871).

CHAPTER XVII
CHILE

THE Republic of Chile is a narrow ribbon-like country, stretched between the Cordillera and the Pacific Ocean, in one part 250 miles wide, but through most of its length varying from 50 to 100 miles or little more; its area about two and a half times that of the British Isles, yet extending from north to south some 2660 miles, approximately 18° 15′ to 56° south latitude. Thus, if this long strip could be rolled up and then unrolled on the corresponding northern latitude, it would reach from Edinburgh almost to Timbuctoo. No other country in the world has so great a latitudinal extent or such extremes of climate, from the rainless deserts of the north to the southern forests, swept by winds from the Pacific and soaked with summer rain and winter snow. It may seem strange that a country so diverse should have resisted Iberian centrifugal tendencies and maintained unity, bound by a vigorous national sentiment; but it should be noted that, although there were scanty settlements as far north as Copiapó and as far south as Valdivia and (later) Osorno, the historical country of central Chile extended only some 500 miles from Coquimbo to Concepción, a fairly uniform region, propitious for pasture and tillage and having communication by sea as well as by land. Settlements south of the River Bio-bio were scanty and precarious owing to the struggle against the Araucanians, a stern school of national unity. Moreover from 1776, when Chile became a separate kingdom and by a fortunate amputation was deprived of the Province of Cuyo, the country had strong natural boundaries, to the north an uninhabited desert (its later mineral wealth unknown) and to the east a colossal mountain range. This physical isolation gives the country almost an insular character. Chilian policy has steadily preserved unitary government, avoiding federal tendencies; for federalism would endanger unity in a country where political divisions would cut the republic into climatic zones.

In the later nineteenth century both ends of Chilian territory received population and industry, the northern nitrate fields and the sheep-pastures of southern Patagonia and Tierra del Fuego. But both these extensions were almost in the nature of colonies, separated from central Chile by uninhabited regions, but connected with the centre by steam navigation. Chile had taken stable form before extending her habitation into the tropics and into Antarctic snows; nor had these extensions strength to stand alone. Remote from Europe, Chile has received little migration, so that her growth has been her own. The peasantry show a strain of Indian blood: but this heritage from the vigorous Araucanians, blended with Spanish ancestry, produces a stalwart population, all intensely Chilian. The Chilian aristocracy, which includes British, Irish and French names—testimony of old alliances—has always practised with distinction a culture of European type.

Chile, alone among South American countries, possesses both abundant mineral ore and native coal. The coalfield of Coronel and Lota, conveniently situated on the coast, supplies fuel by sea to the copper-producing region of Coquimbo: a complementary working of two Chilian industries.

At the epoch of independence, Chile, even more than to-day, was a country of aristocratic Creole families and great territorial magnates, every one of them almost judge and lawgiver to many dependents on his vast estate. Accordingly the early stages of independence were orderly, conducted—after Spanish traditions— by conservative aristocrats and trained lawyers. The accepted hero of independence is Bernardo O'Higgins, son of a famous Captain-General of Chile (afterwards Viceroy of Peru) and of an unmarried Chilian mother. Educated in Europe and spending three years in England, Bernardo had heard Miranda's enthusiastic utterances and admired English institutions. In 1810, aged thirty-two, he was administering his southern estates and held a militia commission; marked out for leadership by education, wealth, position and physical endowments, and later by his qualities as soldier and commander. In his visits to Concepción, the capital of the south, O'Higgins came under the influence of Martínez de Rosas, a lawyer who had been legal assessor to two Spanish Governors and now became guide and inspirer of the first movement towards independence.

In 1810 agitation, stirred by Spanish events and fanned by the Buenos Aires revolution, reached Concepción. But the centre was Santiago, where in July 1810 a cabildo abierto induced the Spanish Captain-General to resign his post into the hands of an octogenarian Creole noble. Two months later, on 18 September 1810— the date now annually observed as Independence Day—this aged Governor yielded power to a Junta of seven men, which, paying nominal allegiance to Ferdinand VII, set up in fact a republican Government by a series of revolutionary measures. Reactionary tumults were suppressed, with the execution of one leader: the Audiencia was dissolved: troops were raised: aid was sent across the Andes to the Argentines. But this first phase of independence was brief and stormy: an agitated and not strictly representative Congress, three successive Juntas, three military *pronunciamientos* headed by José Miguel Carrera; a young, handsome and popular aristocrat who in July 1811, a year after the first revolution, arrived in Santiago from Spain, where he had earned promotion as a dashing cavalry officer in fight against the French. Carrera headed the advanced radical party (*exaltados*) who were a minority in the Government: he won the devotion of the garrison and the admiration of the populace, suppressed the moderates, gave power to the *exaltados* and then, finding his efforts unrewarded, set up a brief dictatorship, aided by his two soldier brothers. Rivals were thrust aside, including the precursor Martínez de Rosas, who was banished to Mendoza and there died without witnessing the Spanish reconquest.

For this unformed and divided State, which had never ousted the royalists (many of them Chilians) from the south and was now distracted by civil strife between O'Higgins and Carrera, fell before royalist troops despatched from Peru by sea, despite outward reconciliation between the rival patriot commanders. A crowd of fugitives, following the two rivals,[1] streamed across the Andes to Mendoza; and for three years, 1814–17, Chile was once

---

[1] Carrera, though he made repeated attempts to reconquer his position, never returned to Chile. His later adventures, ended by a firing party at Mendoza seven years later (September 1821), surpass all romance. His two brothers had preceded him in violent death. Accused of sedition, they were shot at Mendoza in April 1818, three days after victory had been won at Maipú.

more a Spanish 'kingdom', ruled by a royal Governor. The first Governor, Osorio, was not excessively tyrannical; but his rigour increased; and his successor, Marcó del Pont, was a stupid and vindictive autocrat, the unconscious promoter of fresh revolution.

The popular hero of this dark triennium was the guerrillero Manuel Rodríguez, an educated man, once secretary to Carrera. Raising bands of irregulars (including brigands) he fell upon detached parties and garrisons: twice with a few followers he dashed into important posts, surprised the garrison, seized the treasury and galloped away. The Governor divided his forces in hopeless pursuit. Already a legend in his lifetime, Rodríguez would enter the barracks in disguise and mix with the soldiers, insinuating desertion. Everywhere he kept resistance alive, announcing the deliverance to come from beyond the mountains.

The passage of the Andes, invasion by San Martín, his co-operation with O'Higgins, the progress of the war and the crowning victory of Maipú have been related in Chapter VII. But already in February 1818, two months before Maipú and in the midst of reverses, the independence of Chile had been proclaimed on the first anniversary of Chacabuco in a solemn public ceremony, not by a Congress—for none was in existence—but by O'Higgins, who for a year past had been Supreme Director with unlimited powers.[1] San Martín, preferring to be the power behind the throne, leaving office to a native Chilian, had twice refused that post, offered by a cabildo abierto. O'Higgins' military dictatorship, which was necessary at first for the conduct of the war, has to its credit victory at home, the reconquest of the south by Freire, the formation of a naval squadron, police measures against brigandage, educational progress, the naval successes of the Chilian Admiral Blanco Encalada, and—most notable of all—the Argentino-Chilian expedition in 1820 for the emancipation of Peru.

O'Higgins, although he or his underlings were not entirely guiltless of innocent blood, was no terrific tyrant: indeed he had strong though ill-defined democratic views, and was almost the

---

[1] Before proclaiming independence, O'Higgins had arranged a peculiar kind of plebiscite. In every town blank books were opened, where names might be signed for or against independence. No contrary signatures appeared.

only great revolutionary leader in South America who never
favoured monarchy, other than his own. But he had not the conciliatory patience needed for guiding the young State to firm
growth. He offended the clergy by granting a cemetery to Protestants and the aristocrats by demolishing carved escutcheons:
matters which might have been left to time. On the other hand
radical discontent with personal rule was embittered by his enmity
to Carrera's friends and by suspicion that he was concerned in the
execution of the Carrera brothers and in the fate of the popular
hero Manuel Rodríguez, who had burst into Government House
at the head of armed men, had been arrested for this sedition and
—ostensibly on his way to another prison—was murdered by his
guards at the roadside. Besides, no one liked the raising of funds
for urgent financial needs. At last in 1822 the dictator yielded to
demand for reform, calling a Constituent Assembly: but he
nominated the members, believing this to be the duty of an orderly
Government. A short-lived Constitution emerged, which granted
another ten years of autocracy to O'Higgins. This did not avert the
coming change, hastened by a bad harvest—possibly also by an
earthquake. In Concepción a Junta sprang up, supported by
General Freire, commander of the garrison: his troops—who protected the country from brigands, from the Araucanian Indians
and from the southern royalist remnant—were unpaid, ill-clad and
ill-fed and were jealous of the well-treated garrison of the capital.
At last in January 1823 O'Higgins yielded authority to a Junta in a
histrionic scene. He passed his remaining nineteen years on a farm
in Peru, not far removed from poverty.

The best defence of O'Higgins' rule is Edwards' account of
what followed: 'Ten years of effervescence...unbridled constitutional orgy of a decade....During its first tempestuous decade the
adolescent Republic was destined to see a long succession of
Governing Juntas.' The first three years (1823–6) comprise the
stormy dictatorship of Freire, aged thirty-five years, a fine soldier,
but no statesman. His rule was marked by quarrels with a series of
Congresses and other bodies; by one liberal measure, the suppression of slavery; by another Constitution; and by an expedition, led
by Freire himself, which in 1826 captured the last royalist strong-

hold on the island of Chiloe. Six months later Freire retired from office but not from reappearances on the political stage. The invention of nicknames about this time marks the split of parties, the *pelucones* ('periwigs'), the old-fashioned conservatives, and the *pipiolos* ('youngsters'), the innovators.

After Freire's withdrawal a federal experiment divided the country into eight autonomous provinces: this caused hopeless rivalries of authority and was abandoned next year (1828). This phase of 'military corruption and meteoric governing juntas... civil war...anarchy and disorder' demands no more than this sentence from Edwards. It culminated in the Battle of Lircay near Talca (April 1830), where Freire, wearing the strange guise of a liberal champion, was beaten by General Prieto, leader of the conservatives and defender of the last of a rapid series of feeble Presidents in Santiago. Yet the era of feebleness and disorder was now ended: before Prieto's victory Diego Portales, hitherto known as a capable business man, but now to be known as the maker of modern Chile, entered the Ministry. Desiring no personal prominence, preferring the uncensored ease and gaiety of private life, satisfied with the ambition of 'ruling those who ruled', Portales set himself to 'purify' the administration, expelling disaffected officials or colonels and repressing disorder by imprisonment or banishment, without much regard to law, but also without the sanguinary excesses of his Argentine contemporaries. Under Prieto—who became President in 1831, inaugurating thirty years' rule by the Pelucones—Portales continued to discipline, to organize, to reform finance. He engaged the Venezuelan scholar Bello to draft a Civil Code, a task completed in twenty years' labour.

Prieto was the first of four Presidents who ruled, each for two five-year terms, thus giving to the country a long period of orderly progress; not uninterrupted, but for fifty years Chile enjoyed a rare tranquillity under the Constitution promulgated in 1833, which stood, with some modifications, for nearly a century: an oligarchical system which by a restricted franchise and other familiar methods placed power in the hands of some 500 landowning families. By controlling elections they were masters of Congress, which in turn supported and worked with the President;

who accordingly was less of a personal despot than in any other Spanish-American State but was the centre of a powerful aristocratic oligarchy to whom he owed his power. The conflicts, which thrice—in 1851, 1858 and 1891—interrupted this order, differed from the chronic or recurrent strife elsewhere. They were short, sharp and decisive. Their aims and results were clear-cut and thorough. Each was followed by an amnesty and by the firm restoration of order.

In 1836 Prieto was re-elected President; but Portales' rule, as Minister, over President and people was becoming tyrannical. General Freire, who with other Chilian refugees had found asylum in Peru, sailed thence southward on 7 July 1836 with two ships carrying Chilian exiles and Peruvian adventurers, to rouse a 'liberal' revolt in Chile. He reached the island of Chiloe on 4 August: but he failed utterly, was near being shot as a rebel and passed into permanent exile.

'While Freire was organizing in Peru his unfortunate expedition, another sailed from Valparaiso...entrusted with the task of seizing the Peruvian fleet.' So writes the Chilian Edwards, dismissing entirely the plea that the Chilian expedition, which reached Callao on 21 August, was a reprisal for Freire's adventure; a plea which the dates, here given, seem to make conceivably possible, though most improbable. On the other hand Freire's undisturbed preparations in Peru must have been known in Chile. The two Chilian warships entered Callao harbour, apparently as amicable visitors. But that night they seized three undefended and unarmed vessels, the whole navy of Peru: 'a piratical act' declared the Peruvian Foreign Minister; 'a purely precautionary measure', replied the Chilian commander Garrido (a Spaniard by birth), 'to ensure the peace of both nations.' A conference followed on board a British warship and Garrido signed a treaty. He sailed home into Valparaiso harbour with brooms hoisted in sign of having swept the sea of enemy vessels! The grievances alleged by Chile against Peru, certain financial and commercial matters, were not excessive; and as to the activities of Chilian exiles in Peru, the grievances were not all on one side. It was in fact the beginning of a 'spirited foreign policy' by Prieto and Portales. The Bolivian dictator Santa

Cruz had invaded Peru a year earlier and was now forging the Peruvian-Bolivian Confederation. The rulers of Chile were determined to thwart this possible menace to Chile, and they began by forcibly removing, in time of peace, the only obstacle to their command of the sea. They repudiated Garrido's treaty, rejected amicable offers from Santa Cruz, who, intent on his great design, was averse from foreign war: and after negotiations which were menacing rather than conciliatory, they declared war on Peru in November 1836, having resolved to destroy the Peruvian-Bolivian Confederation and the autocracy of Santa Cruz.

A domestic tragedy marred military preparations. The coming war puzzled many or most Chilians. Portales was not universally beloved. And the officers of a regiment in training at Quillota, near Valparaiso, determined to mutiny and stop the war, believing that the army would join a 'liberal' revolution. Portales, despite warnings, visited Quillota. As he was reviewing the troops, he was seized and fettered by the officers. Two days later the mutineers, taking Portales with them in his own carriage, approached Valparaiso, the army headquarters. Losing men by desertion and faced by loyal troops, they retreated at night before musketry fire. The officer in charge of Portales, angered at the failure and impatient of the encumbrance, shot his prisoner by the roadside. The crime shocked the whole people. Portales received a public funeral. His work survived: the form of government, chiefly framed by him, endured; and the war which he had planned—a less worthy title to fame—was pursued with decision.

The first expedition failed. The veteran Admiral Blanco Encalada invaded Peru with about 3000 ill-equipped Chilian troops and a Peruvian contingent, hoping for a general rising in Peru against Santa Cruz. But the people were apathetic or hostile; and Encalada, isolated and outnumbered, signed, without fighting, a treaty recognizing the Bolivian-Peruvian Confederation, thus surrendering the main object of the war (November 1837).

This capitulation angered all Chile: the treaty was disavowed and the war became a national undertaking. In July 1838 a Chilian squadron convoyed northward a fleet of transports carrying 6000 men under General Bulnes, a veteran of the Revolution and of

Araucanian war. He had a difficult diplomatic as well as military task. For Orbegoso, ruling in Lima over 'North Peru', although he hated the imperious supremacy of Santa Cruz, treated the Chilians as enemies, not liberators. However, Gamarra, past and future President of Peru, brought 2000 men to aid Bulnes. Ramón Castilla, of later fame, brought another contingent: and in January 1839 this 'United army of Restoration' defeated Santa Cruz in the sanguinary battle of Yungay. The Bolivian-Peruvian Confederation collapsed and the two countries resumed independent life.

Bulnes, the hero of Yungay—an imposing martial figure of massive countenance and head—became President in 1841, began his rule by a general political amnesty, and for ten years wielded an authority on the whole conciliatory, appointing Ministers of various complexions. It was a time of economic progress, the beginning of railway construction; of steamers from Liverpool coasting the Chilian shore; the opening of the coal-mines south of Concepción and of the copper-mines about Copiapó; advance into the region of guano and nitrate farther north (the beginning of a dispute with Bolivia); foundation of a Chilian settlement at Punta Arenas on Magellan's Strait (the beginning of a dispute with Argentina); improvement of education; growth of a vigorous Press, largely the work of Argentine exiles, fugitives from the tyranny of Rosas; arrival at Valdivia of German immigrants escaping from the European troubles of 1848, valuable workers in the development of southern Chile; some steps towards religious toleration in the interests of European immigrants.

But a modern generation was appearing, impatient of oligarchy. The firing over Parisian barricades in 1848 re-echoed in Santiago; and the approach of the 1851 election brought fusillades; many street casualties in Santiago and elsewhere; repression, imprison-ments, banishments. The official candidate, Manuel Montt, was elected. The defeated candidate led a revolt in Concepción, which was crushed by Bulnes in the battle of Loconvilla, with 3500 killed and wounded. A revolt in Serena-Coquimbo was quelled with less bloodshed. Order had been restored with characteristic Chilian thoroughness; and Montt, the first civilian President (1851–61), did his work with equal thoroughness: a man only forty-two years old but experienced in public life, a determined upholder of authority, but also a laborious public servant, a promoter of education and of public works; whose memory is honoured by his countrymen. His rule ended with another outbreak; the extreme conservative clericals, scandalized by the President's uncompromising attitude to the clergy, joined forces with the liberal opposition. Excitement over the congressional election of 1858 flamed out into civil war, complicated by a serious rising of Araucanian Indians. To end strife, the official candidate for the Presidency withdrew and a compromise candidate was peaceably elected, José Joaquín Pérez, one of Montt's Ministers, but acceptable to the opposition. It was the beginning of a new era, the end of the 'autocratic republic' (1831–61) and the beginning of the 'liberal republic' (1861–91), according to the convenient rather than strictly accurate interpretation of the Chilian historian Galdames. For there was no sharp break with the past; but a lightening of repression; the grant, almost complete, of religious toleration; and one notable change, a law forbidding presidential re-election. Thus Pérez was the last President to hold office for ten years, a decade of tranquillity and orderly material progress, only interrupted by a brief war with Spain, narrated in Chapter XXI, and by the Spanish bombardment of Valparaiso which inflicted damage of above two million sterling.

Chile's part in that war is notable. The Republic had no quarrel with Spain: but when Peru was unjustly attacked, Chile made common cause with a sister Republic against the European invader and suffered in the cause of *Americanismo*. Chilians claim that theirs is the only country which has made sacrifices and shed her blood in defence of the principles of the Monroe Doctrine.

The three civilian Presidents of the period 1871–86, years of internal peace and order despite a grave financial crisis in the 'seventies, belonged to the ruling class holding the traditions of old Chile: but they had to accept infringements of those traditions and to see presidential authority yielding to that of Parliament through modifications of the Constitution during the decade 1874–84. Abolition of clerical *fueros*, extension of religious toleration, civil marriage, wider franchise, limitation of the presidential veto were changes which followed the tendency of the age. But Congress, growing in power, did not grow in character or public esteem. The congressional elections of the 'eighties were agitated by fraud, turbulence and some bloodshed. During this period of internal peace (on the whole) and political development Chile plunged or was plunged into the War of the Pacific, sometimes called the Nitrate War, sometimes, more colloquially, the War of Ten Centavos, the greatest war which has divided Latin-American nations. Since this struggle involved three republics and concerned others, it demands a separate chapter. The victory of Chile in the war was largely due to the stability of her Government and the comparative unity and discipline of her people: it also proved the vigour of the peasantry and the strong national sentiment pervading all classes. Moreover, the victorious troops returning from the capture of Lima in 1881 were sent to suppress a serious Araucanian rising. Stern surgery healed the age-long sore of this hostile element within the Republic. To-day the surviving descendants of these valiant aborigines live at peace on reserved lands.

The territory won from Bolivia and from Peru in the War of the Pacific brought wealth to Chile and also large revenue from the export duty on nitrate. In the 'nineties sometimes 100 four-masted iron sailing-ships of three or four thousand tons lay in the roads of the Chilian port of Iquique, loading nitrate for the voyage round Cape Horn to Europe. Much also went to the United States. But reliance on one accidental source of revenue was to prove disastrous later.

Within a decade of victory in foreign war, civil strife afflicted the country. In 1886 the favour of the retiring President and a brief union of liberal groups raised to the presidency José Manuel Balmaceda, War Minister during the Pacific War, a man representing in his person the aristocratic *pelucón* tradition and in his policy the contemporary reforming movement. Ten years earlier Balmaceda as Minister had proposed a programme of electoral liberty, wider suffrage, stronger municipal and local institutions and separation of Church from State. As President, he exerted all his official influence to achieve part, at least, of these reforms, together with costly schemes of public works and popular education, attempting in vain to unite the dissident liberal groups into a reforming party. The result was a rapid succession of short-lived cabinets; friction with Congress; the appearance of a small but tumultuous 'democratic party'; a hostile majority despite official pressure in the congressional election of 1888; an attempt to rule through Ministers disliked by Congress, against the custom of the Constitution, though not, as Balmaceda insisted, against its express terms; then an attempt to designate a successor. During 1890 this liberal reformer was using dictatorial methods: espionage, muzzling of the Press, opening of letters, arrests, barbarous punishments. In October Congress adjourned, having voted supply only up to 31 December. So far, in dealing with Parliament, Balmaceda had kept the letter of the law. But now, instead of summoning Congress to ask for supply (which would have meant surrender), he decreed, at the New Year, the continuance of the previous year's budget. This was autocracy. On 7 January 1891 Captain George Montt hoisted his flag at Valparaiso as Commodore of the Fleet, which declared for Congress. Civil war had begun. It is a question which side was fighting for civil liberty and democracy. On one side was a member of a wealthy and distinguished family; a man of fine presence; a gifted orator; an aristocrat in temperament, bearing and mode of life; in office the determined upholder of a strong executive, but also an aggressive radical reformer. On the other side was an elected Congress not truly representative, split into groups and seldom producing a clear majority on any great question, but holding the power of the purse and constituting in theory the democratic element in government.

Most of the army supported Balmaceda. The congressional leaders, claiming to be a Governing Junta, embarked on the warships for the northern nitrate fields. They secured a shore base round Iquique and in the course of six months beat in detail the troops in all that region, recruited men, gathered revenue from the export duty on nitrate, and, having command of the sea, procured from abroad rifles and ammunition. For the Balmacedists, powerless at sea, could not send troops against them by land across the intervening desert. Thus practically the insurgents formed an insular maritime power: and geographically the war was between two separate territories, Tarapacá and central Chile, inaccessible to one another by land. Only by a maritime invasion of central Chile from the north could Balmaceda be ousted.

The thing was done. In August 9240 men and some field artillery were conveyed in transports from a bay near Iquique, and were landed in specially constructed flat-bottomed boats on an open beach in Quinteros Bay, twenty miles north of Valparaiso. The Balmacedists, having 32,500 troops distributed among six garrisons from Coquimbo to Valdivia, failed to concentrate enough men to demolish these few intruders. On the day after landing, the invaders forded, under heavy fire, the River Aconcagua and routed a force more numerous, but badly commanded, exposed to fire from the ships and having antiquated muskets against modern rifles. A week later another victory laid open Valparaiso. This swift campaign, remarkable in plan and execution, ended the war; for Balmaceda's cause now collapsed in Santiago. That cause, during the seven months of war, had lost ground, largely owing to his increasing tyranny. People were shocked when some youths, who had tried to raise a guerrilla band near the capital, were deliberately conveyed to the scene of their rash attempt and were there shot.

On the fall of Valparaiso, Balmaceda repaired to the Argentine Legation in Santiago. A week later, on the last day of his term as President, he turned his pistol on himself. His position had been regularized, after a fashion, by the meeting of a Congress elected under his potent influence and subservient to him: but a sham election could not save him.

European opinion viewed with merited attention this hard-fought contest; a contest of principles, not merely personal aims; a genuine conflict between an oligarchical parliamentary system and a ruler promoting democracy through autocracy, whose sincerity and public spirit, despite his later excesses, gave dignity to the crisis.

For the next five years George Montt, who had done more than any other man for the victory of Congress, was President, an honourable man, moderate and discreet, who laboured to heal the hurts of strife. Galdames calls the post-Balmaceda period 'Democratic Republic', a designation whose justice depends on interpretation of the hard-worked term 'democracy'. Ostensibly representative institutions had vanquished dictatorship: but in fact there emerged a parliamentary oligarchy less guided by dignified traditions than that of the old *pelucones*: wealth now counted for more; nitrate and copper had a greater part in public life; modes of election and parliamentary proceedings did not gain in public esteem. Yet decency and stability were still the notes of Chilian public life. Until 1924 members of Congress received no salary, and the Presidents generally observed constitutional custom by working with Congress and maintained public order. The peaceful settlement of frontier questions with Argentina strengthened that order.

As elsewhere, the early years of this century brought labour troubles, and also some measures for education and for welfare of workers. The programme, which Balmaceda had tried to push through rapidly, was in part gradually accomplished by concession to modern tendencies.

The Great War at first upset economic life and then, through the allied demand for nitrate and copper, increased both general wealth and public revenue, aided by the opening of the Panamá Canal, which halved the voyage to New York or Southampton. This temporary prosperity, the source of lavish optimism, was followed by post-war disaster; nitrate *oficinas* idle, huge stocks unsaleable; thousands unemployed; Congress discredited, perhaps not quite fairly, for failure to remedy widespread misery and dangerous social unrest.

Arturo Alessandri, a politician of advanced social views but in his past career as a Senator discreetly adaptable, was the liberal candidate in 1920. Alessandri, one of the most striking of Spanish-American personalities, had preserved, although past fifty, the aspect, vivacious vigour and physical energy of a young man; something also of the impulsive eagerness of youth. He fought the election not merely by the usual party pressure but also by a fiery campaign of popular oratory, and emerged from a doubtful conflict as President, determined on a settlement with Peru, financial reform and costly social legislation; but he was hampered by opposition in the Senate and also by general scarcity and a grave economic crisis. Chafing at his impotence, he used dictatorial and military violence in the congressional election of 1924 and so secured not, as he hoped, a satisfactory liberal majority, but a set of greedy place-hunters who promptly voted themselves a salary— at executive suggestion, it is true—a measure in itself reasonable and customary in other countries, but unfortunate in the moment of its adoption.

General discontent found a voice in the army. In September 1924 a military *coup d'état* moved the President to resign and leave the country. A Junta of three senior officers took charge, soon to be turned out by a Junta of junior officers, headed by the coming man, Major Carlos Ibañez, which invited Alessandri to return and, pending his arrival from Europe, governed dictatorially. Alessandri on his return received a popular ovation, resumed his uncompleted presidency and carried through—in a manner not quite regular but accepted by the country—a liberal reform of the Constitution, which diminished the power of the Senate, strengthened the executive, increased local government and separated Church from State by an amicable arrangement which left to the Church its property and the right to teach. But in October 1925 Alessandri, finding his War Minister Ibañez intractable, resigned again. After several experiments Ibañez, now General, emerged as dictator and three months later legalized his position outwardly by election as President.

Maintaining order by force, Ibañez strove at the same time to reform administration, to employ tried public servants, to further economy and to carry out the financial plan recommended by an American expert: in short a benevolent autocracy replacing a discredited parliamentarism. But financial disaster let loose the discontent which besets government by force; nitrate prices sank: foreign trade dropped to almost nothing. In 1931 Chile, hitherto impeccable in foreign obligations, suspended the service of the public debt, which had vastly increased since 1922. After a riot in the capital—20 killed and 200 wounded—Ibañez fled across the Andes.

An acting President took charge without disorder. After several bloodless experiments or *coups d'état*, Alessandri was elected

President in 1932. His request a year later for extraordinary powers to check socialist and communist agitation is hardly a breach of restored normality. Social welfare has since received greater attention from Government. But the abiding discontent among the *rotos*—the unflattering designation given by the upper classes to the peasants and workers—is disquieting. To save later repetition it may here be added that in February 1936 martial law was proclaimed for two months in southern Chile on account of labour troubles officially attributed to communist agitators connected with foreign organizations: a symptom and a diagnosis which trouble several other republics.

Chilian troubles during the years 1924–32 were largely due to the German invention of synthetic nitrate, which, together with production of other fertilizers, broke up the Chilian monopoly. The consequent misery and unemployment were no fault of Government, except that no scheme of pensions or insurance was in existence. But the collapse of public finance was due to the error of successive administrations which, abandoning normal systems of taxation, gathered the public revenue chiefly from export duties on one mineral product. The years of changing experiment brought little disorder or bloodshed. Chile suffered, not a series of revolutions, but a revolution—largely economic—which began in 1924 and, so far as can be seen, reached political solution in 1932. The more difficult economic solution is now in progress through a remarkable recovery, partly due to another unexpected post-war event, the rise in the price of gold, which is a Chilian product. A fractional service of the debt was resumed in January 1936 and economic advance has continued. An attempted left-wing 'popular front', numerically strong if its component groups hold together or are allowed to do so (an unlikely event), indicates how far Chile has travelled from the aristocratic parliamentary oligarchy of former days.

NOTE. Agustín Edwards, *The Dawn* (London, 1931); A. W. Hancock, *History of Chile* (Chicago, 1893); I. J. Cox, in *Argentina, Brazil and Chile* (Washington, 1935); Haring (ch. v); G. F. S. Elliot, *Chile* (London, 1907), is a good account of the country, with a chapter on history.

CHAPTER XVIII

THE TROPICAL REPUBLICS

'Democracy requires a disciplined people.'

In the Republics of the south temperate zone the aboriginal element and the (much smaller) negro element have been for the most part eliminated or absorbed; the European character has in the main prevailed, much strengthened in the River Plate by immigration. Those countries have no sharp ethnological line between classes or regions; nor, especially since the beginning of the railway age, any great internal barriers to communication. Accordingly, in spite of some recent disturbances largely due to the world-wide depression and not unparalleled in Europe, they have achieved cohesion and historical continuity. Their recent *coups d'état* were conducted with little violence, few casualties and a notable absence of immoral personal ambition. Nor do these temporary breaks in their political life impair the confidence inspired by their previous record.

But in both continents the tropical Spanish-American republics —for Brazil stands apart—present wholly different conditions. These lands are traversed by vast mountain ranges and split up into regions which seem to belong to different worlds. The mountains, ravines and woods befriend the guerrillero, the rebel-politician and the outlaw. Within a few miles, difference of height causes extreme contrasts of temperature, of environment and of character in the population. Moreover, those countries do not possess ethnological or linguistic unity. The proportions vary in different countries; but in tropical America as a whole, the pure Indians outnumber the reputed whites; in some countries the aborigines are a majority, in others half or somewhat less. For the most part they have, except recently in Mexico, no sense of citizenship and no community of feeling with their white masters; they only desire to be left alone, to be allowed to cultivate their plots of land in peace, never to see a magistrate and to avoid being swept into official or revolutionary armies. And in the Andine republics there has been no considerable European immigration, such as the Italo-Spanish influx which has transformed life in the River Plate or the European stream absorbed by southern Brazil. Since the Peruvian, García Calderón, finds in the early life of these tropical countries 'no history, properly so called...no continuity...the political comedy repeated periodically —a revolution, a dictator, a programme of national restoration', a European historian must not inflict on his readers the details of these melodramatic scenes, which only become clearly intelligible when a prominent actor, the tyrant, holds the stage for a time.

Justice dictates one observation. The men who, sometimes from humble beginnings, have pushed their way to the front as dictators, have won and maintained their dominance not merely by violence, but also by virile personal qualities, indomitable resolution and powers of leadership, firm self-confidence and (except among the submissive people of Paraguay) an intrepidity which dared those perils of revolt or assassination which beset an upstart throne. The bayonets and guards of the more unscrupulous, their spies, dungeons, tortures and terrorism would be useless without this vigorous personal strength. Most of them also— quite apart from moral qualities—have been endowed with something of those indefinable personal gifts which attract men and hold them in an almost unreasoning loyalty, sometimes shaken but always revived in presence of the leader. 'He had some quality in him which commanded respect....It was something born in the man', says Mr W. P. Burke, in the course of relating the devious courses of an aspirant for presidential autocracy and the terrorist working of that autocracy. The Norwegian anthropologist Lumholtz, no fanciful person, speaks of 'the fascination which the magnetic personality of Porfirio Díaz exercised on all who came into contact with him'. Of Santa Cruz the British Consul wrote: 'I approach this Indian with greater respect than I feel for the King of England.' There is similar testimony about other despots. Calderón eulogizes these autocrats: 'The national spirit is concentrated in the *caudillos*; absolute chieftains, beneficent tyrants. They rule by virtue of personal valour and repute and an aggressive audacity....Progress is the work of the autocracy....

The great *caudillos*...by imposing long periods of peace, favour the development of economic forces....The newly created interests sought for peace and for the internal order which favoured their own expansion.'

'The Age of Dictators' (an inaccurate phrase) varied chronologically in different republics and is not everywhere extinct to-day. But from about the mid-nineteenth century and more distinctly from the 'seventies this increase of wealth and industry, improved communications, more intercourse with foreign countries and better education favoured more peaceful conditions; and towards the end of the century lawyer-presidents (but not everywhere) were replacing the soldiers. More recently military autocracy, of a less ignoble type than formerly, has gained ground.

Mention of the territorial area of the six tropical South American republics (including Brazil) may be misleading. The vast interior of the continent—forest, plain and hill—is mostly undeveloped, unoccupied and in great part unknown: among the thickets and on the river-banks lurk many tribes of unsubdued Indians, some of them naked cannibals, always at war with one another and with all strangers. Hitherto the only paths through these wilds have been the rivers, the multitudinous upper waters of the Orinoco, the Amazon and the River Plate. About one-half of this untouched or half-touched region lies in western Brazil; the other half belongs unequally to Bolivia, Peru, Ecuador, Colombia and Venezuela. Thus the territorial area claimed by each of these republics means the area delimited by political agreement, extending far beyond the land occupied or developed. These interior wilds have been traversed here and there by explorers and by searchers for rubber or gold, and to-day the motor-car and the aeroplane penetrate their secrets. But they are destitute of cities or villages or civilized habitation, stretching far into equatorial regions beyond the reach or even the knowledge of the citizens of those several republics. Here were all the materials of difficult frontier questions: all the South American States have had such questions with all their neighbours, sometimes causing conflicts narrated in this volume. But since the mid-nineteenth century most disputes have been settled by arbitration or agreement and have thus become problems of survey, not always easy in jungle and mountains. A recent traveller, W. P. Burke, relates how a Peruvian exploring party, during one day's peregrination, crossed the Equator eight times.

THE INCA LANDS

The great territory of mountain and coast, where once the Inca emperors held sway, is divided to-day mainly between three republics, Peru, Bolivia and Ecuador, which have a general physical resemblance, although they differ in the fact that Bolivia since 1880 does not touch the sea and that the Peruvian coast is rainless, whereas the wider coastal plain of Ecuador is a typically tropical lowland of forest and swamp, traversed by winding rivers and annually soaked in the rainy season. The resemblance is also ethnological, the strata of classes mainly corresponding to racial origin. There is a large indigenous population speaking native languages, mostly Aymará in Bolivia and Quichua in Peru-Ecuador.

The Indian inhabitants of the Bolivian-Peruvian sierra live in squalid native villages, mostly in a state of semi-servitude, often having but a dubious tenure of their beloved plots of land or grazing grounds, unwashed, apathetic, more given to alcohol than to hygiene, hating all authority, regarding the republics under which they live as something alien and inimical, and depending much on the character of landlords, employers and district magistrates. Although opinion is now moving in the matter, the duty of Government to the Indians has hardly yet been seriously faced. On the bleak Bolivian highlands, where life is hardest, the Indians have occasionally risen in fierce but futile insurrections, sometimes exploited by contending 'white' politicians. Here much of the Indian land is held in common by immemorial groups of families, gradually diminishing but tenaciously defending their common lands—sometimes in miniature battles—against the encroachments of purchasers or land-grabbers, mostly *cholos*. In Ecuador, where the less lofty plateau affords kindlier soil, the Indians have a less abject lot.

The *cholos*, half-castes recognized as such, mostly bilingual, perhaps one-third of the inhabitants of these three republics, form a 'lower class'—small traders, overseers, minor officials, farmers— but distinctly above the level of the Indians. When they rise in the world, the *cholos* take to the ways of the whites or reputed whites.

These last form a leisured aristocracy of city-dwellers and land-owners: but many of those who pass for white, possessing the pleasant social culture and lively intelligence characteristic of Spanish America, have traces of Indian or, in the coastal region, of African blood. Pure white blood is rare. Whatever their complexion, the upper class in each republic, landowners, professional people, merchants, politicians, are Spanish or hispanicized in speech and mode of life.

Each of the three republics has a centralized unitary Government, which controls municipal and local authorities. A remark of James and Martin (p. 253) applies to all three republics: 'As in most of the other Latin countries, politics in Peru is in the hands of the small propertied and professional classes.' The recent startling violation of their privileged preserve by soldiers in La Paz and Lima will be told in the following chapters.

CHAPTER XIX

BOLIVIA

OF the Spanish-American Republics Bolivia is fifth in extent, more than four times greater than the British Isles. Walled off from the Pacific by the western Cordillera, the country is cut in two by another stupendous range. Eastward of this barrier lies a vast region of forest and plain, difficult of access, undeveloped and in part unexplored, stretching towards the centre of the continent, traversed in the northern part by the innumerable upper waters of the River Madeira, which flows into the Amazon. This eastern region, comprising two-thirds of the country and containing much fertile land, has but a small part of the population. The true Bolivia, one-third of the whole, is the great Andine plateau, varying in height from 10,000 to 13,000 ft. above sea-level, seamed in the northern part by deep and fertile tropical valleys, but bleak and half-desert in the loftier southern part. This table-land, once fabulously rich in silver, yields to-day a more prosaic metal, tin.

It has been told in Chapter XI how, when Bolívar left the country early in 1826, Sucre reluctantly remained as President, supported by his victorious Colombian troops. He strove to restore order in a country tossed by long war and entangled in financial confusion. But he found that the Bolivarian Constitution was unworkable and that he and his Colombian troops were regarded as alien intruders. In April 1828 Sucre was wounded and narrowly escaped assassination in a military mutiny. Peruvian troops invaded the country to expel the Colombians, and after a troubled reign of some thirty months Sucre perforce departed in August 1828.

An intrusive President was murdered after a few days, and early in 1829 the ambitious, able and energetic Santa Cruz, who had held brief authority in Peru, became President of Bolivia, to rule as dictator for eleven years. Santa Cruz, son of a Spanish father[1] and

[1] It has sometimes been said that Santa Cruz was of Indian parentage on both sides. But this is improbable. His father was a foundling, left at the door of a Spaniard named Santa Cruz, who adopted the child. It is unlikely that the Spaniard would have adopted an Indian child. Moreover, although Markham thinks otherwise, the portrait of Santa Cruz does not suggest pure Indian parentage.

of an Inca princess—an ancestry which pleased his pride—had fought for the royalists, had then served under San Martín and afterwards under Bolívar. Although intriguing and faithless in pursuit of his ambition, he was a resolute, able and laborious administrator, of unimpeachable financial integrity and a born master of men. As President of Bolivia, he suppressed turbulence, promulgated a Constitution, brought some order out of financial chaos, organized an efficient army and imposed a much-needed strong authority. Probably hoping to found a semi-Inca dynasty, he loved the decorative apparatus of imperial pomp; and to the baptism of his child he summoned the Cabinet, the Diplomatic Corps, the cabildo in full state, all civil and ecclesiastical dignitaries and a military band: the Vice-President of the Republic bore the infant in his arms and pronounced an allocution in honour of the young citizen and his illustrious progenitor.

The dictator's imperial design (apart from personal aims and dubious methods) was in itself a notable effort to overcome regionalism by uniting Bolivia and Peru. But, lest Peru should absorb Bolivia—smaller not in territory but in population and wealth—Peru was to be split into two States, North and South, each to have its President, subordinate to Santa Cruz as Protector of the triple Confederation.

Despite the weak points of this artificial hierarchy, Peruvian factions opened the way to Santa Cruz. Gamarra, Peruvian ex-dictator, flying before his successful rival Salaverry, joined Santa Cruz—only to find himself duped. For Orbegoso, *de jure* Peruvian President, also made overtures to Santa Cruz, who astutely accepted Orbegoso as his confederate or creature in Peru, without a word to Gamarra. The indignant Gamarra, on discovering the deception, turned against the Bolivian, too late. Santa Cruz, accompanied by some Peruvian adherents of the Confederation (among them General Miller, the hero of Valdivia and Junín) entered Peru in June 1835 and defeated Gamarra. Salaverry then organized resistance, but was decisively beaten in February 1836. Salaverry and other officers surrendered to Miller, upon his promise that their lives should be spared. Santa Cruz, repudiating the promise, ordered Salaverry and eight others to be shot: a senseless cruelty which horrified every Peruvian. However, conventions in North and South Peru accepted his plan and in August 1836 Santa Cruz rode into Lima as Protector of the triple Confederation.

This alarmed Argentina and Chile. Chilian action, begun in that same month, has been already told. An Argentine expedition, sent by Rosas against southern Bolivia in 1838, was defeated; but by diverting the forces of Santa Cruz, it weakened his resistance to Chile. His autocracy did not survive defeat by Bulnes in January 1839, and he disappeared into exile.

Gamarra, now President of Peru, invaded Bolivia in 1841, alleging hostile intrigues among partisans of Santa Cruz but in fact intending conquest or annexation. He was defeated and killed in the Battle of Yngavi, which finally secured Bolivian independence. Ballivián, victor in that fight, member of an aristocratic Creole family and father of a future President, ruled Bolivia for seven years (1841–8), a country afflicted by the misery and squalor which follow civil war: for these Peruvian-Bolivian conflicts had the desolating character of civil war. Ballivián, an autocrat of the more moderate and cultured type, was overthrown by military mutiny. Of the period after Santa Cruz Dawson writes: 'Bolivia...entered upon an epoch of civil war, pronunciamientos and dictatorships which lasted nearly half a century. A recital of the literally countless armed risings and of the various individuals who exercised or claimed to exercise supreme power would throw little light on the progress of the country.'

Two names merit ignominious notoriety. General Belzú, who after a year of confused struggle thrust himself into the presidency (1848–55), was supported by the army and by the half-caste mob of the city whom he flattered and fed. 'Ignorant and violent', he let 'the guerrilla bands do as they pleased. Rapine, robbery and riot became almost the normal condition of the country, while the better elements never ceased their conspiracies.' After him, ten years of frightful anarchy ended in the victory of Melgarejo (1864–71), a rude soldier of great physical strength and intrepidity, but a grotesque tyrant, an habitual drunkard, who governed by brute force and terror, fleecing his subjects, killing a rival with his own hand and crushing in blood every disturbance until at last armed revolt drove him in flight across the Peruvian frontier.

The conflicts of this confused period, 1840–80, were not quite devoid of principle or public motive. Rivalry between north and south gave Bolivia two capitals, La Paz and Sucre, down to 1906. Nor were the universal motives, liberal and conservative, wholly wanting; on the one side central government with authority in Church and State; on the other side local or 'federal' tendencies, restiveness under control whether dictatorial or ecclesiastical, desire for free press, education, toleration, a real and wider suffrage. But the bulk of the population were unlettered Indians indifferent to all these things and viewing all governments with equal apathy or dislike. Thus civic aims meant little in the conflicts of chieftains and their satellites for power, place, and control of revenue; so much so that even in 1888, during comparative peace when the worst disorders were past, the rival chiefs concluded that their programmes did not differ and agreed that one chief should become President and retire after two years in favour of his rival, who meantime was to be Vice-President. Evidently the two 'parties' had one common aim, the mastery of those two posts and of everything depending on them. The compact soon faded away.

Bolivia, deprived of her western coast by the results of the Pacific War (1879–83), confined to her inland mountains and plains, and sending her exports abroad by railways traversing Chilian or Peruvian territory, proceeded to set her house in order. General Daza (1876–80), who had seized power in the customary manner, was the last rude hard-drinking caudillo-President of the old school: and with his forcible deposition in 1880 the country entered upon a new era, interrupted indeed by disturbances and coups d'état, but far better than the earlier anarchy and tyrannies. The change was partly due to material progress, to the great increase in silver mining and the later production of tin, also in part to improved education among the cultured classes. A Constitution promulgated in 1880, less ephemeral than its nine predecessors, lasted until 1936. In 1880, although peace was not yet, Bolivia withdrew from active part in the disastrous war with Chile. Thenceforth the Doctor-Presidents outnumber the Generals, and most of the Presidents have completed their term of office. But not all. Rippy counts sixty military uprisings, ten constitutions and six murdered Presidents between 1826 and 1898. And it was by armed victory that General Pando became President in 1899, thenceforth to guide his country in the path of peace, progress and civil government.

A question with Brazil threatened to disturb the peace of the comparatively tranquil modern period. Early in the present century Brazilian rubber-gatherers made their way, unobserved at first, up the River Acre into rubber-producing forests lying within Bolivian territory but neglected by the Bolivians, being far from inhabited Bolivian regions and only accessible by way of the Amazon. President Pando succeeded in leading an expedition thither in 1902, but, after some fighting and a brief pretence that the Acre territory was an independent republic, it was agreed that Brazil should have that territory, paying an indemnity to Bolivia and constructing a railway round the Madeira cataracts. The railway was built, providing an outlet for Bolivian rubber and other products by the Amazon to the Atlantic. But, owing to the fall in the value of rubber, the result has been disappointing. The importance of the episode lies in the peaceful settlement of a territorial dispute between two republics.

Pando's progressive work was continued by his successor, Dr Montes, an able and public-spirited lawyer, who, after an interval, was President a second time. In the years 1899–1917 four presidential terms were duly completed. Yet in 1910 the Bolivian historian Arguedas scathingly denounced the hollow corruption of civic life and republican forms, the falsity of ministerial utterances and the pretence of public education. Dictatorial methods and personal conflicts were still strokes in the political game played by a small aristocracy. But a game less violent than formerly. In 1920 a 'liberal' tyrant was displaced without tumult or bloodshed. The more tranquil management of this and some minor episodes, together with the evidence of public works and improved material apparatus of life (financed by heavy borrowing in the United States) won for Bolivia a reputation as one of the more stable tropical republics. The revolt of 1930—one of the visitations of republican *coups d'état* about that time—did not shake that esteem. Discontent, the prologue to political unrest, was stirred by sinking tin prices, falling exports, idle mines with consequent unemployment, and by an attempt at remedy through larger taxation and smaller salaries. Already President Siles was disliked for a tyranny which he declared to be necessary owing to disputes with Paraguay. In 1930 he postponed the presidential election, setting up a provisional Government to perpetuate his own power. This cynical usurpation provoked a counter-stroke. A military Junta took charge, genuinely favouring reform and civil liberty; and after six months fulfilled its promise of a free presidential election. This act of restoration—to prevent a revolution, not to create one—was a novel and promising event. In January 1931 Dr Salamanca, founder of the Republican party (which might perhaps be described as the Constitutional party) was peaceably elected. 'Bolivia was the first of the South American revolutionary countries to return to constitutional government: this took place in March 1931 with the inauguration of President Salamanca.'[1]

Disaster in war blurred this hopeful promise. The fall of the Bolivian stronghold Ballivián in 1934 brought the fall of Salamanca and his party. An emergency President undertook the task of carrying on the war as long as possible and then accepting the best possible terms of peace. The war brought a grave economic shock, coinciding with a fall in value of exports during the depression. Although most Bolivians live by the soil, public prosperity and, in some degree, domestic peace, depend on the production and price of tin. The diversion of labour to war dislocated the mining industry; and many of the fighters and released prisoners, on returning home, were slow to resume their former tasks. Nor was imported labour a success in the rarefied Bolivian air.

Bolivia soon followed Paraguay in a praetorian *coup d'état*, due to unrest after the exhausting war and vexation at the 'State of War' maintained after fighting had ceased. In May 1936 a group of officers, headed by Colonel Busch—son of a German physician —dislodged the Government, proclaiming as provisional President

[1] Overseas Report, 1931.

Colonel Toro, a war hero who hastened from the Chaco by air. A 'nationalist' programme was announced, including a tax on absentees and owners of unused land; nationalization of transport; limitation of commercial profits; provision by the State of labour or maintenance for every citizen; obligatory labour for every man from eighteen to sixty years of age—in a country where *gente decente* regard manual work as degrading.

The administration was soon purged of civilians; and soldiers filled all important posts. The movement bears out the remark of an American historian that Bolivia, 'like most of South America, has her eyes turned to Europe for intellectual stimulus and social standards'.

In July 1937 Toro, returning from a health cure, found that he was no longer President and that Colonel Busch, announcing adherence to the 'principles of the revolution of May 1936', had quietly resumed authority, pending a promised election. As a step towards greater individual liberty, three civilian Ministers were appointed, the other eight portfolios being held by soldiers. The press, uncensored, applauded the change; which, like that of the previous year, was commendably tranquil. In 1938 Busch was elected 'Constitutional President'.

NOTE. There is no history of Bolivia in English. Margaret A. Marsh, *The Bankers in Bolivia* (New York, 1928), well describes the country and people. G. M. MacBride, *The Agrarian Indian Communities of the Highlands of Bolivia* (New York, 1921) is a valuable study.

CHAPTER XX

PERU

THE Republic of Peru—four times greater than the British Isles —has three distinct regions: the rainless coastal belt between mountains and sea, traversed by some fifty irrigated river valleys and having an oil-field (Lobitos) in the north; the Andine mountain-mass with its triple range and lofty plateau broken by many rocky heights; and thirdly the forest region, the *selva* or *montaña*, extending east of the Andes far into the Amazonian valley. Two railways, which surmount the western Cordillera by passes exceeding Alpine heights, link the plateau with the coast. But the *montaña* is difficult of access from the capital and the coast. Before 1913 the route for troops or for any considerable transport was to navigate the Pacific southward from Callao, traverse Magellan's Strait, sail northward by the Atlantic and ascend the Amazon to the Peruvian port of Iquitos, the limit of navigation for ocean-going ships: a voyage altogether of some 8500 miles. The opening of the Panamá Canal has shortened the voyage, providing a route by the Caribbean Sea to the Amazon mouth. Efforts are being made to link by road or rail the plateau with the navigable upper waters of the Amazonian system, and a regular air service conveys passengers and mails between west and east. But the *montaña*, though rich in rubber, has had little part in Peruvian history. The coast and the mountain have lived the real life of Peru, but not always in harmony. Arequipa in its alpine valley and Cuzco on the plateau differ from Lima and also from one another; and Arequipa has at times been a centre of resistance to the capital. There are said to be six million inhabitants; more than half being Indians of Quichua speech.

The first four heads of the State were not Peruvian born. The Creole aristocracy of the viceregal capital had done little for independence; and it is hardly strange that those who brought them independence became dictators, first San Martín and then Bolívar. Next the Bolivian Santa Cruz took charge and then the Quiteño La

Mar. The three men most prominent in Peru after 1826 had all served in the royal armies before they joined the patriots after the Spanish Revolution of 1820: a fact which reminds us that the War of Independence was a civil war and that the history of these republics is a continuation of Spanish history.

Most Peruvians regard the departure of Bolívar in September 1826 and of the Colombian troops a year later as the removal of alien tyranny. And in truth Bolívar's ways had been dictatorial. García Calderón, a Peruvian, is more dispassionate: 'The Colombian hero returned to his own country, and at once President followed President and revolution revolution. The history of the first twenty years of the republic records only the clash of the forces of society. . . . Generals and "Doctors", autocracy and anarchy, the oligarchy of the viceroyalty and the advancing democracy, all were at war among themselves.' But since Peruvians to-day remember these early chieftains with pride, their deeds call for record. A gallery of portraits would be the best history of these personal agitations; and Markham, who loves the Peruvians, writes sympathetic descriptions of the prominent actors.

Santa Cruz, the future dictator of Bolivia, had reached the rank of lieutenant-colonel in the Spanish army before he joined San Martín in 1822. Although only thirty-six years of age, he became President of the Council at Lima on Bolívar's departure: an able and energetic magistrate, he laboured effectively to improve the inchoate administration. A Constituent Congress summoned by him elected La Mar as President, and promulgated in 1828 a unitary bicameral Constitution of the normal type, which was thrice modified during the following generation but was not profoundly altered for nearly a century. After a year, in August 1827, Santa Cruz gave way to La Mar, his senior by fourteen years and a native of the Kingdom of Quito, duly elected President by a Convention. When La Mar joined San Martín in 1821, he had served twenty-seven years in the Spanish army, had taken part in the famous defence of Zaragoza, had been a prisoner in France, had escaped back to Spain by long circuitous travel, and had fought for the King in Peru during six years with the rank of brigadier.

As President of Peru in 1827 he plunged into bellicose adventures, sending Gamarra (afterwards his supplanter) to expel the Colombians from Bolivia, and himself leading an expedition to wrest Guayaquil from Colombia. He was defeated, agreed to a humiliating treaty and in June 1829 was arrested by Gamarra's men and deported to Central America. Two months later, Gamarra, a Peruvian born, who had served twelve years in the royal armies before he joined San Martín in 1821, was elected President for four years. Nothing could be more damaging than Markham's apologies for his rule. 'Gamarra loved his country; but...he knew of no way, save force, to solve a question in politics....There were arbitrary increases of taxation, citizens were exiled without trial and other acts were committed which showed a disregard for legality.' His last year of office (1833) brought tumults, a revolt at Arequipa crushed by bloodshed, agitation about the succession.

A Constituent Convention which was in session chose a rich landowner named Orbegoso, 'a tall handsome man of good reputation and noble lineage', who was duly installed on the last day of the year. The proceedings, though not quite regular, were reasonable and should have brought peace. But four days later Gamarra proclaimed as Supreme Chief Orbegoso's competitor Bermúdez, an obscure rebellious figure who passed quickly from the scene after the shedding of much blood. For the two chiefs met in battle in the heights of the western mountains. Orbegoso was defeated, and his army was saved from destruction by a dashing young cavalry officer named Salaverry, who protected the retreat. A few days later the victorious troops of Bermúdez deserted their commander, and the contending troops fell on one another's necks in brotherly embrace, both armies proclaiming Orbegoso, who re-entered Lima as President. But a fresh revolt in Arequipa called him away. In his absence the garrison of Callao Castle rose against him: Salaverry by an audacious *coup de main* dashed into the place, suppressed the mutiny, became Governor of the Castle and won the devotion of the soldiers. A month later (February 1835) the same Salaverry, hitherto the main support of Orbegoso, led out the garrison of the Castle, galloped at their head into Lima and proclaimed himself Supreme Chief of Peru, declaring that Orbegoso was as tyrannical as Gamarra.

Such was the prologue to the attempt of the Bolivian dictator Santa Cruz to dominate Peru. The moment seemed propitious, for there were two rival supreme chiefs, Salaverry in Lima and Orbegoso in Arequipa, while Gamarra was a fugitive in Bolivia, to be used by Santa Cruz and then dropped.

The adventure of Santa Cruz has been already related; Orbegoso's time-serving agreement with Santa Cruz; the Bolivian invasion of Peru, aided by many Peruvians; the Confederation of Bolivia with North and South Peru; the armed intervention of Chile and the overthrow of the dictator and his confederation.

Salaverry, a Basque born in Lima, joined San Martín in 1820, being then an impulsive schoolboy of barely fifteen years. He served in nearly every action of the war and afterwards in La Mar's invasion of Quito. He was now a handsome black-whiskered cavalry officer of commanding stature, six feet two inches, in a land not of tall men; an inspiriting leader of engaging manners and dashing courage. Disgusted with civil strife, he protested in writing against Gamarra's tyranny, was arrested in March 1833 and deported to the remote Amazonian north-eastern region. There he was soon drilling Indian troops on his own account, but was arrested and brought to Cajamarca. Here the garrison of the place joined him and he marched to Trujillo, fought a sanguinary battle against the officer sent to arrest him, was defeated, escaped, was arrested again, escaped a third time and (although by Gamarra's order a proscribed outlaw, to be shot wherever found) he re-entered Trujillo at the head of troops which had joined him. Thence he marched to serve President Orbegoso against the rebel Bermúdez, and, as already related, saved from destruction the President's defeated army. Then—after yet another gallant act at Callao Castle—he turned against Orbegoso and, at the age of twenty-nine declared himself dictator of Peru.

Salaverry's romantic career and tragic end—shot by Santa Cruz —perhaps partly account for Markham's surprising appreciation: 'Among the best examples of gallantry and patriotic devotion, impelled by high and lofty aspirations and generous thoughts, Peru will always cherish the honoured name of Salaverry.' Elsewhere he writes: 'He was overpowered by personal ambition. He knew what was right, but his life was a series of actions against his better judgment. His career explains the history of his country for twenty years after independence. It was a nation of Salaverrys.' This passage is the most damaging indictment which could be framed of Salaverry and his contemporaries.

The fall of Santa Cruz in 1839 brought no peace. Gamarra became Provisional President with the title of 'Restorer'. Having suppressed an insurgent caudillo named Vivanco, self-styled 'Regenerator', Gamarra declared war on Bolivia, invaded that country and was killed in the Battle of Yngavi (November 1841) at the age of fifty-six. Four years later Congress declared Gamarra *benemérito de la patria*, and in 1849 his bones were conveyed home and a monument set up to his memory.

Menéndez, President of the Council, now legally became President. But the generals would have none of him: they 'took', Markham quaintly says, 'a most erroneous view of their duties'. Confused civil war flamed out everywhere. Three rival heads of the State appeared, and the 'Regenerator' Vivanco emerged on top. His reign was brief; for the true regenerator of Peru now appeared upon the scene, 'a little quiet, rough, unpretentious soldier', named Ramón Castilla, 'who for twenty years had been modestly doing his duty': a small, spare, wiry man of iron frame; downright, resolute and honest both in character and in his rugged humorous countenance; a characteristically Latin type in spite of an Indian grandmother. Nearing fifty years, he had seen many campaigns and as Governor of his native Department of Tarapacá had acquired political experience.

A Peruvian by birth, Castilla had joined the royal army in Chile at the age of fifteen, was taken prisoner after the patriot victory of Chacabuco and sent to Buenos Aires. He was released and, after many adventures by sea and land, joined San Martín in 1821, was twice wounded at Ayacucho, commanded the Peruvian cavalry who fought against Santa Cruz at Yungay, was taken prisoner at Yngavi, and returned from Bolivian captivity to find Peru torn in pieces by contending generals, the rebel Vivanco for the moment supreme and Menéndez, the legal President, a fugitive. Castilla, hating civil strife and defending law where he could find it, determined to restore Menéndez to his lawful place: he landed at Arica with five men, was twice fired upon, increased his numbers to fifty, then to 200 and added, by a ruse, a hostile force to his own. Vivanco, deserted by one chief after another, was beaten in battle by Castilla and fled to Chile (July 1844). A general amnesty was proclaimed. Menéndez, restored to his office, summoned a Congress which in April 1845 elected Castilla President of Peru for six years. They were years of beneficent administration and honourable autocracy, of a peace and security desired by all except a few disappointed adventurers, and years also of economic progress, material prosperity and financial regeneration.

This last work, seemingly hopeless at first, was made possible by a strange and exceptional gift of nature. Countless millions of sea-birds nest and hatch their young on the desert islands and rocks of the Peruvian coast, feeding on the marine life carried northward by the cold Antarctic current which refreshes all these shores. In the course of ages huge accumulations of guano or bird manure were thus piled up in the rainless air. On three small islands in Pisco Bay, the Chincha islands, the deposits were fifty feet deep and exceeded twelve million tons. The Lobos islands, farther north, were heaped up with other millions. These were the principal but not the only accumulations; for along the desert shore stretching to the southern limits of Peru and beyond, every islet and every rock unapproached by man had its colony of cormorants and gulls and some deposit of guano. The use of this manure had been known to the Incas. Indeed, the word *guano* or *huano* is Quichua. But local use was no more than a small toll on the annual addition, and the island deposits went on mounting, until, in the early eighteen-forties, through increased oceanic communication and the growing needs of Europe, this fertilizer, gathered from the desert, became a valuable commodity of international trade. Since the islands were no man's property, the guano belonged to the Peruvian Republic; and the State, without expense, sold the guano (which needed only the labour of Chinese coolies with spade and shovel) to foreign merchants and shippers. About the same time a Frenchman named Cochet (who gained nothing by his discovery) made known that in southern Peru the sterile desert might yield another fertilizer from the thick hard crust of nitrate of soda, inexhaustible in quantity, which lay in patches here and there beneath the surface. Since blasting, crushing and treatment in factories were necessary, the State did not work these deposits, but granted concessions, chiefly to foreigners, and levied export duties which yielded large revenue. The inland oasis of Tarapacá became a populous place; a port was created at Iquique: and in the early 'forties the annual export of nitrate exceeded a million tons. Through these two sources of revenue, which took the place of almost all normal taxation except import dues, Castilla funded the arrears of interest on the external debt, consolidated the internal debt, excluding all creditor claims after a fixed date, constructed public works, improved the navy and liberally satisfied the naval and military services. In the rapid exploitation of these opportunities there was much overspending and improvidence. Castilla, a fine soldier, an honest man, an efficient administrator, had not the rare virtues of the trained economist: nor did matters depend on him alone. But the country owed much to his financial work.

Under Castilla's successor, Echeñique, peace lasted three years: but the allurements of nitrate and guano were too much for official honesty. Extravagance, corruption, concessions, extension of the time-limit for claims on the Treasury in order to admit fraudulent claims from Ministers or their friends: these things aroused scandal, discontent and finally open revolt. After long reluctance Castilla joined the revolt, which found a centre in Arequipa. For a whole year, 1854, Peru was in a state of disruption and for six months in a state of active civil war, until in January 1855 Castilla marched victorious into Lima. Six months later he initiated his second term as President (1855–61), a period of honest administration and also of peace, with one serious interruption: for in December 1856 the former 'Regenerator' headed a revolt in Arequipa. The fleet mutinied and joined the revolt, which lasted for fifteen months and was only suppressed after serious street fighting. The revolt was local; the mutinous fleet resumed allegiance, and in 1862 Castilla retired from office, having given his country nearly twenty years of comparative peace and prosperity after twenty years of turbulence.

The succeeding President died after six months, and the Vice-President, Pezet, an old soldier of the War of Independence, hastening back from Europe, assumed office in August 1863, to find himself at once involved in a dispute with Spain; a matter which demands preliminary exposition.

A dozen years earlier a Spanish frigate, cruising round the world, entered the harbour of Callao, and, although Spain had not yet acknowledged Peruvian independence, the courtesies customary between sovereign nations were observed, exchange of saluting salvoes and of official visits. A year later (1851), after some informal indications of amity, a Peruvian envoy named Osma was sent to Madrid to negotiate a treaty of recognition, was cordially received and in September 1853 signed a Treaty of recognition, peace and amity. But the Peruvian Government, disliking certain clauses, refused to ratify it. Osma remained in Madrid without communicating this refusal to the Spanish Government. That Government, accustomed to dilatory ways both at home and in the daughter lands, thought little of the delay; and in 1855 a Peruvian consul in Madrid and a Spanish consul in Lima received the *exequatur* from their respective Governments.

In 1862 a Spanish squadron under Admiral Pinzón sailed from Cadiz for the Pacific; at an unlucky moment, for the Spanish expedition to Mexico and the reincorporation of Santo Domingo in the Spanish Empire had roused apprehension throughout Spanish America; moreover Peru had lately refused the *exequatur* to a Spanish consul as not being *persona grata*. Thus relations were not quite happy when the Spanish squadron reached Callao in July 1863. A month later a group of Basque emigrants employed on a Peruvian cotton estate protested against their treatment. The estate manager, alleging a mutiny, assembled an armed party and fired on the Spaniards, killing one and wounding four. The assailants were acquitted except two, who were condemned to four months' imprisonment.

Admiral Pinzón, disobeying an order to sail for Cuba, sent home an account of the event by one Salazar, a Spanish ex-M.P., who happened to be with him. Salazar, an indiscreet person, returned to Peru with the strange title of 'Special Extraordinary Commissary', charged by the Spanish Government to demand justice. The Peruvian Government refused to receive him in that capacity, but offered to receive him as 'confidential agent' of the Spanish Crown. Thereupon Salazar persuaded Pinzón to seize the Chincha Islands, rich in guano, declaring that this was an act of 'revindication', since Spain had not acknowledged Peruvian independence. The diplomatic corps in Lima, after several Ministers, including those of the United States and of Great Britain, had protested against this doctrine of 'revindication', sent a commission consisting of the envoys of Chile, France and Great Britain, to request that the islands should be evacuated and should remain in charge of the diplomatic corps until the question should be settled. Pinzón refused the request, thus increasing the indignation in Lima.

Salazar now returned to Madrid, telling an imaginative story of insults and injuries. The Spanish Government, hastily accepting his improbable tale, sent to Lima a list of arrogant demands, and although disapproving the seizure of the islands, ordered Admiral Pinzón not to give them up. A Spanish-American Congress, representing seven republics, which had assembled at the invitation of the Peruvian Government, sent a note to Pinzón affirming their amity for Spain, but declaring that the occupation of the islands affected the rights of the whole continent, and that Peru was ready to consider any just claims as soon as her territory should be restored to her. Meantime Pinzón, since his action had been disapproved, had surrendered the command to Admiral Pareja; and this communication, interesting as a manifestation of *americano* sentiment, had no result.

The Peruvian Government having rejected the Spanish demands, Admiral Pareja, obeying orders from Madrid, sailed into the harbour of Callao and demanded satisfaction within forty-eight hours. President Pezet thought resistance impossible, and on 27 January 1865 preliminaries of peace were signed; salutes and visits were exchanged; the islands were restored, Peru paid an indemnity, and Pareja departed to chastise Chile, which had made common cause with Peru.

The Chilians having refused his demands, Pareja declared a blockade of Chilian ports: thereupon Chile declared war on Spain

(September 1865) and two months later the Chilian steamer *Esmeralda* captured the Spanish gunboat *Covadonga*. Pareja, upon this disaster, committed suicide. In December Chile signed an alliance with Peru. Three months later (March 1866) Commodore Méndez Núñez, successor to Pareja, bombarded the defenceless town of Valparaiso, inflicting damage of above two million pounds. After this senseless revenge he departed to attack Callao.

The peace preliminaries accepted by Pezet had caused violent indignation in Lima, where it became known that Pareja in demanding an indemnity had exceeded his instructions. President Pezet, to avoid civil war, retired before a revolt headed by Prado, Governor of Arequipa. Prado, as Provisional President, repudiated the preliminaries, recalled from Madrid the Peruvian negotiator for a definitive peace, and in January 1866 declared war on Spain. Bolivia and Ecuador also declared war. In April 1866 Méndez Núñez passed from the bombardment of the open town of Valparaiso to that of the fortifications, recently strengthened, of Callao.

In a five hours' action the fleet suffered much damage and lost about 200 men. The shore defences lost 2000 and were almost silenced. The Spanish fleet, unable to maintain itself in the Pacific, then sailed home and active hostilities ceased, though the war of cabinets continued five years longer until 1871, when an armistice was concluded. But it was not until 1879 that Spain concluded definitive treaties of peace with the four republics which had declared war. Thus in 1879 Spain accorded formal recognition to the Republic of Peru. Spain had previously recognized the Republics of Ecuador in 1840, of Chile in 1844 and of Bolivia in 1847.

Prado, who had risen to power by a *pronunciamiento*, was overthrown by another led by General Balta, who, after a brief interval, became Constitutional President in 1872. Balta opened a new era, apparently brilliant, in fact disastrous, plunging into gigantic schemes of public works, railways constructed at enormous cost (which were expected to put an end to revolutions), harbour works, steamers on the Amazon and its affluents, embellishment of the capital, a national exhibition, an expanded civil service and, to pay for it all, huge loans which multiplied the public debt tenfold. As always in such cases, a wave of wild speculation, fortune-hunting and intrigue followed public extravagance. Balta at the end of his term was murdered in a mutiny of no political significance. His successor, Pardo, the first civilian President and generally esteemed the best of the Peruvian presidents, was already known as an upright and able Minister, particularly in the department of finance. 'His intellectual and moral force', says Dawson, 'gathered about him the educated and property-holding classes.' He thus became the founder of the 'civil' party, opposed to military methods, advocating gradual and cautious reform, and generally supported by lawyers and business men, a party which has since been a steadying influence in Peruvian politics and has provided most of the presidents, including Pardo's son, who twice held that office, with general esteem, in the twentieth century (1904–8 and 1914–19). Pardo strove to introduce economy, to promote education, to amend the administration and to ensure justice for all, including the immigrant Chinese labourers. But his struggle against bankruptcy, the legacy of previous extravagance, was unavailing. A revolutionary outbreak, headed by the turbulent and ambitious Piérola, Minister of Finance in the recent administration, although it was easily suppressed, did not conduce to economy. The price of guano, the basis of Balta's extravagant schemes, fell, and the deposits had already been much reduced by careless exploitation. In 1875 Pardo, apparently influenced in part by interested advice, attempted a remedy: he declared nitrate to be a Government monopoly, and bought out the owners of the nitrate works, paying them in Government bonds. This measure eventually proved disastrous and is said to have been a contributory cause of the Chilian war. But in any case no immediate benefit from it was possible. The service of the debt was suspended in 1876, in which year the civilian Pardo was succeeded by General Prado, President a second time.

Prado undertook a critical task, for the dispute with Chile was imminent: yet Piérola chose this moment for a second harebrained sedition: his followers seized by a ruse the ironclad *Huascar*, which fought the rest of the squadron for two hours, was declared a pirate by President Prado, exchanged shots with a British warship and finally surrendered, with Piérola on board. It is significant of the prevalent political spirit that this criminal and violent treason of an ex-Minister, who knew the need of unity to meet coming danger, was not treated very seriously, and Piérola was allowed to return to Chile.

A separate chapter is given to the War of the Pacific, the heroism of the Peruvian resistance and its failure. The war brought strange internal dissensions. In December 1879, in the midst of disaster, the soldier-President Prado sailed for Europe, 'to raise a loan and buy ironclads', handing over his post to the Vice-President. The troops in Lima mutinied. The populace declared revolution; Piérola, returning from exile, headed the movement and became 'Supreme Chief of the Republic'. Fourteen months later, when Lima fell, Piérola, unable to organize further resistance, resigned and departed for Europe. The attempt to form a Government in Lima during the Chilian occupation collapsed. A Peruvian Congress then met at Arequipa; but the only real authority was that of two rival generals, Cáceres, who still held out in the southern highlands, and Iglesias in the north. Iglesias at last abandoned futile resistance. His rival Cáceres, stubbornly fighting, was defeated by Chilian troops. Iglesias then declared himself President. He was recognized as ruler of Peru by Chile and, endowed with this irregular authority, negotiated the Treaty of Ancón, signed in October 1883.

On the departure of the Chilians in March 1884, Cáceres attacked Iglesias: after eighteen months of civil war, he captured Lima, and as President (1886-90) entered upon the 'dreary task of reorganizing Peru. The treasury was empty, the population had been decimated by a horribly destructive war during four years, the flourishing coast valleys with their cotton and sugar plantations had been laid under contribution, the mines had ceased to be worked, the guano and nitrate revenue was gone, the country was weighed down with a debt which could never be paid.'

In the last year of Cáceres' term, a notable contract was signed which relieved the country of the external debt, the bond-holders (now formed into the Peruvian Corporation[1]) taking in exchange a

[1] The ordinary stock of the Peruvian Corporation, amounting to nine millions sterling, is now worth about 30s. per £100 nominal. The Preference Stock (seven millions and a half) is worth about £7 per £100.

sixty-year lease of the railways built with their money and undertaking to restore them from their ruinous condition and extend
them, receiving a money payment for thirty-three years and a large
quantity of guano. The Government further reduced its obligations
by a less reputable transaction, enforcing payments in coin and thus
repudiating—to the ruin of many Peruvians—the paper money
issued during the war.

The Peruvian historian, Carlos Wiesse, gravely records that 'the
four years of Cáceres' presidency passed without armed revolutions'. He was succeeded by a friend and fellow-soldier, who died
in 1894. Thereupon Cáceres by customary methods procured his
own re-election. But the glamour, which had surrounded his person
as champion against the invader, faded away when men saw the
highest office in the State treated as a thing to be enjoyed by him
and his friends, while humbler civil servants went unpaid. Guerrilla
bands appeared in the mountains. The restless Piérola, returning
from Chile, put himself at their head, suffered several reverses but
always recovered and finally entered Lima in March 1895. Cáceres'
enemies in the capital joined the insurgents, and for two days
barricade fighting went on in the streets with much carnage.
Gradually losing ground, the stubborn Cáceres at last yielded to
the representations of the foreign Ministers: a provisional Government was formed, and Piérola emerged as President (1896–1900)
by a really popular vote. For this restless caudillo, whose unruly
ambition had twice shed his countrymen's blood in rash insurrections, was the most popular of presidents. His handsome, good-
humoured countenance, his attractive manners, dashing courage,
romantic history and success in that guerrilla warfare which the
people understood, won him general applause. Nor was the
popular intuition at fault. Sobered by age and responsibility,
Piérola proved an excellent administrator, reconciler of parties,
preserver of order, promoter of economic progress; and he quietly
delivered his power into the hands of his constitutional successor,
who was elected without opposition through an agreement between
parties. The same agreement produced a list of parliamentary
candidates, unopposed and all duly returned. This period of internal
peace and of material progress—the revenue doubled in the five

years 1895–1900—continued unbroken under presidents of the 'civil' party down to 1908. At the approach of the presidential election of that year an opposition group of liberals and democrats rose in revolt. The revolt was suppressed in a week (1–8 May) by the prompt measures of an organized Government, and the 'civil' candidate became President, Augusto Leguía, a resolute and able man of forty-four years, who announced a programme of moderate liberalism. Eight months later (May 1909) a revolutionary group burst into the palace, seized the President, a small frail man weighing about seven stone, dragged him through the streets and demanded his signature to an order placing the garrison at their disposal. The President, roughly handled and his clothes torn, stoutly refused. The troops came to his rescue and, though men were falling round him, he escaped, and three years later handed over office to his successor, Billinghurst, one of the conspirators of 1909, and soon afterwards retired to a comfortable exile in London. Billinghurst's dictatorial methods, together with dissatisfaction over his treatment of the scandal of Indian slavery in the Putumayo rubber district, provoked a revolt headed by Colonel Oscar Benavides, a soldier who had received part of his training in France; and after a short *interinato* the moderate and conciliatory Pardo emerged as President a second time to serve for a term (1914–19), disturbed by some labour troubles but generally prosperous owing to the high value of exports during the Great War.

In July 1919 Leguía, now returned from England, unseated Pardo and seized power by a minor and probably unnecessary *coup d'état*, a month before his legal election, to initiate an imperious and arrogant dictatorship of eleven years, thinly disguised by the form of three re-elections. Like other autocrats, he proclaimed a liberal Constitution, and—at all events in outward form—pursued a programme of nationalist liberalism: social reform, improvement in the condition of peasants and workers, abolition of Indian peonage,[1] nominal raising of the Indians to citizenship (a movement

---

[1] Peonage, a form of serfdom, had been abolished by law, but not in fact, in 1915. Nor were Leguía's enactments in favour of the Indians observed even by the dictator himself. But they are indicative of an interesting movement, carried out more effectively in Mexico.

symbolized by the institution of an 'aborigines day' annually celebrated with joyous ceremonies), and a large measure of local government. At the same time, relying on the brief and delusive post-war prosperity, he promoted vast schemes of public works: irrigation, highways, railways; financed partly by increased taxation, but chiefly by huge borrowing, mainly in the United States. Already a despot, an abortive revolt in 1922 and an attempt to assassinate him in 1923 provoked him to cruel tyranny, imprisonments, exiles, summary executions, torture, muzzling of the Press, closing of the University under the name of reorganization. Leguía's wise and truly patriotic action in accepting the settlement with Chile and surrendering the claim to Arica brought him undeserved odium. His recognition of the Colombian claim to Leticia, a small port on the Amazon, and to the district behind it pricked the touchy pride which is always ready to effervesce in any Latin-American republic; and the President was regarded as a betrayer of the nation's interests and the national dignity. His cordial friendship for the United States and his lavish acceptance of American capital alarmed nationalist apprehensions. His strong favour to the established Church and intimate relations with the Vatican, although they secured valuable support by the clergy, did not win universal approval.

Discontent gathered. The liberal enactments, duly legalized by a packed Congress, were illusory; for the will of the dictator and his nominees overrode everything. Taxation was heavy. The national debt swelled alarmingly. Besides public extravagance, the dictator was suspected of corruption and misuse of public money. His autocracy, already intolerable, was shaken by the economic crisis of 1930, by a fall in the value of exports, diminution of revenue, failure to raise a foreign loan, and a budgetary dispute with Congress. Leguía was ageing and unwell. Colonel Sánchez Cerro, a leader of the old caudillo type, revolted in Arequipa and found popular favour. In August 1930 Leguía resigned and tried to escape to England. He was pursued by a warship, brought back and imprisoned on an island in Callao harbour. After long investigation he and his sons were ordered to pay or repay to the Treasury above a million and a half sterling. He lingered in confinement, wretchedly ill, for eighteen months, tended by his son, but lacking all comforts, until in February 1932 he was taken to hospital, too late to save his life.

After a stormy experimental year, Cerro became President at the end of 1931, to undertake a bewildering task, all the more so because a *cholo* (for such he was) on the presidential throne was to many an outrageous offence. Unrest was general, and radicalism took form in the association known as *Apra (Alianza popular revolucionaria americana)*. As the last word indicates, the movement was meant to include all Spanish America, forming a united international front of manual and intellectual workers, with the aim of real democracy and social justice for the Indian. *Apra* found many active adherents in Peru but few or none (except in sentiment) outside Peru. An *aprista* revolt at Trujillo in July 1932 was put down, after much bloodshed, by aeroplanes sent from Lima.[1] An international difficulty arose from the filibustering adventure of a few Peruvian civilians from Iquitos, who seized the Colombian port of Leticia in defiance of the late President's recognition of Colombian possession. Sánchez Cerro, instead of disallowing this unauthorized aggression, yielded to a quasi-patriotic popular outcry and kept Leticia. In September 1932 hostilities broke out, fortunately confined in the main to the region under dispute. In April 1933 Sánchez Cerro was murdered and the presidency passed to General Benavides, who had overthrown the incipient dictatorship of Billinghurst in 1914 and had afterwards carried out with distinction a military mission in France. 'Benavides made it one of his first acts to bring about a truce with Colombia. The new President followed up his successful efforts in the international field by selecting a cabinet of moderate responsible men of good standing who restored internal calm and inspired general confidence.' (Overseas Report, 1934.)

Furthermore, the new Government accepted the suggestions of the League of Nations; and in May 1934 a settlement of the Leticia dispute was accepted by both countries at a conference held in Rio de Janeiro.

---

[1] In recent years the aeroplane has proved an efficacious police weapon in the hands of authority in other republics also.

In the presidential election of October 1936, when after three days' counting (uncompleted) it was clear that the radical candidate would have a big majority, the Cabinet resigned and Congress annulled the election on the ground, tardily but conveniently discovered, that the support given him by *Apra*, an international association, was illegal. Congress then granted to Benavides unrestricted powers for three additional years. Protesting strikers and left-wing agitators were quickly suppressed. All the leading *apristas*, including many of the most distinguished men in the country, fled into hiding or into exile. The omnipotent President, with six soldiers and two naval captains as Ministers (replaced in November 1937 by a Cabinet, half military, half civilian), evidently resolved to 'dish the radicals' by dictatorially giving to the people what is good for them. He announced a programme of social improvement, housing, sanitation, insurance and limitation of hours for workers; popular education; a Council charged with the interest of the Indians—apparently at last an object of real solicitude to Government. The working and the results of the recent military Paraguayan, Bolivian and Peruvian autocracies—of a novel kind in America—cannot yet be judged. In Peru the oligarchical and propertied political elements appear to have accepted or been obliged to accept autocracy as preferable to radical victory. In Bolivia and Paraguay the soldiers, proclaiming a popular cause, swept aside the politicians.

Since in these countries, perhaps even more than elsewhere, political and social well-being depend on economic conditions, another sentence may be quoted from the same Overseas Report: 'Peru is indeed fortunate in the diversity of her agricultural products, not only because she is capable of growing almost everything which she requires for her own needs, but also on account of steady demand for her main agricultural exports of cotton, sugar and wool.' Copper and silver from Cerro de Pasco and other parts of the Sierra still maintain the secular reputation of the Andes for mineral wealth: and the agitated story of guano has had a happy ending. Shocked at the careless waste of this national asset, a voluntary association undertook, early in the present century, the task of preserving it. The Government accepted and continued their work: and to-day trustworthy guards are in charge of the islands to prevent any trespass or depredation, including the occasional raids of condors on the eggs. And the sale of guano, regulated in accordance with the annual deposit, brings in a steady revenue.

NOTE. C. R. Markham, *History of Peru* (Chicago, 1892).

CHAPTER XXI

THE WAR OF THE PACIFIC

THE Chilian Constitution of 1833 begins thus: 'The territory of Chile extends from the desert of Atacama to Cape Horn.'[1] This phrase does not define the northern limit towards Bolivia, the word 'desert'—an empty thing, useless to any one—apparently sufficing. Yet in the eighteenth century Spanish authority had fixed the Rio Salado (in latitude 26° 20′) as the boundary between Chile and the jurisdiction of the Audiencia of Charcas, which Bolivia claims to inherit. A whale's jaw-bone, set upright in the ground, at a place called Hueso Parado ('the Vertical Bone') near the river mouth, marked the frontier. Then in 1801 some Chilian fishermen settled at El Paposo in latitude 25° and were placed under Chilian jurisdiction. Thus Chile, by the *uti possidetis* of 1810, had a reasonable claim as far as El Paposo, but no farther. The fact that Spanish geographers mistakenly gave the latitude of El Paposo as 24° makes no difference. The place itself was the division. But the division was in a desert. The most northerly Chilian town was Copiapó, and at the time of independence habitation extended little beyond that town. But about 1840 the discovery of copper beyond Copiapó—to-day one of the richest copper-producing regions in the world—drew Chilian enterprise northwards. Then came knowledge of the value of guano and then the working of nitrate in the Peruvian Department of Tarapacá, in which some Chilians took part and learnt that rich deposits of nitrate and much guano lay south of the Peruvian frontier. Chilians were soon at work extracting nitrate northwards of the Upright Bone; and President Bulnes, vanquisher of the Bolivian dictator Santa Cruz, declared in 1842 that the northern limit of Chile was 23°. Bolivia protested and Bulnes in reply argued that, just as a frontier between countries is traced along the middle of a dividing river, so also, where a desert inter-

[1] Markham's statement (p. 184) that the laws of the Indies place the boundary at El Paposo is an error. The law which he cites merely says that the district of the Audiencia of Charcas is bounded on the south by that of the Audiencia of Chile, but says nothing about the frontier.

venes, the frontier should divide the desert, giving half to each country. The Bolivians disagreed, and for nearly fourteen years the Bolivian claim north of Paposo was not effectively disputed by Chile, although there were occasional Chilian encroachments, some clashes between Chilians and the Bolivian authorities at Cobija, and an intermittent diplomatic correspondence. During those years enterprising foreigners worked the nitrate with concessions from the Bolivian Government. The labourers were mostly Chilian and the seat of the business was Valparaiso.

At last in 1857 the Chilian Government dealt a sudden blow; they took possession of the Bay of Mejillones, the best anchorage on a harbourless coast, lying a little south of 23° and not far south of Cobija, the place chosen by Bolívar in 1826 to be the Pacific port of Bolivia, developed as such in some degree by Santa Cruz and containing a Bolivian custom-house and political authorities. Protests against the seizure from Bolivia, torn by civil war and doing nothing to work the nitrate, were vain. Chile kept Mejillones. In 1863 war was imminent. Chile declined in turn mediation offered first by Peru and then by the United States. The conflict was postponed by the dispute between Spain and Peru, in which Chile and Bolivia made common cause with Peru against the invader.

After the departure of the Spanish fleet in 1866 Chile and Bolivia concluded a 'Treaty of Mutual Benefits', which provided that the dividing line should be 24°, but that for one degree on either side of this line, that is to say between 23° and 25° Chile and Bolivia should divide the customs.[1] Chile duly paid to Bolivia thenceforth half the customs collected by her between 24° and 25°; but Bolivia, torn by disorder and despising accountancy, did not pay the half due from her between 23° and 24°. Not long afterwards, nitrate having been found in Bolivian territory near Anto-

[1] The Bolivian Foreign Minister, Muñoz, who negotiated this treaty, afterwards declared that during the conferences Chile offered to 'aid Bolivia to acquire by armed occupation' Tacna and Arica 'as compensation for the cession of the Bolivian littoral to Chile' on the ground that the port of Arica is the only natural outlet of Bolivia to the Pacific. Whether or not the Chilian proposal amounted to an offer of aid in a war of conquest, it is certain that some such secret proposal was made and that it became known to the Peruvian Government before long. Peru was to be robbed in order to repay Bolivia for her cession of territory to Chile.

fagasta, a Chilian company, aided by British capital, was permitted by Bolivia to work this nitrate. The workmen were mostly Chilians; and in the desert there sprang up a port at Antofagasta, nitrate factories in the neighbourhood and a mining camp which grew into a town of 5000 people at the silver mines discovered farther inland at Caracoles: all created by Chilian enterprise and labour, to their own profit and that of Bolivia also. A French visitor to the country humorously remarked that out of a score of people about Antofagasta there were seventeen Chilians, one Peruvian, one Englishman and one Bolivian colonel.

Thus the Chilian economic hold on the Bolivian littoral strengthened year by year. But the awkward dual arrangement caused much friction. Then in 1871 came a sudden stir, when a filibustering expedition of Bolivian exiles sailed from Valparaiso and attempted to seize Antofagasta—with the connivance of the Chilian authorities, according to Bolivia, an accusation strenuously denied by Chile. The incident aroused alarm in Peru, which was intensified when in the same year Chile ordered the construction of two cruisers in England.

Chilian-Bolivian attempts to amend the unsatisfactory treaty of 1866 came to nothing. But in 1873 Bolivia granted to the Antofagasta Company a fresh concession, undertaking not to increase the export duty on nitrate for fifteen years, on condition that the Company should make certain improvements at Antofagasta and Caracoles, improvements which were fully carried out. Two years later (1875) Chile and Bolivia agreed by treaty that the non-increase of duty should be extended to twenty years; and Chile cancelled her claim, both past and future, to half the export duty.

Meantime Peru had become uneasy at this Chilian peaceful penetration northwards, all the more because enterprising Chilians were also concerned in the Peruvian nitrate fields of Tarapacá: and in 1873 Peru and Bolivia concluded a 'secret' treaty of defensive alliance, each Government undertaking to defend the other against aggression but reserving the right to define aggression. This treaty was part of a scheme to induce Argentina (which had frontier disputes with Chile) to join Bolivia and Peru in a triple alliance of Chile's three neighbours. Overtures from Peru were favourably considered and publicly discussed in Buenos Aires, thus becoming known in Chile; but they led to nothing: and Argentina adjusted her disputes with Chile separately.

Within a few months the 'secret' treaty of 1873 was known in Chile; and it was also known in Peru that Chile was hastening the construction of her two cruisers in England. The expropriation in 1875 by the Peruvian Government of the nitrate works in Tarapacá, some of them owned by Chilians, did not improve relations.

The treaty of non-increase of duty, although not ratified by the Bolivian Congress, was observed for four years. Then in February 1878 the Bolivian Government, in place of existing taxes, imposed an export duty of ten centavos per hundredweight of nitrate 'as a minimum tax', a phrase which hinted at more to come. Whether this was an increase on former taxation (as seems probable) or merely a more convenient mode of levy, in any case it was a new tax and possibly the beginning of more. The hard-drinking caudillo-President of Bolivia, Daza, evidently did not realize the significance of his act. And although both the Antofagasta Company and the Chilian Government protested against the tax, for over half a year there was no excitement and apparently no crisis. However, in November 1878 Chile sent a stiff note to Bolivia. Daza replied that the complainants could apply to the Bolivian tribunals and that there was no diplomatic question. Thereupon Chile declared that, if the tax were collected, she would 'revindicate' her claim to the 23° boundary. Proposals of arbitration from each side led to nothing owing to the conditions attached to each offer. Finally, in January-February 1879 Daza imprisoned the Company's manager—an Englishman, for much of the capital was English—cancelled the concession to the Company, seized all its works, stores and manufactured nitrate and ordered their sale by auction.

In February 1879, just before the date fixed for the auction, a Chilian squadron appeared off Antofagasta and landed 600 troops who occupied the place and, advancing inland to Caracoles, defeated a company of Bolivian troops. War with Bolivia had begun. A dispute about manure, more precious than gold or silver, started the greatest war (in respect of the extent of its operations) which has been waged between Latin-American nations.

So far, in a large historical sense, apart from juridical considerations, it was a case of the occupation, by those competent to use it, of territory neglected by its nominal political owners: a case which finds a parallel in the westward expansion of the United States. The next step, the encroachment on what was indisputably Peruvian territory, is less defensible; for Peru had not neglected this territory, although bungling over its use. But the diplomatic handling of the whole matter by Peru is only explicable either by supposing complete ineptitude or by supposing that Peru expected or intended war with Chile and was confident of victory. Ineptitude and unstable government are the likely explanation, for Peru was unprepared for war. But Peruvians probably cherished a delusive sentiment that Peru and Bolivia united, with twice the population of Chile, would somehow be too much for their opponent.

The disappointed holders of Peruvian bonds, given in exchange for nitrate works in Tarapacá in 1875, some of them Chilian, others European and North American, agitated in Santiago for war with Peru. But their intrigues probably had little to do with Chile's determination to push northward. When Chile seized Antofagasta and Caracoles, Peru offered mediation; Chile replied by producing the 'secret' Peruvian-Bolivian treaty of 1873 and demanded a repudiation of the treaty and a declaration of Peruvian neutrality. The demand was refused. Chile declared war on Peru in April 1879, and a Chilian squadron blockaded the Peruvian port of Iquique. Meantime Chilian troops, without meeting serious resistance, had taken possession of all the Bolivian coastal region.

The sixteenth-century Spanish historian Zárate wrote concerning these Pacific countries: 'He who commands the sea is master of all that land.' This war was to prove the truth of his remark.

The relative strength of the two fleets may be studied by experts in Admiral Clowes' narrative. But the main strength on each side consisted of two ships. Chile had two new twin-screw ironclad cruisers, the *Almirante Cochrane* and the *Blanco Encalada*. Peru had an ironclad turret-ship or monitor, the *Huascar*, and an armoured frigate, the *Independencia*, both of them single-screw ships. The two guns in the *Huascar's* turret were more powerful than any Chilian guns. With this exception, the armament of the Chilian cruisers, much larger ships, was superior and they were better protected by thick armour. The nominal speed of the four ships was nearly equal, but the Peruvian ships were about ten years older than the Chilian. On the fate of these four ships depended the naval war; and the land war depended on the issue of the naval war.

The Peruvian naval and military headquarters, with President Prado in supreme command, were at Arica. The squadron was commanded by Captain Grau of the *Huascar*, 'an officer of the highest capacity and bravery, remarkably quiet and unassuming and an excellent seaman'. In May Grau, hearing that most of the Chilian squadron had left Iquique for the north, sailed with the *Huascar* and *Independencia* for Iquique, where the Chilian admiral had left his two least serviceable ships, the gunboat *Covadonga*, taken from the Spaniards thirteen years earlier, and the twenty-five-year-old wooden sloop *Esmeralda*, whose damaged boilers could only get up two or three knots, commanded by Arturo Prat. The *Esmeralda* was attacked by the *Huascar* and also by a shore battery. The *Independencia* engaged the *Covadonga*, which after an hour's fight steered southward, followed by the *Independencia*. Meantime the *Esmeralda* fought the *Huascar* with musketry and gunfire, although the latter, except for the moral effect, was useless against her opponent's armour. Out of forty shots from the *Huascar's* heavy turret guns, one only hit the sloop, killing the engineers and disabling the engines. The *Huascar* then proceeded to ram her helpless opponent; ineffectively, for her engines were stopped too soon. As the ships touched, Prat leapt on the deck of the *Huascar* sword in hand and rushed along it, followed by one man. Both fell at once. At the second attempt to ram, equally ineffective, Lieutenant Serrano, followed by twelve men, boarded the *Huascar*. All were cut down. At the third attempt the *Huascar* rammed her opponent which, after a fight of over four hours, sank with colours flying and guns still firing. Prat's self-sacrifice was not aimless: for Grau declared afterwards that, if Prat had been followed by his crew (who did not hear his order to board) they might probably have taken the *Huascar*, so demoralized were the crew of

Peruvian Indians. The result of the whole fight was disastrous to Peru, for the *Independencia*, pursuing the little *Covadonga* and attempting to ram, was led by her into shallow water, piled up on a rock, was pounded there by the *Covadonga* until the approach of the victorious *Huascar*, became a total wreck and was burnt by Grau. Only the *Huascar* now stood between Chile and the command of the whole Pacific coast.

The much-damaged *Huascar*, after a short southward cruise, returned to Callao to refit, chased by the two Chilian ironclads and escaping with difficulty. Having refitted his ship and recruited new men, including many foreigners (mostly English), Grau early in July set out southward on his famous three months' cruise, in which he played hide-and-seek with the whole Chilian navy, avoiding (in obedience to Prado's orders) any action which might risk his ship, but looking into port after port, destroying Chilian boats, capturing merchantmen with valuable stores and a transport with a regiment of cavalry, checking Chilian trade, interrupting transport of troops and stores, and (in the words of a Chilian historian) 'paralysing the operations of war'.

Returning to Arica in September, Grau reported to Prado that the *Huascar* needed overhauling at Callao to restore her impaired speed. Prado said 'no': and Grau sailed southwards from Arica in October, against his own judgment, accompanied by the wooden corvette *Unión*. A week later he was attacked by the two Chilian ironclads off Cape Angamos. The *Unión*, faster than the Chilian ships, made off; in obedience to orders, as was afterwards alleged. Early in the action a shot struck the *Huascar's* conning-tower and blew Grau to pieces: his successor in command was killed: in a fight lasting ninety minutes, out of 200 men 80, including the four senior officers, were killed or wounded. When the ship became helpless, full of wreckage, on fire in eight places, with her turret jammed and her steering-gear damaged, the officers determined to sink her; but some of the crew waved handkerchiefs; and when the Chilian fire ceased at this signal, they hauled down the Peruvian flag. Boats put out from the Chilian ships and their officers boarded the *Huascar* just in time to prevent the engineers from opening the valves and sinking the ship. The captured *Huascar* was overhauled at Valparaiso and in two months joined the Chilian fleet, bearing on her deck a commemorative plate on the spot where Prat had fallen seven months earlier.

To generations of Peruvian youth the life and death of Grau are a heroic saga and its hero a demigod. The hero of the Chilian navy is Arturo Prat.

After the battle of Angamos the Chilians, although unable to blockade all the ports on the long coast or to prevent some supplies from reaching the Peruvian army at Arica, were able without hindrance to reinforce and supply their own army of some 15,000 men at Antofagasta and to pursue their second land campaign against the Peruvian region of Tarapacá, Tacna and Arica; for their first campaign, the occupation of the Bolivian littoral, had been successfully concluded. On 2 November a Chilian force landed near Pisagua, captured that place after heavy fighting, and three weeks later took Iquique. Prado thereupon withdrew from the command and departed for Lima, to sail soon afterwards for Europe 'to buy ironclads' as he said. About the same time President Daza, who had proved wholly incompetent, was deprived of the command of the Bolivian contingent by his own men. After the capture of Iquique, a Chilian force of 2000 infantry with a few cavalry and some field guns attacked the inland oasis of Tarapacá: they were defeated with heavy loss. But next day the Peruvian commander abandoned the place with all his stores, retreating to Arica. The province of Tarapacá was now in Chilian hands.

Next came the invasion of Tacna and Arica. To isolate the Peruvian forces in that region, the Chilians occupied in the early months of 1880 the Peruvian ports and towns to the north-west, Ilo, Islay, Mollendo, Moquegua. In May Tacna, defended by some 13,000 Bolivian and Peruvian troops and attacked by about an equal number of Chilians, fell after heavy losses on both sides. The Bolivian troops, unable to save anything for Bolivia, then went home; and Bolivia, though no peace was made, withdrew from active hostilities. Thenceforth it was a war between Chile and Peru. Ten days after the fall of Tacna, Arica, attacked by land and sea, was taken. In the citadel which crowned the Morro, the Gibraltar-like

rock overlooking Arica Bay on the south, the Peruvian commander
Bolognesi held out to the last, refusing surrender, and fell with most
of his men. Thus Tacna and Arica passed into Chilian possession.

When the war began, mediation was offered by several European
and American governments, without result. The neutrals most
affected by the fighting were Europeans, largely English, who saw
their commerce interrupted by blockade and their property on
shore ruined by bombardment. In June 1879 Lord Salisbury in
a despatch to Washington 'stated that Germany and Great Britain
regretted the war which was being waged largely at the cost of
neutrals and desired to know whether the United States would join
those powers to offer mediation'. Secretary Evarts in reply
declined 'a premature effort, or an effort in combination with other
powers which could carry an impression of coercion':[1] Evarts, like
his successor Blaine, was anxious to avert any European action.
But after the fall of Arica the United States offered mediation,
which Chile reluctantly accepted: in October 1880 a conference
was held on board an American warship at Arica. The three
delegates from the United States, who were not agreed in their
interpretation of their instructions, left the discussion entirely to
the belligerent delegates. The Peruvians refused the cession of
territory demanded by the Chilians. Accordingly the conference
was closed and the Chilians prepared for the attack on Lima.

Already for six months past the Chilian fleet had blockaded
Callao and had twice bombarded the place at long range. The next
step was military invasion. As a preliminary, a small Chilian
squadron with 3000 troops was sent in November 1880 against the
defenceless coastal towns and cultivated valleys of the north 'to
effect military occupation' according to the Chilians; 'to make
requisitions of money and destroy property', as the Peruvians
asserted with more reason. At the beginning of 1881 about 23,000
well-equipped Chilian troops, with sixty-three guns, were on the
coast in the neighbourhood of Lima: a remarkably organized
expedition on the part of so small a country as Chile.

All the men in Lima capable of bearing arms had been ordered
to join the Peruvian forces, which were thus raised to about 33,500

[1] Dennis, *Tacna and Arica*, p. 94.

ill-equipped and in great part half-trained troops—many of them boys and old men—but possessing the advantages of the defence and fortified trenches. On 13 January 1881 the Chilians, attacking the first line at Chorrillos, were victorious after hard fighting and heavy losses; and the town of Chorrillos was sacked with much destruction of property. Three days later the second line of Peruvian defence at Miraflores was swept away. The village of Miraflores was burnt and on 17 January 1881 the victorious army entered Lima. There was much destruction and spoliation: the public library, the finest in South America, was turned into a barracks, and its precious manuscripts and books scattered.

Two months later (March 1881) a prominent Limeño, García Calderón, elected Provisional President by a group of citizens and supported by the Chilian army of occupation, assumed office. Great Britain, France and Italy now offered their good offices to Chile for peace negotiations and were refused. But Secretary Blaine, the early apostle of the movement now known as Pan-Americanism, who assumed office in March, exerted for ten months diplomatic pressure to induce Chile to accept a money indemnity without transfer of territory. Desiring to exclude any European political action, he suggested in November a plan to appeal to other American republics to join in an intervention if Chile should reject the good offices of the United States. If this plan meant anything effective, it meant coercion of the kind suggested by President Wilson in 1916. But a few weeks later Blaine resigned. His successor abandoned all suggestion of a strong policy, confining himself to pacific advice; and Chile thenceforth found no obstacle to her resolve to reap all the fruits of victory.

Meantime an attempt to negotiate peace with Garcia Calderón (who had been recognized by the United States) failed upon his refusal to cede territory: Calderón was unseated and arrested by Admiral Patrick Lynch, the Chilian military Governor of Lima. For nearly three years Chilian troops occupied Lima and the other coastal cities; and a guerrilla warfare, marked by some Peruvian successes, continued in the mountains, Cáceres fighting in the southern region and Iglesias in the north. At last Iglesias, seeing the futility of further resistance, assumed authority as head of the State, was recognized as such by the Chilians and in October 1883 signed the Peace of Ancón with Chilian plenipotentiaries. A Chilian detachment remained in occupation of Chorrillos until the treaty was ratified six months later. By this treaty the Peruvian Department of Tarapacá was ceded to Chile for ever. The two Peruvian provinces of Tacna and Arica were to be held by Chile for ten years, and at the end of that term (*expirado este plazo*)[1] a plebiscite of the inhabitants should decide which country should possess them, and the winner of the vote should pay ten million pesos to the loser.

In 1884 a truce was signed between Chile and Bolivia whereby the Province of Antofagasta was ceded to Chile: thus Bolivia was definitely cut off from the sea and confined to her inland mountains and forests.

As the decade 1884–94 drew to an end, negotiations began about holding the plebiscite, but the two Governments could not agree on the qualification of voters, for there was a defect in the Treaty of Ancón. Article III prescribed a plebiscite at the end of ten years but said nothing about the conditions of the plebiscite, about the authority responsible for holding it or (most important of all) about the question whether the voters were to be the inhabitants of 1884 or the inhabitants of 1894. The question remained an open sore. Chile treated the region as her own, encouraging Chilian settlement and making things difficult for Peruvian inhabitants. In Chilian official maps and statistical publications the region appeared as part of the Chilian Republic.

Repeated negotiations, notably in 1898 and 1912, were fruitless, and in 1912 diplomatic relations between the two governments were severed for the second time: nor were matters improved when Chile in the early years of the twentieth century, by linking existing railways and constructing an extension northward, created a state-owned 'longitudinal railway' stretching from Puerto Montt to Tacna. This was an uneconomic proceeding, for a north-to-south

[1] 'At the end of that term' or 'upon the expiration of that term' is the natural and usual meaning of *expirado este plazo*. President Coolidge in his award of 1925 translated the phrase 'after the expiration of that term' and added the words 'after the ten years but no limit was defined'.

railway through the desert, already possessing the sea for a highway, cannot be profitable: it was a strategic railway, designed for passage of troops and munitions. Moreover Peru protested against the Chilian-Bolivian railway agreement of 1904 (mentioned on p. 237) as an infringement of Peruvian sovereignty.

Yet the situation was burdensome to Chile herself; for Tacna and Arica were poor in minerals and costly to keep. After the Great War the international atmosphere favoured the revision of boundaries and the examination of national rights: and when the vigorous reformer Alessandri became President of Chile in 1920, he was determined on a settlement. The Peruvian President Leguía was receptive. At the end of 1921, although no diplomatic relations existed between the two countries and there had been some recrudescence of bitterness, a message from the Government of Chile to that of Peru suggested the holding of the plebiscite. After some negotiation Peru offered to submit the whole matter to arbitration 'through the initiative of the President of the United States'. Acting on this suggestion President Harding invited both Governments to transfer the negotiations to Washington. Six months later (July 1922) it was agreed that the United States President should arbitrate. In 1925 the arbitrator, President Coolidge, gave his decision, that a plebiscite was possible and should be held, that a plebiscitary Commission of three, a Chilian, a Peruvian and an American as Chairman, should conduct the matter and that the voters should be all former residents of the region and their descendants (mostly Peruvians no longer resident) and all residents of thirty months' standing, but not soldiers and civil servants (all Chilian). The Commission of three duly met in August 1925; and the Chairman patiently strove to reconcile contending passions. But besides the delicate business of importing qualified Peruvian voters, the proceedings of the Chilian authorities, who controlled and policed the region, made a fair plebiscite impossible. After ten months of fruitless effort the Commission in June 1926 abandoned their task as hopeless. The dispute seemed as insoluble as ever.

But already before the dissolution of the Commission, direct negotiations had been opened at Washington upon the invitation of the United States Government. Feeling was still high and for two years little progress was made. But at last a compromise was reached, and in 1929 a treaty was signed whereby Tacna was returned to Peru, and Chile kept Arica, undertaking to grant to Peru a wharf, a custom-house and a railway station on Arica Bay.[1] The boundary was drawn parallel to the railway at a distance of ten kilometres, leaving the railway within Chilian territory.

The question with Bolivia had long been settled. In 1904 it was agreed that Chile should possess permanently the province of Antofagasta: Chile was to construct a railway from Arica to La Paz, to permit the passage of Bolivian goods by this railway without paying customs duties to Chile and, after fifteen years from its completion, Chile was to hand over to Bolivia the part of the line passing through Bolivian territory. These provisions were duly carried out.

The Tacna-Arica conflict has a place in the story of relations between Anglo-Saxon and Spanish America and of peace-making in the Western Hemisphere. American historians have little good to say of United States diplomacy during the war, 1879–83. It encouraged Peru to prolong a hopeless struggle and irritated Chile, proud of hegemony in the Pacific, jealous of any other hegemony and mistrusting American impartiality. About the second phase— the arbitral award and its frustration (1922–6)—both Dennis and Haring say some hard things. Yet the plebiscitary Commission, by showing that Chile was responsible for its failure and by clarifying the position, pointed to a solution. In the third phase, the good offices of the United States, leading to direct negotiation at Washington, facilitated that solution. And not only the two countries concerned but the whole of South America owe a debt of gratitude to the United States for their temperate, impartial and finally successful part in helping to compose a quarrel which for forty-five years had divided two sister nations.

NOTE. W. J. Dennis, *Tacna and Arica* (Yale University Press, 1931); Sir W. L. Clowes, *Four Modern Naval Campaigns* (London, 1902); Haring, pp. 163–78; Markham narrates the War of the Pacific with a strong Peruvian bias in his *History of Peru* and in his book *The War between Chile and Peru* (London, 1882).

[1] This arrangement proved impossible: Peru accepted a money indemnity instead.

Northern South America

English Miles

0 100 200 400 600 800 1000

ATLANTIC OCEAN

PACIFIC OCEAN

CARIBBEAN SEA

Little Antilles

HONDURAS

NICARAGUA

COSTA RICA

COLOMBIA

VENEZUELA

ECUADOR

PERU

BOLIVIA

BRAZIL

MATTO GROSSO

B A H I A

Minas Geraes

Galapagos I.s
(to Ecuador)

Martinique I.
St. Lucia
Grenada
Tobago I.
Trinidad I.

Amazonas

CHAPTER XXII

ECUADOR

1830–1935

ECUADOR is a land of contrasts; a broad tropical coastal plain, covered in great part by dense vegetation, haunted by alligators and great snakes and traversed by the devious waters of the River Guayas, which convey to Guayaquil cacao, bananas and forest products; then the great mountains and the lofty plateau or broad valley, a region of perpetual spring, bordered by the famous 'Avenue of Volcanoes' and crossed transversely by several 'knots' or mountain masses; higher yet the snowy peaks of Cotopaxi and Chimborazo, which affront the vertical equatorial sun; eastward, beyond the craggy descents from the heights, the obscure Amazonian region, 'an unfinished world' of dense forests, innumerable streams, yearly inundations and savage Indian tribes, among them expert professional head-hunters. Torrential seasonal rains, tremors of the earth, volcanic eruptions break the passive monotony of life, and, until recent years, recurrent visitations of yellow fever which swept the coastal regions. The Indians of the coastal plain (where there is also much African blood, although few pure negroes) differ from those of the mountains. Guayaquil, the largest city, and Quito, the capital, lie in different worlds. Until the road between them was completed in 1872 they were almost inaccessible to one another in the rainy season and were often the seats of rival potentates.

Such intemperate natural surroundings did not provide an apt domicile for nursing an ignorant and heterogeneous people into an orderly nation. The initial difficulties in 1830 were even greater than elsewhere owing to continued frontier disputes with New Granada and with Peru, in which Ecuador, weakest, poorest and smallest of the three, suffered most: the crowd of idle generals and colonels and the unpaid soldiery, mostly strangers to Ecuador, added to disorder.

The Constitution of 1830 placed the 'innocent, abject and miserable class' of Indians under the fatherly protection of the parish priests: two years later the same Government took measures to check the 'intolerable abuse' of the extortion inflicted on the Indians by some priests. Evidently the Indians were remote from the tumultuous game of politics, in which provisional and constitutional presidents still rise and fall with bewildering rapidity. These vicissitudes are not the stuff of history. But the comparatively (with intervals) constructive period 1830–75 is illustrated by three biographies, those of Juan José Flores (1801–64), Vicente Rocafuerte (1783–1847) and Gabriel García Moreno (1821–75).

Flores, who, after fighting for years under Bolívar, held command in Quito in 1830, was the leader of the split from Colombia, which would, however, have probably happened in any case. Venezuelan by birth and now Quiteño by adoption, he looked beyond the prevalent localism, and enacted through an obedient Constituent Congress a liberal law of citizenship, admitting not only those born in the republic but all Colombians who had fought or lived in the country. He also desired a federation with the republics of New Granada and Venezuela. But this scheme found no favour in New Granada and indeed was hardly consistent with Flores' own position as 'Supreme Chief, Civil and Military' of Ecuador. A fine soldier, resolute in action, a man of pleasant social gifts, seductive manners and jocose humour, Flores had these traits of a dictator; but this young man (barely thirty) had little administrative experience and few gifts of statesmanship except resolute determination, some knowledge of men and a freedom from personal rancour rare among South American despots. He released from prison his bitterest enemy, making him head of the State: amnesty followed his victory in civil strife, except in the case of military mutiny. Having in his power a man who had set a huge price on his head, Flores treated with friendly hospitality this disillusioned bidder for his life. On the other hand Flores, like others of his kind, had his own way of handling public money and was unduly benevolent to his family and friends, many of them Venezuelans.

Flores, named President in 1830 for four years with large

powers, narrowly escaped death at the hands of mutinous soldiers. The mutiny was suppressed and 'some 300 veterans among the founders of Colombia, Peru and Bolivia perished either by assassination or on the scaffold because they could no longer endure hunger and nakedness.' So writes Ceballos.

Liberal opposition to Flores' despotism soon took form in a club and a periodical, *El Quiteño libre*, and found a leader in Rocafuerte, who in 1833 returned to his country after wanderings almost comparable to those of Miranda and demanding here brief retrospect.

Rocafuerte, one of the most remarkable figures of the revolutionary age, although he took no part in the fighting, was born at Guayaquil in 1783, the year of Bolívar's birth, and was educated in the College of Nobles at Madrid, and in Paris, where he met Bolívar. He took some part in the abortive revolutionary movement at Quito in 1809. Elected deputy for Quito to the Cortes of Cadiz in 1812, he visited England to study parliamentary procedure, passing thence to Sweden, to Russia, where he was received by the Empress Catherine, to France and to Italy. Returning to Guayaquil in 1817 he taught French, on condition that his pupils should teach others and should use as textbooks Raynal, Rousseau and Montesquieu. In 1820 he was in the United States and Cuba, whence he travelled to Madrid at the instance of Bolívar, to report on the Spanish radical revolution of 1820 and its possible favourable influence on the South American movement. Then came two years in the service of independent Mexico, representing that Republic as chargé d'affaires in London for some time and as commercial agent in several European countries. He had also engaged in journalism and had published several pamphlets of liberal or republican savour, had been imprisoned in Mexico for a pamphlet on religious toleration and after his release produced a pamphlet 'On Prisons'. Thus, on his return to Ecuador in 1833, his peregrinations had given him that experience in affairs which was wanting in Flores, whose measures—uncontrolled by a Congress meeting in alternate years—were empiric, capricious and sometimes absurd. Absent through illness on the day (September 1833) when extraordinary powers were voted to Flores, Rocafuerte a few days later denounced from his seat in Congress both that vote and the executive with such vehemence that Congress voted his expulsion; and Flores despatched him under guard to be deported to Peru through Guayaquil. But meantime a revolt had broken out in that port, and Rocafuerte, released from his guards, became head of a revolutionary Government, himself fighting for reform and the end of tyranny, but surrounded by a set of self-seeking scoundrels indifferent to all this.

Through their neglect, Guayaquil was soon taken by Flores' troops. But Rocafuerte, possessing the one frigate which constituted the Ecuadorian navy and some small armed vessels, occupied the island of Puná, obtained supplies from Peru, opened a custom-house, proclaimed the blockade of Guayaquil as 'Supreme Chief', and precariously held the adjoining coast against the guerrillas of Flores. After ten months of war—marked by the sanguinary excesses of civil strife and by a pestilence which raged in Guayaquil —Rocafuerte was betrayed by one of his own men into Flores' hands. Instead of the expected four bullets, the captive received proposals of agreement from Flores, who knew his prisoner's capacity, value as an ally and possible services to the Republic. Accordingly Rocafuerte emerged from prison (July 1834) to become, with Flores' support, Supreme Chief of the Province of Guayas, a post which he filled with economy, zeal and efficiency.

Flores needed this moral aid. Refugees from his tyranny, invading from New Granada, won the capital and set up a rival Supreme Chief, who was accepted by two of the three Ecuadorian provinces. But Flores with 1000 troops defeated twice the number of revolutionaries,[1] heavily fined the reconquered provinces and prepared the way for the presidency of Rocafuerte (1835-9).

Schools, hospitals, improved and more economical administration; increased revenue; more honest tribunals; troops well treated and disciplined; some attempt at representative institutions; esteem in the neighbouring republics; comparative tranquillity and order: such were the results of the stern and resolute rule of Rocafuerte—a liberal by choice, an autocrat by necessity—when he handed over the presidency to Flores, returning himself to his former post at

[1] Olmedo, the bard of Junín, commemorated this 'Battle of Miñarica' in an ode; but repented afterwards of having sung 'like Lucan' victory in civil war.

Guayaquil, where he vied with the Bishop in exposing himself in a brave fight against a visitation of yellow fever.

In 1840 President Flores, having been granted 'extraordinary powers', committed the costly eccentricity of leading troops into New Granada, ostensibly to aid the Granada Government in suppressing a revolt,[1] but more probably in the vain hope of winning or recovering the Province of Pasto. So remote was democracy that when Flores, near the end of his term, summoned an extraordinary Congress, only ten members, including Senators and Deputies, presented themselves.[2] The President then summoned a Convention, carefully arranged to consist entirely of civil servants. Having told them that Ecuador was like 'an isthmus of snow between two seas of fire', he urged the need of reform. The examples of Sparta, Thebes, Corinth, Athens, Rome, the Cisalpine Republic and the United States (a typical South-American harangue with a Bolivarian ring about it) proved, so he said, the need of a permanent or long-lived administration. The Convention obediently adopted a Constitution prescribing an eight years' presidency with dictatorial powers and a Congress meeting at four years' intervals and so constituted as to be subservient to the executive. Flores was then re-elected President for eight years, evidently meaning a perpetual dictatorship. Rocafuerte, still Governor of Guayaquil, now denounced his *compadre* Flores, protesting violently in a stormy parliamentary scene against the continuance of a 'corrupt, immoral and pernicious tyranny'. He then prudently retired to Lima, whence he poured a flood of journalistic vituperation on the tyranny of his former protector.

The imposition of a poll-tax at the opening of Flores' third administration in 1843 roused such hot opposition, headed in one place by the women, that the tax was withdrawn, and the year 1844 passed in uneasy peace. But the perpetual autocracy of a self-seeking Venezuelan foreigner was too much for the Ecuadorians. Mutinies, conspiracies and a revolutionary Government in Guayaquil heralded the New Year. After six months of civil war Flores, beaten in the field, accepted in June 1845 an agreement that he

[1] See p. 255.
[2] Yellow fever prevented elections in the coastal regions, but not elsewhere.

should retire to Europe, keeping his military rank and pay, with a grant of 20,000 pesos for expenses. Twice during the following decade the dispossessed potentate tried to force his way back, first from Europe, where he got support in Spain by promises to enthrone a Spanish prince in Ecuador. He fitted out three ships in England. At the instance of an Ecuadorian envoy in London, Lord Palmerston forbade them to sail. Five years later Flores appeared before Guayaquil with armed vessels from Peru, but met with no response and departed, beaten a second time.

Rocafuerte, who took a leading part in the 'Revolution of 'forty-five' and in framing the inevitable new 'liberal' constitution, survived for two years only. He left no worthy successor; and, except as explaining or perhaps justifying the stern autocracy which followed, the period 1845–60 is not memorable. A mulatto President, Roca (1845–9), moderate and conciliatory, maintained comparative peace. Then for a decade (1849–59) a restless 'liberal' military caudillo, Urbina, dominated affairs, either as self-appointed President (1852–6) or by controlling his predecessor and successor, not always quite docile. Frequent ebullitions of discontent at last culminated in 1859 in a general uprising. A provisional Government appeared at Quito, which nominated a triumvirate and, as first triumvir, Gabriel García Moreno, at the time an exile in Peru, a lawyer and scholar of proved experience and capacity, as the following sketch of his previous career will show. Born in 1821 of Spanish parents, Gabriel was distinguished in the University of Quito by rare industry and power of work—only possible to the most vigorous physical constitution and determined will. At the age of twenty-four he joined the revolt against Flores and undertook the delicate task of collecting the tax which financed the revolution. A year later he attacked with mordant pen the liberal tendencies of the new Government in his ephemeral periodical *El Zurriago*, 'The Lash', followed by *El Vengador*, 'The Avenger', and *El Diablo*. Some months spent in Paris soon after the European revolutions of 1848 imbued the young lawyer with a hatred of those movements and strengthened his reverence for the traditional authority of Church and State. This Parisian interval was devoted not to diversions but to mathematical and physical studies, 'sixteen hours daily' he declared, 'which would have been forty had the day contained forty-eight hours'. After his return home his influence with the administration procured the admission of the Jesuits banished from New Granada in 1851.[1] But his opposition to Urbina led to exile for more than a year (1854–6), spent in Paris, a time of study and political observation. Upon his return he became Alcalde of Quito, Rector of the University and Senator for Guayaquil. His outspoken censure of the Government in the Senate earned him a second exile, which he passed in Peru. He was summoned thence, chosen in his absence to be leader in a revolt against 'the misrule of the military chiefs, miscalled liberals, whose government was a compound of oppression for their enemies and license for their friends.'[2] Moreno accepted the call, landed at Guayaquil and, after a campaign of several months against a disreputable pretender named Franco, was appointed President for four years (1861–5) by a special Convention. Flores, *El padre de la patria*, having returned from exile, presided in this Convention, retrieving, at the age of sixty, his past vagaries. Thenceforth, as Commander-in-Chief of the army, Flores gave valuable support to the Government of Moreno, serving both against internal enemies and against Granadan aggression on the northern frontier until his death on active service in 1864.

For fifteen years, 1861–75—except for a brief interval of radical and anti-clerical reaction during his absence on a diplomatic mission in Europe in 1866—Moreno ruled the country as an autocrat, thrice as President and in the intervals as the directing power, one of the few civilian South American despots. His portrait shows his character, stern, austere, resolute; the very antithesis of the adventurous, ambitious military caudillo-autocrat; resembling rather a formidable scholastic disciplinarian. Of all Latin-American autocrats he was the most rigidly upright, the most laborious and devoted to duty, the least self-seeking and ambitious. His most famous work is the exaltation of the Catholic Church to a position above the State. Papal Bulls and briefs were admitted without the

---

[1] After a year they were banished from Ecuador by Urbina, but were readmitted later by García Moreno as President.

[2] T. C. Dawson, vol. II, p. 334.

government's 'pass'. Education was entrusted to the clergy, the Catholic teaching associations and the Jesuits, who were recalled by him. But Moreno refused to sign a Concordat defining the privileges and liberty of the Church until provisions were added by the Vatican for much-needed reform of the secular clergy and the Religious Orders. The arrival of European clerics—probably a necessary measure—to effect these reforms caused some heart-burning. The path towards theocracy was pushed forward, only Catholics being recognized as citizens, until in 1873 the Republic was dedicated in a solemn ceremony to the Sacred Heart of Jesus; and a symbolic picture of the Sacred Heart was set up in the Parliament House.

The prominence given, both by admirers and by detractors, to Moreno's theocratic polity has tended to obscure his educational, administrative and constructive work. Schools for the people were opened everywhere. Zealous for science and for higher education, Moreno founded an astronomical observatory and invited from Europe eminent scientific men belonging to the Jesuit Order to be professors of mathematics and physics. He himself explored at some risk a volcanic crater for scientific observation.

Moreno was equally thorough in civil administration and in promoting the welfare of the people. He found salaries unpaid, a miserable revenue and debts piling up at ruinous interest. He increased revenue by organizing taxation, suppressing fraud and contraband and founding a mint. His salary he gave to public use. He constructed waggon-roads—a strange novelty—radiating from Quito and a telegraph to Guayaquil: at last in 1872 after ten years' labour the great mountain road was completed from the capital to the port. His energy and probity made themselves felt everywhere. 'The laws were better enforced, life and property safer and material prosperity increased. Government was centralized and the semi-independence of departments abolished.'[1] Needless to say, free speech and free press were barred: every seditious symptom was rigidly suppressed. Moreno, like other dictators, maintained his authority by force of arms in case of need, and sent leaders of revolt to execution as traitors.

[1] T. C. Dawson, vol. II, p. 337.

Liberal or anti-clerical opposition, impotent and mute within Ecuador, was loud-voiced in exile. Its spokesman was the fiery liberal Montalvo, whose masterly prose has won a recognized place in Spanish literature. From his retreat in Peru, Montalvo—a man of pure Spanish descent, like Moreno himself—poured out his eloquent diatribes upon the despotism and the theocracy of Moreno. And when in 1875 García Moreno, just after his election to another presidential term, was struck down by assassins in the plaza of Quito, Montalvo boasted, 'it was my pen that slew him'.

García Moreno, who perished in the prime of life for a statesman, left no successor. The story of brief administrations, *coups d'état*, local *pronunciamientos* (mixed with banditry), alternate pro-clerical and anti-clerical ascendancy demands no detailed narrative. The general tendency, embodied in new constitutions or constitutional revisions, was a reaction against theocracy and against centralized authority. The administration of Antonio Flores, son of *el padre de la patria* (1888–92) was an interval of comparative peace. At last in 1895 Eloy Alfaro seized power, to become President two years later. For twenty years past he had been a militant 'liberal' caudillo, had suffered exile under García Moreno and in 1882 had exercised a violent but ephemeral local dictatorship in Esmeraldas. For more than twenty years (1895–1916) two liberal leaders, Alfaro (1895–1900 and 1905–10) and Gutiérrez Plaza (1900–4 and 1912–16), alternated in power, with two brief intervals. During one of these in 1911, Alfaro, now an old man, rose in revolt: after sanguinary fighting he was made prisoner, dragged from his dungeon by a mob and murdered. Those two decades were marked by material progress, notably the completion of the Guayaquil-Quito railway in 1908 and also by successive inroads on the privileges and independence of the Church and on the property of the Church and of the Religious Orders.

The year 1925 brought a *revolución*; and after a short-lived civilian Junta, a group of soldiers took charge. Since that time Ecuador has never recovered normality. During the eight years 1926–34 six Presidents held office, all either 'provisional' or quickly deposed, or resigned. One of these *revoluciones* in 1932 brought a week of sharp fighting at Quito between two sections of the army, part attacking the capital, part defending behind barricades. The dead were reckoned at 800.

Bright and seemingly well-justified hopes attended the inauguration in September 1934 of Velasco Ibarra, a young man generally *simpático* and acceptable to moderate men of both parties, fifth head of the State since 1831. Widespread approval greeted his deposition eleven months later by a group of officers, acting ostensibly on behalf of an outraged Parliament against a despotic President. Ibarra had assumed dictatorial airs, had imprisoned or exiled opposition leaders: and when Congress, in face of the menacing insults of a crowd of Ibarristas, suspended its sittings, he dissolved the Chambers and proceeded to summon a Constituent Congress. To-day he is an exile. His successor, Dr Páez, installed by the soldiers after a confused interval, reigned for two years, surviving a momentary shock when in December 1936 part of the Quito garrison revolted. They were crushed after about 100 casualties (according to official figures) in street fighting. But in November 1937 the dominant group among the officers deposed Páez and set up a Cabinet, half military, half civilian.

To dwell upon political history alone would leave, as in the case of other Hispanic republics, a mistaken impression. The indefinable but unforgettable culture of old Spain still lingers in the domestic patios and in the churches of Quito. More tangible pursuits— history, science, literature, archaeology—all have their devotees. As to modern conditions, the British chargé d'affaires in Quito reported in 1934 that 'unemployment, in the ordinary acceptance of the word, does not exist in Ecuador' and he commends the efforts of the Government and the municipalities to improve the housing of the workers. Two recent progressive and civilizing steps are due to the *Americanos del Norte*; the regulation of finance in 1929 with the advice of American experts; and, ten years earlier, the cleansing of Guayaquil, the commercial capital, formerly a hotbed of yellow fever and other tropical ailments, now a reasonably healthy place, thanks to the munificence of the Rockefeller Foundation and to the beneficent labours of Colonel Gorgas and his colleagues, welcomed and aided by the Government of Ecuador.

NOTE. See list in the Preface. C. R. Enock, *Ecuador* (London, 1914), gives much information about the country. A recent account of García Moreno in Spanish by Dr Agramonte, Professor of Psychology in Havana University, gives, in a strange and difficult vocabulary, a damaging but unconvincing description.

CHAPTER XXIII

COLOMBIA

COLOMBIA, known as New Granada until 1863, famous in past days as surpassing all the provinces of the Spanish Crown in the yield of gold, rich also in emeralds and pearls, is fourth in extent and third in population of the Spanish-speaking republics, with an area about four and a half times that of the British Isles and with over eight million inhabitants.

The key to the history of Colombia is the configuration of its mountains, rivers and valleys. Nearly two-thirds of the territory lies in the almost empty plains of the Orinoco basin and the Amazonian forests, only inhabited by scanty tribes of savages, some of them cannibals. The remaining one-third, the inhabited part, the New Granada of history, mainly comprised in the Andine region, fills the north-west corner of the continent in an irregular oblong shape, with a coast-line on both oceans. The dominant feature of the country is the gigantic triple range of the Andes. This vast mountain system, gathered into a 'knot' (an entangled mass) of active volcanic peaks north of the Ecuadorian frontier, opens out northwards, like the ribs of a fan, into three Cordilleras, eastern, central and western, enclosing between them the deep valleys of the Rivers Magdalena and Cauca, the chief natural channels of internal communication. But even from north to south communication, except recently by air, is slow, laborious and often interrupted. Transport from the northern ports to the remote capital on its lofty plateau—most of the way by shallow-draft river steamer—took normally ten or twelve days until recent construction of rail and road from the up-river ports, together with speedier boats, is supposed to halve the time. But passage is still sometimes interrupted for a month or more owing to low water in the river. Before the age of steam the journey from the coast took from forty to seventy days, and a civil war in Panamá, yet more remote and only accessible by sea, might be fought out before news of the

outbreak reached the Government in the capital. Journeys from
east to west, across the deep valleys and lofty mountains, are
indescribably difficult and often dangerous. A separate mountain
system of more than alpine height, the Sierra Nevada, rises west of
the Magdalena delta. Thus the country, divided into several
regions distinct in climate, occupations and partly even in population, besides the numberless smaller subdivisions into mountain
valleys, had a long struggle to achieve national unity. The remote-
ness of the capital and the absence of any convenient centre of
national life increased the difficulty.

The two coasts, Atlantic and Pacific, although both typically
tropical in character, differ from one another. The Caribbean
region, having a wet and dry season, touched by the trade winds,
and accessible from Europe, early invited settlement and possesses
the chief ports. But the northern part of the Pacific coastal region,
the Chocó, suffers constant drenching rain which swells the
volume of the River Atrato: here dwell few inhabitants except
naked Indians and groups of semi-barbarous negroes. Farther
south, however, the port Buenaventura is now linked by rail with
the railway of the Cauca valley and provides an alternative land
route to the capital. The opening of the Panamá Canal brings this
Pacific region into nearer contact with the world known to
history.

Nowhere, not even in Mexico, do the American tropics offer more
striking contrasts of climate and of racial character within short
distances, from the sweltering valley of the Lower Magdalena to
the pleasant upland dales and tablelands and thence to wind-swept
páramos and lofty peaks. The plain of Bogotá at a height of 8500 ft.
enjoys a perpetual but not unclouded spring. The peasantry of the
Caribbean coastal region are largely negroes and mulattoes: those
of the mountain parts are native Indians, people of small stature
but of great physical strength and endurance: they supply the rank
and file of Colombian armies. The Goajira Peninsula is owned by
an Indian tribe, horse-breeders and horse-dealers, who stoutly
preserve a real though not officially recognized independence. The
Motilones Indians of the Sierra de Perija on the Venezuelan
frontier shoot from their hidden thickets wooden arrows of deadly

force which bar all approach. Even in the heart of the Republic, in the jungle stretching between the Magdalena and the eastern Cordillera south of the River Sogamoso, scanty groups of Indians still hunt their game with poisoned arrows and successfully resist all contact with men wearing clothes. But these small survivals, although they demand record, are not typical of the whole country. To count the people of pure white origin would be unprofitable; one in ten according to some, one in twenty, say others. Such figures give a mistaken impression of character: for fully one-third of the population, even if many of them be tinged with other blood, are Spanish or hispanicized and provide the governing class. The official estimate for 1933, interpreting generously the term 'white', counts the pure white to be 35 per cent.; and the Hispanic character penetrates much farther; for the Church, as Bolívar hoped and planned, retains a great influence, and one which favours European traditions. No decided bar divides colours or race. Merchants, professional men and politicians number in their ranks men of mixed blood and educated Indians. But the portraits in the *Historia de Colombia* by Henao and Arrubla show that—as in the other continental republics—including Mexico—the European type prevails among the ruling and guiding classes. Few European immigrants have entered the country since Spanish days. But the people of Bogota pride themselves on having preserved on their lofty *sabana* a social and literary culture which derives from Europe. A culture of more rural type finds a home in the beautiful and fertile valley of the upper Cauca at a height of some 3500 ft.; a region which with its varied crops and pastures yields almost all the necessaries of life.

Although rich in minerals—oil, platinum, gold and silver—Colombia is mainly an agricultural country of primitive farming methods; coffee outweighs all minerals. Vast estates (now to be broken up, if unused) are few and peonage is rare.

The physical contrasts of the country are reflected in the contrasts of its history, which may be summarized in a sentence: long years of tremors, upheavals and conflicts in the nineteenth century; and then, by an astonishing and sudden transformation, a full generation of internal peace; and now, for twenty-seven years past, tranquil constitutional government—a pattern and a hope for all tropical America. Even the troubled period meant something more than fights between unscrupulous caudillos. These were frequent enough, but many had worthier aims. García Calderón, with over-emphasis but with much truth, writes: 'In Colombia men have fought for ideas... exalted convictions are the motives of political enmities.' And the Colombian statesman Núñez remarks: 'We have had too much political dogmatism.' Thus constitutional history means something in Colombia.

In no other American country had the Church such a hold on the people. The conservative party, which took form about 1840 and was in power till 1849 and again in 1857–60, sincerely desired to maintain Church privileges and to base education on the Catholic religion: they believed in the need of strong government and the suppression of disorder, including seditious speech or writing. The liberals—holding office (with a brief interval 1857–60) from 1849 to 1880—were with equal sincerity anti-clerical, and desired the fullest individual liberty, freedom of speech and of writing, with popular control over officials. Both parties were led by vague aspirations to adopt in the 'fifties a scheme of local autonomy and extreme decentralization, miscalled federalism but in fact meaning disintegration; until the conservatives were converted by experience to the unitary system. Then in the last quarter of the nineteenth century one party contended for the Church and for strong central government, the other for the secular state and 'federal' decentralization. But if many of the leaders fought for deeply felt principles, not so the unfortunate Indians, swept into contending armies by the press-gang and sometimes caught by the lasso to be thrust into the firing line, so that the 'very word *reclutamiento* (recruiting) spread alarm and desolation in the fields'. These submissive recruits stood with stolid indifference to shoot and be shot at; and, if made captive, they fought with equal stolidity on the other side. But besides these official or revolutionary armies, there were always in time of civil war wandering guerrilla bands of volunteers, in reality bandits marauding and wasting in the name of liberty or of order. Yet Colombia has suffered no long dictatorships, and two attempts at military autocracy (1859 and 1867) were promptly crushed. For this reason the biographical method of history is less applicable to Colombia than to most of her neighbours. But three very different personages may be selected to illustrate that history: the adventurous caudillo José María Obando (1797–1861); Tomás Cipriano Mosquera (1798–1878), thrice President; and the reformer Rafael Núñez (1825–94).

The Republic has had four names. Beginning in 1830–2 as the 'Republic of New Granada', it became in 1861 'Confederación Granadina', in 1863 the 'United States of Colombia' and in 1886 (upon the defeat of federalism) 'Republic of Colombia', the name which it still bears. The chief political landmarks are the federal Constitution of 1863, the unitary Constitution of 1886 and the peace of 1902. To narrate the civil wars would be impossible. A Colombian writer, Holguín, reckons twenty-seven; Haring counts 'ten civil wars which were national in scope'; the Colombian historians Henao and Arrubla emphasize five, which may be mentioned here in anticipation: (a) the revolt of *los supremos* in 1840–2; (b) the war of 1860, due to the division into autonomous states; (c) the conservative revolt of 1876; (d) the radical revolt of 1885; (e) the three years' war of 1899–1902, also mainly a radical revolt or series of local and general revolts.

Yet to talk of seventy years of turmoil is unjust. From 1830 to 1860 New Granada shows a better record than her neighbours to the south, a record interrupted by one prolonged general civil war (1840–2) which was preceded by nine years and followed by at least twelve years of tranquil progress. The real turmoil came after 1850 and—since Colombians love ideas—was partly due to two ideas; the 'federal idea' (not a federal reality) and the 'revolutionary idea', Colombian theorists, especially the youth, being apparently imbued with the notion that the French example of 1848 taught revolution to be in itself an admirable thing.

The earlier troubles which followed Bolívar's retirement in 1830 were solved, after some fighting, when Santander, summoned from exile by a Constituent Congress, became President under the centralized but liberal Constitution of 1832. The Vice-President, José Maria Obando, who had played a leading but somewhat ambiguous part in the recent conflicts, acted as Head of the State until Santander's arrival. Obando, a fine soldier and a hero of the revolutionary war, was a man of handsome exterior, engaging manners and an attractive air of distinction, set off by careful dress. With fair complexion, blue eyes, tall and stalwart frame, he looked like a British officer. But his school of action had been the ultra-savage warfare of Pasto, his native place; and his wayward ambition caused much evil. Moreover there clung to him throughout his life, even as President of the Republic (1853-5), the suspicion of complicity in the murder of Sucre.

Under the firm rule of Santander and his successor the country enjoyed nine years (1832-40) of peace, prosperity and stability in public finance. Schools were opened, business improved, and the conflict with Spain was ended when in 1837 Spanish ships were admitted to the ports of the Republic; a concession reciprocated by Spain.[1] This tranquil period was interrupted rather than ended when the people of Pasto, who had fought so stoutly for monarchy and tradition, took up arms in the name of religion because, with episcopal approval, some almost deserted convents had been closed. The revolt, apparently ended by agreement and amnesty, was revived by the unscrupulous ambition of Obando, proclaiming liberty, federation and religion, and was only crushed with the aid of Ecuadorian troops.

But the real trouble came when Obando, who had fled on foot from the field of defeat, appeared at the head of the widespread revolt, strangely known as *La Revolución de los Supremos*, because a dozen or more provincial 'Supreme Chiefs', beside the ex-interim-President Obando, were fighting for power. After hard fighting, in which the capital was in imminent danger, the revolt collapsed owing to these divisions and in 1842 there was peace. But the progress of a decade had been wiped out by two years of strife: industry ruined, trade destroyed, crops and cattle consumed by devastating hordes, who spread in their passage a plague of small-pox. Obando, the chief mischief-maker, was banished; and, with due poetic justice, General Herrán, who had defeated him in the field, assumed the Government, having been already elected President—to be succeeded in 1845 by his second-in-command

[1] Diplomatic recognition by Spain was delayed till 1881.

Mosquera. The twelve[1] years' peace which followed is largely due to Herrán, a quiet magnanimous practical man, who announced 'amnesty for the past, stern severity for the future'. He kept order under the inevitable new Constitution, which strengthened the executive, even enabling the Government to nominate civil servants to sit in Congress: a provision obviously inviting challenge although in fact less dictatorial than the customary Latin-American method of nominating the whole Congress by means of a managed election. Herrán and his successors advanced the works of peace: the treaty of 1846 with the United States; steam-vessels on the Magdalena; twenty-five miles of carriage-road, the first in the country, on the *sabana* of Bogotá; some improvement in the mule-tracks which served for roads elsewhere; the Panamá railway; monetary reform; a geographical survey of the country; organization of education, at first under the Jesuits, recalled to the country in 1842, but expelled nine years later by the liberals.

The portrait of Mosquera in García Calderón—a portrait which might serve as frontispiece to some heroic romance—shows him as a peremptory, irascible soldier, accustomed to command, impulsive but resolute, with muscles tough and pliant as steel wire and an inexorable will, tough but not pliant. His dominant personality, heroic aspect and the memory of his war-service as aide-de-camp to Bolívar, gave him a political prominence not justified by statesmanship or by consistency of conduct. Mosquera was thrice President for brief periods between 1845 and 1867. Although in his first administration (1845–9) he continued the conservative work of Herrán, these twenty-two years were a time of liberal movement, which took definite form in 1849 when a crowd, excited by news of the recent Parisian 'Revolution of July', forced upon a reluctant Congress—about to appoint a conservative—the election of the liberal José Hilario López. 'I will rule by the party: anyone not my friend is my enemy', was the ominous pronouncement of López, who filled the civil service with his own men, fit or unfit. Under him and his successor Obando (returned from exile and raised to the presidency), the Jesuits, who had been admitted by the con-

[1] Rather seventeen years, 1842–59, interrupted by a serious but frustrated military *coup d'état* in 1854.

servatives in 1842, were banished, clerical *fueros* abolished, religious communities suppressed, bishops and clergy subjected to the ordinary tribunals not only in civil and criminal cases, but also for neglect of their religious duties: a strange provision which turned the clergy into civil servants paid and supervised by the State. Protesting bishops were exiled: sporadic conservative revolts led to a more bitter anti-clerical movement and to the separation of Church and State in the constitution of 1853. A brief conservative administration in 1857 brought a reversal of these anti-clerical measures—soon to be reimposed and reinforced by Mosquera.

The decade 1853–63 brought three successive constitutions, a 'pact' and several constitutional enactments, which are best treated as a single movement, vehement experimental liberalism, culminating in the notable Constitution of 1863. The Constitution of 1853 enacted universal secret suffrage, complete freedom of the press, popular election of provincial governors and even of judges, and granted 'utmost municipal power' to the provinces, which proceeded to enact constitutions for themselves. Obando, the former champion of federalism, now President, aggrieved by this weakening of the executive, connived at a barrack rising, which held the capital for half a year but was finally suppressed. The President was impeached by the Chamber before the Senate and deposed from office for neglect of his duties.

Next came an 'additional act' which declared Panamá to be a 'federal sovereign State, an integral part of New Granada', and provided that a law might erect any part of the country into a State. All the provinces caught the infection, and during the following two years (1855–7) seven other States were constituted by law, comprising, with Panamá, the whole Granadan territory: each State adopted a constitution and chose a Governor or President. The new system, thus strangely formed, was defined in 1858, when eight states 'confederate themselves for ever and form a sovereign ...nation' under the significantly weak title 'Confederación Granadina'. The whole movement was in fact not federative but regional and disruptive. But the 'federal idea' had mastered everyone, including the conservatives, who hoped—with some reason but with disappointing results—that many of the new States would set up conservative governments. Indeed it was a conservative administration (1857–60) which produced the Constitution of 1858. Accordingly peace and a general agreement appeared to prevail: after suppression of the *cuartelazo* of 1853 the army was reduced to 400 men, and the 'fifties were a time of progressive public works, already noted on p. 256.

It was a delusive peace. A law passed by the conservative administration, empowering the executive to scrutinize votes in elections, was denounced as unconstitutional by the liberal press and by some State legislatures. But it was local trouble within the new States which kindled a general conflict. Hardly had these been created when in half the States the 'ins' and 'outs' were at odds. In one State the conservatives revolted against a liberal administration, and, on suffering defeat, carried their arms into the adjoining State. In another the liberals drove out a conservative Governor and installed their own. Civil wars were soon raging within four states.

The decisive event, early in 1860, was a conservative revolt in Cauca against the veteran warrior Mosquera, Governor of that State, a man dangerous to provoke. He thoroughly beat down his opponents in a sanguinary civil war within his State. But meantime the national conservative Government raised troops to restore order in the States and strengthened their own hands by legislation. Thereupon Mosquera, victorious in Cauca, demanded the abrogation of the obnoxious election law and, not obtaining this, severed relations with the central Government, claimed complete sovereignty for Cauca and, with the consent of half the States, named himself 'Supreme Director of the War'—a war of his own making. Further incited by liberal emissaries from Bogotá and by the liberal press of the capital, he attacked the national Government and the States loyal to it. For a whole year (May 1860—May 1861) sanguinary conflicts desolated the country. It was said that in one battle almost all the combatants on both sides were killed or wounded: in another half the combatants. Twice, on one occasion after severe defeat, Mosquera accepted terms of peace from commanders in the field, which the Government refused to ratify. Obando, who cannot be accused of changing sides, brought from the south his Pastusos to aid his old enemy Mosquera—now fighting, like himself, to oust authority. On the eve of final victory Obando fell by a lance-thrust in an obscure skirmish. In May 1861, two years after the first local outbreaks and a year after his challenge to the Government, Mosquera entered the capital as victor, shot three innocent men, sent the ex-President and his friends in fetters to a dungeon in Cartagena, declared himself 'Provisional President of the United States of New Granada', and summoned a Congress of Plenipotentiaries (a significant term) from six of the States—for two still resisted—who concluded (September 1861) a 'Pact of Union' as basis of a Constitution for the 'Granadan Confederation'. But serious fighting continued for three months and sporadic guerrillas for more than a year, and it was not until February 1863 that a convention of delegates—all 'liberals' as a matter of course—assembled from the States (now nine in number) and three months later (May 1863) promulgated the famous 'Constitution of Rio Negro', 'the work of a single party, the victor in the struggle', as the Chairman of the Convention remarked. By this Constitution, 'Nine sovereign states unite and confederate...and form a sovereign nation', an enigmatic pronouncement. The Constitution practically empowered the States to make war on one another and forbade the national Government to intervene or restore order except with consent of Congress. This strange contradictory system was in effect declared to be immutable, for the provisions for amendment were quite unworkable.

The new Constitution limited the presidential term to two years, in order to check the dangerous power of Mosquera, who, as conqueror, became interim President for a year and then, after a biennium of diplomatic posts in Europe, reoccupied that seat in 1866. As head of the nation this champion of State rights found that non-intervention in State civil wars made government impossible. Faced by a hostile radical majority, the old soldier assumed a military dictatorship after the typical *americano* fashion. His *coup d'état* was countered by another: the officers of the palace guard seized him in his bed: the army, the Parliament and the people applauded the stroke: Mosquera, after imprisonment in the astronomical observatory, was impeached by the Chamber before the Senate, deposed and condemned to two years' imprisonment, soon commuted to banishment.[1] Thus a juridical plaster covered up an abnormal but probably defensible breach of the peace.

After 1863 the nine sovereign States proceeded once more to form their several constitutions and 'thus began...the era of conflicts and civil wars. In these local struggles, which exceed forty, conservatives and liberals fought for power'.[2] In 1876 these local conflagrations spread over the whole country, when the conservative administrations of two States revolted against the radical national Government and roused their sympathizers to guerrilla warfare in three adjoining States. In one battle the contending armies numbered 3000 against 4000, in another 5000 against 7000. After six months' fighting the radical Government won the day. But the conflicts within the several States were ceaseless.

The end of anarchy was heralded by the election in 1880 of Rafael Núñez, a lawyer and political author aged fifty-five, who had travelled widely in Europe. His grave, thoughtful and pacific countenance, his charm of manner, his persuasive intellect, his diplomatic tact and subtlety gave him a remarkable ascendancy over men. As President of Congress and as Finance Minister Núñez had served the radical Government. But, a sincere Catholic and believer in the beneficent influence of the Church, experience and responsibility made him a conservative reformer. As President (1880–2) he worked to strengthen central authority; and during the interval[3] before his second presidency (1884–6) he urged the need of reform by an able press campaign. His inaugural address (August 1884) contained the words: 'Revolutions have become a safe and lucrative profession. We see them coming and we perceive the methods of checking them. But existing institutions forbid the use of these methods.' Three months later the

[1] After some years Mosquera returned from his exile at Lima, and became once more 'President' of Cauca and Senator for that State. He died at his home at Popayán, aged eighty, in 1878.
[2] Henao and Arrubla.
[3] The State of Panamá chose Núñez, a native of Cartagena, to be President of Panamá for the biennium 1882–4: a signal proof of his reputation. He never took up the office, being engaged in preparing for his second national presidency.

Governors of four States revolted against Núñez' Government: in other States revolutionary bands arose. Soon, despite efforts to suppress these local outbreaks, the whole country was aflame. It was in the main a radical revolt to regain the lost predominance. For eight months, January to August 1885, there was hard fighting, both a general war and local struggles everywhere.

'Señores, the Constitution of 1863 is dead.' So Núñez announced from the palace balcony when victory was in sight. Eighteen delegates, selected rather than elected, two from each State, drew up a plan of reform which was submitted—by an interesting resumption of traditional Spanish methods—to the 619 municipalities of the country. Only fourteen voted 'no'.

The resulting Constitution of 1886, which set up a unitary Government for 'The Republic of Colombia' and which with some modifications prevailed for fifty years, 'provides for political centralization and administrative decentralization'.[1] Its main points are a strong central Government which appoints Governors of Departments[2]—the former States; elected assemblies in the Departments with powers of local taxation and regulation; religious toleration, but the Roman Church protected by Government as the religion of the people. Núñez was President of Colombia until his death in 1894, usually residing for reasons of health in his native city of Cartagena and exercising control through a deputy in the capital: he declined a pension voted to him by Congress.

Occasional revolts against the new system were suppressed. But in 1899 the weakness of an aged President and the financial confusion bequeathed by civil wars tempted the radicals, the party excluded from power, to revolt. Local outbreaks, apparently insignificant at first and not treated with sufficient decision, spread into a general conflict which lasted for three years. In May 1900 in fourteen days' fighting 15,000 Government troops defeated near Bucaramanga 14,000 revolutionaries, who never recovered from the blow yet fought on doggedly for two years longer. 'The Government was victorious, but the three years' war caused in-

[1] Haring, p. 200.
[2] The Departments now number fourteen. The remote and thinly inhabited regions are administered by the central Government.

calculable harm: at least 100,000 men perished on the battle-field; many were left permanently unfit for work; commerce was ruined, communication hindered; production almost nothing; and paper money, increasingly issued by the Government...was depreciated until a paper dollar was worth less than one cent gold.'[1] And then, in less than a year came a stunning blow, the secession of Panamá.

Yet the victory in 1902 of the conservatives, who remained in office until 1930, was the beginning of a new era, the era of peace. Thenceforth the history of Colombia is, happily, not spectacular and only conspicuous for those qualities which need no record. One imminent danger, fortunately averted, demands mention: in 1904 General Reyes, an able and vigorous man who had served the State in the recent civil war, entered on a six years' term as President. Impatient of control and delays, he assumed within six months a dictatorship, imprisoning opposition deputies, dissolving Congress and creating a packed assembly to pass his own decrees. As the end of his term approached, he demanded that the presidential term, for him alone, should be lengthened to ten years. But public opinion was so stirred by this move and yet more by Reyes' proposal to recognize the independence of Panamá in return for a money payment that Reyes quietly resigned and went abroad in 1909. The country owes much to his successor Restrepo, a conciliatory and moderate man, who formed a coalition administration of conservative complexion, scrupulously observing constitutional forms and respecting local liberties. The succeeding conservative governments maintained order but—unless possibly in their protection of the Church and of religious education—cannot be called reactionary, pushing forward labour legislation, measures to encourage peasant proprietorship and extensive public works, notably road and rail, largely financed by heavy post-war borrowing in the United States. Departments and municipalities also borrowed on the security of specified local revenues; a proceeding obviously open to criticism. American corporations have also worked at supplying public utilities and developing resources, particularly oil, precious metals and banana planting.

In 1930 a split in the conservative party and the vacillations of

[1] Henao and Arrubla.

the Archbishop—invited to umpire between the merits of two conservative candidates—gave an opportunity to a liberal candidate, Olaya Herrera, Colombian Minister in Washington, who arrived in an aeroplane and, after a whirlwind electoral campaign, secured a majority of votes. No violent partisan, the liberal President continued the fifty years' conservative tradition of moderation; so also his successor, President Alfonso López (1934); although the conservatives, as the liberals in the previous period had done on occasion, now sometimes abstained from voting, which seemed to them a delusive form. Under López' influence the Constitution of 1886 was modified in 1936. The new Constitution grants immediate Colombian naturalization to any Spanish American or Brazilian who asks for it. Education is declared to be 'free' (that is not necessarily Catholic in character) subject to State supervision. All forms of worship 'not contrary to Christian morals' are permitted. 'The Government may conclude agreements with the Holy See, subject to subsequent approval by Congress, in order to regulate, upon bases of reciprocal deference and mutual respect, the relations between the State and the Catholic Church.' This seems to indicate that Colombian liberalism is discreet and conciliatory. Another clause suggests the possible rationalization of industry, subject to parliamentary consent: a hint at the bureaucratic or executive control characteristic of the times. In his allocution for the year 1936, the President appealed to his fellow-citizens on behalf of 'Christian civilization', endangered elsewhere by 'combats and horrors'.

Colombia, although sorely tried by the depression, is the only South American Republic which suffered neither *coup d'état* nor revolt in the years 1929–32. Those who doubt the future of these tropical republics of mixed Spanish, Indian and African blood may find in this history reasonable ground for hope.

THE ISTHMUS

The later international prominence and domestic turmoil of Panamá obscure the fact that until the mid-nineteenth century— that is to say until the 'federal' and Californian period—this was the most tranquil of the Granadan provinces and also relatively insignificant, no longer—as in days long past but still remembered —a treasure mart between Europe and Peru and not yet a frequented gateway between the two American coasts and two oceans.

The disorders following the disruption of Great Colombia in 1830–2 were quelled, not without some bloodshed, and Panamá was at peace until the general revolt of *los supremos* in 1840 brought some disturbances: but the leading citizens of Panamá quietly assumed independence and looked on in isolation at the two years' general chaos. This happy abstention was due to the fact that Panamá was, in relation to the rest of New Granada, practically an outlying island, being inaccessible by land. The usual route for troops and officials was by sea from Cartagena to Colón and thence across the Isthmus to the city of Panamá. The Pacific Ocean route to Panamá from Buenaventura was seldom used owing to the difficulty of the mountain paths to Buenaventura. This geographical isolation and temporary independence of Panamá in 1840–2 must be remembered in connexion with the secession in 1903.

When the Bogotá Government recovered peace and strength in 1842, the Panameños quietly submitted, accepting a general amnesty. 'From 1840 for sixteen years peace prevailed, save certain (local) disturbances';[1] a peace largely due to harmony between the administration and the clergy, whose powerful influence favoured authority and order.

But the singular geographical position of the Isthmus and the possibility of a canal were always in mind. In 1846 New Granada, apprehensive of supposedly possible British encroachments, concluded a treaty with the United States, whereby New Granada granted to the United States and to her citizens transit of the Isthmus by any existing or future modes of communication; the United States guaranteed the neutrality of the Isthmus 'that free transit may not be interrupted or embarrassed', and also guaranteed to New Granada her 'rights of sovereignty and property...over the said territory'. The treaty, although it assigned to the United States not only the right but also the duty of protecting free transit, was not intended nor was it interpreted by the United States as authorizing political intervention. They confined themselves to

[1] Bancroft.

protecting transit in case of need, abstained from all part in local
factions and on occasion urged upon the Granadan Government
the duty of protecting transit from the Granadans themselves.

In 1850 the sovereignty of New Granada was reaffirmed in the
Clayton-Bulwer Treaty between the United States and Great
Britain, in which the provisions concerning a Nicaraguan canal
were expressly applied also to a Panamá canal, the two contracting
powers binding themselves 'never to obtain or maintain any exclusive control over the ship canal; never to fortify or exercise
dominion'.

In that same year an American company, by contract with the
Granadan Government, began the construction of a railway from
Colón to Panamá. For, upon the finding of gold in California in
1848, the Isthmus had become once more a passage-way for
emigrants, fortune-hunters and treasure, as well as the resort of the
mixed crowd of plunderers who always hang upon such movements.
In 1854, after protests from eight foreign consuls against the
want of protection to passengers, who paid a transit tax, a guard
was formed, with the Governor's consent, by some citizens and
foreigners, who quietly pursued and hanged many malefactors,
frightened away the rest, and after eight months disbanded, handing
over to the local authorities a pacified land. Yet in the following
year a mob, upon very slight provocation, attacked a number of
American passengers sheltering in the railway station at Panamá.
The police, who were called in to quell the riot, joined the mob and
fired on the foreigners, of whom sixteen were killed and as many
wounded. The attacking mob had fourteen casualties. Much
baggage was·looted, and the Governor, terrified of the mob, sat by
inactive.

In 1855 two events opened the stormy modern period: the completion, after five years' labour, costly in money and in human life,
of the railway from sea to sea through miasmic swamp and jungle;
and the grant of complete Home Rule to Panamá as a 'sovereign
State'. Between 1855 and 1903 Professor Parks counts forty chief
magistrates and thirteen landings of American marines. British
marines landed thrice, in 1860, 1863 and 1873. Revolts, sham
elections and fights were ordinary incidents. In 1860, Mosquera's

civil war having touched Panamá, British marines protected the railway. From the rest of the civil war (1861–3) Panamá, semi-independent, held aloof. The Federal Constitution of 1863 and a new State Constitution brought fresh tumults. It was the era of forty local civil wars throughout Colombia: but special sources of disorder afflicted Panamá; the constant passage of foreigners, many of them rough men prone to drink and quarrels; the unruly ambition of the negroes, now all free, who far outnumbered the whites or quasi-whites and often sallied out in revolt from the negro quarter of the city of Panamá: in 1868 they poisoned a too active President. The third cause was the indefinite relation between the 'sovereign State' and the nation of which it was an 'integral part'. The local authorities failed to keep order, yet resented any police or military action by the national authorities. In 1873 the American chargé d'affaires in Bogotá demanded that the national Government should protect transit against local factions. After 1880 the introduction of thousands of workmen by the French Canal Company added to the disorder. In the general revolt of 1885 against Núñez' Government a tardy declaration of neutrality by the President of Panamá was ineffective. American forces took charge at both termini and aided the authorities against a revolutionary rabble who burnt down the town of Colón.

The unitary constitution of 1886, reducing Panamá to the condition of a Department of the Republic of Colombia under a Governor nominated by the central executive, brought neither peace nor content; there were complaints that the country thenceforth was treated as a dependency and exploited by officials sent from Bogotá. Accordingly the 'Three Years' War' of 1899–1902 brought a revolt in Panamá or rather a series of four revolts led by Belisario Porras, afterwards twice President of the Panamá Republic. The revolts failed, and the Isthmian war was ended by a peace signed in November 1902 on board the American warship *Wisconsin*. A year later Panamá was a sovereign republic.

That event was the culmination of the canal story—to be here resumed.

In 1878 the Colombian Government granted to a Frenchman named Bonaparte Wyse a concession for the construction of a canal.

The concession was transferred to a French Company, which began excavations at both ends in 1881, despite President Hayes' declaration, 'The policy of this country is a canal under American control', and despite the efforts of his Government between 1880 and 1883 to ignore or modify the Clayton-Bulwer Treaty, being unwilling to 'perpetuate any treaty impeaching our right and long-established claim to priority on the American continent'. These diplomatic efforts were renewed in the 'nineties after the failure of the French enterprise; for in 1889 the French Company, after scandalously wasteful expenditure and the death of thousands of workmen by fever, stopped work, but nevertheless managed to keep alive the concession from the Colombian Government.

The Spanish-American War of 1898 brought the matter to a head. American naval action against Spain in the Caribbean was delayed while the warship *Oregon* steamed at full speed 13,000 miles from the North Pacific round Cape Horn to reinforce the American Atlantic squadron: a convincing proof that a canal under American control was a national strategic necessity. Diplomatic obstacles disappeared when, by the Hay-Pauncefote Treaty of 1901, Great Britain—the only European Power which had not been anti-American during the Spanish War—abrogated the Clayton-Bulwer Treaty, only stipulating that the canal should be open on equal terms to the ships of all nations. The United States then purchased from the French Company the canal concession, which, however, granted no right of political control. Accordingly an agreement was signed—the Herrán-Hay Convention—granting to the United States, subject to ratification by the Colombian Senate, a lease of a strip of land across the Isthmus, with sovereign rights, in return for money payments. In August 1903 the Colombian Senate, being dissatisfied with the terms and also incensed at an arrogant note from the American Minister in Bogotá, rejected the treaty, but did not consider the matter closed and intended further negotiations. On 31 October the Colombian Senate closed its session, having done nothing more about the matter. But next day the executive declared that negotiations should continue. Two days later a revolt broke out in the city of Panamá, incited—like most Spanish-American revolts—by a few men and at first confined to the city of Panamá and unknown in Colón. An American naval commander at Colón, obeying cabled orders from Washington, prevented Colombian troops from crossing the Isthmus to quell the outbreak, orders to prevent their landing at Colón having arrived too late. The leaders of the revolt—a bloodless movement—proclaimed independence. Within three days the United States recognized that independence. A fortnight later (18 November 1903) a treaty was signed between the United States and the Republic of Panamá, which granted to the United States, in return for a guarantee of independence and for payment in money, the leased sovereignty of a strip of land ten miles wide, with the right of fortification, the right of policing in case of disturbance the adjacent cities of Panamá and Colón, and also the occupation and control of any lands or waters outside the zone which might be necessary for the canal works or their defence: a provision which empowered the United States to take possession of any Panaman territory at their own discretion.

Professor Parks, in his full and fair exposition of these events, finds no evidence that President Theodore Roosevelt himself instigated the revolt in Panamá. His action has been variously judged by American historians. Some condemn it, others consider that the urgency of the case and the unreasonable attitude (in their view) of the Bogotá Government justified or excused his prompt support of the revolt, rapid recognition of independence and violation of the 1846 treaty: for the view held by some, that the treaty which guaranteed Colombian sovereignty obliged the United States to protect the peace of the railway even against Colombian troops, need not be seriously considered. But it might be argued that the guarantee of sovereignty implied a reciprocal obligation that sovereignty should be effectively exercised: and Colombia had failed to govern the Isthmus.

But throughout Spanish America judgment was universal, unequivocal and unanimous. Colombia protested against what she regarded as high-handed robbery. 'The shock', so writes Eder, 'was felt throughout Spanish America: a quiver of indignation ran through the southern continent', an indignation repeatedly voiced during the following generation in every part of Spanish America. Some American proposals of reparation to Colombia came to nothing. At last in 1914 President Wilson brought forward a more generous proposal which Colombia was willing to accept. An uncompromising group in the American Senate delayed this arrangement for seven years, but finally, influenced, in part at least, by the discovery of oil in Colombia and by the desire of removing obstacles to American business, this opposition gave way in 1921. It was then agreed that Colombia should recognize the Republic of Panamá and should receive from the United States twenty-five million dollars in five annual instalments, besides certain rights in the Canal zone as a route between her Atlantic and Pacific coasts. Thenceforth relations between the two republics have been amicable, although hardly entirely cordial until President Franklin Roosevelt's announcement of his 'Good Neighbour' policy. President López of Colombia, accepting in a cordial letter in February 1936 President Roosevelt's invitation to the Peace Conference at Buenos Aires, writes: 'We Colombians understand the policy now developed by the President of the United States to be a radical and favourable modification of the policy which formerly aroused uneasiness and mistrust among the Latin-American peoples.... Since the beginning of Your Excellency's Government a fundamental change of direction has been effected, which all the American peoples justly value and which is a new cause of sympathy and of prestige for the United States.'

In the Republic of Panamá disorder has been checked by American guidance and by occasional interventions, including supervision of elections thrice. But when a *coup d'état* overthrew the Government in 1931, the United States did not interfere and acknowledged the new President. The country has less than one-third the area of the British Isles and less than half a million people, varying in gradations from white to black. Unconquered Indian tribes, interesting to anthropologists, subsist in the forests, but the citizens have little Indian blood. Panaman history since 1903 is simply the tale of anomalous relations with the United States, which has been admirably expounded by Dr McCain but can barely be touched here. An outcry about postal arrangements and tariffs infringing Panaman sovereignty was allayed by the 'Taft Convention' of 1904: but for thirty years there was friction about the nature and limits of sovereignty; competitive trading in the zone and smuggling thence into Panama territory; the right of police intervention and 'the right of the United States to extend the Canal zone as it chose'; also about the prohibition of a trans-Isthmian road and of any road or rail affecting canal strategy. A Convention drafted in 1926 to remedy these grievances fell through. But in 1936 the 'Good Neighbour' policy of President Franklin Roosevelt abrogated the rights of territorial expropriation and of police intervention, permitted the construction of a Colón-to-Panamá highroad, made generous concessions about possibly unfair trading and kindred matters, and disavowed any protectorate by withdrawing (in form) the guarantee of independence. Some co-operation—probably formal rather than essential—in defensive arrangements for the canal approaches, is also promised.

During the thirty years of injured pride the Panamans got great benefits from their contact with the United States: the total and most desirable disbandment of the Panaman army, improvement of internal peace, of health, of security to life and property, of justice and of the decencies of life generally, besides the material adjuncts of modern civilization. 'Colón and Panamá city had grown from malarious villages into beautiful modern cities of 33,460 and 74,409 inhabitants.' The two great events of Panaman history—not the work of the people themselves—were the construction of the canal and the preliminary sanitation in the zone and in Colón and Panamá city. Minute and costly preventive organization, based on experience in Cuba, kept off the pestilence which had swept away the workers of the French Canal Company. The canal itself, 'the greatest liberty man has taken with nature', with its two great systems of locks, was opened to world traffic in 1914.

We are concerned here not with the effect of the ship canal on world-wide trade routes, but with its more immediate Latin-American bearings. It has made the west coast of South America continuous with the east coast of the United States, bringing Guayaquil, Callao and Valparaiso within easy maritime distance of New York and New Orleans. It has also brought that west coast into nearer contact with the Old World: it has brought a stream of traffic past the northern coast of South America, to the benefit of the principal ports.

The fact that the Canal Treaty was made with the little Republic of Panamá has had one notable result. If the Herrán-Hay Treaty had been ratified, the United States would have had constant delicate questions, not with a little republic almost created by herself, but with Colombian officials on the Isthmus and with the Government at Bogotá; matters which would have caused frequent concern to all Colombia's neighbours. For example the United States were able to check, with very little disturbance, a frontier quarrel between Panamá and Costa Rica, obliging the two republics to accept a common-sense interpretation of an arbitral award given by President Loubet in 1900. Had the quarrel been between Colombia and Costa Rica, it would have been a much more awkward matter. As things are, the United States has been able to fix a limit to her more immediate political influence at the southern end of the North American Continent, the Isthmus being her strategic and economic frontier and 'part of her coast line', since it is the sea-route from New York to San Francisco. All that lies south of that line stands historically in a relation to the United States differing from that of the small Central-American and Antillean republics, which will be considered in the next two chapters.

NOTE. J. M. Henao and G. Arrubla, *History of Colombia*, translated by J. F. Rippy (Chapel Hill, N. C. 1938); Haring, ch. VII; Wilgus, *The Caribbean Area*, ch. XXII; E. T. Parks, *Colombia and the United States** (Durham, N.C., 1936); W. D. McCain, *The United States and the Republic of Panamá* (Durham, 1937); P. J. Eder, *Colombia* (London, 1907, and several reprints), a description from intimate knowledge; F. L. Petre, *The Republic of Colombia* (London, 1906); W. L. Scruggs, *The Colombian and Venezuelan Republics* (London, 1900).

CHAPTER XXIV

VENEZUELA

THE Republic of Venezuela—officially 'The United States of Venezuela'—with a territory about three and a half times that of the British Isles and a population estimated at three millions and a quarter, comprises four main regions: (1) the flat region about Lake Maracaibo and the narrow northern coastal strip between the Caribbean Sea and the mountains; (2) the mountainous region, of Alpine height in the west, but towards the east declining to gentle altitudes and containing fertile uplands and beautiful valleys, among them that of the capital; (3) the *llanos*, the plains of the Orinoco and of its western affluent the Apure, a grassy expanse parched in the dry winter and drenched in summer,[1] extending to the forests of the west and of the south; and (4) the Guayana (Guiana) highlands towards the Brazilian border, a region of mountain, dense forest and running streams, only inhabited by scanty tribes of Indians. These are the main divisions in a country of infinite diversity: indeed the western region of Maracaibo and in the east the great delta of the Orinoco, a country of jungle, swamp and rivers (the thirty-six mouths of the Orinoco) are distinct regions in themselves. The River Orinoco, navigable to ocean ships of moderate size as far as Ciudad Bolívar, provides, with its affluents, access by lighter vessels to a vast interior, especially in the rainy season; for the Orinoco, like the Amazon, has a seasonal rise and fall of 40 ft. or more.

The country possesses a cultured white or rather quasi-white aristocracy: but the mass of the people are of mixed origin, European, Indian and (particularly in the coastal region) African.

The northern coast of Venezuela, like that of Colombia, faces across the Mediterranean Sea of the New World towards the southern shore of the United States. Thus the country belongs to

---

[1] The rainy season, May to November approximately, is locally called winter (*invierno*). The dry season, in reality the winter months, is called summer (*verano*).

that Caribbean Area, of close concern to the United States. Venezuela also is singular in having a European people as neighbour, for her eastern border touches British Guiana, and the British island of Trinidad, within sight of her shores, has much commerce with Venezuelan ports and supplies a retreat for Venezuelan exiles or for men who have worked and saved in Venezuela. Angostura bitters, formerly made at Angostura (now Ciudad Bolívar), are now made under safer conditions in Trinidad.

The 'United States of Venezuela' nominally form a Federation of twenty autonomous states—each possessing in theory its own legislature and constitution—besides a Federal District and three Territories administered by the central Government. The Territories, with few inhabitants, comprise nearly half the national area. As will appear from this chapter, no real federation exists. The States, known as 'provinces' until 1864, have numbered at different times eleven, thirteen, twenty-one, twenty, eight, nine, twenty, thirteen and again twenty. Evidently they are not essential entities joined in a federal union, but are the result of a succession of experiments in decentralization and local government. Seven of the States have less than 100,000 inhabitants apiece and five of these considerably less. An American historian remarks, 'no genuine attempt has been made to establish the federal system as we know it in this country',[1] and relates that a business man of his acquaintance in the city of Valencia did not know whether the State had a constitution. On the other hand the division into twenty-four parts for purposes of local government is quite reasonable, and the word 'federation' is used partly from misunderstanding, partly because it is a popular party symbol, representing liberalism, local institutions and theoretical limitation of central authority. Obviously, however, the administration has certain federal elements.

Venezuela suffered more than any other South American country from the war of independence—'war to the death'—which here, even more than elsewhere, was a ruinous civil war, Venezuelans fighting and killing one another in opposing hosts in the name of King or of *patria*. From Venezuela armies went out to New Granada, Quito and Peru, whence not many returned. Earthquake

[1] W. W. Pierson in *The Caribbean Area*, p. 422.

added to the destruction; and Venezuela lost in these struggles from one-fifth to one-third of the population. Most of the whites perished, the Creole aristocracy from which Bolívar and Sucre had sprung. Thus here more than anywhere was reconstitution difficult. The twenty Venezuelan constitutions are said to prove Venezuelan unsteadiness, not quite fairly; for three of them are the war-time constitutions of 1811 (Caracas), 1820 (Angostura) and 1821 (Cúcuta). The moderate Constitution of Valencia (1830) which granted considerable local autonomy, the first Constitution of independent Venezuela, stood for twenty-seven years. Some of the later constitutions have been dictatorial enactments rather than republican experiments. 'Dictatorship', says Professor Pierson 'has been the real constitution, whatever the formal written instrument...may have been'. Yet the republic has had an agitated life. Without including minor uprisings, historians record, in the seventy years after 1830, above fifty serious revolts (mis-called 'revolutions'), of which twelve succeeded in overthrowing government.

Nevertheless, for seventeen years after separation from New Granada (1830–46) Venezuela had a sounder Government than any other Latin-American republic except Chile, and a Government more moderate and liberal than any, thanks to Páez, the llanero horseman, now allied with the educated classes, reconciler of parties, twice President (1831–5 and 1839–43), and leader of the conservative oligarchy which ruled until 1846. Páez himself rode out to crush four long-drawn-out revolts with all his old furious dash, enhancing his legendary renown by strange exploits against rebels and brigands. But his painstaking and peaceful administration is an equal title to fame; Páez was singular among dictators in his respect for law. In 1835 he vacated the presidency, retiring to his beloved cattle-farm, soon to be summoned thence in order to crush revolt against his successor. During the seventeen years of his influence schools were opened (for the unlettered chieftain valued education); strict integrity ruled the Treasury; much public debt was paid off, despite the great cost of suppressing rebels; the army was reduced to 800 men, merely a police force; roads were improved; religious toleration was proclaimed in 1834. In that year an English Church was opened in Caracas. In the unaccustomed field of external affairs the conservative oligarchy went astray, declining or allowing to lapse a favourable offer from Lord Aberdeen concerning the British Guiana boundary question.

Páez had never liked Bolívar's warmth towards the Church. Religious houses of men were now suppressed; and the bishops, on pain of exile, were forced to swear solemnly in church to the Constitution of 1830. The President himself, separated from his wife, frequented the theatre and other public places accompanied by his 'official' mistress, who, however, commanded no monopoly of his attentions.

A former henchman of Páez, A. L. Guzmán, was the spokesman of liberal opposition, founder in 1840 of a newspaper El Venezolano, in which he urged democratic reforms in vehement popular journalism and later in violent personal abuse. In 1846 he stood for the Presidency, was held responsible for armed uprisings in support of his candidature and was arrested before the election.[1] Páez backed José Tadeo Monagas, like himself an unlettered son of the plains, who with his younger brother José Gregorio had fought for independence and had been rewarded with gifts of land. The brothers had led two military revolts against the Conservative Oligarchy; yet Páez believed him to be the most likely continuer of his own work. Monagas had other views but encouraged this opinion. Duly elected, he founded the 'Dynasty of the Monagas', also strangely known as the 'Liberal Oligarchy'. Monagas, professing liberalism and winning support from genuine liberals, nevertheless protected clerical and military fueros, to gain that valuable two-fold alliance. A crowd of officials, including provincial Governors, were displaced by Monaguistas. After a year of growing autocracy and financial corruption, the House of Deputies prepared to impeach the President before the Senate and took the precaution of providing itself, quite legally, with a police guard and voted an adjournment to the safer air of Puerto Cabello.

The President's reply was prompt. On 23 January 1848 shots

---

[1] After the election Guzmán was condemned to death for sedition but was allowed to pass into exile. He soon returned, to become Vice-President under President Monagas.

were fired outside the Parliament: two of the police guard fell and two of the assailants. Next day a turbulent crowd, supported or at least not impeded by troops, threatened the assembly. Some deputies were killed in attempting to escape. The whole body issuing from the House were driven back by musket fire. After several other deputies had fallen, the diplomatic corps persuaded Monagas to 'pardon the lives' (his own phrase) of the rest, who made their way to safety, many seeking refuge in foreign legations. A later subservient Congress appointed 24 January to be a national holiday, to celebrate the 'establishment of liberty'.

Páez denounced the outrage on Parliament and organized a revolt in the west. But whereas he had always succeeded in raising forces to defend authority, few followed him in revolt. Defeated, he fled into New Granada, returned thence to renew his attempt, was captured and confined in a damp airless dungeon; and in 1850, deprived of titles, military rank and pay, the 'father of his country' was exiled and departed for the United States.

After four years José Tadeo Monagas passed on the presidency to his younger brother, who duly handed it back to José Tadeo four years later. This Monagas dynasty, which in spite of repeated revolts endured for twelve years, carried out one liberal measure— the abolition of slavery in 1854. Some slaves had been already freed by a manumission fund, established in 1821 for Great Colombia but much neglected, and also by the *libertad de vientre* dating from 1830. And now the remaining 13,000 slaves and 27,000 *manumisos* (freedmen still owing some service) were liberated and an indemnity was provided for their masters.[1]

Another supposedly liberal measure, passed in 1849, forbade the death penalty for treason and conspiracy; 'a law', says Gil Fortoul, 'which was rightly held to be eminently humane in a country of endemic revolution, where there was hardly a public man who did not conspire against the Government'. Others hold that the prevalence of these offences called for severity rather than lenity.

[1] New Granada abolished slavery in 1851, Ecuador in 1852 and Peru in 1855: evidently slavery was out of date in the Spanish republics: but this does not lessen the merit of the younger Monagas and his advisers. Peonage, however, continued in Venezuela and is not quite extinct to-day.

In 1857 José Tadeo Monagas, in order to secure his own (illegal) re-election, enacted through an obedient Congress a new Constitution, which swept away the laws prescribing slow and cautious amendment of the Constitution. The thirteen provinces, with their Governors, assemblies and officials, were now abolished and replaced by twenty-one provinces, in order that the President might nominate twenty-one governors, who should secure for him the support of twenty-one new assemblies and of all the subordinate officials. Thus the object of this 'federal' constitution was to strengthen and perpetuate a central dictatorship. But a year later general discontent, increased by financial scandals, overthrew Monagas—condemned to 'perpetual exile', which lasted two years. In 1859 a Convention at Valencia, elected by universal suffrage, decreed a Constitution resembling that of 1830, but providing a wider franchise and an extension of local Government. This Constitution hardly had a trial, for in the same year began the *guerra larga* between the constitutionalists or reds and the federalists or yellows, a war of 'innumerable guerrilla bands who gather, disperse and reassemble daily without decided advantage to either side for nearly five years'. In 1861 Páez, now over seventy, reappeared from exile, took command of the constitutionalists and maintained a precarious dictatorship during two years of war, until in 1863 the federalists were successful owing to the skill of Guzmán Blanco, a dashing guerrillero leader and a persuasive negotiator, son of the liberal journalist A. L. Guzmán. Páez, vanquished, passed once more into exile and died ten years later in New York, aged eighty-three.

These and later conflicts were not wholly aimless. It is true that unfortunate peasants were forced or decoyed into the ranks of the nearest 'general' without much notion what it all meant; but the federalist leaders were contending not indeed for real federalism but for decentralization, local government and some check on central authority; and notwithstanding the dictatorships which followed, they achieved something.

In 1864 a new 'federalist' constitution erected twenty provinces into States, adopted the name 'United States of Venezuela', and restricted presidential office to two years. But this experiment brought no peace. During a stormy five years and a succession of revolts, Guzmán Blanco strove for settlement. But ex-President Monagas reappeared in arms and seized the Presidency. He died in office, but was succeeded by his son, third of the dynasty. Guzmán Blanco, driven into exile, organized an expedition in the Dutch island of Curazao, mastered the capital and the central region, and, ruthlessly crushing several uprisings (for there were no more amnesties) extended his sway over the whole country. In the prime of life (forty-one), a man of firm courage, inflexible determination and a personality which took hold of his people, this son of the liberal publicist, himself professing federal liberalism, ruled the country as dictator for nearly twenty years (1870–89), sometimes as Constitutional President, sometimes in nominal retreat, spending these intervals as Venezuelan Minister in Paris and sending orders thence to his nominee in Caracas. His 'unbending, corrupt, progressive autocracy'[1] had a farcical, capricious, bombastic side, as when a solemn academic commission was appointed to assign the prize among some hundreds of school essays on the set subject of The Glory of the 'Illustrious American', his chosen title. He declared that he had 'undertaken an infinite voyage towards an infinite future'. He grew rich at the public expense, treating the custom-house as his own property, but did much for financial reform and for education. Like other dictators, he promoted economic progress by public works and, most of all, by ensuring peace.

A dispute with the Archbishop over a matter of little moment pricked the dictator's susceptible vanity and was one motive for his policy of contemptuous anti-clericalism: a policy which has never since been reversed. Nunneries (already few in number) were suppressed:[2] clerical *fueros* were abolished: civil marriage was established: marriage of clergy was authorized: funds appropriated for clerical salaries were ridiculously small and half the parishes were vacant. He even talked of a national Church independent of Rome.

In 1887 the dictator withdrew a third time to his luxurious diplomatic retreat in Paris. It was once too often. Two years later

[1] Gil Fortoul.
[2] Seminaries, training colleges for the priesthood, were also suppressed, but were restored after Guzmán Blanco's time.

an exultant mob was smashing the half-dozen effigies of the 'Regenerator', which adorned or disfigured the capital, while Congress denounced his autocracy and deposed his nominee.

Disorders followed. But General Crespo, the best of Guzmán Blanco's men, an honourable and devoted public servant, ruled as President from 1892 to 1896, was the mainstay of his successor and seemed to be the best hope for the future. Unhappily he was killed in a skirmish against rebels in 1899.[1]

From the succeeding anarchy there emerged in that same year another strong dictator, Cipriano Castro, 'the Lion of the Andes', a man of mixed blood, owner of land and cattle in the western mountainous region. A bold and skilful guerrillero leader, he started an insurrection in the west, aided by a neighbouring cattle-farmer, Juan Vicente Gómez, like himself an Andino of mixed blood. Gathering recruits by force, eluding or beating or adding to his own forces successive bodies of Government troops, he entered the capital after a campaign recalling that of Bolívar in 1813. He proclaimed liberty, became Provisional President, then President and in effect dictator for nine years of cruel and repulsive tyranny. He crushed repeated outbreaks with dauntless courage and also with ruthless penalties.[2] Mere suspicion of disaffection brought a man to prison. Dreadful stories are told of pestilential dungeons, torture, long imprisonments, lingering deaths. It was a strange autocracy, for Castro was unimposing in appearance, ignorant, shamelessly sensual, wantonly cruel, insolent in his dealings with foreign nations, possessing few gifts of statesmanship except intrepid courage, self-confidence and resolute determination. He owed much to his deserved military fame and to the firm discretion of his right-hand man Gómez. For nearly a decade Castro wielded

[1] When, on the occasion of the Cleveland message in December 1895, Caracas burst into wild excitement, beflagged processions and harangues glorifying the United States and vituperating Great Britain, President Crespo maintained a dignified patience and noncommittal reserve.

Crespo, having been advised by his physician to visit the seaside village of Maiquetia, was reminded that the President could not leave the Federal District without permission from Congress. 'Put Maiquetia in the Federal District', said the President; and this was done.

[2] G. Garibaldi, in *A Toast to Rebellion* (London, 1936), chs. VI–XII, describes the most serious revolt against Gómez and the fate of the captives. G. W. Crichfield in *American Supremacy*, 2 vols. (New York, 1908), describes, from his own experience, forced recruiting: vol. I, pp. 278–81.

despotic authority, supported by bayonets, served by a host of spies and surrounded by submissive adulation. Like other dictators, he promoted public improvements and he gave his country peace. Castro was married; but his personal indulgences exceeded all that could be imagined in Ruritanian farce. He was reputed to have seven houses in different parts of the city, each inhabited by a lady: the street outside each house was brilliantly illuminated, as a means of police protection. But he ranged much farther afield in his indulgences. At the end of 1908 Castro, his health ruined by excess, departed for Europe to consult surgeons, leaving in authority as Vice-President his old companion Gómez, so astute a manager of men that he was nicknamed *el brujo*, the wizard.

Castro, on returning to Venezuela, was forbidden to disembark by Gómez, who quietly took the place of the dethroned chieftain and initiated a dictatorship which lasted twenty-six years until the death of the dictator at the age of seventy-eight in December 1935.

When Castro left in 1908, the national finances were chaotic: debts were repudiated: several powers, including France, had broken off relations, and the Netherlands Government had sent gunboats to requite an outrage. Gómez changed all this: diplomatic relations were renewed and debts punctually paid. By 1931 the whole foreign debt was redeemed and four years later the internal debt. Aided by wartime high prices Gómez had begun to work this miracle even before foreign corporations, mostly American, opened up, from 1918 onwards, the great Maracaibo oil-field, enriching the Government and—together with monopolies and other profitable affairs—bringing a colossal fortune to Gómez and abundance to his family and friends. Gómez was unmarried, but his known children numbered some scores.

Gómez nominated the Congress and dictated the laws, sometimes as President, sometimes (declining unconstitutional re-election) as Commander-in-Chief directing a puppet President. An early riser (5 a.m.), frugal and a hard worker, he ruled the country from his country house at Maracay, in a beautiful valley seventy miles south-west of Caracas, secured by military roads, adjacent barracks and an aeroplane camp. The whole Venezuelan population was disarmed and carefully watched. Ebullitions of revolt and repeated incursions of exiles were quelled. Captured revolutionaries, suspects and men denounced by the ubiquitous spies suffered hideous penalties. Censorship filtered all news for abroad, and concealed the gravity of the outbreak in the capital among students and part of the garrison in 1928. Peace was preserved, credit was high and—like Porfirio Díaz before his fall—Gómez was regarded abroad as the creator of a new and solvent Venezuela. A Venezuelan authority, quoted by Mr Pierson, sums up the work of Gómez: peace; increased commerce, agriculture and industry; improved education and hygiene: but unworthy officials, enriched by office; corrupt manipulations of oil concessions; business and industries exploited by presidents and officials (this was a huge scandal); Constitution and law violated; prisons full of political prisoners subject to infamous punishments; exiles, arbitrary rule legalized.

Upon the dictator's death—or more probably at his command before his death—Congress appointed as Provisional President General Contreras, Minister for War, a moderate man of known prudence and energy. The stir of half-incredulous relief throughout the country on news of Gómez' death naturally brought some disorder, but singularly little. In the capital a general strike was provoked by an arbitrary edict from the Governor of the Federal District, at whose orders (apparently) troops fired on a demonstrating crowd. The crowd, surging before the President's residence, demanded a free press, the dismissal of all Gómez' officials and the restoration of civil rights. The first two demands were granted. As to the third, the moment was hardly opportune for defining civil rights. The Governor of the Federal District fled into hiding and was replaced by a released prisoner. The houses of Gómez' kinsmen and friends were sacked and the contents made bonfires. Many officials were dismissed, among them two State Governors, replaced by returning exiles; for the refugees and the proscribed now returned home, while the dictator's family and political friends, fleeing from retribution—some of them with fat purses—filled the hotels of Curazao. The Venezuelan Government later claimed about £6,750,000 from the estate left by Gómez: and many suits have been brought against that huge estate by those who suffered in person or substance and by the surviving relatives of his victims.

Contreras, having completed the unfinished term in April 1936, became President for seven years, the term fixed in the Constitution enacted by Gómez. While maintaining strong rule and watchful precautions, Contreras has reversed the previous system without serious disturbance. Social services, public works and the welfare of workers have been his care, and also an attempt to give more reality to State Governments. A new Constitution, together with a detailed 'basic law', shortens the presidential term to five years and grants full civic rights to all save communists and anarchists. The mere profession of those doctrines is treason. Thus formal legality is given to measures commonly practised in other republics by executive authority; and the formation of a 'popular front' of left groups was forbidden on the ground that some of the groups were banned by law.

The transition from the Gómez period is one of the most promising passages in recent South American history. There is something in Gómez' boast that he was breaking the revolutionary habit and enforcing the custom of peace. But the conspicuous fact is that a strong man has guided the transition. Much depends on the successor to the sexagenarian Contreras.

FOREIGNERS AND FRONTIERS

Venezuela's frontier questions with her neighbours, Colombia, Brazil and British Guiana, have been settled by arbitration. The last of these questions, the long dispute about the eastern frontier, concerns the external relations of Spanish America.

The Republic of Venezuela was heir to the Spanish Captaincy-General of Venezuela. Great Britain on the other hand by treaty with the Netherlands in 1814 acquired the settlement of Demerara, Essequibo and Berbice, which had been recognized as Dutch by Spain in the Treaty of Münster in 1648. But in these treaties the limits were not fixed; nor could they be fixed in those unexplored and uninhabited regions. The crux of the matter was the control of the southern shore of the Great Mouth or Ocean Mouth of the River Orinoco, upon which shore Point Barima (later the western limit of the British claim) is a strategic point.

In 1822, upon the formation of Bolívar's Great Colombia, the

Colombian agent in London was instructed to inform the British Government that 'The colonists of Demerara and Berbice have usurped a considerable territory which, according to the last treaties between Spain and Holland, belongs to us, on (this) side of the River Essequibo. It is absolutely indispensable that these colonists should place themselves under the protection and obedience of our laws or should retire to their former possessions.' Great Britain not having recognized Colombian independence, the matter dropped; and when the treaty of recognition and friendship was signed in 1825, Colombia, intent on other matters, did not raise the question, which remained dormant till 1840.

In that year the British Foreign Office instructed the Prussian geographer and explorer of British Guiana, Robert Schomburgh, to trace and mark with posts the western boundary. This he did, placing the first post at Point Barima and tracing thence a line generally in a southerly direction but following the winding course of hills and rivers. The Venezuelan Government protested, claiming again the Essequibo as boundary.[1] Lord Aberdeen replied that the posts were meant not as a definite claim but as a basis for negotiation. The matter then rested ('owing to difficulties interposed by Great Britain', according to Gil Fortoul) until 1844, when Fortique, the capable Venezuelan Minister in London, reopened negotiations, again claiming the Essequibo boundary. Lord Aberdeen disagreed, but proposed a line which left the whole Orinoco estuary and the adjacent country in Venezuelan possession, starting from a point (the mouth of the River Moroco) some 150 miles east of Point Barima. Thus he surrendered the northern part of the Schomburgh line, but claimed the southern part, ceding the extreme British claim on condition that Venezuela undertook to protect the Indian inhabitants and never to cede the territory in question to any other power. Fortoul remarks that the extreme British and Venezuelan claims were equally unfounded, but that Venezuela missed this opportunity of settling the matter by fair negotiation. 'Unfortunately', he says, 'the Venezuelan Government impeded the

[1] The Venezuelan Minister in London was, however, instructed to make 'gradual concessions' in order to reach a satisfactory agreement. He apparently ignored these instructions.

negotiations of their able Minister in London by useless delays and superfluous observations...they regarded the British conditions as offensive to national sovereignty....Such conditions did not in the least affect the sovereignty of the Republic....Upon urgent messages from Fortique that so favourable an opportunity should not be missed, the Venezuelan Government decided to withdraw their objections, on condition that the non-alienation clause should be made reciprocal' and that the Indian clause should be modified. This decision never reached the British Government; for upon the sudden death of Fortique the Venezuelan Government dropped the matter ('owing to foolish parsimony', says Gil Fortoul) and Lord Aberdeen received no reply to his offer. Gil Fortoul adds that the matter then 'could have been easily concluded and would have saved to the Republic troublesome questions and final defeat'. And J. M. Rojas, an older historian, who as Venezuelan Minister in London had to deal with the question later, writes: 'we have never been able to grasp the reasons why the Government did not accept an agreement which would have avoided the later thorny complications.'

The matter then rested until 1850, when a Venezuelan decision to fortify Barima Point brought a protest from the British Government, which declared that they had no intention of occupying the contested area but were not indifferent to Venezuelan occupation. Venezuela then accepted a mutual agreement not to occupy. Both sides broke this agreement, the Essequibo colonists by casual westward encroachment on empty lands, the Venezuelan Government by a more definite act, the foundation of a settlement in 1858. In that year the Governor of British Guiana visited Caracas in hopes of effecting an agreement, but reported that nothing could be done owing to disturbed conditions.

The 'extreme claims' on either side differed in kind. Venezuela claimed lands inhabited and cultivated by colonists of British and Dutch origin. Great Britain claimed, on behalf of those colonists, empty lands where political sovereignty was hard to find. This point is illustrated by the Venezuelan historian L. Duarte Level,[1] who, after giving a damaging account of the Spanish missions in

[1] *Cuadros de la historia...de Venezuela* (Madrid, *c.* 1920).

Guiana, adds that Venezuela owes them gratitude: 'in our frontier question with British Guiana, our only solid and incontestable argument for rights over Guiana was the work of the missionaries there. We owed it to them that we did not lose all. Our frontiers reached as far as the advance of the evangelizing Capuchins. In planting the Cross they fixed the limits of Venezuela.' These Capuchin missions were destroyed by the Venezuelan republicans in 1817. Of the forty-one missionaries, eleven escaped, ten died in prison, the rest were executed.

From 1858 the matter again rested for eighteen years. The second phase of the dispute opened in 1876 under changed conditions: gold had been discovered in the Cuyuní valley. To a Venezuelan note reopening the question, the British replied that they would await the expected arrival in London of Langdon, Governor of British Guiana, before replying. Venezuela then sent a memorandum to Washington, reviewing the controversy, and declaring that Venezuelan representations to Great Britain 'had only met with manifestations of annoyance'. Two American investigators, Perkins and Possum, find no ground for this complaint.

The British Government was, however, strangely dilatory. Two years passed; Governor Langdon did not arrive in London; and the Foreign Office was silent. At last, in 1879, Rojas, Venezuelan Minister in London, reopened the question, proposing either a settlement according to historical right or a 'boundary of accommodation, each side conceding a little'. Lord Salisbury replied preferring the second method, but declaring that the Essequibo boundary was inadmissible, as it would mean the abandonment of 40,000 British subjects and of territory which had been in Dutch possession for 200 years. After fruitless correspondence extending over two years, Lord Granville in 1881 made another proposal, less generous than the Aberdeen offer of 1844, but still ceding Barima Point. Venezuela sent no reply to Lord Granville for two years, throwing away (so Perkins considers) a good opportunity for favourable settlement. Instead of this, Venezuela again applied to the United States, mentioning the Monroe Doctrine. In 1886 the United States offered to Great Britain their good offices with a view to arbitration; but the offer was declined. Acceptance of this offer might have saved later trouble without loss of dignity. The Colonial Office List for 1885 had this note: 'It is impossible to specify the exact area of the colony, as its precise boundaries between Venezuela and Brazil are undetermined, but it has been computed to be 76,000 square miles.' The List for 1886 has the same paragraph, but the last words run: 'computed to be about 109,000 square miles.' To-day's estimate is 98,480 square miles.

In 1887 President Guzmán Blanco handed the British Minister his passports and 'in the name of the immortal Monroe' appealed to the United States to insist on arbitration of the whole Venezuelan claim. All this time, although the matter was gaining attention in the United States, neither the State Department nor the general public were profoundly stirred or disposed to take a hand. But in 1894 Venezuela appointed as Agent in the United States a vehement advocate, W. L. Scruggs, formerly American Minister to Colombia and Venezuela. His widely distributed pamphlet *British Aggressions in Venezuela; or the Monroe Doctrine on Trial*, published in 1894 and reprinted (to supply demand) in 1895, prejudged the whole question both in the first two words of the title and in the pamphlet itself. His words stirred the Anglophobe feeling of certain sections of the American population and, by representing the Monroe Doctrine in danger, touched a more general sentiment. In the spring of 1895 Scruggs visited the Secretary of State, Olney, and a little later President Cleveland. In July 1895 Olney sent his famous despatch to Lord Salisbury declaring that 'distance and 3000 miles of intervening ocean make any permanent political union between an European and an American State unnatural and inexpedient.... The States of America, south as well as north, by geographical proximity, by natural sympathy, by similarity of Governmental Constitutions, are friends and allies of the United States.... To-day the United States is practically sovereign on this Continent,[1] and its fiat is law upon the subjects to which it confines its interposition.... There is a doctrine of American public law... which...requires the United States to treat as an injury to itself

---

[1] The context shows that the word 'Continent' is here meant to include both American Continents. The despatch, which reads like a didactic lecture, is given in A. B. Hart's book on the Monroe Doctrine and also by Alvarez.

the forcible assumption by an European Power of political control over an American State.' Olney—as Monroe had done in 1823—bases his argument on possible injury to the United States. And of this he writes a detailed and gloomy forecast.

Lord Salisbury, after four months, sent a reply more categorical than conciliatory, denying that the Monroe Doctrine was international law or applicable to this particular case. President Cleveland then submitted the correspondence to Congress, with a message which implied that Great Britain by an extension of boundaries was taking 'possession of the territory of one of our neighbouring republics'. He added the words: 'The Monroe Doctrine finds its recognition in those principles of international law which are based upon the theory that every nation shall have its rights protected and its just claims enforced.' He proposed that a Commission should be appointed by the United States Government to examine the question and make a report and he concluded with the words: 'When such report is made,... it will in my opinion be the duty of the United States to resist by every means in its power, as a wilful aggression upon its rights and interests, the appropriation by Great Britain of any lands... which after investigation we have determined of right belong to Venezuela.'

Accordingly the United States Government appointed a Commission to investigate in Washington the dispute between Great Britain and Venezuela. This Commission never reported, for Great Britain now concluded at Washington a treaty of arbitration with Venezuela, only stipulating that occupation should confer a title. The United States, acting on behalf of Venezuela, agreed that fifty years' occupation should be taken as conclusive. The decision of the Arbitration Court, sitting in Paris, was disappointing to Venezuela; but this is an insignificant part of the episode. Its real significance lies in the fact that Great Britain, after denying the right of the United States to intervene, nevertheless accepted their intervention. Thus United States policy achieved a novel and striking development, of profound significance for the Republics of Latin America. Opinion in those Republics universally approved the action of the United States in this instance; and from a practical point of view, apart from political theory, that action was beneficial to both the litigants by settling, with the moral, although not formal, guarantee of the United States, a vexatious question. A valuable precedent for the settlement of disputes by arbitration was also established. On the other hand Olney's claim of supremacy in the Western Hemisphere—apparently connected with the Monroe Doctrine—has not been maintained by later American statesmen.

People in England generally knew nothing and cared little about the Guiana boundary, but cared much about any trouble with the United States over a matter so remote, and were much relieved by Lord Salisbury's pacific concession. Whitehall can hardly have regarded British interests as seriously endangered. But the Foreign Office was trustee for the people of British Guiana—English-Dutch in origin and denizens of America no less than the Venezuelans—and was bound to make the best possible terms for them. In Anglo-Saxon and Spanish rivalry in the New World this incident is a small episode, in which the United States, in consequence of the events of 1775–83, were quite reasonably advocates for the Spanish side.

Six years later came a more direct clash with European powers. When, after years of destructive civil war, the ignorant and violent despot Castro mastered the country, he was soon faced by claims for reparation from ten foreign countries, including the United States and Mexico, partly for injury to persons and property, partly for non-payment of Government obligations. Two of these powers were particularly insistent, Great Britain and Germany. Castro, eager to win patriotic applause by showing contempt for the foreigner, refused arbitration. His fair-sounding offer to submit the claims to a Venezuelan Commission was reasonably rejected, since it simply meant submitting the claims to Castro himself, who had lately imprisoned several judges of the Supreme Court for a mere hint at some possible legal decisions unsatisfactory to the executive. In the course of 1902 Great Britain and Germany agreed upon joint coercion of Venezuela unless satisfied. In November 1902 Great Britain communicated this coercive intention to the American Secretary of State, John Hay, who replied 'that the United States Government, although they regretted that European powers should use force against Central and South

American countries, could not object to their taking steps to obtain redress for injuries suffered by their subjects, provided that no acquisition of territory was contemplated.' Germany some months earlier had signified to Washington her intention and had received a similar reply.

On 7 December 1902 the British and the German Ministers in Caracas each presented a strong note demanding satisfaction and then left the country, committing the interests of their nationals to Mr Bowen, the American Minister. Two days later a German frigate, aided by British sailors, seized four Venezuelan gunboats at La Guaira. Castro at once arrested all the Germans and British in the capital. The Governors of provinces, in obedience to telegraphed orders from the dictator, did the same, and these unfortunate foreigners were confined in horrible Venezuelan prisons for some days, until the American Minister and the American Consuls throughout the country insisted on their release and took all German and British property under American protection. On 11 December Great Britain proclaimed a blockade of several ports and two days later, in reprisal for the seizure of a British ship and an affront to the British flag, the antique forts at Puerto Cabello were bombarded, without loss of life.

On that day Venezuela submitted through the United States a limited proposal for arbitration, which was accepted in principle by the allies, including Italy, which had now joined the blockade. President Roosevelt was invited to serve as arbiter but declined, and it was decided to refer the matter to the Hague. At a preliminary diplomatic conference in Washington, Bowen, American Minister at Caracas, represented the Venezuelan Government. Negotiations were difficult, particularly as to priority for the claims of the blockading powers: nor were they facilitated by a German bombardment of a fort at La Guaira: but finally these matters were referred to the Hague, and on 13 February 1903 the blockade was lifted, two months after it had begun. The Hague tribunal arranged that ten mixed Commissions should sit in Washington to judge the ten claims, preference being given to those of the blockading powers. Great Britain and, at British suggestion, Germany also had already reduced considerably their pecuniary demands, and the Commissions largely reduced all the claims. The least excessive of these proved to be that of the United States. That power throughout had acted a moderate and conciliatory part, devoid of animus and effective towards a solution.

The influence of this Venezuelan episode on Anglo-American relations does not here concern us. But this, the last European intervention to enforce pecuniary claims, marks a stage in the relations of Latin America with Europe and with the United States. It also gave occasion for the suggestion sometimes known as the Drago Doctrine. On 29 December 1902 Señor Drago, Argentine Minister for Foreign Affairs and afterwards a member of the Hague tribunal, propounded to the United States on behalf of his Government the view that the forcible collection of debt from any nation was inadmissible. He argued that this view was implicit in the Monroe Doctrine 'to which this Argentine Republic has hitherto solemnly adhered'; and he invoked the 'sentiment of Continental brotherhood'. In 1907 Drago in an article in the *American Journal of International Law* repeated this view, expressing his regret at the Treaty concluded in that year between the United States and Santo Domingo, which—so he declared—violated the Drago principle.

NOTE. *The Caribbean Area*, especially chs. XXIII and XXIV, by W. W. Pierson; T. Rourke, *Tyrant of the Andes* (London, 1937) is a biography of Gómez; W. L. Scruggs, *Colombian and Venezuelan Republics*; Dr Possum carefully relates the Guiana boundary dispute in vol. VIII of the *Hispanic-American Historical Review*, and Professor D. Perkins reviews it in *The Monroe Doctrine, 1867–1907* (Baltimore, U.S.A., 1937).

CHAPTER XXV

BRAZIL

BESIDES the difference of origin and language, Brazil, or Portuguese South America, differs from Spanish South America in three fundamental points, unity, monarchy, slavery. (1) Portuguese South America, claiming about half the continent, remained politically united, while the other half broke up into nine Spanish-speaking republics. (2) Brazil, suffering no violent break with the past and having almost no war of independence, continued to be ruled by a branch of the hereditary Braganza dynasty down to 1889. (3) The basis of the social industrial system in Brazil until near the end of that period was negro slavery. The slave-trade, though theoretically illegal by treaty with Great Britain from 1831, continued until after 1850; and slavery itself, much diminished towards the end of the period, down to 1888.

As to the maintenance of political union, Brazil, despite its vast extent, its want of economic unity, the difficulties of communication in former times and the difference in character between (for example) the sugar-growing tropical lands with their negro and 'coloured' peasantry, the coffee-growing red-soil uplands of São Paulo and the 'gaucho' State of Rio Grande do Sul, is not split up by natural barriers. Yet, but for the unifying authority of the monarchy, 'federalist' movements might have become dangerously separatist. For ten years, 1835–45, the pastoral country of Rio Grande do Sul maintained, by guerrilla warfare, a precarious independence until imperial authority was restored by force and an amnesty proclaimed; and the long-standing dissident sentiment of the north, centred in Pernambuco, although suppressed in 1817 and 1824, flared up again in 1848 but had to deal with a firm and stable government.

Brazil, a Federation of twenty semi-autonomous States, measuring above 2600 miles from north to south and somewhat more from east to west, is in itself almost a continent; but, traversed by the Equator and lying principally within the tropics, the country has in effect much less range of latitude than Chile or Argentina. The dominant features are the equatorial forest-clad valley of the Amazon; the great plateau, seamed by the deep ravines of several rivers, rising into two mountain-chains and facing the Atlantic across the coastal plain for 2000 miles with an edge 2000–3000 ft. high; and the great forest (Matto Grosso) of the western lowlands. The capital, most magnificent of all the inhabited places of the world in its natural setting and now a city worthy of that setting, stands just north of the Tropic of Capricorn; and a rect-angular extension of Brazilian territory stretches thence southward through a sub-tropical region into the temperate zone to the border of Uruguay, providing a home for many agricultural 'colonies' or villages of Germans, Poles and Italians, many of them introduced with help from the National Government or that of a State.

Possessing a territory three times that of Argentina, or twenty-seven times that of the British Isles and a population officially estimated to be 42,400,000 in December 1936, less than earlier estimates but still about half the population of South America, Brazil might seem to demand a space in this volume equal to that given to the nine Spanish-speaking republics. But since each political entity calls for separate narrative, this cannot be: nor is it needful. For during the half-century of Pedro II's reign (1840–89), a period of 'almost unbroken peace' and tranquil economic progress, the monarchy of Brazil was happy in having no history. That period demands interpretation rather than narrative; and the troubles of the preceding period (1822–40), trifles compared with the storms raging in neighbouring republics, may be briefly treated as introductory to the settled era. Since the concerns of Brazil with the River Plate—the occupation of Uruguay (1817–25), the war with Argentina (1825–8), the overthrow of Rosas (1852) and the war with Paraguay (1865–70)—have been already told, and also the acquisition of the Acre territory (1903), this chapter may deal with internal history from the achievement of independence in 1822.

At that moment Brazil already possessed a 'constitutional' head of the State, who had, before proclamation of independence, summoned a Constituent Assembly. There was also a Prime Minister, José Bonifacio Andrada, and a Cabinet, having some constitutional character carried on from the Regency. In June 1823 amid great rejoicing the Constituent Assembly met. The deputies were men of parts, magistrates, clergy, professional men, but inexperienced in affairs: they were fifty instead of the intended hundred, for most of the seats assigned to the northern provinces were vacant owing to some reluctance or difficulty in those parts. The Emperor, Pedro I, in an opening speech, undertook to defend the coming Constitution 'if it were worthy of Brazil and of me' and wished the assembly to produce a Constitution 'worthy of my imperial sanction'. The words alarmed the Assembly, but were warmly defended by the Andrada brothers, who stood as opponents of democracy and champions of authority—in reality their own authority, since they regarded themselves as the authors of independence and superior to the throne. They used the familiar methods of Spanish-American autocrats: espionage, arrests, banishment of men suspected of disaffection to independence. The Emperor resented their attitude: and when the Andrada brothers backed up the ultra-nationalist and anti-Portuguese elements in the Assembly and thereby drove the extreme right wing into alliance with the left in hostility to the Government, Dom Pedro seized the opportunity to dismiss the two brothers from the ministry. These at once threw themselves into violent opposition, attacking the changed administration in the Press. Finally the Emperor dissolved the Assembly, which declared itself 'in perpetual session' and sat all night, 'the night of agony', in futile protest. The two Andradas, with several others obnoxious to the Emperor, were deported to France.

The Emperor, rejecting the Constitution drawn up by the defunct Assembly, promised another 'twice as liberal'. A committee appointed by him drew up a Constitution, which was submitted not, as promised, to another National Assembly but—by a quasi-constitutional arrangement resembling Spanish custom—to various municipalities, was accepted by them and in March 1824 was promulgated with the ceremonious oath of the Emperor and chief dignitaries. This Constitution of 1824 was 'with slight modifications the fundamental charter of Brazil up to 1889...considering time and circumstances, extremely liberal in character'.[1]

In 1824 by his father's death Dom Pedro became King of Portugal; and although he soon abdicated in favour of his infant daughter María, his connexion with the Portuguese throne drew him closer to the Portuguese elements in Brazil, alienating the nationalist majority. The liberals resented his dissolution of the Constituent Assembly and his refusal to summon Parliament till 1826. Further causes of dissatisfaction were a costly and disastrous war with Buenos Aires (1825-8); financial confusion and extravagance; repeated and inordinate increase of the royal stipend; the Emperor's infringement of his own Constitution, particularly in the matter of ministerial responsibility to Parliament (a point which he probably did not clearly understand), his capricious arrogance, neglect of his wife and favour to his beautiful mistress 'The Marchioness of Santos', who set up and deposed Ministers and became almost the chief of an informal backstairs cabinet. Moreover he failed in the most elementary duty of government, that of keeping order. From 1826 to 1830 there was a rapid succession of unpopular ministries and constant friction with the House of Deputies, which gained courage and authority, while Dom Pedro sank in public favour. In September 1830 news came of the French 'Revolution of July' and the fall of the absolutist Charles X. 'The effect was electric', says Armitage. A group of 'patriots' were soon plotting revolution. In April 1831 Dom Pedro, finding that he could not even rely on the army, abdicated in favour of his 'dearly beloved and esteemed son, Dom Pedro de Alcantara', a child of five years. He appointed José Bonifacio Andrada—now returned from exile—tutor to his children and sailed for Europe in a British warship. The remaining three years of his life—he died aged thirty-six—belong to the history of Portugal.

Against the errors of Pedro I may be set two services to Brazil: he led the country to independence and gave her a liberal Constitution, under which his dynasty endured for nearly sixty years longer. Moreover, in his time parliamentary government took form and gathered strength. Of the first House of Deputies Armitage writes:

[1] P. A. Martin.

'Feeble and vacillating in 1826, querulous in 1827, exacting in 1828, they at length ventured to station themselves as a barrier to the aggressions of the supreme power in 1829.' The fact that Parliament thus regularly met, gained in strength year by year and upon the Emperor's abdication took charge and appointed a regency, sufficiently shows that Dom Pedro, absolutist though he was, was less so than the quasi-republican autocrats of Spanish America or the contemporary Bourbon despots of Europe, and that in a large sense he kept his oath to the Constitution. He has his place among the liberators and law-givers of Latin America.

The departure of Pedro I left the leaders of the Brazilian people free to choose their form of government; for obviously they were not bound to preserve intact the Constitution granted by imperial authority.[1] Their choice was hereditary monarchy: any other choice would probably have meant disruption.

'Woe to the land whose king is a child.' The Regency of three men found disorders everywhere; mutinies in the army, already used to praetorian ways; strife between 'federalists' and 'restorers', the extremists of both wings, also between Brazilians and Portuguese; personal conflicts; banditry; unrest among the native or half-caste people of the north. In Pará a revolt of soldiers, who murdered their officers and the magistrates, led to four years of civil war (1832–6). In 1835 the ten years' war in the south broke out. In Pernambuco the citizens armed themselves against mutinous soldiers. The death of the absent Pedro I in 1834 removed one cause of strife, and a single regent was appointed, Padre Feijó, who had shown vigorous capacity as Minister for Justice and now as head of the State strove for two years to restore order. He created a National Guard or citizen militia to withstand the unruly soldiery and protect the public peace. Although he failed to suppress the southern separatist movement, he upheld authority and unity in general and is remembered among the makers of modern Brazil. But in 1837 he resigned in face of parliamentary opposition; and his successor, the conservative Araujo Lima, could not cope with recurrent disorder and disintegrating forces. Early in 1840, the liberals, among them the brothers Andrada, proposed

[1] The Constitution was in fact amended three years later.

that Pedro II should be declared of age. In July 1840 the two chambers in joint session accepted the proposal. A deputation waited on the Emperor, not quite fifteen years old, who replied: 'I am ready.'

The Regency had not been barren: the education of the young Emperor was a notable work; and also, in the capital and the more settled parts, some degree of political education of the people, who (except the slaves) enjoyed a personal liberty rare in Latin America; for Brazilians a century ago possessed freedom of speech, a free and ably conducted press and a Parliament not indeed elected on any wide and genuine suffrage, but on the whole representative of the more educated classes and possessing not only freedom of debate but powers of legislation.

For some nine years disorders continued: but in 1845 a vigorous campaign, followed by an amnesty, ended the separatist movement in Rio Grande do Sul; and the Crown proved to be not merely a national symbol—in itself a matter of high value—but a unifying force, largely owing to the disinterested character, indefatigable labour and practical sagacity of the Emperor himself. The unanimous testimony of North American historians is notable. 'Under his benevolent despotism, if despotism it could be called,' says James, 'Brazil enjoyed an era of internal peace and development and external prestige. Democratization of the Government would probably have spelled anarchy in Brazil, as it did in all the Spanish-American States after independence. The half-century of Dom Pedro's reign afforded two generations of practice in politics.' Dawson (p. 459) and Rippy (p. 261) write in the same strain; so also Haring (pp. 69, 74) and Martin in his more detailed appreciation (p. 183). The pervasive influence of Dom Pedro diffused through the higher ranks of the administration a spirit of upright integrity. The lower grades of the Civil Service, especially in the provinces, hardly reached the same standard of disinterested probity. But the general record of those days might furnish an example to later politicians. An omnivorous reader, the Emperor was interested in all branches of knowledge and loved intercourse with men of letters and science. His recreation was visiting schools, and during his European travels he perplexed his hosts by his unwearied sight-seeing in the character of a modest and studious observer. The country, largely owing to internal peace and the growing concern of Europe with South America, advanced in wealth and prosperity; but the royal scholar was accused of insufficient attention to material progress and to immigration, which might occupy some of the vacant lands of his vast dominions. A notable event in this connexion was the opening of the River Amazon to the ships of all nations in 1867, largely owing to pressing suggestions from the United States: Brazil, with other powers, had insisted on the opening of the River Plate in 1853 and could not consistently keep closed this great waterway.

The Constitution of 1824, modified ten years later by the *acto adicional*—which gave legislative assemblies to the provinces but left to the Emperor the appointment of provincial governors (a safeguard against separatism)—was the norm of political life. The Deputies were chosen by indirect election for four years. The sixty Senators were appointed for life by the Emperor from a triple list presented by provincial electors. 'Dom Pedro exercised his prerogative of nomination with great scrupulousness and rare impartiality....' If the Senate was an oligarchy, it was an impartial, enlightened and dignified one. But the key of the Constitution was the 'moderative power...entrusted to the Emperor...that he may incessantly watch over the maintenance of the independence, equilibrium and harmony of the rest of the political powers'. The moderative power included nomination of senators, power to convoke and dissolve Parliament, assent to Parliamentary acts, appointment of Ministers and the right of pardon. Inevitably the exercise of this personal power was much criticized. But 'the smooth functioning of the machinery of government year after year without a serious breakdown was due in large measure to the tireless vigilance of the Emperor.... In the phrase of the Brazilian historian Oliveira Lima, "If there was any despotism, it was the despotism of morality."'[1]

The blot on Brazil was slavery, and—far worse—the inexpressibly atrocious slave-trade, the importation from Africa of tightly packed cargoes of negroes for sale in Brazil. By treaty with Great

[1] The quotations are from Martin.

Britain this trade was to cease in 1830; but nothing was done to stop it. The horrors of the Atlantic passage—wherein the North American slave-traders were as guilty as the Brazilian purchasers—have been set forth by Professor Hill. The Brazilian planter preferred buying imported slaves to the trouble and expense of rearing slave-children; and in the decade 1842–52 above 32,000 slaves a year were imported. In 1845 Lord Aberdeen passed through the British Parliament an Act that all slave-vessels should be tried by British admiralty courts instead of the existing mixed British-Portuguese Commissions. This open infringement of Brazilian sovereignty, treating Brazil as a barbarous inferior State, roused hot resentment and caused a large increase in the importation of slaves —60,000 in the year 1848.[1] In 1850 British cruisers were ordered to enter Brazilian territorial waters, including ports and rivers, and to seize all ships fitted for the trade. The Emperor hated the trade and the consequent ill-repute of Brazil, as did also the more thoughtful of his subjects; and in that same year the Brazilian Government passed a drastic law for the suppression of this horrible traffic, which is said to have ceased about 1853.

But slavery still continued, probably under milder conditions than elsewhere, especially in domestic service. But people still living have seen the whip wielded by overseers of stevedores in Brazilian ports, and within the lifetime of men living to-day young girls were forced to parade their physical attractions before the expectant eyes of bidders in the slave-market of Rio. The most inhuman among masters and marketers of slaves were free negroes, sons or grandsons of slaves.

In the 'sixties, especially after emancipation in the United States, the matter could hardly rest. Yet a moderate suggestion concerning emancipation in the Emperor's speech to Parliament in 1867 roused an extraordinary sensation. In 1871 was passed the law of 'free birth', which, however, under certain conditions, bound the free-born to servitude until the age of twenty-one. Thenceforth the cause of abolition gained ground, and was furthered by a strange

[1] Owing to the large infusion of African blood, the colour bar in Brazil, although not quite disregarded, is not rigid. Brazilian statisticians argue that, through European immigration and the prevalence of the stronger type, the African element will in time be eliminated. This is a question for biologists.

economic episode. The Province of Ceará, half-depopulated by the long drought of 1877-9, took to shipping the unemployed slaves, which it could not feed, for sale in the Rio market. The sight of cargoes of slaves shipped for the market shocked a generation posterior to the African slave-trade and furthered the cause of abolition. In 1883 Ceará freed its few remaining and almost useless slaves. Amazonas followed in 1885. In that year the Federal Congress passed a bill liberating all slaves over sixty-five. The abolitionist campaign gathered force, and slaves were deserting the sugar plantations. In 1888 Dom Pedro sailed on a visit to Europe. His daughter Isabel, acting as Regent, although warned that she was endangering the throne, pressed upon Parliament a bill for abolition without indemnity to the owners. In May 1888 the bill extinguishing slavery without compensation was passed amid great enthusiasm. Eighteen months later Dom Pedro ceased to reign.

'The monarchy is an exotic plant on the American Continent.' Such was the slogan of the republican party, small at first, which took form in 1871 and gradually gained influence through its newspaper, *A Republica*. The bearded philosopher on the throne, who described himself as the best republican in his dominions, never checked the spoken or written word, never showed resentment at scurrilous satire of his own person and allowed negro urchins to follow him in the street crying *a Republica* with mischievous comments. The influence of French thought and example, always strong in Brazil, favoured the new party. The clergy, naturally a pillar of monarchy, were alienated by the imprisonment of two bishops in 1874 for an illegal attempt to exclude freemasons from Catholic associations. The abolition of slavery without compensation offended the great landowners and planters,[1] hitherto conservative monarchists: and a new industrial class, lacking the same tradition, was increasing in numbers. The Emperor, grown old in the laborious service of his country, ailing in health and apt to fall

---

[1] It has been suggested that, since the conservative Parliament, which voted abolition, mainly represented this class, abolition may not have much strengthened the republican ranks. But in England we are well accustomed to conservative administrations surprising their constituents by passing, under pressure, ultra-liberal measures, sometimes to the detriment of conservative pockets. Moreover, the history of the Peninsula and of Hispanic America is a series of surprises which constantly defies probability.

asleep while presiding in Council, was losing his hold on men and on affairs. His heir-apparent, the Princess Isabel, was suspected of absolutist and ultramontane tendencies, and her foreign husband, the Comte d'Eu, was disliked.

But the determining factor was a strange indiscipline and political agitation in the army, which had meddled in politics ever since independence. Since victory in the Paraguayan war 'the army had degenerated in morale and discipline. It participated in politics, attacked ministries in Parliament and in the press, aired its private disputes in public, refused to be disciplined by the Minister of War.'[1] The imperial administration had been culpably slack in this matter: an able and persuasive professor in the Army School, known to his countrymen by his Christian names Benjamin Constant, was allowed undisturbed to preach republicanism to the junior officers. The Emperor's tardy efforts to reduce the numbers of the army and to tighten discipline only roused resentment. And the example of Spanish-American *pronunciamientos* was infectious.

In 1889 officers were fraternizing with republicans, and disquieting rumours were current. On 13 November Floriano Peixoto, quartermaster general of the army, assured the Prime Minister that the plotting meant nothing. 'Trust the loyalty of the military leaders', he wrote. Within thirty-six hours General Deodoro Fonseca, a veteran of the Paraguayan War, 'pronounced' before daybreak of the 15th, backed up by Peixoto. Deodoro, with part of the garrison of Rio, seized the Government buildings, was joined by the rest of the troops, proclaimed a Federal Republic under a provisional Government and two days later placed the Emperor on board ship for Europe. Dom Pedro died two years later in Paris. The people of the capital, unaware of what was happening—for there was no disturbance—stood by quietly while the army took charge. President Justo of Venezuela, when he heard the news, remarked: 'The only republic in South America is ended, the Empire of Brazil.' Modern Brazil has since recognized her debt to Dom Pedro; and his body, conveyed from Europe with due ceremony, now rests in his native country.

[1] Haring, p. 73.

PLATE III

PEDRO II OF BRAZIL

The revolution inevitably brought military dictatorship under Fonseca. A Constituent Assembly, convoked by him, produced after eighteen months[1] (February 1891) a Constitution for the 'United States of Brazil' generally resembling that of the United States, but granting to each of the twenty states much larger autonomous powers, including even the right to tax exports.

Rejecting a civilian candidate in order not to provoke the army, the assembly elected Deodoro Fonseca President for four years, with Floriano Peixoto as Vice-President. But Deodoro, an imperious soldier and no statesman; surrounded by an unpopular ministry, a crowd of unscrupulous hangers-on, and a Congress bitterly and increasingly hostile—while everywhere soldiers ignored civil liberties and finance fell into hopeless confusion—found his task impossible. After nine months he dissolved Congress, proclaimed martial law and, alleging monarchical plots, assumed open dictatorship. Resistance to this stroke was so violent, including a military revolt in Rio Grande do Sul, that in three weeks Deodoro resigned, handing over his office to Peixoto, who as a soldier had betrayed the Emperor and as Vice-President had been faithless to Deodoro.

Congress met and declared Peixoto to be President until 1894. But Floriano outdid Deodoro in forcible autocracy, installing his own men as Governors throughout the states. In July 1892 Rio Grande do Sul, grossly misgoverned, rose in insurrection; and in September 1893 the long-brewing revolt of the warships in Rio harbour—partly due to naval jealousy of the privileged army—burst out under Admiral de Mello. Peixoto met the crisis with vigorous determination, raising troops and ordering from abroad munitions and armed vessels. For six months (September 1893 to March 1894) the vast bay of Rio was the scene of a strange civil war; the ships and one fortified island (which had joined the insurgents) firing on the shore forts, whose batteries replied with mostly ineffective fire. But the admiral's hands were tied, for the commanders of foreign warships at anchor in the bay forbade any

[1] The delay, characteristic of South America, was needless, for the Congress adopted with slight modifications a constitution already drafted by Ruy Barbosa, who was the civilian brain behind the military revolution and during the following generation the most prominent liberal statesman, orator and writer of Brazil.

attack on the city, on the understanding that Peixoto on his side should mount no batteries within the city limits.

After three months of indecisive cannonading Admiral de Mello in his flagship[1] sailed out of the harbour before dawn of 1 December between the hasty fire of the two forts commanding the entrance, to join the gaucho leader Saraiva in the south, where an insurgent Government had been set up. He left in command Admiral Saldanha da Gama, a distinguished sailor and a fine chivalrous type of the Brazilian aristocracy, whose personal character, valour and intrepid energy kept the revolt alive for four months longer, although his avowed monarchical leanings brought dissension rather than strength. But his difficulties grew. For some months all the foreign naval commanders accepted Saldanha's order or request excluding merchant-ships from a zone which lay in the line of fire. But in mid-February 1894 the newly arrived commander of the five United States warships refused to recognize this barred zone, authorized two American vessels to discharge cargo within the zone and announced that in case of interference he would fire on Saldanha's ships. It was a blow to the revolt, giving something more than moral support to the Government of Floriano, which some believed to be the republican bulwark against reaction.[2]

The expected help from the south never came. Saldanha, three ships having been sunk and the rest much battered, was preparing to leave the harbour as soon as he should hear from de Mello (who had effected little) when armed ships, ordered from abroad by Peixoto, appeared on 7 March off the mouth of the harbour. Resistance was impossible, and Saldanha with his men took refuge on two small Portuguese warships, whose commander, refusing to give them up to certain death and possible torture, conveyed them to the River Plate, where most of them escaped.

Floriano, who had ruled by terror during the war, filling his dreadful prisons with suspects on the information of spies, was pitiless after victory. Numbers perished by quick sentence by

[1] Akers, correspondent of *The Times*, who was on the bridge of the flagship, gives a good first-hand account of the civil war.

[2] In his *Diplomatic History of the United States* (pp. 758–9), Mr S. F. Bemis, differing from Martin, simply calls the insurgents 'monarchists' and writes: 'At the cannon's mouth, the American admiral refused to permit the anti-republican warships to enforce a blockade on American vessels.'

farcical court-martial: many were simply killed by soldiers, often after torture. Men innocent of rebellion but hostile to Floriano incurred his vengeance. Negro prisoners, who had probably merely obeyed the orders of their chiefs, were flogged, sometimes to death. Civil war, stained by indescribable atrocities on both sides, dragged on in Rio Grande until October 1895, when it was suppressed by federal forces. Saldanha da Gama perished in that war.

A year before that time, in November 1894, Floriano, his legal term having expired, surprised many political prophets by quietly handing over his office to the duly elected civilian President Moraes Barros, a lawyer of São Paulo. Floriano, failing in health, retired into private life and died six months later.

By his illegal, arbitrary and corrupt despotism Floriano had provoked the rebellion. But Deodoro was also partly in fault: and it may fairly be held that, when the rebellion came, Floriano acted throughout with the simplicity and the effective energy of a soldier and that, apart from his cruel methods, the stern maintenance of authority even in defiance of legal methods was necessary to peace and order and the prevention of the confused strife which would inevitably have followed insurgent victory. It is in that character that his countrymen remember him to-day.

Moraes Barros, 'personally honest and respected by the nation',[1] eliminated militarism, restored freedom of speech and of the press, granted a general amnesty for political offences and respected State rights. At the same time he maintained authority and suppressed disorders, of which the most serious was the strange attempt of a religious fanatic named Maciel, 'The Councillor', to set up an independent theocratic community in the interior of the State of Bahia. The suppression of this eccentric movement cost a military campaign and the loss of thousands of lives.

Moraes and his successors down to 1930 'have generally ruled in accordance with constitutional forms'.[1] But under the extreme presidential system prevailing in Brazil, the President has usually nominated his successor by an understanding with the Governors of the States and with the majority in Congress, which first helped

[1] Haring, pp. 76–7.

to manage the presidential election and then acted as arbiter of its legality, a proceeding whereby members of Congress hoped to retain their comfortable and profitable seats. This method, whatever its merits in respect of democratic theory, has raised men of marked ability to the presidential chair, a seat of comprehensive authority and patronage: and the one departure from custom, in 1910, meant a lowering of the standard. In that year the dominant group in Congress, rejecting the President's nominee, put forward a soldier, Hermes Fonseca, nephew of Deodoro. This reaction towards military autocracy produced the rare occurrence of something resembling a popular contest. The liberal orator, writer and diplomatist Ruy Barbosa, author of the Constitution and Brazilian representative at the Hague Conference of 1907, appeared as an opposition candidate, denouncing by the novel method of an oratorical campaign the excessive interference of the executive in everything, including the action of the law-courts. He was beaten, amid much talk of unfair election, by Hermes, who now had full official support.

A strange incident marks the beginning of his term. The negro crews of two new battleships, just come from England, killed their officers and fired on the naval school. The Government were obliged to treat with the mutineers, who surrendered on promise of amnesty. The leaders were taken out to sea and shot, there to find easy burial.

Hermes fortunately had not the makings of a successful usurper: and notwithstanding an increase of extravagant corruption and a serious financial crisis (one of several) in 1913, the four years of reaction were not a serious interruption of the political and economic life of the nation. His successor, Wenceslao Braz (1914–18), first of the restored line of civilian Presidents, enhanced the reputation of his country by handling the difficult war problems with energy, discretion and success, with the loyal aid of the able Foreign Minister, Lauro Müller, a Paulista of German parentage.

The almost dictatorial rule of the civilian presidents in the following period did not pass unchallenged: an attempt in 1922 to restore Hermes to power by a military *coup d'état* was suppressed after some firing on the capital by Hermes' son, commander of a neighbouring fortress. More serious was a military revolt two years later, professing liberal aims, which held the great city of São Paulo for three weeks before yielding to federal troops: but sporadic outbreaks followed in many parts of the republic, partly due to the autocratic methods and unpopularity of the President Silva Bernardes (1922–6). Indeed, a complete history of Brazil would require separate histories of the principal States, particularly the wealthy and advanced coffee State of São Paulo with its magnificent capital, its cultured aristocracy and its jealous local patriotism; Minas Gerães, neighbour and rival of São Paulo; and the growing State of Rio Grande do Sul, where in 1923 a revolt against an autocratic Governor, ruler for nearly a generation past, assumed, once more, a separatist intention. The diversities of the regions which make up Brazil may be illustrated by a contrast between São Paulo with seven million people and the four northern States of Pará, Amazonas, Maranhão and Piauhy, together comprising a million and a half square miles, but containing only three million inhabitants, of whom the rural part live in most primitive conditions.

Yet the vast mass held together. The President had the right, under some theoretical restrictions, of declaring a state of siege (suspending civil rights) in any part of the Federation and of 'intervening' in any State in case of emergency, at his own discretion. But on the whole it was the interest of State Governors, autocrats in their several capitals, influential in national affairs and often hoping for high federal office, to keep on terms with the executive in Rio: and an outbreak here or there may be likened to a hurt in the limb of a giant which may bleed again but does not indicate amputation. The system, though sometimes strained, continued intact till 1930, the epoch of general depression.

The Empire, largely owing to the costly Paraguayan war, left a legacy of debt to the Republic. And the Republic, over-confident in the future, had multiplied the debt by repeated borrowings and lavish expenditure, much of it productive, but much extravagantly bestowed. The crisis of 1898, when the menace of national bankruptcy was averted by the Funding Loan, the later borrowings and the disaster of the depression years cannot be here narrated.[1] A glance at the present quotation of Brazilian Government loans may provide a comment. Nor have individual States a happy financial record. The fault lies partly with British financiers and credulous British investors; and, after 1914, in part also with North American financiers and investors.

The republican period, together with the last decade of the Empire, comprises approximately the period of great material and economic advance in Latin America, particularly in the Atlantic republics. Four and a half million European immigrants, many of them sturdy and thrifty Portuguese peasants, are said to have entered Brazil since 1820; most of them during the past half-century (1885–1935), the period of improved transport and influx of capital from northern Europe and later from North America. Amazonas and Pará were enriched and their cities, Belem and Manaos, grew rapidly by export of forest rubber in the late nineteenth century, an export supplied in great part by the flight of the half-Indian peasants from the drought-stricken province of Ceará to become rubber-gatherers along the remote waterways of the Amazon. This abnormal prosperity, leading to lavish public expenditure, was transitory and was followed by financial disaster due to the competition of cultivated rubber from the East Indies, raised from seeds or plants taken from Brazil to Kew and there nursed to maturity.[2] More lasting has been the wealth derived from coffee on the rich red soil of the plateau of São Paulo and the adjoining States, whence for fifty years past has come half or more of the world's consumption of coffee and nearly one-third of the federal revenue of Brazil. The error of over-production and of reliance on one crop, the official efforts to regulate supply and price, the fall in the price of coffee and the burning of vast stores of unsaleable coffee can only be briefly mentioned here.

But economic progress has been manifold. The outbreak of the Great War roused Brazil from a strange negligence. Although a bean, dropped in the tropical soil, will grow in a few days, Brazil

[1] *His Majesty the President*, by E. Hambloch (London, 1936), gives a history of Brazilian loans.

[2] The loss has been in part repaired by export of Brazil nuts and other forest products.

had hitherto imported beans, the chief food (as in Portugal) of the working man. Necessity soon remedied this defect. Under the same stimulus, Brazil 'suddenly became aware that she owned thirty million head of cattle', as a Brazilian lecturer told us in London at the time. The number, conjectured rather than known, induced a too large optimism; for these neglected millions were not the best beef: but, to meet instant demand, freezing establishments of North American foundation were set up. Later, with gradual improvement of breeds, the cattle industry grew and is extending to-day through clearings in the far western forest whither the motor-truck has forced its way. Cotton of home growth and manufacture now supplies most of the people's need.

A great achievement early in the present century was the cleansing —by drastic sanitary measures—of the capital, which for half a century had been the home of yellow fever, probably brought in a slave-ship about 1850. To-day Rio is one of the healthiest of tropical cities; and also one of the most beautiful. For during the prosperous rule of President Rodríguez Alves (1902–6), the capital with its narrow crowded streets was transformed by demolition and reconstruction at great cost both then and later (for the work still goes on), causing some murmurs in other parts over tax-paying for the benefit of the federal capital. Not less notable was the cleansing of Santos, the coffee port, contiguous to swamps and formerly a hotbed of disease, now a seaside holiday resort.

Brazil has had frontier questions with all contiguous States, that is to say with all South American countries, except Chile and Ecuador which do not touch her borders. The Paraguayan frontier was fixed under the Empire: all the other questions were solved by the Republic. The settlement, usually by arbitration, has in every instance been favourable to Brazil, and, except in the case of Acre, has been entirely peaceful.

Yet Pierre Denis in 1909 wrote paradoxically: 'Brazil has no inland frontiers' except towards Argentina and Uruguay. He explains his meaning: that the real Brazil, the country occupied by civilized people, was not an inland continental country, but a country mainly bordering on the Atlantic, except for a sparse population on the navigable rivers; that the only considerable external commerce and the only custom-houses worth mentioning were in the Atlantic ports; that Brazil had not yet colonized its vast interior and had not pushed population to the political frontiers. Yet this illuminating statement needs qualification; for Brazil was already in contact, not profoundly important contact, with eastern Peru by the Amazon, in a less degree with Bolivia by the Madeira, and with Paraguay through Brazilian settlement on the River Plate system. Yet even to-day, in spite of an almost feverish push westward, communication in Brazil is mainly by water, by the Atlantic and by the navigable rivers. The only railway system is in the south, from Victoria south-westward and westward. Elsewhere each principal port is linked by a separate railway with its productive hinterland, although something has been done to join these separate lines. But in the present century Brazil has been taking possession of her remote and hidden territory. Railways have been pushed westward as colonizing enterprises under Government direction into lands only known to savage Indians and first revealed by the surveys of the railway engineers, who were left to choose their own line to the points to be reached; the advancing railhead becomes a movable village; settlers accompany and follow the progress of the line. A railway now traverses the whole country from the Atlantic coast through São Paulo to the Paraguay, penetrating the woods of Matto Grosso. Another line has been pushed towards the river port of Cuyabá, which is reached by motor from the western railhead. For in recent years the work of the railways has been continued through waste and forest by road-construction and by the motor-car. The maintenance of forest roads and bridges through tropical rains, local inundations and sometimes dusty drought is not easy. But any trail along which a motor-lorry can force its dangerous way counts as a road. Homesteads, growing their own crops, spring up in the natural savannahs and in the forest clearings, and in a few years cattle are being driven thence to the markets and *frigoríficos* of the Atlantic region. The hard work of this expansion—rough and laborious work despite the picturesque romance of pioneering—is largely done by foreigners, but the result is Brazilian. Yet there still remain vast spaces, particularly in the equatorial region of the Amazon basin, which

are untouched by white settlement and even untrodden by explorers. An interesting side of this movement is conciliatory
contact—partly by means of gramophones fixed in trees—with the
scanty tribes of suspicious and resentful Indians.

President Washington Luis Pereira de Souza (1926–30), ex-
Governor of São Paulo, was faced towards the end of his term by a
financial crisis, imminent owing to overborrowing for fifty years,
but aggravated by the world depression. A drop in coffee prices
to one-third of the former level, a heavy fall in the value of exports
and in the national revenue, no more borrowing possible and a
huge sum annually needed for debt service: these were the elements
of an economic disaster for which, as everywhere, the Government
was blamed. Thus economic discontent and actual suffering con-
duced to political trouble. But the immediate cause of that trouble
was personal action and excessive presidential authority. Since
1889 the heads of the Republic, except two, had come from São
Paulo or Minas Gerães, and latterly those States had alternately
sent a President to Rio. In 1930 it was Minas' turn; but just before
the election the Governor of Minas declared for Dr Vargas,
Governor of Rio Grande do Sul. President Pereira de Souza
refused to agree and put forward a Paulista, Dr Prestes. This move
towards something resembling a Paulista dynasty united a dozen
groups in support of Vargas. But, as usual, the President's nominee
headed the poll. Widespread protest, alleging unfair election, took
the usual form of revolt. Pereira de Souza, who was still in office,
attempted to hold his ground; but his own troops turned against
him, and in October 1930 a group of generals entered the palace,
arrested the President (who refused to resign) and after six weeks'
confinement, shipped him for Europe. Vargas, installed as Provisional President by a military Junta, was dictator for above three
years, ruling and legislating by decrees, well-intentioned and often
liberal in character. He dismissed the National Congress, the State
legislatures and the municipal councils, setting up 'interventors'
in the States.

Two years of this autocracy kindled into flame the perennial
Paulista discontent with government from Rio and with the financial
treatment of the State, whence came one-third of the national

revenue; and now the overthrow of the Paulista Constitution and the dismissal of a host of Paulista officials to make way for Vargas' nominees roused bitter resentment. In June 1932 São Paulo rose in arms: 70,000 federal troops were despatched against the State, which was roused to an impassioned resistance resembling that of an invaded nation. Armies, outnumbering anything hitherto known in South America, engaged in conflict. But the contest was unequal; and after seven weeks the Paulista insurgents were forced to yield: some leaders were deported to Europe; others to northern Brazil; the rest were pardoned.

Vargas after victory was conciliatory, and the Paulistas in turn believed that they had helped to 'reconstitutionalize' the country. Bitterness died down. In November 1933 a National Assembly met and after some months produced a Constitution which defined the President's powers, but without much likelihood of diminishing those powers: it empowered the House of Deputies to summon any Minister to give information about his department: but this 'interpellation' did not imply complete ministerial responsibility, that is to say the obligation to resign upon an adverse vote. A novelty in this constitution was the election of fifty deputies (about one-fifth of the whole number) by professional classes; agriculture and stock-raising; industry; commerce and transport; and liberal professions, including civil servants. Except in the last class, employees as well as employers had the vote. The Constitution contained an element of State socialism and also of extreme nationalism in respect of industrial enterprises and the control of natural resources. Under this Constitution in July 1934 Vargas was elected constitutional President. The National Assembly became a Parliamentary Congress and 'the change from a discretionary to a constitutional Government was quietly accomplished'.

Thus wrote, in September 1935, experienced observers in the British Embassy and Consulate at Rio. Two months later military revolt shook Brazil. Troops, led by non-commissioned officers, seized Natal, capital of Rio Grande do Norte, apparently hoping to set up an independent 'communist' State in the north. There was a revolt in Pernambuco, and some fighting in the adjoining States; also outbreaks far to the south in Paraná, and then in Rio itself.

Although the northern leaders were sergeants, many officers led or joined these revolts. The Government acted with decision. A state of siege was proclaimed. Loyal troops—and the army in general was loyal—were sent to suppress the revolts: above 5000 persons were arrested in Rio, and thousands elsewhere. Complaint was made to Montevideo that the Soviet Legation in Uruguay was the root of communism in Brazil. The Uruguayan Government responded amicably by dismissing the entire Soviet Legation.[1] In March 1936 Dr Vargas (announcing that 'a grave situation, comparable to a state of war, existed in the nation') decreed with consent of Congress 'a state of war' for ninety days, thereby assuming unlimited powers and legalizing capital punishment, forbidden by the Constitution: twenty-eight military officers were arrested in May 1936, and the Government at last succeeded in finding and arresting in the capital itself the communist chief, Captain Prestes, said to be the author of the November revolt, a famous guerrillero and a legendary militant figure but no political guide. Indeed, the fighters for 'communism' had little notion of its meaning and no clear aim; nor have the green-shirt 'integralists' of fascist and anti-foreign tendencies—who also trouble the Government—any distinct regenerating plan.

The revolts of 1935 were not wholly, probably not mainly, communist. Many joined the revolt weary of the irresponsible autocracy of successive presidents, unchecked by any effective parliamentary criticism, since the only opposition in Congress was a group of 'outs' wanting to get in and the only possible vote of censure was insurrection. Among the revolutionaries were 'young Brazilians' who talked of an intensely native culture, anti-European, seeking primitive Tupi-Guaraní affinities, hating all the politicians and sympathizing with Mexican indianism and with a native-minded group of Peruvian *intelectuales*.

Vargas, described by a competent authority as 'broad-minded and progressive...a man of talent and vision', a friend of social justice and of the working man, declared himself 'not unfavourable

[1] This meant the severance of relations between Uruguay and the Soviet Union. The Soviet Government brought the matter before the League of Nations, which discreetly patched up the quarrel; and relations were renewed between the two countries.

to the liberal idea'. Many of those arrested in November 1935 were released, but others were arrested in unknown numbers, but certainly many thousands. In January 1936 many arrests followed the discovery of a 'nest of communists' in Rio. The nervous alarm about communism was genuine. 'Agents from Moscow' were discerned in the most unlikely persons, and relations were severed with the Madrid Government on account of its communist tendencies. But the number of arrests and the known character of many political prisoners indicate that the accusation of communism was often a pretext and that martial law is a political weapon aimed in more than one direction. There is strong evidence of rough treatment (to use a mild term) of some prisoners. Recent events give almost a prophetic colour to Keyserling's comparison of Brazil with Tzarist Russia. 'Backward and culturally non-homogeneous peoples' he says 'cannot be ruled according to the ideas of modern democracy. In both cases there is a country of immense vastness governed by a small minority; the latter culminates in one individual who is omnipotent as long as the term of his office lasts.... The Brazilian high official and that of Tzarist Russia resemble one another like two brothers.'

The 'State of War', renewed in successive ninety-day periods, lapsed on 17 June 1937, when the 1934 Constitution was restored. But on 10 November 1937, amid the agitated preliminaries of a presidential election, Vargas—declaring that corruption, disorder, communism and personal faction required strong central authority —dismissed Parliament and produced a new Constitution, to be submitted to a plebiscite. His Constitution—which provides a six-year presidential term, sets up a National Economic Council and continues Vargas' 'mandate' until the plebiscite—is, according to its author, federal, presidential, representative and democratic, 'not fascist but purely Brazilian'. At the same time presidential decrees suspended the service of the public debt, extinguished all political parties and forbade party badges. These measures have already provoked two green-shirt or integralist conspiracies, followed by many arrests and more stringent autocracy.

Brazil possesses a strong parliamentary tradition, dating from the events of 1826–8, mentioned on p. 295. To say more or to gauge the hopes roused by political stirrings since 1930 would be premature. In any case the vast and varied resources of the country promise a secure future.

NOTE. J. Armitage, *History of Brazil*, 1808–31, 2 vols. (London, 1836); P. A. Martin in *Argentina, Brazil, Chile*; H. G. James, *Brazil after a Century of Independence** (New York, 1925); L. F. Hill, *Diplomatic Relations between the United States and Brazil** (Durham, N.C., 1932); A. K. Manchester, *The Rise and Decline of British Preeminence in Brazil** (Durham, N.C., 1932); R. Nash, *The Conquest of Brazil* (New York, 1926); M. W. Williams, *Dom Pedro the Magnanimous* (Chapel Hill, N.C., 1937).

CHAPTER XXVI

MEXICO

MEXICO, first in population ($17\frac{1}{2}$ millions) and second in extent (seven times that of the British Isles) of the Spanish-American Republics (excluding Brazil) is a federal republic comprising twenty-eight States and three Territories; a land of complex diversity both in physical features and in population, which includes above 100 tribal Indian groups and above fifty still surviving native languages. These divisions explain the comparative ease of the Spanish conquest and also the fact that to this day the conquest is incomplete, since in that broken country the piecemeal occupation of every valley and every tribal mountain district was impossible: scanty tribes, hardly touched by Mexican authority, still live in primitive paganism, tinged in parts by traditions left by Spanish missionaries. But these separate tribal aborigines, speaking only native tongues, are a minority of the population. Railways, roads, petrol, aviation, industrial advance, a decade of civil war (1810–20) and the progressive policy, educational and agricultural, of the present Government have broken into this polyglot isolation. Most of the Indians are sedentary villagers understanding some Spanish and working on the land or in the mines side by side with their mestizo and white neighbours.

The country, cut in half by the tropic of Cancer, is the only Latin-American Republic extending into the north temperate zone, although in reality the more temperate parts are not in the north but on the cool tropical tablelands, notably the famous valley or plateau of the capital, 7400 ft. above sea-level. Mexico also differs from its southern neighbours in having a long frontier bordering a non-Latin state, a neighbourhood which has profoundly affected Mexican history: a momentous proximity. From the two coastal belts, Caribbean and Pacific—both of them typically tropical in character and known as the *tierra caliente* or hot land—rise the irregular heights of the Sierra Madre, the mountain-system which fills most of the country and encloses between its towering heights a tableland or rather a series of tablelands imperceptibly sloping

northward from a height of 8000 ft. in the south near the capital to
half that height or less at the northern frontier and providing a way
for road and rail which link the chief centres of population with
those of the United States. A volcanic belt, some of its peaks
piercing above the snow-line, crosses the country from east to
west between parallels 18° and 21°, the capital standing midway
between these lines. The tropic of Cancer approximately divides
the fertile and more populous southern half of the country, producing sugar and other tropical crops, from the less fertile and more
primitive northern half, which contains great cattle ranches and
wide deserts. Although above three-fourths of Mexican exports
consist of oil, silver and other minerals, most of the people live by
labour on the soil; and the true economic structure of Mexico rests
not on mineral exports but on crops of maize and beans which feed
the people. Every illustrated book on Mexico shows a picture of
Indian women grinding and kneading maize into *tortillas*, the flat
cakes which are the daily bread of every peasant family. Three-
fourths of the people, including about six million pure Indians and
about the same number of mestizos, are villagers, living in simple
fashion as peasants and labourers. To estimate the number of pure
whites, descendants of Spaniards or Creoles, would be unprofitable.
Those who may be roughly regarded, without close scrutiny, as white
or Europeanized in mode of life are probably about one-fourth.

When after long civil war (1810–21) independence came, Mexico
had more than double its present area, almost roadless, in great
part barbarous, with wide wastes separating the inhabited places,
about seven million inhabitants, more than half of them Indians.
Yet the more settled part, roughly south of the tropic of Cancer,
was the most populous and best ordered part of Spanish America.
Imperial Spain, aided by the wealth in silver, left her impress:
stately cities, magnificent churches, public institutions, solid
dwellings; a basis, as it seemed, for fairly tranquil historical continuity. Yet for thirty-two years (1823–55) revolts, *pronunciamientos*, barrack mutinies are countless. Mexican history is
punctuated by 'Plans', beginning with the Plan of Iguala, most of
these Plans being merely manifestoes by a 'pronouncer'. Presidents,
acting presidents and deputy presidents rapidly pass, some in a few

months, others after a year or two, none but generals holding office for long. Military officers, often largely outnumbering privates (at one time 24,000 officers for 20,000 nominal rank and file) were a privileged class of salaried but often unpaid idlers, every general a possible leader of mutiny.

Finance meant confusion and chronic insolvency. It is true that the long civil war (1810–21) was costly and the failure in 1826 of a London bank, agent for the Mexican Government, brought heavy loss. But in Spanish days, despite waste and corruption, the Mexican treasury, enriched by dues on silver, had supplied local needs, had sent subsidies to Guatemala, Venezuela and Havana, and in addition had furnished considerable revenue to Spain. The Republic was insolvent owing to extravagance, waste, corruption, contraband and salaries of superfluous civil servants while private soldiers and lesser functionaries, unpaid or under-paid, pilfered to live. The Mexican Teja Zabre, in a semi-official history, notes that the history of the years 1823–55 is a drama constantly repeated, 'alternating periods of military dictatorship and anarchy', and attributes revolution to 'the weakness of our imperfect democracy for remedying electoral frauds except by force'. Bancroft, narrating this period, twice hints at the need of dictatorship: 'the only question was its abuse.'

In twenty-three years (1824–47) four Constitutions appeared, not merely amended instruments, but each displacing its predecessor, federal in 1824, centralist in 1836, ultra-centralist and dicta-torial in 1843, federal once more in 1847. All this was the work of a small dominant class, 'possessors of power or aspirants'. The Indian or half-Indian peasants and labourers endured a servitude worse than that of the Spanish period; for now men working in the fields might be seized, drilled into rough shape by a liberal use of the sergeant's cane and then marched over deserts and mountains to fight for they knew not what under incompetent officers, some of them mere boys. In 1853 Brantz Mayer, almost in the words of present-day reformers, describes the Indians as 'hereditary slaves of the estates where their ancestors have worked for centuries'. He tells how the landowner's shop takes back most of the wages and how the Indian is often tempted by alcohol to sell himself for life.

Almost prophesying the devastation wrought after 1910, he says the Indians knew that 'if the Creoles could expel the Spaniards, they had a far better right to expel the Creoles.... The revolt of the copper-coloured race would indeed be a fearful spectacle.'

Bandits plied their trade everywhere: indeed local insurrections sometimes differed little from brigandage. Travellers could not pass between the capital and Vera Cruz without armed escort. Murders in the city were unnoticed incidents. The Mexico described by Señora Calderón in 1839–41 and by Brantz Mayer a little later had degenerated sadly from the New Spain described by Humboldt in 1803. The institutions of art and science, eulogized by him, were now empty shells. The staunch republican Mayer speaks of 'Mexican decadence: citizen is armed against citizen... politicians are constantly seeking to aggrandize themselves either in wealth or power without a thought of loyalty to the constitution.' Yet some honourable and disinterested men strove to serve the State, notably the liberal Gómez Farías, perhaps too hasty a reformer in his brief opportunity in 1833–4; the conservative Terán, noblest of the fighters for independence who at last lost his mental balance and fell by his own sword on the tomb of Iturbide; and the hispanophil historian Lucas Alamán, lover of order and justice.

Nor was political strife aimless, especially at first. Two parties soon appeared, federalists, who were usually liberals, desiring reform in State and Church, and centralists (corresponding to the South American 'unitarians'), who were commonly, though not exclusively, conservatives, standing for 'religion and *fueros*', for the privileges of Church and Army and for the immense property of the Church and of the Religious Orders. The two parties were organized in rival masonic lodges popularly known as 'oil and vinegar'; the Scottish rite (conservative) backed by the British Minister Wade; and the York rite, inspired by Poinsett, his American colleague and antagonist.

During this period the Republic suffered four shocks: (1) a Spanish invasion in 1829; (2) the revolt and secession of Texas in 1836; (3) a French attack in 1838; (4) war with the United States in 1846–7. The Texan and American history demand later narrative. The Spanish and French episodes may here be briefly told by anticipation.

In the fond belief that monarchy was revered in Mexico, 2600 troops from Havana landed in July 1829, high summer, in the unwholesome region of the River Pánuco, expecting a cordial welcome and easy march to the capital. They found the town of Tampico deserted; no adherents and no supplies.

Santa Anna, stationed at Vera Cruz, acted promptly; raised a forced loan, sent cavalry by land, embarked infantry on an improvised flotilla—about 2000 men of both arms—and attacked Tampico. Fresh troops arrived under Terán, best of the veterans of independence. The Spaniard, losing men by disease and bullets, must soon have yielded; but Santa Anna, eager for glory, hastened the surrender by a sanguinary attack. The surviving Spaniards were conveyed to Havana. Santa Anna's exploits, magniloquently told, prepared his way, a popular hero, to the presidency four years later.

In 1838 Santa Anna, discredited by defeat and captivity in the Texan war, was retired among his fruit trees and fighting-cocks near Jalapa, when the 'Pastry War' brought him hurrying as a volunteer to Vera Cruz. A French squadron had blockaded the Caribbean ports, claiming indemnity to Frenchmen for losses and injuries during civil strife, including 60,000 dollars for a pastry-cook, whose shop and wares had suffered in 'revolution'. The French admiral, his ultimatum being disregarded, bombarded the castle of Ulua (which was much damaged) and landed troops against the defences of Vera Cruz. Santa Anna, who was now in command, mounted his white charger and led a party to cut off some Frenchmen retreating to their boats. A discharge of grape-shot killed his horse and wounded his left leg, which had to be amputated. This episode and the victim's pathetic eloquence retrieved past errors and again led him to the presidential chair. The Mexican Government agreed, through British mediation, to pay most of the French claim for pastry and all else.

It remains to summarize civil history, 1823–55, omitting details of confused conflicts and revolts. After Iturbide's abdication a triumvirate of guerrilla chieftains, Victoria, Bravo (who had fought beside Morelos) and Guerrero, ruled for twenty months (1823–4) while a Constituent Congress was discussing the merits of federation and centralism. The stalwart republican Father Mier declared that 'federation meant union of what had been separated...but the provinces of Mexico had always been united; there was nothing to federate'. Of all the *próceres* of independence, even including Bolívar, Mier was the only one who grasped this fact. But the federalists prevailed; and accordingly the country was artificially divided into nineteen autonomous States and four Territories. 'When the federal Constitution was drawn up', says Justin Smith, 'it became necessary to assume that there were separate political entities to combine, for otherwise a confederation was impossible; and hence they (the provinces) were called forth into a theoretical existence.'

Guadalupe Victoria, elected President, held his ground for four years (1825-9), suppressing a revolt led by the Vice-President Bravo, whose strange example was infectious. Guerrero, though beaten at the poll, became the second President after a confused scuffle in which the capital was partly sacked. Under him negro slavery was abolished—the Indians were already free in theory—and the Spanish invaders were repulsed. But he was unseated by the revolting Vice-President Bustamante; and, attempting to hold out on the Pacific coast, was betrayed to his pursuers and was 'executed'. Bustamante, now aged fifty, an able administrator and henceforth a prominent political figure, had studied for Holy Orders, had practised as a physician, then entered the royal army and finally served under Iturbide. His present triumph was brief; for Santa Anna, 'the king-maker', victor over the Spanish invaders, was watching his turn and using Bustamante as a stepping-stone. In 1833 Santa Anna became President, or rather dictator, and thenceforth for twenty years was the foremost personage in public life; astute, watchful, persuasive and plausible; endowed with all the external and picturesque graces of a leader in peace and war; singular in his power of winning and holding men; a masterly composer of specious manifestoes. His semi-legendary renown was partly due to his valour in the field and to the fact that, having been a soldier since the age of sixteen, he was, in the crowd of republican generals, the only one regularly trained as an officer and competent to organize and discipline troops. Although he had no gifts for high command, was sometimes disastrously careless and was beaten in all large operations, it is fair to add that he was handicapped by the incompetence and indiscipline of his subordinates. His many mistresses (though he was twice married) and his passion for cock-fighting—where he rubbed shoulders with the mob, betting lavishly and excitedly—did not damage his reputation with his countrymen. When things went ill, he talked of ill health and retired to his beautiful estate in the pleasant climate of Jalapa, sometimes leaving a nominee in charge—on one occasion two, alternating in power—sometimes apparently retired but waiting the turn of the wheel; posing as a liberal at need, but clever at adapting any constitutional form to his own ends. Twice he regained the summit after apparently irretrievable failures, and six times between 1833 and 1855 he held brief power as President, or rather dictator.[1]

In his first presidency, 1833–5, Santa Anna assumed complete autocracy, dismissing Congress, all State legislatures and all municipal councils, and installing his own nominees. This upset of State rights and of the Constitution was unspeakably stupid; for amid inevitable armed outbreaks in several States, it gave some constitutional justification to the revolt which was brewing in Texas. Santa Anna laid down the civil power to take command in the war of Texas; and in the following year, 1836, a newly elected or newly appointed Congress abrogated the Constitution of 1824 and established a Central system. In that year Texas was lost to Mexico.

The federal Constitution of 1824 had been an error: but its abrogation was a greater blunder. Several States (now reduced to Departments) revolted, claiming their lost autonomy. Yucatán, after a destructive Indian rising and a civil war, made alliance with independent Texas and seceded from the federation in 1837, to return half-heartedly to the fold later. Bustamante, who became President 'for eight years' under the new Constitution, kept his

---

[1] In 1833, 1841–2 (by the Plan of Tacubaya, to be presently narrated), 1843, 1844, 1847 and 1853 (as 'Serene Highness'). Muñoz, a recent biographer, gives eleven brief presidential terms to Santa Anna; but he includes the occasions when Santa Anna was deputy for someone else and also the occasions when he replaced his own deputy and resumed authority.

seat, despite these troubles, for four years, until he was overthrown
by the 'Plan of Tacubaya', upon which two contemporary wit-
nesses, Señora Calderón, the English wife of the first Spanish
Minister in Mexico, and Brantz Mayer, an American diplomatist,
throw a lively light. There was a preliminary attempt to unseat
Bustamante in July 1840, when a party of barefooted soldiers crept
into the palace by night and arrested the President as he leapt from
his bed to seize his sword. But General Valencia, commander of
the citadel, remained loyal. For a fortnight cannonading alternated
with negotiations between the citadel and the *pronunciados* in the
palace. Finally these had to give way: an amnesty was proclaimed
and Bustamante, who had escaped from his captors, recovered his
authority.

That authority was brief. General Valencia, defender and magni-
loquent eulogist of Bustamante, turned against him in August 1841
when Paredes, the most respectable of the generals, 'pronounced'
at Guadalajara against gross misgovernment and oppressive taxation and in favour of 'a citizen worthy of confidence'. The revolt
spread. Santa Anna, the 'citizen' indicated, marched inland from
Vera Cruz. For five weeks there was fighting in the city: 'every
turret and belfry is covered with soldiers and the streets are
blocked up with troops and trenches. From behind these turrets
and trenches they fire at each other, few soldiers falling, but
numbers of peaceful citizens; shells and bombs falling through the
roofs of the houses, and all this "for the public good".' So writes
Señora Calderón. Finally Santa Anna and his supporters met at
Tacubaya, a village near the capital, and there proclaimed the
'Plan' that all the authorities should be abolished except the judges,
and that the 'Chief of the Revolution should nominate a Junta to
choose a Head of the State'. Accordingly Santa Anna nominated
a Junta, which in turn elected Santa Anna. Bustamante, the
champion of centralism, tried to hold his ground by proclaiming
federation; but, after more fighting in the capital, destruction of
property and killing of civilians, he left the country. Victory in
revolt received the customary rewards: in Paredes' division alone
eleven generals were appointed; and a crowd of newly fledged
colonels blossomed out into gay uniforms.

Santa Anna received an ovation in the capital, as did also, separately, his severed limb, which was interred with an oratorical panegyric under a stately monument. He now legislated at his caprice by rapid and often contradictory decrees, varied by frequent visits to the cock-pit and occasional retreats to his estate, leaving a deputy to bear the hopeless burden of the executive. Requisitions from the Church and from the convents and repeated forced loans supplied for a time his ostentatious extravagance and his gorgeous regiments, while revolts broke out everywhere and trouble with the United States loomed nearer. The tragic farce lasted three years, until in September 1844 his old associate Paredes 'pronounced' in Jalisco. Seizing money from the mines and from everywhere, Santa Anna took the field with (so it is said) 12,000 men and 100 guns (!). His army melted away by desertion, and the President was soon wandering foodless and shelterless with three companions among trackless mountains. Then he narrowly escaped death at the hands of Indians. Next, he passed some months in prison, awaiting trial for treason. His buried limb was torn from its mausoleum and dragged through the streets by a vituperating mob. But, his successor not finding favour, his faults were half forgotten. An opportune earthquake, felt as a sign of divine displeasure, was the occasion of an amnesty; and in June 1845, exiled 'for ten years', he embarked for Havana, where he met his dethroned predecessor Bustamante and won large sums at the cock-pit from the Spanish officers.

Within a week of his departure the cry of 'Santa Anna and Federation' was heard in Mexico. Nine months later, war being imminent, American ships blockaded the Mexican coast. But, believing that the exiled hero would work for peace, the American authorities allowed him to land at Vera Cruz in August 1846. Six weeks later, he set out for the north as commander, soon to become President. The disastrous war with the United States demands a separate chapter. Santa Anna was thrice defeated, in the north, in the west and in the valley of Mexico. When in September 1847 the victorious invaders entered the capital, he resigned the Presidency. Six months later (April 1848) he passed into exile by favour of the American victors, having had no share in the negotiations which yielded to the United States half the territory of the Mexican republic.

After five years he reappeared as President-dictator to deal with general confusion: strife within every province, strife between the provinces, strife between the national Government and every province; banditry everywhere. His remedy was to appoint in every province a dictator, who in turn appointed sub-dictators in every district and they in their turn set up smaller despots in every municipality: pure autocracy; espionage, a muzzled press, legislation by decree, forced loans, forced recruiting, a huge army, no Congress, soldiers in every ministry and all prominent posts; and to decorate the scene, absurd ostentation, lavish extravagance and —at the age of sixty—dissolute indulgences. To secure his power, the dictator contemplated inviting a European prince to reign as King in Mexico, while he himself should rule as Mayor of the Palace. Some Mexicans had always leaned towards monarchy, notably General Paredes and the historian Lucas Alamán, an able and estimable person, several times Minister for Foreign Affairs. And now Santa Anna gave some countenance to Gutiérrez de Estrada, a Mexican living in European exile, a self-appointed champion of monarchy for Mexico, who for ten years past had been importuning European statesmen to aid his plan, a plan which bore fruit ten years later.

This last tyranny of Santa Anna lasted two years, until, after revolts, conflicts, skirmishes, executions, it was swept away by the Plan of Ayutla, which closes the Santanista period and initiates that of Benito Juárez. Santa Anna passed once more into exile. Years afterwards he was allowed to return to his Mexican home, where he died in poverty and obscurity in 1876 at the age of eighty-two, having survived to see the beginning of the long autocracy of Porfirio Díaz.

NOTE. Priestley, chs. xv–xix; Brantz Mayer; Bancroft, vol. v; F. E. Calderón, *Life in Mexico* (Boston, U.S.A., 1843 and reprints); W. H. Callcott, *Santa Anna* (Norman, Oklahoma, 1936); Justin H. Smith, *The War with Mexico*, 2 vols. (New York, 1919), gives a good preliminary narrative of Mexican history.

CHAPTER XXVII

TEXAS AND CALIFORNIA

'Manifest Destiny.'

THE secession of Texas, incorporation in the United States, consequent war and loss of half the Mexican territory are no mere phase of Mexican history but the longest stride in that expansion which has made the United States the richest and strongest country in the world. The world-wide aspects of that movement do not here concern us: but this immense advance of the 'Colossus of the North' is a crucial event in the history not only of Mexico but of all Latin America. The causes of that event were the failure of Mexico to use or occupy those lands and the inevitable westward expansion of the United States, not to be debarred from idle and empty lands by invisible diplomatic barriers. But the historical antecedents of the movement go back nearly a century. Indeed, the rivalry between Spanish and Anglo-Saxon America dates from Elizabethan times and took solid form with the British conquest of Jamaica in 1656. The foundation in 1733 of the British colony of Georgia, pressing close on Spanish Florida, brought British America into contact and friction with Spanish America. But the first great step in the encroachment of Anglo-Saxon America upon continental Latin America is the British conquest of Canada; temporary conquest of Havana, in which 4000 colonial troops took part; and annexation of Florida[1] in 1759–63; for British attacks on the American possessions of the two allied Latin powers, Spain and France, were parts of the same imperial movement. The second great advance is the acquisition of Louisiana by the United States forty years later: this demands brief retrospect.

In 1761 the vast region of Louisiana, having its capital at New Orleans but extending in the main to the west of the Mississippi, was ceded by France to Spain, which exercised a dubious sovereignty for forty years. In 1801 Napoleon compelled the Spanish

[1] In 1783 Florida was restored to Spain, which kept it for only thirty-three years.

Crown to retrocede the country to France: but two years later, having failed in his transatlantic designs through the maritime war with Great Britain and the consequent collapse of the French expedition to Santo Domingo, he sold Louisiana to the United States. That Government claimed that Louisiana included Texas, extending to the Rio Grande. But by the treaty with Spain which in 1819–21 added Florida[1] to the Union, the United States, in order to facilitate the treaty and gain the immediate object, withdrew the claim to Texas and accepted the River Sabina as the boundary between American Louisiana and Spanish Texas. This withdrawal was bitterly criticized by American opponents of the administration and was not forgotten later. The Mexican inhabitants of Texas, a country as large as France, probably then numbered about 3000, mostly in the capital, San Antonio. Of the Spanish missions nothing remained a few years later but half-ruined buildings. The country in general was left to Indians and wild beasts, a vacant land, although subject to a recognized but idle and unused Mexican sovereignty.

But already American adventurers and pioneers were crossing the boundary from Louisiana into these empty Texan lands, some of them pursuing wild political aims. Regular and permitted colonization followed, when in 1821 the Spanish Viceroy, during the last days of Spanish authority in Mexico, admitted into Texas 300 American families, who were to accept Spanish allegiance and profess the Roman Catholic religion; this last evidently a vain stipulation. Then, after Mexican independence and the federal Constitution of 1824, the vast region of Texas became, provisionally, merely part of the State of Coahuila. The Government of that State at once admitted numerous American colonists, under the strange belief that these American settlers would form a bulwark against American political aggression. Naturally these English-speaking and mostly non-Catholic immigrants were not absorbed

[1] This cession of Florida was in the nature of a retrocession. From 1763 to 1783 Florida was in British hands and attached to the region of the Thirteen Colonies. In 1819–21 the former British Colonies, now independent, recovered Florida; and thus the whole Atlantic coast of North America became once more Anglo-Saxon, as it had been in 1763–83. This instance of the vicissitudes of imperial expansion illustrates the fact that the spread of the United States is a continuance or resumption of British imperial advance in America.

into Mexicanism, and demanded in vain that Texas—according to promise—should be separated from Coahuila and constituted as a State. Offers from Washington to purchase Texas were rejected by Mexico. Bitter indignation was stirred up in Texas when in 1830 Terán marched into the country with Mexican troops to enforce an odious decree which restricted colonization near the boundary and upset existing contracts. Resentment against the Mexican Government grew, and by the end of 1831 a kind of provisional Texan Government had been set up. During the following months parties of Texans, that is to say American immigrants (now Mexican citizens) revolted and captured several Mexican garrisons.

The trouble came to a head when in 1834-5 Santa Anna swept away State rights, illegally abolishing the State legislature of Coahuila-Texas and ordering that the Texans should be disarmed. He thus provoked a general insurrection, the Texan insurgents protesting that they were not rebels, but that, like their neighbours in Zacatecas, they were defending the Constitution of 1824 against an 'illegal usurpation'. But the fiction of loyalty to Mexico could not be kept up, and in November 1835 a Convention of Texan delegates set up a Government which four months later (March 1836) proclaimed an independent Texan republic.[1] This meant open war. Santa Anna, assuming command, set out north-eastwards from Saltillo with 8000 raw recruits on a wintry march of 300 miles across desert country to the Rio Grande, leaving a trail of abandoned stores and of corpses, both men and animals, and thence 150 miles to San Antonio. Alamo, a thick-walled mission station converted into a fortress defended by Texan guns, stood in his way, refusing a summons to surrender. Hoisting a blood-red flag in sight of the garrison in token of 'no quarter to rebels', Santa Anna attacked with some 4000 men, took the place by assault, losing 400 men, and slew the 183 defenders. A second massacre followed when the Texan garrison of Goliad, another mission station, attempting to retreat, were surrounded, compelled to surrender and next day were deliberately shot, above 400 in all.

---

[1] The attitude of Washington towards this whole movement is described by R. M. McElroy in *The Winning of the Far West* (New York and London, 1914).

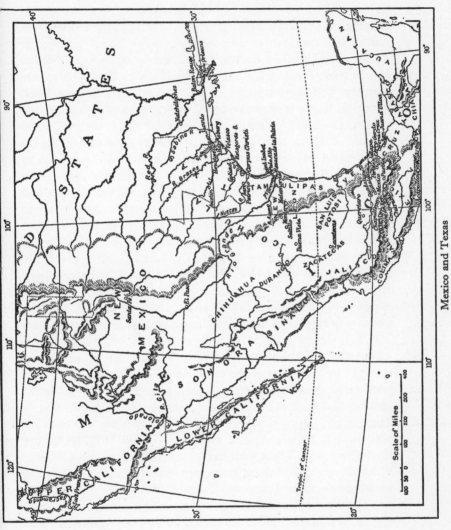

Mexico and Texas

Three weeks later Santa Anna met his nemesis. Encamped with about 1200 men on a hill-side by the River Jacinto, facing an enemy—about 800—encamped in a wood below, Santa Anna was sleeping the siesta one sultry afternoon (April 1836): the men were resting and the sentries were nodding, when Sam Houston, the Texan commander, a man who had lived and hunted with an Indian tribe, crept to the attack. There was no battle, only rout, slaughter and the surrender of half the fugitives. Santa Anna, fleeing on foot in a peasant's dress, was caught and brought to the victor's camp. The Texans clamoured for the execution of the butcher of Alamo and Goliad; but Houston knew better. At his dictation the captive commander sent orders to all his officers to retire and (although as a prisoner he had no right to do so) undertook to recognize the independence of Texas. He was then allowed to pass to the United States and had an interview with President Jackson, who sent him home to Vera Cruz in an American warship.

The independence of Texas, now a fact, was recognized by the United States in 1836, by France in 1839, by Belgium and Great Britain in 1840: and the new Republic soon had a flag (one star), an army, a naval flotilla and a considerable commerce. But Mexico still contended that Texas was merely part of Mexican territory in revolt. In 1842 Santa Anna sent some ineffective raids into the country and threatened invasion. This brought armed volunteers from the east to aid Texas. Mexican sentiment, already inflamed by the aggressive action of an American naval officer in a Californian port, swelled in bitterness against the United States. In 1843 Santa Anna, as President, announced to the American Minister in Mexico that the Mexican Government 'will consider equivalent to a declaration of war...the passage of an act for the incorporation of Texas with the territory of the United States'. The first application from Texas (not unanimous) to Washington for admission to the Union was declined. But as time passed, there was apprehension at Washington lest independent Texas should absorb New Mexico and California, possibly even Oregon, and bar the westward expansion of the United States: there was also uneasiness about the policy of Great Britain and France concerning Texas and Mexico and, more particularly, about their supposed designs upon California. At last, early in 1845, the United States Congress ended the anomalous situation by passing an act to admit Texas to the Union. In July a Texan convention accepted this invitation.

Henceforth war was inevitable, although the Government at Washington still worked for peace 'if peace could be maintained without sacrificing our just demands' (including some pecuniary claims) and at the same time attempted to purchase New Mexico and California; regions which, if war should come, were viewed as the prize of victory.

California, rich and extensive, containing probably some 10,000 Mexicans and a few hundreds of foreigners, mostly Americans, was almost detached from the rest of Mexico. The Spanish missions, which had made California, had been swept away under the Republic. The chief port Monterey (not to be confused with the capital of Nuevo León) was a miserable village. Authorities sent from the federal capital were thrice driven out; and at this time the Californian Government, so far as government existed, was a local triumvirate. Present-day California cherishes a picturesque tradition of the generous, careless life led in those days by the great landowners among their horses, their fighting-cocks and their countless herds of cattle, a primitive aristocracy who knew no law but their own rude code of equestrian chivalry.

New Mexico, then containing probably nearly 100,000 Mexicans (besides independent Indian tribes), was more in touch with the rest of the Republic, being traversed from north to south by the 'Santa Fe trail' along which passed armed convoys of wagons carrying American goods to Mexico and paying exorbitant customs in Santa Fe. The people, unprotected from the Indians, knew the Governor and garrison chiefly as rapacious oppressors and had no love for the Federal Government.

But Texas was the crucial point. Mexico was uncompromising and, regardless of the chances of victory, determined to invade. Accordingly in the autumn of 1845 some 4000 American troops under General Taylor were sent into Texas to meet this menace. In March 1846 Taylor approached the Rio Grande, which the Americans claimed to be the boundary of Texas; a claim not admitted by the Mexicans, who considered that a smaller stream, the Nueces, further to the east, was the boundary. The inevitable clash came in April 1846, when Mexican troops crossed the Rio Grande and surrounded a small party of American soldiers, killing some and capturing others: 'American soil invaded by the Mexicans' according to the American view: 'Mexican soil invaded by the Yankis', as the Mexicans declared. It was a tragic day for Mexico.

During the war which followed (May 1846 to February 1848) civil conflicts within the Mexican Republic never ceased: the generals, few of them real soldiers, seemed to be more anxious to thwart one another or to injure their own Government than to resist the invader. 'The saddest chapter of the tale', says Teja Zabre in a semi-official history, 'is that the same *pronunciamientos* which paved the way for the entry of the invader, served to escort him when he left.' General Grant writes: 'The Mexican army of that day was hardly an organization. The private soldier was picked up from the lowest class of the inhabitants...his consent was not asked. He was poorly clothed, worse fed and seldom paid, and well-nigh uninstructed in the use of the inefficient weapon with which he was supplied. The officers of the lower grades were but little superior to the men.' Justin Smith remarks: 'in a sense we seem to be watching children.'

The war had three phases, which can only be briefly summarized: (1) Taylor's invasion from the north; (2) Scott's invasion by way of Vera Cruz, which was the decisive move; (3) Kearney's westward march and the conquest of New Mexico and California. In May 1846 Taylor defeated a Mexican force far outnumbering his own, crossed the Rio Grande and marched into the undefended Mexican town of Matamoros. In August the regular invasion of Mexico began. Taylor, moving westward, took Monterey after hard fighting in September; Saltillo fell to him in November, and, far to the south, Victoria in December.

Meantime Santa Anna, appointed to supreme command, was gathering an army at San Luis Potosí and raising scanty supplies of money by strange expedients. At the end of January 1847 he led out thence 18,000 ill-equipped and ill-trained troops against

Taylor, who with about one-third of that number, was encamped to the south of Monterey. Having lost 3000 men by sickness, exhaustion and desertion in his three weeks' wintry march, Santa Anna attacked the invaders at Buena Vista on 22–23 February and, having had victory almost in sight, was obliged to retreat. Sick, miserable and starving, less than half of the men who had set out staggered back into San Luis Potosí; but Santa Anna, announcing triumphant success, travelled in his swift carriage to the capital and assumed the presidency. In the same month in which the Battle of Buena Vista was fought, Mexicans fought one another in the capital for nine days over the proposal to raise funds from the Church, and afterwards the city was a battle-field of civil conflict for a month (22 February to 23 March).

The invasion from the north by General Taylor was cut short and, by orders from Washington, the Vera Cruz route was chosen. Scott, as Commander-in-Chief, having disembarked his army unresisted to the south of the city, took Vera Cruz on 29 March 1847. Santa Anna with fresh energy prepared to resist this, the real invasion. With 12,000 men[1] and artillery he fortified a defile which he believed to be impregnable. But, neglecting precautions, he failed to make it so. The Americans, surmounting the obstacles of thick woods and pathless crags, outflanked and routed the defenders, taking many prisoners and guns.

Jalapa fell before the invaders, then Perote, and on 15 May Puebla. Thenceforward for three months, although both sides increased their forces and strengthened their positions, it is hard to say how far fighting was serious. For on 5 May an emissary from President Polk reached Vera Cruz to negotiate for peace. A month later negotiations were opened through the British Legation; and it was understood that on the conclusion of peace Santa Anna was to receive a million dollars. The American advance, begun on 7 August, from Puebla to the valley of Mexico was almost unresisted. But Santa Anna, for his own reputation, now had to fight in earnest. People accused him of treason. His authority was crumbling: there were dissident movements in the

[1] 'Mexico', says Brantz Mayer, 'possesses a wonderful facility in the creation of armies or in the aggregation of men under the name of soldiers.'

north-west: six central States formed a coalition which almost threatened secession. But he had a last and great military opportunity when Scott led his little army of some 10,000 men over the eastern rim of the mountains which encircle the valley of Mexico, apparently descending into a trap; since about 25,000 Mexican levies, including a body of 200 hard-fighting deserters from the American troops, were holding fortified places on ground most difficult for attack. But defence was ill directed, and the reciprocal hatred between Santa Anna and the obstinate General Valencia brought severe defeat. The Americans, overcoming extraordinary difficulties of ground and losing heavily, but much less than the Mexicans, won two victories. A brief armistice (24 August to 7 September) brought no conclusion. On 13 September the citadel of Chapultepec was taken by assault and escalade after heavy fighting, the defenders having failed to explode mines, previously prepared, under the assailants' feet. Next day the invaders marched into the capital. Santa Anna resigned the presidency and departed on a futile attempt to cut the American communications by attacking Puebla. Mob violence in the capital and continued attacks on American posts and communications were suppressed by stern measures. Finally, a provisional Mexican Government at Querétaro accepted the Treaty of Guadalupe Hidalgo, ratified in May 1848, whereby the United States, paying fifteen million dollars to Mexico, acquired or rather kept California and New Mexico: for those regions had been in American hands since the end of 1847. Kearney's unresisted march through New Mexico and the conquest of California at the cost of a few skirmishes and one temporary reverse during the latter half of 1847 read more like a story of romantic adventure than sober history. The details belong to the history of the United States rather than to that of Mexico. Doniphan's astonishing march to Chihuahua, with a victory on the way against an apparently impregnable position, is a further episode of little military importance except for its striking effect on Mexican opinion.

Five years later Santa Anna, once more President-dictator, sold to the United States, on his own authority, the Mesilla valley, known as the 'Gadsden Purchase'.[1]

---

[1] The Texan frontier was adjusted or extended by agreement in 1850.

Teja Zabre, even while stigmatizing these proceedings as a 'spoliation carried out by force', remarks, 'a great part of Mexico's territory was lost because she had been unable to administer and settle those regions . . . that which Spain had been unable to colonize and the Republic unable to settle, was occupied by the stream of Anglo-American expansion'.

United States expansion to the Rio Grande and the Pacific has nothing to do with theory or doctrine. It was a matter of expediency, almost of national necessity; the natural expansion of a growing nation over lands nominally possessed by people doing little to use them. President Polk, quite legitimately, used every contributory argument to conciliate reluctant public opinion, pointing to possible French or British action and citing Monroe's authority. His apprehensions were reasonable in view of future possibilities: but they were not the reason for national expansion, which requires no theoretical explanation. United States' foreign policy, like that of every nation, has been guided by the needs of every emergency as it arose and not by abstract principles.

Polk's special mention of North America in connexion with the Monroe Doctrine does not concern the present topic. But, with reference to Latin America, he added the 'no-transfer' principle: for when in 1848 the seceding Government of Yucatán offered 'dominion and sovereignty' to the United States, to Great Britain and to Spain in exchange for aid, Polk wrote to Congress objecting to a 'transfer of dominion and sovereignty to any European power'. This rule, which had previously been adumbrated, later took more definite form, forbidding to all Latin-American States the voluntary cession of territory or of sovereignty to a non-American State.

NOTE. Justin H. Smith, *The War with Mexico**, 2 vols. (New York, 1919); *The Annexation of Texas** (New York, 1911).

CHAPTER XXVIII

MODERN MEXICO

REFORM, INTERVENTION, AUTOCRACY, REVOLUTION

(i) *Reform*

THE departure of the Americans left chaos: revolts, disorders, brief administrations; liberal attempts to curb the power of army, clergy, and landed aristocracy; reaction under Santa Anna's last autocracy (April 1853 to August 1855), which brought no peace and was overthrown by the radical movement known as the Plan of Ayutla; this set up a liberal Government with the Zapotec Indian Benito Juárez in the Cabinet.

The son of Indian peasants, an orphan in infancy, at the age of twelve a shepherd boy ignorant of Spanish and of the alphabet, Juárez had been educated for the priesthood by a friendly Franciscan, had preferred to study law, had sat in the National Congress and for five years, 1847–52, had ruled his native state of Oaxaca as a just and capable Governor. To the credit of the Mexican people, his squat figure and unprepossessing aboriginal features did not impede his public career. Imprisoned by Santa Anna at Ulua in 1853, he had escaped to New Orleans, where he supported himself by work in a cigarette factory. He returned thence to join the Plan of Ayutla and take office as Minister of Justice in a liberal Cabinet. At once he passed through Congress a law abolishing ecclesiastical courts, making the clergy amenable to the ordinary civil tribunals and thus sweeping away the medieval privileges (*fueros*) of the clergy: a just but over-hasty measure which provoked the battle-cry of 'religion and *fueros*', giving shape to the struggle between privilege and reform. Comonfort, the most moderate of the Ayutla men, consented to become Provisional President in December 1855 in the vain hope of calming passions. Next came the banishment of the Jesuits, and then the famous 'Ley Lerdo', so called from its author Miguel Lerdo, which forbade the Church, the largest landowner in the country, to own land except for purposes of worship and thus compelled the clergy, not indeed to surrender their property, but to sell their lands. The hope of thus creating peasant proprietors was disappointed: small men dared not buy; and the Church lands were sold in huge estates to rich Creoles or to speculators. Then clerical fees were limited and cemeteries placed under lay control. Next a Constituent Congress produced the Constitution of 1857, which proclaimed full individual liberty, freedom of speech and of the press and, by silence concerning religion, recognized no State Church: no substantial change was made in the federal, parliamentary and presidential arrangements, which, in theory, resembled those of the United States. Tannenbaum, a sympathetic historian, justly remarks that the constitution was 'unenforced and unenforceable'. Juárez, its real author, was in too great a hurry.

The 'War of Reform' which had already begun and continued to rage for four years over this Constitution was (says Teja Zabre) the 'cruellest and longest civil war in the history of Mexico'. Comonfort, now 'Constitutional President', joined a revolt against his own Government and, having failed to ride the whirlwind, resigned and fled. Juárez, as Chief of the Supreme Court, became acting President. But one Zuloaga, a 'general' of shady antecedents, elected President by a nominated Congress, held the capital through the military successes of a young soldier named Miramón. The Republic had two Presidents, Zuloaga in the capital, supported by the army and the ruling classes, Juárez 'wherever he happened to be'. Zuloaga took the strange step of sending General Almonte, an able and active man who had been prominent among Santa Anna's adherents, as an emissary to Europe to solicit French and English intervention in support of the Government in the capital. Vera Cruz, with its profitable custom-house, was the seat of Juárez and his Cabinet. Miramón besieged the place in vain for six weeks; and returning to the capital, slaughtered all the officers who after a recent battle had surrendered to his ferocious colleague Marquéz, including physicians tending the wounded.

In 1859 Juárez assured his position when, recognized as President of the Republic by the Government at Washington, he publicly received the American Minister McLane in his presidential residence at Vera Cruz. Somewhat later two armed ships, fitted out by Miramón's orders at Havana to attack Vera Cruz by sea, were seized as pirates by American warships at Juárez' request. Meantime the European powers recognized the President—alternately Zuloaga and Miramón in bewildering interchange—who ruled in the capital by confiscation, blood and terror.

In July 1859 Juárez, after announcing a daring liberal programme, including a plan for breaking up the great estates, promulgated by decree the three famous 'Laws of Reform': (1) disestablishment and disendowment of thè Church; (2) marriage a civil contract; (3) civil. not clerical, registration of births, deaths and marriages. All confraternities and male religious houses were suppressed. Nunneries, forbidden henceforth to receive novices, were thus to disappear gradually.

Juárez' cause gained ground. His officers were victorious in the field; for Juárez himself was always the black-coated lawyer-President. In January 1861 Juárez triumphantly entered his capital. An amnesty was proclaimed and there was no bloodshed. But Juárez expelled the Spanish Minister, the Papal delegate and five prelates, perhaps justly but with indiscreet and autocratic zeal. Miramón fled abroad. Marquéz took to the mountains to pursue a sanguinary guerrilla war.

Some exalt Juárez as a great all-round statesman. Lord Acton speaks plainly: 'Incorruptible...he had risen slowly, without perfidy and without violence, a patient, steadfast man....But he proved incapable as a ruler and utterly unequal to the desperate task of restoring order in a country distracted by passion and ruined by anarchy.' He attempted at one sweep to carry out the principles of 1789 which had cost eighty years of struggle in France. His rapid autocratic decrees provoked the resignation of his three best ministers; then of the whole reconstructed cabinet. He was blamed for negotiating the McLane-Ocampo Treaty, 'granting to the United States', says Priestley, 'perpetual unlimited transit across the Isthmus of Tehuantepec and across the north Mexican states to the Pacific under conditions which meant practical derogation of Mexican sovereignty in those areas....The United States was to pay four million dollars, but half was to pay the American private

claims.... Fortunately... the American Senate refused ratification.'
The confiscation of Church property and sale of lands produced
meagre profit owing to waste, mismanagement and dubious
dealings. Juárez, inexpert in finance, was overwhelmed by claims
and was ill served by over-zealous friends, who emulated their
thievish adversaries by seizing much-needed treasure; and Juárez
had to make restitution at great cost. He admitted indebtedness
to Great Britain for funds which had been seized in the British
Legation by 'The Government of Mexico', that is to say by his
usurping rival Miramón. But in July 1861, just when Juárez was
re-elected President, Congress approved, without negotiation or
request for a moratorium, a decree for suspending payment of
interest on external debts for two years. This unfortunate decree
brought on a storm which had long been brewing.

(ii) *Intervention*

Six months later 6000 Spanish troops landed at Vera Cruz. In
January 1862 they were joined by 3000 French and by a British
squadron which landed 700 marines. The diplomatic passages
leading to this joint intervention belong to European rather than to
Mexican history. The ostensible object was merely the enforcement
of pecuniary claims. Juárez replied by preparing defence and by
the famous decree of January 1862 that any Mexicans aiding the
invaders should be tried by court-martial and executed as traitors.
Nor did he neglect negotiations, which led to an agreement that the
intruders should recognize his Government, that they should move
from the unwholesome coast to higher ground near Orizaba, and
that, failing a settlement, they should return to the coast before any
hostile move.

It soon appeared that the exorbitant French claims covered
aggressive designs disapproved by their allies. In April 1862 the
Spaniards and the British withdrew. Napoleon III had hoodwinked
his allies; for he had resolved to set up a Catholic European prince
—Maximilian, brother of the Austrian Emperor Francis Joseph—
as hereditary sovereign of Mexico, thus to win glory and profit for
France and to check any southward expansion of the United States,

who were absorbed in their great internal struggle and were unable for a time to take any action beyond their own borders.

Thus another alien aggression made Mexico a second time the scene of a conflict affecting the destiny of the whole Western Hemisphere. The duel between the peasant-born Indian and the magnificent Hapsburg prince provides a vivid human setting to a conflict transcending Mexican limits.

The French commander, now unhampered by allies, broke his promise to return to the coast and occupied the town of Orizaba. He was joined by the infamous Marquéz and, moving westward, routed the Mexican levies holding mountain defiles. In May, despising his enemy, he attacked Puebla and was repulsed with heavy loss. But 30,000 troops came from France, and a year later (May 1863) Puebla was reduced by starvation after a two months' siege. The French marched, unhindered, to the capital. Juárez, driven from the city, set up his Government as Constitutional President at San Luis Potosí.

In July 1863 an Assembly of Notables voted, at French dictation, for the proposed monarchy. The French commander and this Assembly thus forced the hand of Napoleon, who, finding that he had misinterpreted both the policy of the British Government and the wishes of the Mexican people, was disposed to drop his adventure, but now felt obliged to go forward. Three months later a deputation of grave frock-coated Mexican gentlemen, of respectable and responsible aspect, claiming to represent the President and people of Mexico, waited on Maximilian in his Adriatic castle, and offered him, on their behalf, the Mexican throne. He replied that acceptance depended on a free vote of the whole nation. The French commander readily produced this requirement, and in April 1864 a second deputation conveyed to the Archduke the wishes of an 'immense majority of the Mexican people'. Maximilian, although moved mainly by his own ambition and that of his wife, the beautiful and courageous Princess Charlotte of Belgium, believed that he was the destined regenerator of Mexico, bringing orderly and prosperous government. Despite the awkward fact of support by French troops, with some Austrian and Belgian volunteers, he had no designs against Mexican independence. He meant to rule loyal Mexicans as an independent monarch. The French troops, except a small nucleus, were to be gradually replaced by native recruits: and Maximilian asserted his independence by refusing a French concession in Sonora which covered political designs.

Landing at Vera Cruz, the imperial pair drove through silent and deserted streets; but in the villages where they passed, the Indian peasants greeted them in festal crowds, hoping to find, in the fair-haired stranger from the East, the regenerator of their race foretold in ancient legend. And when their equipage approached the capital in May 1864, there were—besides the clergy—enough monarchists or adherents of the nearest authority to give them a flattering welcome.

Maximilian was a tall, handsome and amiable prince, aged thirty-one, distinguished by a magnificent blonde beard, sailor, traveller, linguist, author (both verse and prose) and recently Austrian Governor of Lombardy. No one could have been more well-meaning or looked the part better: but he lacked common sense, indulging in romantic dreams of greatness.[1] As the French arms advanced, the modest black carriage of President Juárez (now preserved in the National Museum) rolled from northern city to city, and halted at El Paso (now Ciudad Juárez) in sight of United States territory. Here the legitimate head of the nation fixed his capital, convinced of ultimate victory.

Maximilian, despite military progress, was plunged in perplexities. His obligations to France and the daily cost of war brought overwhelming debt. His conciliatory treatment of the liberals, some of whom entered the Cabinet and many received important posts, angered his reactionary supporters. His refusal to cancel past legislation and restore Church property, now owned by the purchasers, turned the clergy and even the Papacy against him. He alienated the landowners by an ultra-liberal decree wiping out arrears of peons' debts and abolishing the whip on the haciendas. He anticipated the 'six-year plan' of to-day by ordering the establishment of schools everywhere. These kindly commands,

---

[1] Maximilian's rules of court etiquette, written by himself, filled a printed volume of 600 pages.

only possible of fulfilment by a loyal and energetic magistracy and police, were a dead letter. Maximilian never summoned Congress.

Yet during 1865 the Emperor's authority seemed to be established. Porfirio Díaz, ablest of the republican commanders, who had long held out in the south, was made prisoner. The more regular republican armies were beaten, and many leaders submitted. Only guerrilla bands remained, numerous indeed, but regarded by the imperialists as brigands. 'As for the Indians', says Bancroft, 'they looked on with passive indifference', except, presumably, those who were swept into the armies on either side. In October 1865 Maximilian decreed that any captured members of guerrilla bands should be tried by court-martial and executed within twenty-four hours. Later events show that this was meant as a menace rather than a deliberate resolution: but just after the decree a republican force was defeated and its leaders were shot by the Mexican General Méndez. Meantime the imperturbable Juárez, although his legal term ended in November 1865 and he postponed the presidential election on his own authority, was waiting undismayed for the approaching deliverance. For, while the imperialists were winning deceptive Mexican victories, the North was winning in the American civil war: men, money and arms were crossing the frontier into Mexico. In February 1866 Secretary Seward told Napoleon that the French troops must be withdrawn.

The last French soldiers departed in March 1867. The Emperor, ill, worn and bewildered, was about to abdicate, but was persuaded by interested or foolish advisers, on the strength of some fleeting success, that victory was coming. The republicans closed in on the diminishing imperialists, who only held out by the press-gang and heavy requisitions or rather extortions. Maximilian, taking the field himself for the first time, was besieged in Querétaro (February–May 1867) and at last made prisoner. He was tried by a court-martial of junior officers, a captain presiding, and was condemned to death. Juárez, imperturbable in defeat, was inexorable after victory and refused all petitions for pardon. And, indeed, clemency would have alienated his supporters and left a possible rival. Maximilian, meeting his fate with serene dignity, was shot with two Mexican generals, Miramón and Mejía. Thenceforth Mexican forms were to be republican.

(iii) *Autocracy*

Two days later Porfirio Díaz marched victorious into the capital, and in mid-July 1867 the restored President entered the city. Reprisals, by Mexican standards, were moderate. But the disbandment of 84,000 troops, accustomed to guerrilla fighting and to living on the country, let loose uncontrollable forces of disorder. Revolts were chronic; banditry everywhere; the franchise, unintelligible to the masses, was worked by politicians; Juárez, asking for exceptional powers to keep order, was accused of usurpation. In 1871, after a managed but indecisive election, Congress declared him to be President once more; and a revolt of Porfirio Díaz, an unsuccessful candidate, proclaiming 'free election and no reelection', collapsed. The death of President Juárez in 1872 appeased strife for a moment, and the Chief of the Supreme Court, Sebastián Lerdo (brother of the late Miguel Lerdo, author of the Ley Lerdo) took his place. Under him the 'Laws of Reform' were incorporated in the Constitution: nunneries were suppressed and Sisters of Mercy were banished. But Lerdo's capricious autocracy was his undoing. In 1876 Porfirio Díaz was successful in a second *pronunciamiento*, defeating the Lerdistas in a sanguinary battle. Lerdo departed for the United States: 1000 cavalry escorted to Vera Cruz a train of twenty-five wagons and fifty mules loaded with his baggage, including 20,000 pesos[1] of public money. Díaz became 'Provisional President', a year later 'Constitutional President' and in 1878, having wisely paid by a forced loan a sum due to the United States, he was recognized as President by that Government and so secured his position in the eyes of the world. Thus began the longest, most famous and apparently the most successful 'monocracy' in Latin-American history, a dictatorship surpassing all others in territorial extent, in the numbers of its subject population and in the almost unruffled strength of its sway.

---

[1] Mexican dollars, worth 10,000 American dollars or about £2100; seemingly moderate presidential loot. But this was probably due to the poverty of the treasury rather than to personal abstinence.

The Díaz autocracy, although nominally interrupted by the presidency of González (1880–4), lasted in fact from 1876 until 1911 through seven re-elections.

Porfirio Díaz, who had some Indian blood, was born in 1830 of a poor working family in Oaxaca. Destined for the priesthood, he preferred to study law; but his true vocation was soldiering. He joined the Plan of Ayutla in 1855; and throughout the War of Reform and the French intervention he fought against reaction, chiefly in his own country of the south, enlisting Indians and forming a disciplined army, not a mere horde of guerrilleros. Twice he escaped from French captivity and, as a victorious general, he occupied the capital for Juárez. His varied adventures and his escapes by land and sea surpass anything imagined in sensational fiction. He was a fine soldierly figure of a man, especially on horse-back; of vigorous frame and constitution, kept in training by abstemious and active life; of an integrity rare among Mexican politicians, but no more scrupulous than other Ibero-American dictators in methods of keeping the peace.

His first task was to secure his power and restore order. An incipient revolt in Vera Cruz was checked by the summary execution of nine 'Lerdistas', probably innocent of revolt. Thenceforth conspirators, subversive leaders and suspects soon disappeared; for spies and willing servants knew their business. For a full generation the country saw no civil strife. Violent crime (unless committed by a magistrate or his friends), banditry and robbery were suppressed by the ready methods of the famous *rurales* or mounted police, many of them ex-bandits. The *ley fuga*, and the report 'the prisoner, trying to escape, was shot', saved trouble to tribunals. Thus Mexico was made as safe as any country in the world except in the waste places of the north and on the turbulent border, infested by savage Indians, smugglers and fugitives from civilization, both American and Mexican. Although, like his presidential colleagues in some other republics, Díaz suppressed disorder by terror, his authority rested not only on terror, but on a loyal acceptance of a rule which brought peace. A packed Congress dutifully obeyed his orders. Judges were appointed and removed by him, in fact though not in form. Men of any former party were welcomed, if they yielded unquestioning adherence. He secured the support of the landowners by much regard for large property and little for labour or peasant proprietorship. In the latter part of his time he also won the general support of the clergy—still a great power in the land despite the Reform Laws—by respectful countenance and by shelving in great part the anti-clerical laws, although he himself was a prominent freemason. Indeed the Church obtained a considerable re-endowment by gifts and legacies, acquiring lands, houses and mortgages held in other names. The dictator gave due attention to the army, his indispensable buttress.

All prominent officials were his friends and also all State Governors. But the great cattle-kings of the north, Governors or Governor-makers in their respective States, were semi-independent potentates who had to be humoured, notably Luis Terrazas, owner of more than seven million acres in Chihuahua and lord of as much again through his kinsmen; and the Torres family, owners of more than six million acres in Sonora. There is some evidence that Díaz himself disapproved increase of debt-peonage and encroachment on Indian village lands. But his power rested on the upper classes; and he knew that a single wealthy hacendado, if aggrieved, could annex a couple of generals and finance a revolt. The slave-driving sisal planters of Yucatán, not so formidable individually, were a powerful group united by self-interest: so also the sugar-planters of Morelos, who are described by one who knew them as 'the most charming people in the world, highly educated, cultured, travelled ...but negligent and over-indulged. They thought of the land in terms of the golden stream that flowed from it into their laps.'[1]

Public works were Porfirio's particular concern. He welcomed capital, chiefly from the United States but also from Europe, for railway building, harbour improvement, mines, factories, public utilities, the draining of the valley of Mexico (a beneficent hygienic work) and, from the opening of the present century, extraction of oil. The national debt increased, but so also did revenue, wealth and population. And under the skilful management of the Finance Minister Limantour, public credit stood high. The alcabala, the

[1] *Tempest over Mexico*, p. 37.

odious and uneconomic tax on sales, was abolished and also (so far as a decree could avail) all internal customs and tolls: but some of these were hard to kill.

Foreign affairs, except for negotiation of loans in Europe, meant for Díaz only one thing, the amity of the United States. He carefully fulfilled all obligations towards that powerful neighbour. Notwithstanding some inevitable friction, his patience and discretion in handling delicate questions about the pursuit of criminals and predatory Indians across the border in both directions were met with cordial friendliness. Mexico welcomed the second Pan-American Conference in 1901–2. Five years later the United States and Mexico joined in an attempt to pacify Central America; and at a banquet in Mexico city Secretary Root declared Díaz to be worthy of the 'hero-worship of mankind'. American opinion was naturally reflected in Europe and was confirmed by the financial punctuality of Mexico. The evils of peonage and of latifundia, mentioned by Brantz Mayer in 1853 and by Lord Acton in 1868, were half-forgotten or ignored until the fall of Díaz,[1] when the chorus of eulogy gave way to a chorus of reprobation.

Yet those evils increased during Porfirio's later years. A law of 1886 allowed any prospector to 'denounce' unoccupied land and to occupy it, paying a small tax. Since the Indian villages seldom possessed a written title to their immemorial communal lands, the hacendados were thus enabled to annex any Indian lands adjacent to or surrounded by the great estates. The landowner or his manager was all-powerful, favoured by the Government, having through the use of the whip almost the power of life and death, and aided by the *rurales*, who treated a runaway peon as a criminal. Debt-slavery for life, transmitted to children, was particularly horrible on the Yucatán sisal plantations. Yaqui Indians (whose tribe had been in part shot down by punitive expeditions) were conveyed thither

---

[1] Mr Kenneth Turner's investigations, made in 1908–9, did not appear in book form, *Barbarous Mexico*, until 1911. De Fornaro's book *Diaz, Czar of Mexico* (1908) was so violent as to be ineffective. Lumholtz, who spent five years in Mexico between 1893 and 1898, says that alcohol tempted Indians into debt-slavery, but speaks of Porfirio's humanity and desire to befriend the Indian. Enock in 1911, after several years in Mexico, mentions debt-slavery but adds that the Indians were not unhappy or oppressed.

from Sonora in slave gangs by long journeys of indescribable hardship in which many died. In addition to debt-slavery and land-grabbing, labour unrest was caused by the contrast between wages paid by foreigners in industrial undertakings (railways, factories, mines, harbours, oil-fields) and the pittance paid to agricultural workers, which remained stationary while prices rose; so that the farm labourer was worse off than under the Spanish viceroys in the eighteenth century. It is fair to add that their miserable condition, like that of the debt-peon, was due in great part to their own apathy and to the cheapness of the besotting *pulque*, the fermented juice of the maguey, the curse of the peasantry.

Yet these evils were not the main cause of the collapse. Díaz was growing old and so also were his associates. He was no longer adaptable; and his cast-iron system, which had crushed anarchy, was obsolete in a pacified and partly industrialized Mexico. Its efficiency had waned and also the integrity, not indeed of the President but of the people about him. He was losing his hold on the upper classes and had not the same hold on the growing business middle class. In 1904, the date of his re-election—for six years this time—he appointed a Vice-President, a possible successor; but, desiring no rival, he chose an unpopular and unsuitable person. There was a rift in Porfirista circles: a group of professional office-holders and aspirants nicknamed *científicos* ('highbrows'), who cared little for the aged dictator but much for the profitable continuance of the Porfirista system, were generally disliked; and there was widespread uneasiness about the footing gained in the country by American investors, including huge land grants in the north.

(iv) *Revolution*

In 1908 Díaz declared to an American journalist, that Mexico was ripe for democracy and that he would not seek re-election in 1910. In the same year appeared a small volume, *La Sucesión Presidencial en 1910*, which went through three editions. The author, Francisco Madero, a nervous-looking little man, not much over five feet in height, a vegetarian and a spiritualist, who had received an ill-digested education abroad, belonged to a wealthy land-owning family in Coahuila, further enriched by mining. Francisco had already broken the traditions of his class by generous philanthropy to the workmen under his charge. His book, although decently respectful to Díaz, was a bold attack on his system and it denounced the Yaqui infamy. Men had been shot for less.

Political agitation grew: an anti-re-electionist party; a democratic party; imprisonment of agitators; an oratorical tour by Madero; his presidential candidature, arrest and escape to the United States; the re-election of Díaz, aged eighty, in July 1910, and in November the publication of Madero's manifesto 'The Plan of San Luis Potosí', in which he assumed the provisional presidency, called on the people to rise in armed revolt against the usurper, and promised restitution of lands unjustly taken from small proprietors.[1] Thus by a political move the spark was unintentionally set to a tremendous conflagration, a revolution more social than political, which is still in progress and must therefore await full interpretation by future historians; a revolution in the proper sense of the word. For Mexican historians justly regard the four *coups d'état* which overthrew four successive chiefs not as so many *revoluciones* but as episodes in a profound and genuine Revolution.

In response to Madero's call guerrilla bands sprang up or gathered strength on the wide northern spaces of Chihuahua. Early in 1911 Madero himself crossed the Rio Grande from the United States with about eighty companions. Pascual Orozco, a clever business man, now a guerrilla leader (at first with twenty-five followers), joined him: 300 men rode in under the bandit Pancho Villa, a burly redoubtable fighter of great physical strength, tempestuous energy and strong mother-wit—he was quite illiterate—who six years earlier as a peon, fleeing from justice or injustice, had taken to the hills and had since been a hunted man but also a popular hero, raiding the Terrazas herds and befriending the poor. Later he was to command 40,000 men.

Despite an initial reverse (March 1911) the guerrilla war spread;

---

[1] This promise of restitution is quite clear and commendably brief: a virtue rare in Spanish-American manifestoes. But there is no mention of breaking up the great haciendas or of labour reform.

parties of federal (i.e. governmental) troops were ambushed; troop trains were waylaid and destroyed; arms and ammunition seized; recruits were gathered in, and on 9 May Madero's captains, Villa, Orozco and Garibaldi (grandson of the Liberator) took the town of Juárez. The news lighted a flame throughout the country. Everywhere insurgent bands arose. In Morelos, to the south of the capital, the peasant leader Zapata with a horde of ill-armed followers took and sacked the town of Cuautla, only eighty-five miles from the capital. Owing to withdrawal of troops to defend the capital, the railway thither lay open to Madero. Porfirio's federal army had failed him, nominally 20,000 men but one-third of them ghosts whose pay enriched officials; the men gaol-birds, the generals old men. On 25 May the aged dictator resigned, and on 7 June 1911 Madero 'The Apostle' entered the capital amid wild enthusiasm. A week later he had a cordial interview in Cuernavaca with Zapata, who had raised the slogan *Tierra y Libertad*, 'Land (for the landless) and Freedom', uniting under his compelling command and reducing to order various bands of pillaging guerrilleros. The Revolution seemed to have triumphed when Madero took the oath as Constitutional President in November 1911.

The Revolution had hardly begun. It was moving not in palace or congress, but in the villages of Morelos, where Zapata in the same month launched his 'Plan de Ayala', in which he denounced Madero as 'inept, a traitor and a tyrant', false to his agrarian promise; he named himself 'Chief of the Liberating Revolution' unless Pascual Orozco should accept that post.[1] He decreed: (1) that villages or citizens deprived of lands to which they held titles should at once reoccupy these lands and defend them to the utmost with arms; (2) that one-third part of every great estate should be expropriated, with indemnity, to provide lands 'for the villages and citizens of Mexico'. This manifesto gave the Revolution a form which was afterwards officially adopted in substance, for obviously 'one-third' is not an immutable proportion. Thus Zapata 'is the

[1] Pascual Orozco was ruled out by his own action: thus Zapata became the self-appointed 'Chief of the Revolution'. Two months earlier, in August 1911, Zapata had waylaid a train in which Madero was travelling with the intention of shooting him as a traitor. But Zapata was persuaded to hold his hand and was publicly embraced by his intended victim and saluted by him as *general integérimo*.

real originator of the agrarian movement which is having a tremendous influence on Mexican life to-day'.

Himself a mestizo tenant-farmer, but near to the Indian peons of Morelos, Zapata was 'a graceful figure of a man with a kind of natural elegance', remarkable for singularly penetrating black eyes. He boasted that he never bought a rifle or a bullet; he took all from the 'federals'. 'The Zapatistas', says one who suffered much at their hands, 'were not an army. They were a people in arms.' The federals, attempting to destroy that people, made it a war of extermination. Hence dreadful reprisals, in which Zapata himself shrank from no cruelty or destruction. For four months in 1915 he occupied the capital; in 1916 the Carrancistas overran most of Morelos, but Zapata was undismayed: a year later he commanded 40,000 volunteers and boasted that in eight southern States the federals held only the capitals and the railways. In one-fourth of Mexican territory Zapata was the only Government, a terrific master, followed and obeyed with a devotion which still enshrines his memory. He fought for nine years, until in 1919 an emissary from Carranza invited him to an interview and treacherously murdered him. Although for years much booty passed through his hands to supply his troops, he took nothing for himself and died poor. He stands third in the trio, Hidalgo, Juárez, Zapata, revered as the deliverers of the Mexican people.

Official history must turn to the capital and the President. Madero (1911–13) was not the man to guide or understand the forces evoked by him. A dreaming and trustful optimist, he vacillated and delayed over the most urgent matters. His treatment of the Zapatista movement was contradictory and even hostile. His family, beloved by nobody and not all as blameless as himself, surrounded him. He employed, perhaps inevitably, some of Porfirio's men, notably General Huerta, a fine soldier of dominating personality, mainly or wholly Indian in blood, a hard but strongheaded drinker, the ablest commander in Mexico.

In March 1912 Orozco, Madero's first supporter, chagrined at not receiving a reward of 100,000 pesos, revolted in Chihuahua, backed up by the hacendado Luis Terrazas. The revolt spread through the north, but was crushed, with Villa's aid, by Huerta: a dangerous victory. Eleven months later, February 1913, Huerta led a barrack mutiny in the capital against the chief whom he despised. For ten days, *el decenio trágico*, the streets were swept by rifle fire in a disturbance preliminary to Huerta's treachery. Madero was arrested and, under promise of safe conduct to Vera Cruz, was persuaded to resign. Huerta, after a brief juggle with constitutional forms, became President and Madero was murdered.

This was the beginning or recrudescence of a chaotic civil war which raged for three years, 1913–16, and broke out repeatedly during the following four years. In this turmoil 250,000 people perished; villages were destroyed and cities ruined; factories, farms and dwellings went up in flames; population decreased,[1] while generals multiplied, many of them 'finger generals' promoted by the pointing of the commander's forefinger after a combat with the remark, 'you are a general'. A strange war, in which an army moved like a nomad tribe, accompanied by its women to forage and cook. If a man fell, his *viejita* found another man or, particularly in Zapata's army, took a rifle and joined the ranks. These *soldaderas* were fierce fighters and ferocious in vengeance.

Huerta, having seized the capital, demanded by telegram the adherence of all State Governors. Carranza, Governor of Coahuila, refused to recognize the usurper, raised troops and proclaimed the 'constitutionalist' cause. Carranza was a rich landowner, ex-Senator and ex-Minister; the type of a respectable bourgeois politician; blue-spectacled, grey-bearded; of mild paternal middle-aged aspect. His call found an echo in the adjoining State of Sonora, where a successful merchant named Obregón[2] raised troops, largely Yaqui Indians, hard fighters and indefatigable marchers. Obregón, who proved to be a capable leader, marched southward through the Pacific States and then through Guadalajara to the capital. Pancho Villa, returning to the fray, crossed from the United States into Chihuahua with eight men; soon to gather

[1] The census gave 13,500,000 in 1900; 15,160,000 in 1910; 14,336,000 in 1920; 16,553,000 in 1930. Thus, but for the civil war in 1910–20, the population would have been greater by at least two millions in 1920, and probably by three millions in 1930.

[2] Said to be descended from one O'Brien, aide-de-camp to the last Spanish Viceroy.

5000, to be appointed 'General of the Northern Army' by the 'First Chief' (Carranza) and to renew his impetuous career of conquest, capturing Torreón in October and (with 8000 men) Juárez in November; then establishing himself as Governor of the State in the city of Chihuahua, where he ruled by decree after the fashion of Sancho Panza in defiance of economy, printing paper money, fixing prices, despoiling haciendas, and distributing confiscated lands. President Wilson got into touch with Villa (who neither smoked nor drank and had now laboriously learnt to read) in case the ex-bandit deserved backing as restorer of order. But Villa spoilt his chances by shooting a British hacendado, and in any case his tempestuous impulses could hardly have regenerated the Republic!

Meantime Huerta, ruling in the capital, was recognized by European powers but not by President Wilson. Many saw in Huerta the strong man who might crush disorder and drive the country back into the path of industrial progress. But he proved to be a military dictator of baser metal than Díaz. He dismissed an inconvenient Congress and began to raise a huge army. Many unoffending people were 'executed' or disappeared. Huerta's press-gangs even seized marketing women in the city to serve as *soldaderas*.

The occupation of Vera Cruz by American forces, to requite an affront to American marines in Tampico and also to prevent the landing of arms for Huerta, probably strengthened Huerta's position for the moment by rousing patriotic animus against the United States. The acceptance of mediation offered conjointly by Argentina, Brazil and Chile and the resulting Conference at Niagara Falls enabled President Wilson to withdraw without loss of dignity from an affair which damaged the United States in the eyes of all Latin America.

The Carrancista or Constitucionalista movement grew, receiving arms from the north, while American arms and recognition were denied to Huerta. In July 1914 Huerta followed Díaz to Paris, and Obregón with Carrancista troops occupied the capital. But there was a set-back; first a revolt in the north, then the defection of the suspicious Villa. The discordant leaders met in conference at

Aguas Calientes and fervently applauded the 'Plan of Ayala' expounded by an emissary from Zapata. But the conference produced nothing solid, and for a time the two guerrillero chieftains Villa and Zapata were almost masters of the country, appointing or tolerating two *fainéants* provisional presidents in succession. For a year, August 1914 to July 1915, while the capital changed hands several times, Carranza was confined to Vera Cruz. There the bewildered First Chief, no revolutionary but borne on the crest of a stormy revolution, was driven to justify his position. From his precarious coastal foothold he issued in December 1914 a programme of agrarian reform (in fact Zapata's plan), labour laws, local government, social legislation.

He thus brought to his side the moderate reformers. In July 1915 Villa, who had lost his bearings and his guerrillero caution and was striking with blind fury at those whom he regarded as traitors and tyrants, was decisively beaten by Obregón. Thenceforth, though for five years more he followed a stormy career in the northern wastes and was once pursued by an American expedition under General Pershing, Villa ceased to be a political force. In October 1915 the United States and nine other American republics recognized Carranza as *de facto* President; and the Revolution reached a definite stage and a pause of comparative peace when in 1916 a Convention met at Querétaro and promulgated the 'Constitution of 1917', which provided for land-grants to villages and to individual villagers by the break-up of the great haciendas, whose owners were to be compensated by interest-bearing bonds: all peons' debts were wiped out. One article (127) is a labour code which, says Tannenbaum, 'in law at least, gave the Mexican workers a status which at that time did not exist in any other country'. All waters were declared to be national property and also everything beneath the soil, so that ownership of the surface gives no ownership of minerals. To the Church was denied the right to hold land, and all church buildings were declared to be the property of the Republic, which should decide which of them might be used for worship. The priest in charge of every such church was to be registered. No foreign ministers of religion are allowed. State legislatures may limit the number of priests. Clergy are denied the rights of citizens, being forbidden to vote or to criticize Government or laws. Thus the Church, so far from being separated from the State, was placed under rigid State control.

Carranza, now constitutional President, almost ignored the new Constitution. He used force against all social unrest and attempted to perpetuate his corrupt autocracy by nominating an insignificant successor. Zapata denounced him as a traitor and pursued his terrific campaign of 'land without master or overseer' until he was murdered in 1919. Widespread disturbances preceded the presidential election of 1920. In short, Obregón, the man who had placed Carranza in power, overthrew him in order to take his place. Carranza departed for Vera Cruz with twenty-one trains, conveying officials, soldiers, baggage and treasure. The line was cut in front of them. The President fled on foot with a few companions. As he slept in a mountain hut, he was shot through the interstices of the wattle wall. Obregón was not responsible for the murder.

Obregón as President accepted the 1917 Constitution, discreetly tempering its extreme elements, but promoting the plans for land and labour. He was succeeded by his principal Minister, General Plutarco Calles (1924–8), the strong man of the Revolution, aged forty-seven, vigorous in frame and countenance. He had been a schoolmaster of modest origin, had risen to be Governor of Sonora and joined Obregón in the overthrow of Carranza. Resolute in crushing and punishing sedition, he was dictator for eleven years (1924–34), pushing forward land distribution and education, and —thanks to the post-war boom—improving roads and much-needed irrigation. To the Church he was 'ruthless and vindictive' (Mecham's words). Obregón, elected to succeed Calles in convenient alternation, was murdered by a fanatic before inauguration; and during three brief presidencies of other men (1928–34), Calles was dominant, authority residing in the National Revolutionary Party, founded and controlled by him.

During the Obregón-Calles period, 1920–34, the Revolution advanced. A disciplined army was organized and three serious revolts were crushed in 1923, 1926 and 1929, besides the minor disturbances of stormy times. Distribution of land continued, despite delays, disputes, difficulties and occasional sanguinary

violence. The labour code—quite distinct from the agrarian movement—grew into a volume, favouring the worker and embarrassing
to industry. The assertion of State ownership of all beneath the
soil brought protests from the United States, almost approaching a
rupture, until it was agreed that the provision should not be retro-
active and that concessions already granted should hold good.
Foreign ownership of land within a certain distance from the
frontier or from ports is forbidden. The Revolution has long since
dropped the service of the foreign debt, with occasional hints at
some arrangement.

In December 1934 General Lázaro Cárdenas, who had served
the State long and honourably, became President. Of inconspicuous origin, largely self-educated and employed as a youth in modest
capacities, Cárdenas had been, at the age of eighteen, editor and
printer (with his own hands) of a journal founded by himself in his
native town of Xiquilpan, when in 1913 he joined the revolt against
Huerta. Serving throughout the revolutionary wars he was several
times wounded, earned every promotion by active service and
became Governor of his native State of Michoacan. President
Cárdenas' masterful policy, of 'left' tendency, closed the Calles
period. In April 1935 Calles, in a published newspaper interview,
severely criticized the Government. For a moment his old political
following rallied to his side with applauding congratulations. Two
days later, Cárdenas spoke, rebutting the charges and appealing
for loyalty to the Revolution. The response was general and
enthusiastic. The administration was purged of pro-Calles elements:
the mass of the people and all officialdom warmly approved; and
six weeks later Calles left for California. In December 1935,
arriving back by air and welcomed by many soldiers and politicians,
he protested against calumnies and declared that dignity compelled
his return to political life. Cárdenas was prompt. Several generals
and colonels holding important posts were superseded and also
four State Governors: pro-Calles Senators and Deputies were
expelled; and four months later Calles was placed in an aeroplane
with three of his supporters and conveyed across the frontier. In
1935 Cárdenas 'intervened' in thirteen States. Only by stern
measures could the Revolution attain peace, eliminating rebellion

and murder as 'elements in political technique' (Tannenbaum's words). Calles declared that he had been exiled for opposing an attempt to 'institute a dictatorship on the Russian plan...communism...a complete dictatorship of the proletariat'.

Political democracy is hard to find in Mexico. 'There has never been', says Tannenbaum, 'any effective suffrage. The administrator has been and still is the law.' Only one 'party' exists, the National Revolutionary Party, 'a State institution' (Teja Zabre's naïve remark) supported by a quota from salaries of all civil servants: political orthodoxy, from which any dissent is perilous, is denoted by the term *revolucionario*, which means not an opponent of Government but a hearty supporter of its advanced tendencies.

One who knows Mexico well, writes in July 1936: 'The situation in Mexico is extremely interesting...many experiments are being tried out and there is one great advantage, laws can be made by a decree overnight and cancelled later if not found workable! There is no public opinion....It is a "totalitarian" State as much as Mussolini's or Hitler's, but with strong leaning towards the workers. It is also, to a certain extent, anti-foreign and anti-capitalistic. In the last ten years there has been a distinct progressive upward trend—idealistic and humanitarian. Recently the President issued a decree forbidding gambling in the Federal District. This decree prohibits the playing of cards—and people have had to abandon their innocent bridge clubs.'

The 'Six-year Plan'—the latest phase of the Revolution—drafted by a Committee of the National Revolutionary Party and zealously promoted by Cárdenas, proposes 2000 rural schools, besides higher-grade and technical schools, a great Polytechnic, fifty children's gardens, 1200 libraries, an intensified agrarian movement, cattle shows, loans to cultivators, official control of industries, especially oil, electricity and aviation. The movement has to deal with the conservative inertia of the Indian villager: and it is a question whether these educational schemes, controlled industrial development and modernization of agriculture, can preserve village arts and traditions or foster (as is hoped) a native Indian culture colouring the national life. But twenty-three million acres are said to have been distributed, and the Revolution has turned or is turning the peon into a peasant-proprietor or paid labourer. The significance of this work touches not only the other tropical republics with their Indian population, but even Chile and Argentina with their many landless workers on broad lands. The efficacy of the work in Mexico depends on peace.

Opinion abroad, especially in Rome and in the United States, has been deeply stirred by 'the denial of religious freedom and official persecution' (Mecham's words) of the Church in Mexico. Although many of the peasantry seldom or never saw a priest, most of the people were professedly Catholic and many were devoted Catholics. The domestic irregularities of some priests and other clerical shortcomings, although they facilitated attack, were not the reason of attack. Anti-clerical legislators were not Church reformers. More damaging to the Clergy were their political and social affinities since Maximilian's time and even earlier, and particularly their recent incursions into politics. They denounced the revolt of 1910–11 and Madero's administration, not merely as citizens but as authoritative religious teachers, and—like many of the upper and middle classes—they supported Huerta. Later, many clergymen weakened their position both with the Government and with their parishioners by opposing the agrarian movement and labour legislation. But obviously reasonable restriction of clerical civic activities did not necessitate persecution of their flocks and of religion.

During the revolt against Huerta and after his fall the Church and the clergy suffered revolting outrages. Then the comparative peace of 1916 brought a respite, and for nine years the 1917 Constitution was not strictly enforced. But in 1925 President Calles decreed full enforcement. In February 1926 the bishops published a 'collective protest' against the anti-clerical laws. Calles responded by arbitrary additions to those laws. He expelled all foreign priests; closed all convents, orphanages and Catholic schools; forbade all religious teaching even in private schools; confiscated all Church property and ordered all priests to be registered.[1] At a hint from Calles, the State legislatures limited the number of

[1] These and other absurdly minute restrictions apply equally to Protestants. Thus American Methodist ministers are forbidden to officiate in Mexico.

officiating clergy, sometimes to one priest for 5000 or even 10,000 inhabitants. The bishops, deeming Church ministrations impossible under these conditions, withdrew in July 1926 all priests from the churches, which were handed over to lay committees. In November 1926 the President forbade private masses.

In 1926-7 armed revolts of *Cristeros* (militant Catholics) broke out in many places, sometimes led by priests; and the Archbishop of Mexico claimed that 'Catholics have the right to fight for their rights by peaceful means first and in extreme cases with arms'. Thereupon he was expelled with five other prelates: other deportations followed and the clergy were subjected to irritating restrictions. During these disturbances thousands of Catholics were arrested and some priests were executed.

In 1929 President Portes Gil (1928-30), successor to Calles, concluded an agreement or at least an armistice with the Episcopate, modifying the rigour of the law. In June 1929, amid great public rejoicings, masses were celebrated in the churches for the first time since July 1926.

Yet in December 1931 a magnificent ceremony at the Guadalupe shrine provided provocation or pretext for renewed attack. President Rodríguez (1932-4) openly avowed that the movement was not merely anti-clerical but anti-Church and anti-Catholic by declaring that he was determined to 'eliminate fanaticism', being apparently unconscious of any fanaticism in the refusal of religious freedom to the Mexican people. The restrictions varied in different States. In Tabasco the disreputable Garrido, dictator of the State for fourteen years under Calles' protection—now in exile since his patron's fall—destroyed every religious building, imprisoned priests, and employed spies to report those guilty of religious worship. Elsewhere many churches were turned into schools or places of business and recreation. In some States laymen performed such services as were possible for them. In 1935 it was found that sixteen States (including the federal Territories) had no ministration of priests, totally forbidden in nine and in seven others non-existent, because no priests were licensed: in other States the licences granted were ludicrously or tragically few: thus in Oaxaca, though the law in theory permitted eighteen priests, only one was licensed[1] for a population exceeding a million. For the 200 churches of the Federal District twenty-four clergy were allowed, but no priest may officiate in more than one church.

Signs have appeared of some mitigation of extreme intolerance. In the town of Orizaba—situated in Vera Cruz State, where all religious practices were forbidden—the police raided in April 1937 a house where Mass was in progress and killed a girl. The outrage elicited such vehement protests, and an investigation ordered by Cárdenas, that for the first time for many years services were permitted in the churches of Orizaba and in other towns of the State of Vera Cruz. In July 1937 1500 Catholics forced their way into a padlocked church in Nogales, a frontier town of Sonora; and both the fire brigade and the soldiers refused to dislodge them. The Supreme Court recently disallowed a decree issued a year earlier by the Governor of Chihuahua reducing from five to one the number of priests for the 500,000 people of that State, a decree which had provoked strife and bloodshed. In May 1937 the Governor of 'Godless Tabasco' announced that—although that part of the State Constitution forbidding celibate priests to officiate cannot be repealed—Catholics henceforth will not be persecuted and may worship before images in their homes. These concessions show what religious liberty means in Mexico.

Yet in spite of this bigoted intolerance, the word idealism, hardly applicable to her southern neighbours, is not amiss—by another Iberian contradiction—in Mexico; for (to quote a competent authority) Mexico is ruled by the dictatorship of an idea, wielded by a minority, the National Revolutionary Party. Both the intolerance and the ideal are expressed in the remarkable wall-paintings of Rivera, the artist of the Revolution.

The space here given to Mexico may seem disproportionate: but Mexican history defies the brevity appropriate to tranquil scenes. Moreover, happenings in Mexico, bordered by the United States and six times trodden by European or 'Yankee' troops, concern all Latin America and, in some cases, all the world. For a

---

[1] The compiler of these figures, K. Grubb, *Religion in Mexico* (London, 1935), cannot vouch for their precise accuracy. Obviously the number of licensed clergy is not invariable. But the figures are sufficiently accurate to show the position of the Church in Mexico.

generation Díaz offered to the United States a firm and respected Latin-American front. And to-day the British Consul-General writes that 'Latin America is watching with general sympathy and immense interest' the social experiment for 'bettering the condition of the masses'. In quite another way Mexican Church policy (which drew a protest from President Leguía of Peru) concerns both Church and people everywhere.

NOTE. Priestley, ch. XIX to end; Bancroft, vols. V and VI; U. R. Burke, *A Life of Juarez* (London, 1894); E. C. Corti, *Maximilian and Charlotte of Mexico**, trans. by C. A. Phillips, 2 vols. (London, 1924); D. Dawson, *The Mexican Adventure** (London, 1935) deals with Maximilian; D. Hannay, *Diaz* (London, 1917); C. Beals, *Porfirio Diaz* (Philadelphia and London, 1932); K. Turner, *Barbarous Mexico* (London, 1911); E. Gruening, *Mexico and its Heritage** (New York, 1928); *The Caribbean Area*, chs. XVII–XXI; W. H. Callcott, *Liberation in Mexico*, 1857–1929 (Palo Alto, 1931); Mecham, chs. XIV–XVI; F. Tannenbaum, *The Mexican Agrarian Revolution** (Washington, 1930); *Peace by Revolution* (New York, 1933); A. Teja Zabre, *Guide to the History of Mexico**, English trans. (Mexico, 1935); B. E. King, *Tempest over Mexico* (London, 1936); W. H. Callcott, *Church and State in Mexico* (New York, 1926); Lord Acton, *Lectures on Modern History*, ed. by J. N. Figgis and R. V. Laurence (London, 1906).

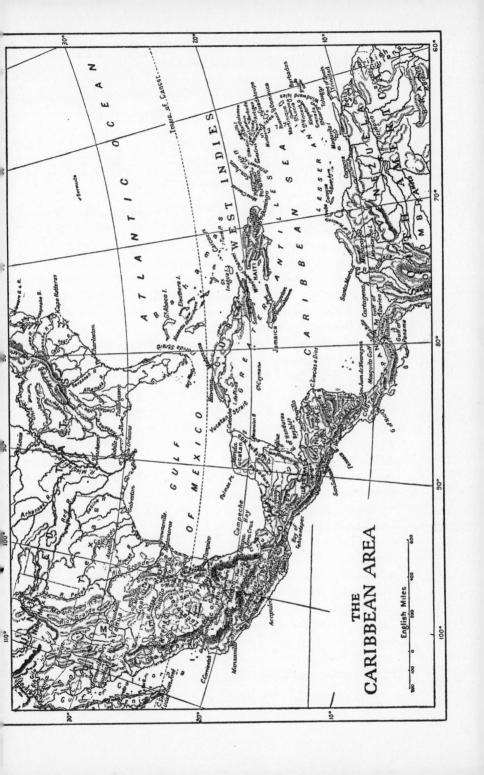

THE
CARIBBEAN AREA

English Miles

CHAPTER XXIX

CENTRAL AMERICA

The attempt to impose upon an unprepared people the political institutions copied from the United States...has not been the most happy.

ROSCOE R. HILL

It has been pointed out on p. 7 that 'Central America' is not a geographical description, but a political term invented in 1823, upon separation from Mexico, to designate the region which formed the Captaincy-General of Guatemala and now comprises five republics, Guatemala, Honduras, Salvador, Nicaragua and Costa Rica. Mexico, Central America and Panamá are part of North America and contain the Isthmian region: and that position is the key to Central American history.

Central America is a strip of tropical land extending in a roughly Z-shaped curve south-eastward from Mexico for a distance of 1000 miles or more. The Cordillera here runs near the Pacific: most of the cities are situated in the mountain valleys whose rich volcanic soil yields harvests of coffee, or on the dry and comparatively healthy Pacific coastal plain. Thus all this region faces historically towards the Pacific except at one point, the valley of the River San Juan in southern Nicaragua. With that exception, the broad Atlantic coastal plain, rain-soaked, torrid, plagued with insects and in great part thick with tangled forest—to-day transformed in part by banana cultivation—had never been subdued by the Spaniards and was left by the independent Governments to a mixed population of Indians and negroes, with no laws or government other than that of rum-drinking polygamous sambo chiefs. In 1821 the Scotch adventurer, 'Sir' Gregor McGregor, who had served in the Venezuelan war of independence, set himself up, unmolested, as 'His Highness the Cacique of the Poyais Indians' in the northern part. From about 1830, the Superintendent of the British Settlement of Belize (now British Honduras) pushed his frontier southward without serious obstacle, occupied the island of Ruatan and tried to extend political influence as far as San Juan (Greytown).

Even to-day the eastern coast is almost a foreign country to the native Central American, and the Caribbean ports of Honduras and Nicaragua are for practical purposes nearer to New Orleans than to Tegucigalpa and Managua. The Caribbean plain is dominated more by the United Fruit Company, which developed it, than by the republican governments in the distant highland capitals. Since the 'white-collar' staff of the company is American and most of the labourers, as well as many of the private planters, are Jamaica negroes, the prevailing language of the banana country is English.

In the mid-nineteenth century 'the Coast' had frequent contact with Jamaica, but almost none with the interior. For nearly two centuries the Government of Jamaica had been on friendly terms— sometimes amounting to political patronage—with the 'King of the Mosquitos' (or Moscos Indians): and in 1844 Great Britain proclaimed a protectorate over the Mosquitos, 'a mixed race combining the blood of negroes, Indians, pirates and Jamaica traders'.[1] The Mosquito coast according to some was 200 miles long, according to others 800 miles. In 1846 Lord Palmerston defined it, liberally enough, as extending from the River San Juan to Cape Honduras.

In spite of the clause forbidding colonization in the Clayton-Bulwer Treaty of 1850, which Great Britain regarded as not retrospective, this protectorate, together with a claim to the Bay Islands and part of the Honduras coast, was maintained until 1859–60, when, after long dispute with the United States, it was withdrawn, with the stipulation that the Mosquitos should retain autonomy under Nicaraguan sovereignty. This autonomy came to an end in 1894, Great Britain declining to interfere. But down to the present century Colombia, which included Panamá, maintained a shadowy claim to the Mosquito Coast as far as Cape Gracias a Dios.

The area of Central America is about one and a half times that of the British Isles; the population approaches six millions, of whom Guatemala claims 40 per cent.: one-fourth of the whole inhabit little Salvador, far the smallest of the five and the only one not washed by both Oceans. There is some product of precious

[1] S. A. Bard, *Adventures on the Mosquito Shore* (London, 1856).

metals, but the whole country or group of countries is mainly agricultural. In Guatemala the native Indians, the bulk of the population, are a class apart from the quasi-white upper classes and live for the most part in a state of debt-peonage apparently less oppressive than that of Mexico; but cheap alcohol plays havoc with them; and forced labour during the coffee harvest is an oppressive abuse.

In Honduras, Nicaragua and Salvador there is a greater fusion of races and a considerable strain of negro blood. But here, as elsewhere in tropical America, property, politics and the profitable professions are mainly in the hands of a distinct upper class, self-styled white and contemptuous of democratic equality. Salvador, more thickly peopled and therefore more apt for combined activity and educational influences, has better preserved her European heritage; and her political agitations have been largely due to the turbulence of her neighbours. Honduras, having three long 'foreign' frontiers, has suffered much from these stormy intrusions.

In Costa Rica the Indians, more barbarous in character, were almost exterminated by the Spanish conquest; and the half million Costa Ricans, the purest European stock of all tropical America, a singularly interesting little nation, inhabit the pleasant and fertile valley or plateau of the *meseta central*, where three cities, at no more than a neighbourly distance from one another, are surrounded by farms of moderate size; the whole forming a community unique in Latin America. The people are said to be descended from the sturdy and industrious Gallegos of north-west Spain, differing from the lighter Andalucian type of their neighbours. Her remote position, the seat of population being far from the northern frontier, has enabled Costa Rica generally to keep aloof from those turbulent neighbours; and her own internal *coups d'état* or *revoluciones*, although sufficiently numerous, have usually been brief and almost bloodless affairs. Indeed for eighty years past Costa Rica has hardly suffered internal bloodshed: a thing rare in any part of the world. The brief autocracy of Tinoco (1917–19) would have hardly merited attention, but for its occurrence in the critical war years. To-day the Costa Ricans boast of having more schools than soldiers.

The Captaincy-General of Guatemala had no war of independence. Through the action of the aristocracy and the higher clergy, Spanish authority was replaced by local authority in 1821, and two years later Mexican authority also disappeared. A Honduran Congress, in impartial hatred of Spain and of Mexico, voted for incorporation in the United States. But finally the five provinces, each adopting a parliamentary Constitution, joined to form a Federation, which abolished slavery and the slave-trade and seemed to be entering on a fair-weather course. Yet Central America became a proverb for the extremes of tumult, anarchy and tyranny. The violence of nature may be a contributory cause of political violence: extreme contrasts of climate, torrential rains, hurricanes, volcanic eruptions, earthquakes, destructive pestilences. In recent years three of the five capitals have been laid in ruins by earthquake.

The preponderance of one member is usually fatal to a federation; and in this case Guatemala, the biggest member, being saddled with the expense and labour of maintaining the system, lost enthusiasm for it. Distance and lack of communication were difficulties. Ecclesiastical questions also roused bitter strife. Here the liberals prevailed: clerical *fueros* were abolished: male Religious Orders, except those ministering to the sick, were suppressed; and in 1832 toleration of all religions was decreed, the Roman Church being recognized as that of the nation. But Central American democracy, whether federal or not, was an absurdity. 'Within a few years', says Munro, 'authority established and upheld by force was the only authority which was recognized or respected, and there was no means of changing the officials in power and consequently no recourse against bad government except revolution. Civil war had thus become an indispensable part of the political system.' The State Governments disobeyed the Federal Government. The Federal Government and the State Government of Guatemala, sitting in the same place, were at variance. The migration of the federal administration from Guatemala to Salvador in 1830 was a futile makeshift; and in 1838 the Federal Congress dissolved, authorizing the five States to form independent governments. The result of this disruption is that each of these five little communities, with its national flag and its spirited national anthem, has to bear the cost of a sovereign administration, and each finds a seat in the League of Nations[1] and in Pan-American Conferences as a sovereign power. The three central States, Nicaragua, Honduras and Salvador, have repeatedly essayed in vain a triple union which Guatemala and Costa Rica might later join.

Yet Central America has a common history: for the conservatives in every State made common cause with their friends in the neighbouring States; and so also the liberals; so that every *revolución* or *coup d'état* in one State found aid in others; a deposed president, crossing the frontier, found a friendly president willing to aid him and his fellow exiles to get home again and work a counter-revolution. Thus a civil war in one State usually became also an inter-state war. Moreover a powerful dictator in one State sometimes strove to dominate the others either by supporting his own creatures as fellow-presidents or by forcibly restoring the form of federation under his own autocracy.

Down to about 1870 the terms liberal and conservative had a meaning. The liberals were the opponents of the aristocratic-clerical group which had countenanced the movement of independence but desired to avoid the consequences of independence and retain their predominance: the liberals also professed to favour federation. But about 1870 the aristocratic-clerical group had lost significance, and federation had collapsed. From that time the terms liberal and conservative denote groups of politicians rather than principles. Five summary narratives, repeatedly overlapping, would be an unprofitable maze of names and disputes. It must suffice to trace salient features and view character without strict regard to order of time.

In the absence of real democracy, the happiest and most prosperous times in each republic have been the administrations of capable and disinterested presidents, exercising autocratic authority and maintaining internal peace. Even turbulent Nicaragua, after forty years of civil strife, enjoyed thirty years of peace (1863–93) under able conservative presidents, who allowed no freedom of

[1] In 1936 three of the five announced their withdrawal from the League.

election but kept order and furthered economic progress. Regional faction was appeased partly by fixing the capital permanently in the neutral city of Managua but much more by the judicious exhibition of force. On the other hand the high lights of the story, lurid lights indeed, are the long dictatorships, particularly the three Guatemalan autocracies of the 'conservative' Carrera (approximately 1839–65), the 'liberal' Barrios (1873–85) and the tyrant Cabrera (1898–1920). To these may be added, in odious eminence, the 'liberal' Zelaya of Nicaragua (1893–1909).

The first of these tyrannies was peculiar. When in 1837 cholera swept Guatemala and some priests told the peasants that the liberals had poisoned the wells, Carrera, a rude illiterate half-breed but energetic, astute and capable, placed himself at the head of a horde of insurgent Indians and dominated Guatemala for a generation. From 1844 to his death in 1865 he was, but for two short intervals, conservative President of Guatemala and the greatest power in Central America, supporting creatures of his own as rulers in the other republics during much of that time. Allied with the clergy, he restored clerical *fueros* and readmitted the Religious Orders.

The liberal reaction after Carrera's death was led by Barrios, President-dictator of Guatemala in 1873–85. He abolished the *fueros*, suppressed the Orders and proclaimed in 1879 a Constitution of anti-clerical tendencies which, with several later modifications, still stands to-day and 'impairs the legitimate freedom of the Church'. He also pursued the traditional liberal programme of federation, first by negotiation, and, when that failed, by force, recruiting a large army and declaring himself 'dictator and supreme commander' of all Central America. Salvador, Nicaragua and Costa Rica resisted liberalism of that type and requested aid against the aggressor from the United States. In the end Barrios, invading Salvador at the head of his troops, was killed in battle. To Guatemalans Barrios is a high-souled patriot who fell in pursuit of a great ideal; to his detractors he is a cruel tyrant. There is probably some truth in both views.

The third Guatemalan dictator, Cabrera, is the least reputable of the three. Having accidentally become acting President on the assassination of the President in 1898, he held power for twenty-two years by the odious arts of military tyranny; espionage; a large army and police force; repression of all political utterance even in private; imprisonment or execution or disappearance of insurgents or dissidents or even suspects. Munro, who witnessed this 'reign of terror', writes that it was approved by many influential natives and by most foreign residents 'on the ground that only a very strong government can prevent revolution and maintain order': but he describes also the atmosphere of fear and suspicion 'which has noticeably sapped the spirit and the self-respect of the people'. When Cabrera was unseated in 1920, his last public act was the bombardment of his capital from the neighbouring heights.

Fourth among dictators is the Nicaraguan Zelaya; who as a very young man, after some fighting and bloodshed, was accepted as liberal President, when in 1893 inevitable dissensions ended the thirty years' sway of the conservative oligarchy. Zelaya is one of the many contradictions of Latin-American history. True to his liberal professions, he opened schools everywhere, sent promising youths abroad for study, improved transport by steamer and railway, and encouraged coffee cultivation. Nor did his tyranny, except in recruiting his army, afflict the poor and inconspicuous. But he was 'a brutal and unscrupulous tyrant who for sixteen years exploited the country for his own personal profit on a scale unprecedented in the history of the Isthmus': to customary repressive methods he added torture. It is said that, on hearing talk of free presidential elections, he permitted his fellow-citizens to vote at choice for one of three names, José or Santos or Zelaya, those being his own three names: a mocking variation of Cabrera's method of sending soldiers to round up voters for one name only, Cabrera.

Nicaragua owes historical prominence to one geographical feature. The Cordillera sinks to a depression in the south, providing a route between the oceans which was much used in Spanish times for trade: vessels sailed from Atlantic waters up the River San Juan and across the Nicaragua Lake, whence transit to the Pacific was easy. Upon the acquisition of California in 1848, this transcontinental route, long talked of as the possible line of an interoceanic canal, became supremely important to the United States as a passage between her eastern and western coasts. In that same year Great Britain hoisted the Mosquito King's flag (of British manufacture) at the village of Greytown (San Juan del Norte), the Atlantic terminus of the route. The result of this forward step was the conclusion in 1850, after long negotiation, of the Clayton-Bulwer Treaty, which placed the United States and Great Britain on an equality with regard to any trans-Isthmian canal which might be constructed.

In 1848 an American Transport Company was formed, with the consent of the Nicaraguan Government, to convey passengers and goods by this route between New York and San Francisco. The constant passage of American vessels, vehicles and men produced a famous or notorious episode. Nicaragua was distracted by rivalry between cities. The conservative city of Granada, seat of the chief Creole families, was at perpetual feud with liberal León, the historical capital, centre of a region of small farmers. In 1854 the faction of León called in the aid of an American filibuster named Walker, already notorious for raids on Sonora and Lower California. Walker landed on the Pacific coast in June 1855 with fifty-seven companions, soon increased to some hundreds. He took the city of Granada and, being reinforced, despite heavy losses, by volunteers from the United States, made himself President of Nicaragua; rescinded all the federal legislation of 1823–38, thereby legalizing slavery and the slave-trade; governed by decree, executed one or two 'traitors' and confiscated the property of his enemies. He was acknowledged by the American Minister but not by the authorities at Washington. He had many sympathizers in the United States, particularly among Southerners, hoping for the incorporation of another slave State. Walker had no such intention: he meant (in his own words) to 'cut the expanding and expansive democracy of the North by a powerful and compact Southern federation based on military principles'.

Costa Rica saw the danger, purchased arms from the British Government (which did not like Walker's adventure) and invaded Nicaragua, at first without success. But the other three republics sent aid to the Nicaraguan conservatives. Walker long held out

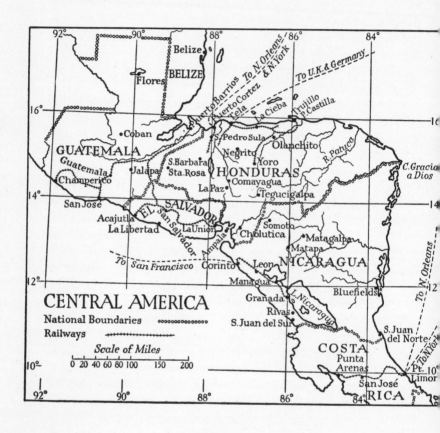

CENTRAL AMERICA

National Boundaries   ∘∘∘∘∘∘∘∘∘∘∘∘∘
Railways   +++++++++++++++

Scale of Miles

0 20 40 60 80 100   150   200

against great odds, even after the seizure of his vessels on the River San Juan cut off his recruiting and supplies. At last he surrendered to an American naval officer in May 1857, two years after his first landing in the country. A later attempt to renew his adventure was stopped by an American warship, and at a third attempt he was taken on the Honduras coast and shot. Walker's enterprise, so soon after the Mexican War, roused uneasiness throughout Spanish America concerning possible American designs. The worst that can be said has been said by Munro: 'The President and the Department of State were by no means unfriendly to Walker's enterprise while it still offered a prospect of success. The American minister in Nicaragua had throughout exerted his influence in favour of Walker, although in so doing he had greatly exceeded his instructions.' This American attitude was partly due to the hope of thwarting unduly persistent British territorial claims on the Caribbean coast and the Bay Islands, claims which were not withdrawn until 1859–60. There was, however, ground for apprehension; for, had Walker succeeded, the United States would inevitably have been drawn into the business, whether willingly or not.

From the opening of the present century the United States felt growing concern about peace and order in Central America owing to the influx thither of American capital and American citizens. Further motives were the 'Roosevelt corollary' of the Monroe Doctrine, American predominance in the Caribbean area and the possibility of a second canal through Nicaragua even after the choice of the Panamá route.

In 1906 Guatemala was at war with Salvador and with Honduras owing to the usual cause, aid given to Guatemalan insurgents against the tyrant Cabrera. President Roosevelt, having failed to persuade peace, invited Porfirio Díaz to join him in offering mediation. Representatives of the five republics, meeting those of the United States and of Mexico on board an American warship, agreed upon peace and the holding of another conference. After further strife—chiefly due to the Nicaraguan tyrant Zelaya—the five republics, at a conference in Washington in 1907, agreed to maintain perpetual amity, to set up certain institutions and practices implying some degree of common citizenship, not to recognize any government established by a *coup d'état*, not to intervene in any civil strife or allow political refugees to live near the frontier and to set up a Central American Court of Justice consisting of five judges, one from each republic, to decide all questions arising between them. At first these agreements effected little, chiefly owing to Zelaya's intrigues; and a general war was only averted by the action of the Central-American Court, supported by the influence of the United States and of Mexico.

Thus far the United States, in promoting concord between the five republics, had avoided any interference in the internal affairs of any republic and (through concert with Mexico) any appearance of Anglo-American dictation to Spanish Americans. But this abstinence was difficult to maintain, since the internal troubles of any one State constantly overflowed the frontiers. And after the Washington Conference of 1907 the United States Government— virtually though not technically a party to the engagements then concluded—was constantly solicited by one republic after another to maintain those engagements. The chief obstacle was Zelaya, who also desired Central American Union, after his own fashion, by stirring up trouble in every republic in order to win predominance over the whole. Furthermore, Zelaya opposed American influence, whether financial or political, in Nicaragua.

In 1909 the outbreak of a conservative revolt and a strong note from the American State Department, backed up by the advice of Porfirio Díaz, induced Zelaya to resign in favour of Madriz, a highly esteemed liberal. But the United States withheld recognition from Madriz and, through the action of American naval forces at Bluefields, enabled a defeated revolutionary movement to recover strength and to overthrow Madriz' Government (February 1910). The resulting conservative administration was only saved from financial ruin and chaos by effective aid from the United States in the organization of finance and in control of the customs, which long continued. But in 1912 further revolts and a request from the conservative President for American support brought the despatch of a warship to Corinto and the landing of American marines, who stormed a liberal stronghold. After this a legation guard of 100 marines, stationed in the capital from 1912 to 1925, together with the frequent presence of a warship at Corinto, kept the Government in office.

In 1916 Nicaragua, in return for three million dollars, granted to the United States the exclusive right to construct an interoceanic canal by way of the River San Juan and Lake Nicaragua, the occupation of two Caribbean islands for ninety-nine years and also the right to establish for ninety-nine years a naval base on Fonseca Bay. Salvador and Costa Rica brought suits separately before the Central-American Court of Justice against this Treaty as infringing their territorial rights. The Court decided in favour of Costa Rica and later in favour of Salvador. Both Nicaragua and the United States declined to accept these decisions, and in consequence the Court, reduced to a nullity, passed out of existence in 1918.

In that year Munro wrote: 'it will be difficult to convince the Central Americans of the sincerity of our goodwill...so long as we...uphold a minority administration in Nicaragua by force of arms.' He speaks of the 'fear and suspicion' aroused in Central America. The suspicion pervaded all Latin America. But the withdrawal of the Legation guard, postponed at the request of the Nicaraguan Government and finally carried out in August 1925, was followed by civil war, bloodshed and confusion. Twice within a year American forces protected the lives and property of Americans and of British subjects in the banana region; and at last in November 1926 the conservative President requested American aid. In 1927 there were 2000 American marines doing police duty in small detachments. The despatch of 'troops' or 'infantry' would have shocked American public opinion. But the landing of 'marines' caused little disquietude. In 1928 these numbered 5600; and during the following three years—a time of general depression and of one stupendous disaster, the destruction of the capital by earthquake—they had much trouble and suffered some losses in protecting the Government against the 'liberal' guerrillero Sandino, whom some regard as a patriot resisting invaders. But the British Consul, in his Report for 1935, speaks emphatically of 'Sandino and his bandits...the terrorism of banditry over a wide area'.[1] Other work of the intervention was supervision of elections, peace

[1] Overseas Report, *Nicaragua*, 1935.

between contending parties and the training of a native constabulary, which made possible the withdrawal of the last marines in 1933.

The twenty years, with a brief interval, of military intervention in Nicaragua threw into the shade briefer interventions in the neighbouring republics. 'We have temporarily intervened in Panamá seven times, in Honduras six times and in Guatemala and Costa Rica once each'; so writes H. E. Barnes. Moreover, Honduras and Salvador accepted in different degree fiscal control, entirely beneficial to their finances. In Salvador, when the customs passed under American control, the debt service was expected to absorb 70 per cent. of the receipts; but so efficient was the new system that 70 per cent. for five months of the year sufficed for the debt service, and the remainder yielded more revenue to the Government than the entire proceeds of the duties in former years.

To weld into a federal nation five provinces while one of them exercises national sovereignty by maintaining a separate treaty with a foreign power, would seem to be a chimera. Yet the fall of the Guatemalan dictator Cabrera in 1920 opened the way to amicable intercourse and to negotiations for federation. Guatemala, Honduras and Salvador (the other two holding aloof) agreed upon a union, which, however, proved to be a hollow affair and, upon a fresh *coup d'état* in Guatemala, seemed likely to embroil all three republics, had not the United States insisted on the observance of the 1907 agreements. A conference of the five republics met at Washington in 1923, which concluded a Treaty of Amity, reaffirmed the arrangements of 1907, set up—on paper at least—machinery for the peaceful settlement of disputes and agreed upon the non-recognition of revolutionary governments. In 1932 Costa Rica and Salvador, partly owing to resentment at American action in Central America, denounced this treaty. But it had not been wholly ineffective: once again the United States had kept the peace among these little communities.

Central Americans, like their Spanish-speaking neighbours in both American continents, are not to be judged solely or mainly by their political history. The kindly and friendly social life of Central America, a life which eschews haste or worry and knows how to enjoy leisure, has a civilized quality of its own. There are many, both 'Yankis' and Europeans, who regret the impact of northern alien vigour on the engaging ways of the unhurried, careless and improvident dwellers in these warm and fertile lands. 'They are children', exclaimed one who knows and loves the Central Americans to the present writer. The remark, meant as a protest against American doings, was in fact an unconscious defence of them. The indolent acquiescent ways of the educated Central American, and his propensity to borrow money on his property without thought of ability to pay, are a handicap in a competitive world. Economic activities pass increasingly into the control of foreigners; not only 'Yankis', for before the Great War Germans had a great hold on Guatemalan property, and they are active to-day in Central America. There are French, English, Levantine and Chinese ingredients in the infiltration from abroad: the many Spanish and Italian traders can hardly be regarded as a novel element: and indeed the descendants of many foreigners are likely to be absorbed into Central American life, modifying in some degree its character.

American intervention saved the Nicaraguans, in spite of themselves, from much bloodshed and from the misery, famine and pestilence which attend civil strife. Moreover, the costly and devoted work of Americans in combating tropical diseases, improving sanitation and teaching hygiene throughout Central America is wholly beneficent. All change brings something to lament; but it does not follow that the change on the whole is to be lamented.

The historian of Central America cannot ignore the banana; a recent industry which in one generation peopled a wilderness, and, before the recent depression, provided nearly 90 per cent. of Honduran exports in point of value, above 30 per cent. of those from Costa Rica and Nicaragua and much from Guatemala. Salvador alone, untouched by the hurrying bustle of this modern business, quietly harvests her coffee crops, as for a century past, in her remote Pacific highlands.

The banana had long nourished the peasantry of Caribbean lands before it touched the palates of New England and of Europe.

From 1860 some had reached New Orleans from Honduras. But the real beginning was in 1870, when the master of a New England schooner carried some bananas from Jamaica to Boston. His first cargo arrived rotten: his second brought large profits: fifteen years later a modest company was founded which grew into the Boston United Fruit Company, formed in 1899. A recent volume, *The Banana Empire*, by two American investigators, one of them for twelve years in the service of the company, tells its story. The United Fruit Company gradually eliminated or absorbed its rivals until to-day it owns, in its own name or that of its allies, four million acres—once derelict and worthless land—on the Caribbean coast of Central America, 1500 miles of railway and a fleet of swift ships. But the company dominates a much larger region, being owner or controller of the only means of transport and export, the chief importer and seller of goods in its own shops to others besides its own people and master of the destiny of private planters. The company 'in its pursuit of profit has transformed tangled jungles into centres of human activity, at least temporarily; it has constructed buildings, railroads and other works of modern material civilization; it has erected (eleven) well-equipped hospitals; and it has reduced...the menace of tropical fevers'. The favour shown to the company by all administrations and the anxiety lest it should move its operations elsewhere, unless gratified, are mainly due to the benefits which it brings to those regions. Yet the two authors balance their catalogue of benefits by describing the high-handed, illegal and devious proceedings of the company, which 'trains its own political representatives to deal with Caribbean governments'.

The careful and sober historian Munro corroborates this testimony, writing thus in 1918, ten years before the company reached the height of its activities: 'The economic development of the last twenty-five years has created a situation in which some of the five republics are almost powerless to protect themselves against the oppression and greed of foreign interests; for corporations, like the great fruit companies and the railroad companies, are able to bring to the support of their projects financial resources which far exceed those of the local Government or of any group of natives. Some of these concerns, by the corruption of officials or by the unscrupulous use of their control of transportation facilities, have obtained special privileges which have been an obstacle to the legitimate business of other foreigners and to the development of the community as a whole.' The position of the company as a sixth political power among the five Central American republics gives point to the words of President Wilson in a historic address to a gathering of Latin Americans at Mobile in October 1913: 'States that are obliged... to grant concessions are in this condition, that foreign interests are apt to dominate their domestic affairs, a condition of affairs always dangerous and apt to become intolerable. What those States are going to see, therefore, is an emancipation from the subordination ...to foreign enterprise.'[1] The promised emancipation still lags.

NOTE. D. G. Munro, *The Five Republics of Central America** (New York, 1918); C. D. Kepner and J. A. Soothill, *The Banana Empire** (New York, 1935); *The Caribbean Area*, chs. XII–XVI; W. O. Scroggs, *Filibusters and Financiers* (New York, 1910); Bancroft, *History of Central America*, vol. III; M. W. Williams, *Anglo-American Isthmian Diplomacy**, 1815–1915 (New York, 1916); I. D. Travers, *History of the Clayton-Bulwer Treaty** (New York, 1900); E. G. Squier, *Nicaragua* (New York, 1852), *The States of Central America* (New York, 1858), *Honduras* (New York, 1870); J. L. Stephens, *Incidents of Travel in Central America, Chiapas and Yucatan*, 2 vols., illustrated (New York, 1841). There is an article on 'The Central American Policy of Palmerston' in *The Hispanic-American Historical Review*, August 1936, and another in vol. III of *The Cambridge Historical Journal*.

[1] See A. Alvarez, *The Monroe Doctrine*, p. 354.

CHAPTER XXX

CUBA

There are strange noises in the island. The Tempest

THE island of Cuba, the 'Pearl of the Antilles', 'the sugar-bowl of the world', stretches long and narrow for above 700 miles—about the length of Great Britain—across the north of the Caribbean Sea, its north-western coast almost within sight of Florida. At either end are the two historic sea-roads from the Caribbean region to the North Atlantic Ocean and to Europe. The island is somewhat more than one-third the size of the British Isles and the population exceeds four millions, part African, part European in origin; for the native Indians were early exterminated. The inhabitants are officially stated to be 70 per cent. white and 30 per cent. coloured. Carleton Beals remarks that these figures would be exactly reversed according to the standards of the United States, where any tinge of African blood is labelled 'coloured'.[1] But immigration from Spain increases the white element. Cuba is a land of varied beauty and wealth. In the east a rugged mountain mass rises above 8000 ft. There are two groups of mountain or hill of gentler elevation. But the real character of the island is in the broad rolling plains, watered by many streams and yielding from fertile soil under a kind climate abundant harvests of sugar-cane and tobacco, besides every sort of tropical fruit. In contrast to the neighbouring almost harbourless continental coast, Cuba possesses many excellent and easily defensible natural harbours.

For over a century the island was an object of external solicitude owing to its singular relation to Europe and to America, a dependency of Spain yet geographically almost a prolongation of the Florida peninsula and having a natural economic connexion with the neighbouring lands through interchange of tropical and temperate products. But for its bearing on these international questions, the unhappy domestic history of Cuba would have made little

[1] Chapter IV of *Cuba illustrated*, by Irene A. Wright (1910), has some apposite remarks on this point.

noise in the world. It may be summarized thus: subjection to Spanish misgovernment in the nineteenth century, with repeated revolt and civil war during thirty years (1868–98); then, after the Spanish-American War, a republican life even more tumultuously violent than that of her continental neighbours, but checked and regulated in some degree by the counsels, the tutelage and occasional authoritative action of the United States.

When Napoleon laid hands on Spain in 1808, the cabildo of Havana, like those of the Indies generally, proclaimed allegiance to Ferdinand VII; and, unlike her continental neighbours, Cuba maintained that allegiance. Cuba had no choice, being an island and the base of Spanish military and naval action against the mainland. The success of the continental insurrection, together with the radical Spanish revolution of 1820–3, naturally caused agitation among many Cubans and some conspiracies. But more than one-third of the inhabitants being slaves and more than one-half coloured, the Creoles generally were not eager for independence, having the dreadful example of Haitian massacres before them. Colombian and Mexican designs for invading and emancipating Cuba in 1826 have been already mentioned.

The wrongs of Cuba were those already noted in Chapter IV as characteristic of the 'Spanish Colonial System'. Parts of that system—exclusion of foreign immigrants, prohibition of foreign trade and legal insistence on religious orthodoxy—were impossible to maintain in the nineteenth century. But this last remnant of the Spanish Indies, Cuba and Porto Rico, still suffered absolute and arrogant government by Spanish officials; excessive, ill-regulated and irritating taxation, not all spent in the island but yielding a revenue to Spain; troublesome commercial restrictions, to favour Spanish trade; exclusion of Cubans from lucrative or powerful offices; corruption and extortion by judges, tax-gatherers and all officials from the Captain-General downward, all (with occasional exceptions) seeking to enrich themselves quickly; supercilious arrogance of Spaniards towards Creoles. These ills, familiar in earlier generations, were a strange anachronism in the nineteenth century and particularly in the age of steam, when Cubans were in constant touch with the United States and with Europe, when many travelled and studied abroad. Moreover, just when the obsolete Spanish system had been swept away on the neighbouring continent, the Spanish monarchy, in order to shut out all liberal contagion and suppress sedition, drew the bonds tighter on Cuba, conferring absolute power—power above the law—on the Captain-General in 1825: an arrangement probably meant to be temporary but in fact maintained for fifty years.

The activities of Captain-General Tacón (1834–8) throw a damaging light both on Spanish administration and on the character of Cuban society. He found filth, neglect and corruption; innocent men in prison untried; professional assassins for pay; blackmailing brigands on frequented highways; 12,000 vagabond parasites in the capital. With imperious rapidity Tacón swept away these abuses. He constructed roads, municipal buildings, a market, a theatre, public fountains, and encouraged the building of the first railway. Upright, drastic, formidable, he forced the island into wholesomer life. But his stern despotism, tactless ways and peremptory assertion of Spanish authority earned hate not only for himself but also for Spain, widening the rift between peninsulares and Creoles. Cuban patriots, deported by Tacón for supposed seditious views, henceforth were discussing in the cafés of Madrid the chances of rescuing Cuba from the tyranny of Spain either by independence or by annexation to the United States, which some thought more practicable.

After Tacón, Cuba sank back into corruption and neglect. Yet for another generation there was no general desire for independence. The Spaniards and the wealthier Creoles had a common interest in maintaining slavery and the slave-trade, in preventing unrest among the coloured population and in producing slave-grown sugar to compete with the free labour of Jamaica and Barbados. Despite a treaty with Great Britain for the extinction of the slave-trade in 1820, the horrors of that trade continued to the 'sixties and struggled on even later, the Captain-General receiving a fee from the importers for every African slave landed. Slavery, already much diminished, was abolished by decree in 1880 but lingered till 1886.

The annexationist movement in the United States between 1845 and 1860 found little response among Cubans and therefore did not profoundly influence Cuban history: but it won such prominence as to demand brief treatment. American policy and American public opinion were quiescent concerning Cuba until the mid-century. It is true that Jefferson and Adams in confidential letters expressed their hope and belief that in the natural course of events Cuba would become part of the United States: but neither they nor their successors for nearly twenty years sought to hasten matters. President Polk in 1845 brought a change of view. Vice-President Dallas publicly toasted 'the annexation of Cuba'; and three years later, after the Mexican war, Polk suggested to Spain the purchase of Cuba, without result. Despite loud-voiced popular agitation for annexation, succeeding administrations (1849–53) opposed expansion and issued stern proclamations against fili-bustering, but failed to check the adventurer Narciso López. López, born in Venezuela, had risen to be general in the Spanish army and Governor of Valencia. In 1843, holding a high post in Cuba, he lost that post and all rank and pay through a revolution in Madrid. He then settled in Cuba, engaging in business and in conspiracy against Spanish rule. Obliged to flee to the United States, he organized in 1850–1 two expeditions—of 250 and 400 men respectively, mostly Americans—which sailed from New Orleans for Cuba, evading the vigilance of the federal authorities. They found no effective support in the island, and López in his second venture was captured and executed with many of his men. Spain was sore over this affair, over the impunity of López after his first venture and his vogue as a popular hero in the United States. On the other hand the provocative meddling of Cuban port officials with American trade and the dilatory evasions of Madrid in handling complaints were exasperating.

President Pierce (1854–7) favoured expansion and appointed as Minister to Spain Pierre Soulé, an impulsive French-American who had publicly eulogized López and in the American Senate had vehemently urged the forcible seizure of Cuba. Soulé was empowered to 'negotiate...concerning...cession of the Island of Cuba...to the United States'. During his brief diplomatic career in Spain (October 1853 to February 1855) he made it his 'one aim and ambition to acquire Cuba...by purchase; by favour...by threat of war'; so writes Dr Ettinger. In October 1854 the American Ministers at Madrid, Paris and London; Soulé, Mason and Buchanan (a former Secretary of State) drew up the Ostend Manifesto, which declared that if Spain should refuse a price for Cuba 'far beyond its present value' and if Cuba in Spanish possession was found 'seriously to endanger our internal peace and the existence of our cherished Union...' then 'by every law, divine and human, we shall be justified in wresting it from Spain'. This conclusion was disapproved by the State Department.

Buchanan's outspoken desire as President (1857–60) to 'add Cuba to the Union' and his proposal for purchase found no favour in Congress; and the presidential election of 1860 was adverse to his views. Then came the American Civil War, which eclipsed the agitation about Cuba. That agitation had been partly due to suspicions of Great Britain, whose territorial claims in Central America gave colour to these suspicions. Spain, during this time of apprehension, had repeatedly sought French and British aid. Lord Palmerston had advised her to win Cuban loyalty by liberal reforms, and to counter the southern desire for acquisition of a slave-state by liberating the Cuban slaves.[1] But the stubbornness of Spain provoked revolt at last.

El padre de la patria was Carlos Manuel de Céspedes, a typical aristocratic Creole landowner, aged forty-nine, a graduate of Barcelona University, a qualified advocate in Madrid, a traveller over half Europe. In 1855 he suffered a year's imprisonment for his insular liberalism. He then resumed his place on his eastern estate and in Havana society, until in 1867 long discussed Spanish promises of reform vanished with illusory 'special Laws' which simply re-enacted the existing system.

On 9 October 1868 Céspedes, having freed his slaves, raised at the gate of his sugar estate 'The cry of Yara', the call to independence, forcing into action his cautious partners in conspiracy. His 147 companions grew into a motley ill-armed host. Despite an initial reverse, the east of the island was soon aflame and by the end of the year 10,000 men—some say 26,000—were in the field. In

---

[1] He also warned Spain against war with the United States, pointing out that Cuba and the Philippines were vulnerable.

vain the Captain-General tried negotiations. The 'Ten Years War' had begun. An improvised Constituent Congress drafted a Constitution with President (Céspedes), Cabinet and Parliament. Mediation offered by President Grant came to nothing. The itinerant 'Republican Government' failed to get recognition, even as belligerents, from the United States. Throughout the war—notwithstanding troublesome interference with American trade, the destruction of American property in Cuba and the shocking condition of the island—the Washington Government preserved correct neutrality, preventing, with great trouble and cost, expeditions from the United States in aid of the insurgents, but not preventing their purchases of arms: and filibusters occasionally slipped through. A rupture was near when in 1873 the ship *Virginius*, conveying munitions and men (mostly Americans) to Cuba under the American flag was seized by a Spanish gunboat far from Cuban waters and towed to Santiago, where fifty-two of the men were shot. Hot indignation, war preparations in the United States, diplomatic protests on both sides finally died down when it was found that the *Virginius* had no right to fly the Stars and Stripes. Spain compensated the families of the dead and released the ninety-three living.

The horrors of civil war between men of Spanish speech and blood need not here be reiterated, nor yet their stubbornness in guerrilla war and their patience in bearing hunger, exposure, sickness and nakedness. Criminals were released to swell the Government's ranks. Ill-disciplined irregulars known as volunteers did garrison duty after their own fashion on the same side, noted for their sanguinary ferocity. The insurgents responded to the murderous edicts of the Captain-General (afterwards modified) by burning the houses, crops and sugar-mills of pro-Spaniards. The insurgent cause was weakened by dissensions: Céspedes, wanting in conciliatory patience, was thrust aside in 1873 and was killed in a Spanish raid on the village where he was living unprotected in retirement. Estrada Palma, afterwards first President of independent Cuba, an estimable and cultivated man of disinterested integrity, took his place. The ablest insurgent leader was probably Agramonte, a man of the same class as Céspedes; but the popular military hero was Máximo Gómez, a native of Santo Domingo, once a sergeant in the Spanish army, now a general and a master of guerrilla warfare who taught his mounted levies—expert horsemen all of them—to charge the Spanish infantry with the machete, their accustomed rural weapon, which proved an effective cavalry arm. A young mulatto, Antonio Maceo—the 'bronze Titan'—also won renown as a spirited and astute leader. But in 1875 Gómez suffered defeat; and the war, still dragging on for three years, degenerated into raids and banditry. The leaders quarrelled, and many abandoned the cause. The Carlist War, which had tied the hands of Spain, was now over. In 1878 Martínez Campos, a moderate and conciliatory Captain-General, by promises of political concessions, induced those still in the field to accept the Pact of Zanjón. The Spaniards had lost 140,000 men, chiefly from fever: the insurgents had lost more than 40,000. The last ebullition, a negro revolt known as 'the little war', in 1879 was repressed without undue severity and was followed by the extinction of slavery, decreed in 1880 and effected in 1886.

The desolated island sank back into exhausted peace, but not into content. Spanish promises again proved illusory: the system was scarcely changed, and Cuba was saddled with an immense debt, the cost of the civil war. Yet Cubans were not unanimous: many landowners and business men were not eager for change. Some favoured 'autonomy', Home Rule under Spain; others annexation to the United States. But the party for independence held the strongest ground. The soul of this party was José Martí, 'the apostle'. Martí was the son of a Spanish sergeant who had become captain of rural police in Cuba. A quick-witted boy, he owed his education to the kindness of a schoolmaster who taught his pupils to call Cuba *patria*. Early in the Ten Years War Martí, aged sixteen, for a private letter which savoured of sedition, was condemned to six years' hard labour. For six months he was among the fettered prisoners who laboured under the lash in stone quarry and limekiln. His sentence was then commuted by special favour to exile. He spent four years in Spain, making his eager voice heard—while still in his teens—among Cuban exiles, and graduating in the University of Zaragoza. Then came residence in

Mexico and in Guatemala under the unwelcome rule of native despots; then, after the Pact of Zanjón, return to Cuba and, inevitably, a second expulsion when he censured the Spanish administration.

His second exile—fifteen years—was mostly spent in New York, teaching, translating, writing in journals, working in a business house. In 1881 he sought a home in Venezuela, 'cradle of American liberty', but after half a year Guzmán Blanco, missing the accustomed adulation, told him to depart. His reputation grew in the Spanish-American world; writing in Mitre's famous Buenos-airean paper, *La Nación*; appointed Argentine Consul in New York: a post which—with its much-needed emoluments—he resigned when the Spanish Consul complained of his colleague's agitation against rule in Cuba. Martí urged on Cuban committees in American cities not merely autonomy or annexation to the United States but independence, to form part of a larger fatherland, *la patria hispano-americana*. He raised funds by persuasive speech and writing, taught that negroes and whites were equal as citizens of Cuba, risked his reputation by checking premature attempts. With the 'nineties the time seemed to have come. Frail in body and bearing a permanent injury from the Havana stone quarries, he multiplied his energies; addressing meetings of Cubans in the cities of Florida with a fiery and sincere eloquence, journeying to Central America, to Jamaica, to Santo Domingo to animate and reconcile leaders. At the end of 1894 all seemed ready, when a heavy blow fell. Three ships loaded with munitions, about to sail for Cuba from United States ports, were seized by federal authorities. Yet the revolt was pushed on, since all had been prepared in the island. Máximo Gómez and Martí landed in Cuba on a stormy night of April 1895 and joined the insurgent host of Maceo near Santiago. Six weeks later Martí, eager to be under fire before resuming his work in the United States, thrust himself needlessly into a skirmish and fell, one of the first casualties of the three years' War of Independence. The anniversary of his birth, 28 January, is annually kept as a public holiday in Cuba.

The moment for revolt was well chosen. From 1891 to 1894 the sugar industry had prospered owing to a reciprocity treaty between

Spain and the United States. In 1894 the treaty was denounced, at great loss to Cuba. Poverty and hunger proved excellent recruiting agents, and swelled the forces which galloped with Gómez and Maceo to renewed exploits. Once more a Republican Government was improvised in the east.

The horrors of this civil war surpassed all that went before. The insurgent leaders destroyed whatever might aid the enemy, and by deliberate destruction drove the homeless peasantry into their own ranks. They broke through the defensive lines drawn across the island by the unmilitary strategy of Martínez Campos and raided the centre of the country, approaching the capital. Early in 1896 Martínez Campos was replaced by 'the butcher' Weyler, a small spare man, but instinct with relentless force. He drove the country people into garrison towns and concentration camps where, despite provision on paper for their sustenance, they starved. The insurgents vied with the Captain-General in destruction. In December 1896 the mulatto Maceo fell by an ambush, to the jubilation of all Spain. Gómez, past seventy yet vigorous and elusive as ever, fought on grimly in the east, but was losing ground. Weyler seemed to be grasping victory, when in October 1897 he was replaced by the more moderate and conciliatory General Blanco: the vehement indignation of the American people, voiced by official utterance, had had its effect. In December 1896 President Cleveland, after mentioning the large American investments in the island and extensive trade, hinted at possible intervention. In December 1897 McKinley spoke yet more strongly, but declared against annexation. Two months later the American warship *Maine* blew up in the harbour of Havana and 264 men perished. When Captain-General Blanco heard of it, he burst into tears exclaiming 'this is the saddest day for Spain'. All Americans believed that the explosion was a Spanish act; and although McKinley for a time negotiated for peace, events moved rapidly to war.

The details of the brief Spanish-American War (May–August 1898) hardly concern Latin-American history. American victory was swift and complete. At the peace Puerto Rico was ceded to the United States and became a dependency of that power. With regard to Cuba the United States kept their promise and declined annexation, which was urged upon them by Spain as the best security for Spaniards and Spanish property in Cuba. For three years the island was ruled by American Governors. Honest administration (a novelty which astounded the Cubans); the starving fed and restored to their homes; the ruin of war, so far as possible, repaired; Gómez' army paid off at American expense; tribunals improved; schools founded; civil servants made to work; the University (which had 400 students and 96 idle professors) made a reality; a general hygienic cleansing: such was the work of the two American Governors, particularly the second, General Leonard Wood, a genial autocrat of herculean strength and energy. His best service to Cuba and to all tropical America was the conquest of yellow fever. Dr Finlay, a Cuban physician, had failed to win acceptance for his discovery that a certain kind of mosquito conveyed the infection. The American doctors proved its truth and the exact mode of transmission by experiments on men who offered themselves: one of them, Dr Lazear, died of the disease. Thorough sanitation, by destroying the insect and isolating patients, was effected; and Havana, a plague-spot and a source of infection to neighbouring lands, was made a healthy place.

The main task was to prepare Cuba for republican government. A Convention met which framed a Constitution and made an agreement with the United States, including the famous 'Platt Amendment', whereby Cuba granted coaling or naval stations (later reduced to one at Guantanamo) to the United States, undertook not to contract any debt without adequate provision from the ordinary revenue and consented that the United States...'may intervene for the preservation of Cuban independence (and) for the protection of life, property and individual liberty'.

In December 1902 Wood handed over the Government to the elected President, Estrada Palma, who gave four years of reputable and economical administration to the country. But the approach of the 1905 elections brought grave disorders; and Palma's Ministers, zealous for his re-election, managed matters so thoroughly that the votes cast for him largely outnumbered the total of electors. This was too much for the 'liberals', who after trying to get American intervention, rose in arms. Palma then asked for intervention. In response President Roosevelt, anxious not to intervene, sent two commissioners, Taft, Secretary of War, and Bacon, Assistant Secretary of State. Finding that the recent re-election had been fraudulent, the commissioners opened negotiations with the insurgents, without result. Palma insisted on resigning, and in September 1906 Taft named himself Provisional Governor, to be succeeded a fortnight later by Charles E. Magoon, sent from Washington as Governor of Cuba. Jenks, an unsparing critic of American policy, nevertheless thinks that the Platt Amendment saved Cuban independence: the United States were bound by the Peace Treaty with Spain to provide a stable government for Cuba; and had there been no provision for intervention, a protectorate might have been the only remedy.

For twenty-six months Magoon ruled Cuba by decree through Cuban civil servants, while a commission, with Colonel Crowder as chairman, revised the system of administration and the electoral law. The intervention brought one great benefit: owing to neglect of preventive measures by local authorities, yellow fever had reappeared. Thenceforth the national Government undertook the work of sanitation and the plague was conquered.

In January 1909 Magoon handed over the Government to the newly elected President José Miguel Gómez (1909–13), a jovial person of attractive personal presence and quick intelligence, fifty years of age, who had fought the Spaniards in 1875 and 1895, had fought Palma in 1906 and later was to fight in vain for his own return to power. He followed 'the tradition that Government existed for the benefit of the office-holders' and soon made a fortune, but all this with such engaging geniality as not to scandalize his indulgent fellow-countrymen, who remember him as a true Cuban.

A revolt of dissatisfied war veterans in 1911 was pacified by a strong warning from Washington. A more serious revolt of coloured men in 1912, complaining of inequality in public life, brought the landing of American marines.

Gómez' hopes, set upon re-election, were dashed by a liberal split, which let in the conservative candidate, Menocal. Since during the twenty years 1913–33 the terms liberal and conservative were little more than labels of rival groups and since elections were normally fraudulent and seldom quite bloodless, persons rather than principles or policies concern the historian. Two generals dominate this period, Menocal, President for two consecutive terms (1913–21), who nominated or accepted his successor Zayas, and Machado (1925–33). Menocal, a man of culture, educated in the United States, had earned distinction in the war of 1895–8 and in civil life the reputation of an excellent man of affairs. His administration began well, but, surrounded by relatives and friends, he soon became infected with the presidential virus. The abnormal prosperity due to large crops and high prices of sugar during the Great War gave him singular opportunities. His re-election in 1916, by customary methods, provoked a 'liberal' revolt in February 1917, when American marines were landed to keep the peace and protect American property. The revolutionaries—particularly the irrepressible ex-President Gómez—were disappointed in their hopes of intervention in their behalf, and Menocal's declaration of war against Germany on the day after the United States' declaration was probably in part an astute political move.

Meantime what of the Platt Amendment? According to the State Department there was no 'intervention' after 1909, the landing of marines in 1912 and 1917 not counting as such. Washington followed a 'preventive' policy, avoiding open intervention but issuing deterrent warnings in case of disorder or grave scandal. Questions were often referred to Washington, and the American Minister in Havana was much more than the envoy of a foreign power. There was much resentment over this, and anti-American outbursts were a commonplace of political oratory. Yet every administration relied on American support and every revolutionary movement sought intervention: not perhaps a case of inconsistency or of acquiescence but making the best of existing opportunities. So important was internal peace in Cuba for the sake of sugar production during the War that American troops remained in the island with Menocal's consent from August 1917 until 1922. In fact during the War military policy or necessity placed Cuba in the position of a 'subject-ally', particularly in regard to the control of trade and of sugar prices in the interest of the allied cause.

In Cuba everything is extreme. War profits and the post-War boom reached fantastic and demoralizing heights; enormous crops; the price of sugar multiplied; fortunes suddenly made and lavishly squandered; wild speculation; blind extravagance; improvident reliance on one variable product; incalculable injury inflicted on the island by denudation, the destruction of valuable forests to plant cane for immediate and delusive profit. Then came the crash of 1921; rich men suddenly penniless; banks closed; collapse of public finance.

In January 1921, civil war being also imminent owing to electoral disputes, General Crowder, a man of exceptional qualities and experience, to whom 'Cuba was a religion', unexpectedly arrived as President Wilson's personal representative, apparently to occupy a position somewhat like that of a British Resident at the court of an Indian prince, but without definite legal standing. He remained two years, appeasing strife, obtaining an American loan on condition of administrative and financial reforms, and procuring the appointment of an 'Honest Cabinet' in June 1922. Ten months later (Crowder having departed) President Zayas dismissed this Cabinet, to resume the customary profitable ways. In 1923 Crowder returned to Cuba with the rank of Ambassador: a significant recognition of the dignity of the Cuban Republic. For thenceforth the United States supported the people in power and kept the Platt Amendment in the background. In the same year a Cuban presided over the fourth Assembly of the League of Nations. A year earlier a Cuban had been chosen as a judge of the Hague Permanent Court, and in 1927–8 Cuba held a temporary seat on the Council of the League of Nations.

Machado, a veteran of the war of '95, big, solid, self-made, a farmer's son, a man of the people, of proved capacity in business, took office amid high hopes in 1925, appointing honest and able subordinates and working for improved administration, aided by a brief spell of economic prosperity. But within a few months 'political assassinations, deportations of alien agitators, imprisonment of labour leaders without trial' marked 'the tyranny of Machado's remote imitation of Mussolini'. So wrote Jenks in the early part of Machado's rule, declaring at the same time that

Machado and the group of brilliant young leaders who have his confidence have adhered with marked tenacity and intelligence to their programme of national revival'. There is no inconsistency here: dictatorship often means reform.

In 1927 the President prescribed a new Constitution extending the presidential term to six years but forbidding re-election *except for Machado himself*. In February 1928 President Coolidge, addressing the Pan-American Conference at Havana, declared that the Cuban people were 'independent, free and prosperous, enjoying all the advantages of self-government' and spoke of the ' stability of their Government in the genuine expression of opinion in the ballot-box'. Eight months later Machado, self-appointed, entered on his second term amid growing discontent and ominous disorder.

The general depression of 1929–33, aggravated by an increase in the American customs duty on sugar in 1929, caused the failure of many sugar estates, unemployment, misery, want, brigandage: the seed of revolt; for, owing to excessive reliance on one crop, the price of sugar is a political barometer in Cuba. To meet growing opposition, terrorism grew. The University and all secondary schools were closed, to check student agitation; spies were everywhere; criminals were released from gaol to recruit the *porra* (bludgeon), the body of gunmen who removed Machado's enemies or suspects. Murder, torture, solitary confinement, 'disappearances' were methods of government. A revolt in 1931 was suppressed. The hideous and inhuman terrorism provoked retaliatory violence and the formation of a secret society, 'the A. B. C.', ruthless in method but theoretically constructive in aim. Still Machado held on, supported by 12,000 well-paid troops.

A delusive truce arranged in 1933 by Sumner Welles, the American Ambassador, was followed by renewed violence, a paralysing general strike, machine-guns turned on a festive crowd rejoicing at the false news of Machado's resignation. At last in August 1933 the army turned against the President. He escaped for his life in an aeroplane across the sea, execrated by the whole of Spanish America, while a hungry mob sacked the palace and his country house. Then came a furious man-hunt of *porristas*, spies, gunmen, Machado's underlings, dragged from their hiding-places and done to death in the streets.

Céspedes, son of *el padre de la patria*, became Provisional President, supported by American destroyers, but 'no intervention'. Within a month he had fallen; on 4 September 1933 a group of sergeants, headed by First Sergeant Batista, a court shorthand-writer, deposed their officers, seized all barracks, forts and ships, and set up a Governing Junta. Two days later President Roosevelt took the novel and significant step of inviting to the White House the Ambassadors of Argentina, Brazil, Chile and Mexico, to tell them that the United States desired to avoid intervention and see the Cuban people obtain a Government of their own choosing and able to maintain order. Roosevelt did not recognize the President installed by the Junta; but when after four months the Junta itself removed him, Roosevelt summoned to the White House the representatives of seventeen republics to tell them that he was ready to recognize President Mendieta, who had assumed office with a more reputable basis of authority. Five months later (May 1934) President Roosevelt's 'Good Neighbour' policy abrogated the right of intervention and thus gave formal independence to Cuba. Mendieta's rule was brief and shaken by disastrous strikes, arson, rioting, martial law, the army in charge. Mendieta was the third of six presidents or acting presidents who, after the fall of Machado in 1933, came and went in the course of thirty-two months amid extremist agitation provoked by the recent tyranny and by the breakdown of economic life and amid counter-agitation of 'right' tendencies; while Batista watched and waited, soon promoted Colonel and Chief of the General Staff, in reality head of the army.

At last in May 1936 Cuba appeared to resume 'normality' with the installation of the generally respected Miguel Mariano Gómez, supported by a coalition of political groups and with the reopening, about the same time, of the University, closed for four years past. Seven months later (28 December 1936) the President, failing to satisfy these groups, was deposed. He had vetoed a bill promoted by Colonel Batista for taxing sugar in order to support 3000 'civic-military' schools giving prominence to military education. The President objected to the burden on sugar and also to military or semi-military control of education; but he defended his veto not on these grounds of expediency but on constitutional grounds. He was impeached by the House of Deputies before the Senate, was found guilty, was deposed, and quietly departed to his house accompanied by a crowd of sympathizers, while the Vice-President took his place. The sugar-educational bill then passed and Batista declared himself satisfied. It was a victory for the army or the head of the army and for fascist tendencies almost on the day when the peace agreement was signed at Buenos Aires. Some months later the House of Deputies deposed their Speaker on the ground of disloyalty to Batista, replacing him by a politician of undoubted fidelity to the military chief. A large garrison is housed eight miles from Havana in a garden city, containing pleasant provision for the comfort, welfare and recreation of the soldiers: Batista's residence is in the centre among his troops. Batista permits criticism, and in June 1937 a Cuban Deputy, declaring—with discreet silence as to names—that Mussolini's methods were imitated in Cuba, introduced a law forbidding dictatorship. Cuba has proposed as candidate for the Nobel Peace Prize President Franklin Roosevelt, and in April 1937 the Cuban Foreign Minister pronounced a warm public eulogy of the Pan-American movement.

The question occurs why Cuba, exposed to no external dangers, needs military education. But the tranquil[1] legality of the whole proceeding is noticeable and Cuba appears to have lived down the devastating shock of Machado's tyranny with a political competence which contrasts with her early republican days. Batista, like other intelligent dictators, seeks to conciliate business interests and to win foreign esteem by keeping order. Nor does political history tell the whole truth. The many American visitors to Cuba during the past generation, 'Tourisme' having become a Cuban industry, have found a friendly people inhabiting a pleasant country for travel and sojourn; and two noble Spanish institutions in Havana, the Galician Club and the Asturian Club, bear witness that it is a country where the poor immigrant may make his way. It is a

[1] Tranquil with one exception. During a debate in the Senate on the eve of the impeachment pistols were drawn. The Chairman, a crack shot, restored order by drawing his revolver and threatening to shoot the first interrupter.

delicate question whether or to what extent American political influence has been exercised in favour of American business. Proximity, reciprocal needs and great potential wealth in the hands of improvident and careless people have favoured American enterprise; and American investment has been welcomed and encouraged by Cuban politicians and business men. The result is that great part of the best land of Cuba is owned or controlled by Americans, mostly corporations of absentee shareholders managed by boards in New York. The great American-owned sugar-mills have raised the standard of life for the Cuban peasant, but also have dominated his life.

That great foreign investment does not necessarily mean political control is proved by the 500 millions of English money in Argentina, including 270 millions in railways. But the case is different. Those British railways, so far from dominating the national industry or the land of Argentina, have in great part created the national industry and have multiplied the value of the land for the Argentine owner. In Cuba it is the land itself and the national industry which has in great part passed into foreign hands. How far this is due to Cuban remissness it is hard to say. It is certainly Cuban remissness which leaves most of the retail trade to Spanish immigrants.

On p. 376 mention is made of the 'unhappy domestic history of Cuba'; but it takes more than that to make a Cuban unhappy. Hudson Strode remarks that most Cubans 'are blessed with a joyous sensibility to those aspects of life which have no market value'. Except for the word 'joyous'—not everywhere equally applicable—the remark is true generally of the Spanish American.

NOTE. A. A. Ettinger, *The Mission to Spain of Pierre Soulé** (New-haven, 1932), the best account of American policy towards Cuba; J. M. Callahan, *Cuba and International Relations** (Baltimore, U.S.A., 1899); C. E. Chapman, *A History of the Cuban Republic** (New York, 1927); H. Strode, *The Pageant of Cuba* (London, 1935); L. H. Jenks, *Our Cuban Colony* (New York, 1928); *The Caribbean Area*, chs. IX–XI.

CHAPTER XXXI

HAITI AND SANTO DOMINGO

I have travelled in almost every quarter of the globe and I may say that, taken as a whole, there is not a finer island than Santo Domingo.

SPENCER ST JOHN

ALTHOUGH no larger than Ireland, the island of Haiti or Santo Domingo (formerly Española), a land of mountains and rich plains, is split into two unequal parts. The western part, one-third of the whole, is the negro Republic of Haiti, the most thickly populated part of tropical America, with a population of two and a half millions, of whom a few, the self-styled *élite*, mainly mulattoes, speak French and maintain some contact with French culture, through a French priesthood, through schooling in France and through visits to Paris, commonly paid for until recently by the national treasury. The rest, the illiterate peasantry and workers, are almost a separate people, speaking 'Creole', a partly Africanized French patois. The Dominican Republic occupies the Spanish part of the island, twice the size of Haiti with about half the population, mainly mulatto, little or no pure white blood (except a few Spanish immigrants) but a considerable quasi-white or hispanicized element in the governing class.

Briefest notice of these States might seem enough. But military Government by the United States during some years brought them into the forefront of Latin-American publicity and political agitation, endowing them, as supposed victims of '*Monroismo*', with historical prominence.

Haiti has a peculiar origin. Early in the seventeenth century the rude community of French cattle-hunters (buccaneers) in the west of Española grew into a French colony, which was recognized as such by Spain at the Peace of Ryswick in 1697. During the following ninety years this French colony of Saint Domingue became the richest part of tropical America; a hard-working, free-living, slave-trading, slave-driving, money-making society, providing half Europe with sugar, growing also coffee, tobacco and cotton; and on the poorer lands rearing cattle and swine. This busy productive community was a contrast to the Spanish colony of Santo Domingo, twice the size of the French part and equally fertile but (its mineral wealth long since exhausted) a half-empty roadless country with a scanty population of Spaniards living in patriarchal ease on their estates or inhabiting the decayed city of Santo Domingo, once the metropolis of all the Spanish Indies. There were only 16,000 slaves and, as throughout Spanish America, liberal laws of manumission.

The comparison is not wholly favourable to French Saint Domingue, an ill-cemented community, 'materially prosperous, socially diseased', in which every section was bitterly discontented. There were nearly half a million slaves, more than half of them African-born (for it was cheaper to import than to breed), kept down by fear and themselves a constant fear to their masters. There were about 30,000 free coloured people, many of them slaveowners and landowners, but kept apart by a rigid colour line, debarred by law from the liberal professions and liable to insult and outrage from the lower class of whites. There were about 35,000 whites; European officials, arrogant and aloof; some European planters and merchants; Creole landowners and bourgeoisie, unfriendly to the Europeans, resenting their own exclusion from office and hating the rigid French commercial monopoly, which was evaded in some degree by smuggling and, on the eve of the French Revolution, was modified by slight concessions, unavailing to assuage discontent. The French system, more despotic than the Spanish, had nothing corresponding to the *cabildo*. Official peculation was as customary as in the Spanish Indies.

In 1788–9 came the stupefying shock of the Revolution with its declaration that 'all men are born free and equal'. The Creole slaveowners attempted in vain first to make terms with the Revolution and then to assume autonomy. The rapidly changing Parisian revolutionary Governments, acclaiming liberty but anxious to preserve the colony, issued a series of inconsistent decrees in 1789–92 which only stirred unrest. The reader may trace in Stoddard's narrative the strange cross-currents of strife in the tragedy which fills the years 1791–1804, a tragedy whose horrors can hardly be paralleled in all the records of history. The story is complicated by the fact that the colony, small though it was, was divided into three provinces; North, West and South; separated from one another by marked physical features. The story opens with three roughly simultaneous movements in 1791-3. The few whites drifted into revolt, but never a united revolt, against the power of France and welcomed the British and Spaniards, enemies of republican France, who invaded the colony in 1793.

The mulattoes rose in the west and south, at first in unstable alliance with royalist whites, but finally setting up—except in one or two strong places—their own racial supremacy under an able leader named Rigaud, maintaining the slavery of the negroes whom they despised, but also enlisting negro regiments. In the north—the richest and most populous province—the negro slaves rose in blind destructive fury, torturing and killing all whites within reach, burning crops and buildings. Their movement gathered substance when in September 1792 three Jacobin commissioners arrived from France, violent revolutionaries, who, after provoking civil war among the whites, called the negro marauders to their aid against the white 'aristocrats', allowed these savages to sack and burn the capital, Cap Français,[1] offered freedom to any slave serving as a soldier and in August 1793 decreed the emancipation of all the slaves in the north. Thus France herself destroyed her colony. The French, threatened by an overwhelming black flood, were at war with one another. And even had there been a change of policy in Paris, France was powerless in Saint Domingue owing to the European war, and particularly the maritime struggle with Great Britain.

A few months later the predatory and unintelligent negro revolt found a clear-sighted leader, Toussaint l'Ouverture, 'the first of the blacks'.

Toussaint was a black slave, now aged fifty, who as coachman on a sugar plantation near the capital had found leisure to learn reading and the rudiments of writing. Joining the negro insurrection late in 1791, he soon rose in rank. When war broke out with Spain in 1793, he led 600 negroes eastward to join the Spaniards. Through military success and the force of his compelling person-

---

[1] Now Cap Haitien.

ality—which impressed whites as well as his own people—he soon commanded 4000 well-armed negroes trained by European officers. In May 1794 Toussaint suddenly massacred the Spanish soldiers under his command and led his negro troops across the frontier into Saint Domingue. Toussaint astutely saw that, whereas Spanish service led to nothing, the impotence of France in Saint Domingue owing to the European war, and particularly the maritime struggle with Great Britain, opened to him the way to winning the supremacy of his own race and of his own person through nominal service to France.

In 1795 Spain by the Peace of Basle ceded to France the Spanish part of the island, retaining the administration provisionally but disbanding black troops, most of whom joined Toussaint. During that year the English invaders, wasting through yellow fever and attacked by Toussaint's negroes and by Rigaud's mulattoes, were losing their hold on the island; for the invasion was as ill-managed as the other British side-shows of the revolutionary wars. At the end of the year Toussaint led 10,000 troops to the aid of a bewildered French Governor in the capital, and thereby won extraordinary official recognition from France in 1796. Then, by lucky accidents and by the handy method of 'electing' inconvenient Frenchmen as deputies to the French legislature, Toussaint gradually got rid of the French officials who stood in his way. In May 1798 the British commander surrendered the two places which he still held, signing an agreement with Toussaint, who was received with regal honours. Five months later the last French representative in Saint Domingue was expelled.

There remained Rigaud and his mulattoes (1798–1800). Toussaint gradually fought them down, adding their troops to his own, aided by his black generals, Cristophe and the infamous Dessalines, an able commander but a ferocious savage from the Congo. Dessalines, appointed Governor of the South to complete the work, gradually killed off the mulattoes, generally by new and exquisite tortures, his own inventions.

In January 1801 Toussaint's armies marched eastwards. Within a month he entered the city of Santo Domingo, treating the Spanish inhabitants with brutal insolence. To the French, on the contrary, he was conciliatory, desiring now, after the duplicities and cruelties of his upward progress, to found a civilized state incorporating European elements. Abstemious, indefatigable and intelligent in business, imperious in decree, maintaining regal state, attended by a bodyguard of 1500 cavalry, master of 20,000 veteran troops besides unnumbered irregulars, Toussaint strove for two years (1800–1) to reorganize the devastated land. He welcomed the French planters back to their estates, giving them negro labourers. To produce wealth, the means of commerce and of customs revenue, the negroes, now legally free, were made to work the soil harder than ever under the pitiless Dessalines. The ports were opened to the trade of all nations. In August 1801 a Constitution, generally liberal in character but naming Toussaint Governor for life, with a mere acknowledgment of French sovereignty, was sent to France for approval. It was a challenge to the First Consul, to whom the sea was now opened by the preliminaries of Amiens.

In January 1802 a French fleet appeared carrying 12,000 troops under Leclerc, Bonaparte's brother-in-law. Toussaint saw at once that all his work was undone and ordered his generals to burn the ports, kill all the whites except some hostages and retire into the interior. His orders were only obeyed in part. Leclerc, without waiting for 7000 expected troops (who arrived a fortnight later), inflicted a series of rapid blows, and on 1 May received the submission of Cristophe and Dessalines, who both entered the French service. Toussaint also surrendered, received a pardon and retired to his estates.[1] A fortnight later, before conquest was complete, came the yellow fever: 3000 Frenchmen died in a month, then 160 daily: French reinforcements, increasing the death-roll, brought dubious strength. In September 4000 died; in November Leclerc died in the midst of a revolt of the mulatto troops provoked by news that Bonaparte had restored mulatto disabilities and the slave-trade. Cristophe revolted, then Dessalines. The French started a war of extermination, letting loose upon the negro population man-eating bloodhounds from Cuba. As fresh troops came during the winter and some recovered from the fever, the French gained

---

[1] Afterwards he was treacherously arrested and died in a French prison of consumption or perhaps rather of cold and neglect.

ground and conquest was in sight, when in May 1803 war broke out with Great Britain. Hostile fleets blockaded the island: at the end of the year a few thousand Frenchmen were prisoners in Jamaica, the survivors of 50,000 troops sent to the island during the past two years. Thus ended the Napoleonic dream of American empire. In December 1803 Dessalines, leader of the final revolt, proclaimed the independence of Haiti, reviving the Indian name of the island. After a fierce struggle with rival chiefs, he crowned himself Emperor, imitating Bonaparte, in 1804. He invited the French landowners to return to their estates, promised protection to the whites, and then massacred them.

Thus the French part of the island started its independent life with a negro population under an African savage; its roads, sugar-factories, irrigation works and country houses in ruins. The educated people had been almost exterminated. But enough survived to furnish clerks and secretaries. The thinly inhabited Spanish part of the island, where there was less to destroy and there had been less fighting, had suffered less: and a small French garrison, attacked in vain by Dessalines, still held Santo Domingo city.

In 1806 Dessalines fell in a revolt, provoked by his cruelty. After him Cristophe reigned, in the north only, as King Henry I. He built a gorgeous palace and crowned the highest neighbouring peak with a stupendous citadel, of which it was said that every stone cost a man's life. In 1820, prevented by a paralytic stroke from mounting his horse to check a revolt, he shot himself. His subjects then joined the republic to the south. For the true founder of the Haitian Republic was an educated mulatto who had served in the French army, Pétion, President for eleven years (1807–18) and author of a Constitution providing a life-presidency. Defying King Cristophe, he ruled in the south with a milder autocracy. Pétion gave an asylum to Bolívar, a fugitive after defeat in 1815–16 and provided him with munitions to renew his efforts, only stipulating that Bolívar should free the Venezuelan slaves. After him Boyer, also a mulatto educated in France and formerly a soldier of France, ruled for twenty-five years (1818–43), and for twenty-two years ruled the whole island; for on the death of

Cristophe in 1820 his little kingdom accepted Boyer's rule, and a year later the Spanish region was added to Haiti. Thus for thirty-six years the young republic—except for the frontier war against Cristophe and the conquest of Santo Domingo—enjoyed internal peace and a Government which was well-intentioned and (except in the conquered Spanish region) not unduly oppressive, although Boyer, to get the land tilled, forced his negro subjects to work under armed guards. He also burdened his country with a heavy debt by paying a large indemnity to France on account of the dispossessed landowners in return for French recognition of Haitian independence.

In 1843 Boyer was deposed, and the resulting troubles in Haiti enabled a group of patriots in Santo Domingo to shake off the odious Haitian domination and form the Dominican Republic, Spanish in speech and tradition. Thus since 1844 the island has comprised two distinct States; the Haitian and the Dominican Republics. Of these the Spanish-speaking Dominican Republic claims priority of narrative, since American intervention—the decisive event in both histories—came first there.

The Dominican Republic

Since the cession to France in 1795, not followed by effective French occupation, Santo Domingo has passed six times under foreign dominations: (1) 1801–5 bullying oppression by the negro conquerors Toussaint and Dessalines; (2) 1805–8 French dominion, maintained by General Ferrand, who by the force of his personal qualities kept the tricolour flying almost single-handed for three years; (3) 1809–21, revolt, aided by British ships, against France, to the cry of *Viva Fernando Séptimo*, and rule by Spanish Captains-General for a dozen years; (4) 1822–44, after a few weeks of independence and a futile proposal of union with Colombia (December 1821–January 1822) conquest by Boyer; stupefying and oppressive rule by negro Haitian officials, hostile to everything Spanish and everything white; (5) 1861–5, a Spanish colony once more, after various solicitations of American or French or Spanish 'protection' or rather protectorate; (6) 1905–24, gradually increasing American control, at first fiscal then also political, culminating in eight years (1916–24) of American military government.

During the stormy years 1791–1805 and during the odious Haitian domination of 1822–44 some 40,000 whites, one-third of the population, had migrated to neighbouring lands. Thus Santo Domingo, which in Spanish days had possessed a white aristocracy, moderately slave-owning, had now become largely mulatto, and so remained, although some of the white exiles, urgently invited by the republican governments, returned to their abandoned lands, now thickets of weedy growth and exposed to the chances of civil war. For within six months of winning independence, the Dominicans were fighting one another.

Their early history is the story of two men, Santana and Báez, representatives of two sides of Dominican life, comrades in the fight for independence, afterwards—owing to Santana's jealous ambition—rivals and enemies.

The first Republic lasted seventeen years (1844–61). Santana filled ten of these years in three non-continuous presidential terms. Báez, twice head of the state, filled six years. During those seventeen years there were three other heads of the State. Santana was a big uncouth ignorant caudillo, in whose broad countenance the negro element predominated over European and Indian strains.[1] His bodily strength, prowess in fight and commanding personality won him the hero-worship of his peasant-neighbours. A hard fighter for independence, victor, at the head of a ragged troop, over an invasion of the savage Soulouque in 1849, he was no less a fighter for his own hand, disposing promptly of adversaries or conspirators. Twice he resigned an uneasy presidency, only to fight his way back to power. Having persuaded the reluctant Spanish monarchy to readmit Santo Domingo into the Spanish Empire in 1861, he became the first Spanish Captain-General; but he was not made to obey Spaniards or anyone else; and a year later he retired with a pension and a strangely incongruous Spanish title of nobility. He died in 1864, aged sixty-three.

His rival Báez, five times President or acting President between

[1] The Indian strain discernible in his features probably came from the long connexion between Santo Domingo and Venezuela.

1849 and 1878 and also victor over Soulouque in the second black invasion of 1854, was Santana's complete opposite. Almost white, a cultivated man educated in Europe, his copious mid-Victorian whiskers denoting a European bourgeois character, he desired to 'moralize' the administration and even to respect law. But custom and opportunity proved to be the strongest law, and Báez as President was as autocratic as Santana. He died in exile, aged seventy, in 1884.

The Spanish occupation was a failure, odious to the Dominicans and burdensome to the tottering monarchy of Spain, obliged by the ravages of yellow fever constantly to reinforce the Spanish garrison—13,000 men at one time—and spending large sums in crushing revolts. The end of the American Civil War also indicated the wisdom of withdrawal; and the last Spanish troops embarked in July 1865. They left one legacy—an increase in the white element of the population.

Three years later Báez, despairing—as Santana had done—of maintaining a respectable independence, solicited annexation to the United States. A treaty of annexation was signed in 1869 with President Grant's Government, and was approved by a Dominican plebiscite with the inevitable huge majority;[1] but the United States Senate rejected it. Báez' further efforts for annexation discredited him and he went under in the political vortex which agitated the country until 1899, the chieftains of 'red', 'blue' and 'green' parties contending for the mastery, while ruinous debts piled up, new constitutions pullulated and sometimes two rival and simultaneous governments faced one another.

Anarchy, as usual, led to dictatorship, in the person of the mulatto Ulises Heureux, who, with an interval of nominal retirement (1884–7), ruled for nearly twenty years (1882–99). Physically he was a magnificent specimen of athletic manhood, in character the perfect tyrant; astute, fearless, vindictive, corrupt, unscrupulous, incredibly sensual. His spies were everywhere. His paid soldiers, wanton to all others, were obedient to him, his executioners and bravos ready to kill at a word. In every town he had a

---

[1] 16,000 Dominican citizens voted 'yes'. Báez, thinking that complete unanimity would look bad, provided eleven 'noes'.

mistress, to receive him on his presidential tours and also to act as a spy. His former mistresses were his spies abroad, sending him reports from European capitals. All this cost money, and Heureux borrowed recklessly, treating the Treasury as his private purse. Thus when his own turn came and his enemies—themselves marked for arrest and probable death—shot him in the public street, he bequeathed to his country nothing but intolerable debt.

Yet he had kept the peace, and his fall brought fights between personalist parties, plunging the country deeper into bankruptcy. The chief creditor was an American corporation, containing many British shareholders, entitled the San Domingo Improvement Company, which had acted as Heureux' agent and had managed the custom-houses. After Heureux' death the Improvement Company was turned out of the custom-houses: a measure which increased the financial confusion. Between 1901 and 1904 the Governments of France, Belgium, Germany, Italy and Spain by diplomatic pressure obtained from the rapidly changing and disordered Dominican Government definite undertakings for the respective bondholders. The United States intervened diplomatically on behalf of the Improvement Company and it was agreed that, failing certain stipulated payments by the Dominican Government to the Company, an agent appointed by the United States Government should collect the customs at Puerto Plata and, if necessary, at other ports. The stipulated payments were never made; and in October 1904 a Financial Agent appointed by the United States took over the collection of customs at Puerto Plata.

At once there were protests from France, Belgium and Italy, all claiming promised custom-houses: an arrangement which would have left the Republic without any revenue, while salaries were unpaid and the Government was borrowing at 40 per cent. Accordingly, at a hint from Washington, the Dominican Government requested 'the United States to take charge of the collection of duties'. In February 1905 a treaty was signed enabling the United States to collect the customs and adjust Dominican finances.

Two months earlier, in his message to Congress, Roosevelt had said: 'The adherence of the United States to the Monroe Doctrine may force the United States, however reluctantly, in flagrant cases of...wrongdoing or impotence, to the exercise of an international police power'; and now, in presenting the treaty to the United States Senate, Roosevelt defined his famous corollary to the Monroe Doctrine: 'it has for some time been obvious that those who profit by the Monroe Doctrine must accept certain responsibilities along with the rights which it confers.... It is incompatible with international equity for the United States to refuse to allow other powers to take the only means of satisfying the claims of their creditors and yet to refuse, itself, to take any such steps.' A few months later he told Congress: 'There was imminent danger of foreign intervention...only the actual opening of negotiations ...by our Government prevented the seizure of territory in Santo Domingo by a European power.'

The Senate having refused to ratify the treaty, Roosevelt by executive authority appointed in April 1905, with the consent of the Dominican Government, a customs receiver for that Republic under a *modus vivendi*, which assigned to creditors 55 per cent. of the dues and 45 per cent. to the Dominican Government. Roosevelt disappointed British shareholders in the San Domingo Improvement Company by declining to give any preference to that American concern. The arrangement was profitable to European creditors, and the Dominican Government received more from the 45 per cent. than formerly from the entire customs. After two years this arrangement received legal sanction when the United States Senate ratified a treaty slightly modified from the one rejected in 1905. The new treaty empowered the American Government to give to the General Receiver and his assistants any necessary protection: a provision which authorized forcible intervention in case of need. No such need arose for five years: a time of improved public credit and general prosperity and also a time of internal peace owing to the rule of a strong President, the slayer of Heureux, Ramón Cáceres, a burly genial person and a fine soldier, who maintained a disciplined army and police, scotched every sign of revolt, and with cool common sense worked heartily with the American customs officials.

But every dictator has enemies. In the autumn of 1911 the President during a Sunday afternoon drive was waylaid and shot.

Confusion followed; an 'election' arranged by the military Governor of the capital, a triangular civil war between three ex-Presidents, the arrival of Commissioners from Washington, at whose suggestion the Archbishop, an excellent and able man who had no enemies, became President, but resigned in sixteen months, having failed to reconcile aspiring politicians. Further steps towards American control were: a supervised election in 1913, the appointment of an American financial expert in May 1914 to control receipts and expenditure; then in August 1914 the arrival of Commissioners bearing the Wilson Plan. This was an intimation: (1) that all fighting should cease; (2) that the party leaders should choose a Provisional President, otherwise the United States Government would appoint one; (3) that elections should then be held, observed by American officials; (4) that all revolutionary movements should thereafter cease. The Commissioners were instructed that no argument should be allowed. 'It is desired that you present plan and see that it is complied with.'

The party leaders obediently chose a Provisional President. But the inauguration of a constitutional President in December 1914 brought no peace. In that same month Secretary Bryan urged that the American Customs Receiver should become Controller of the internal revenue with power to prepare the budget, and that American officers should organize a constabulary. Eleven months later these proposals—now insistent demands—were declined by the Dominican Government. Five months later (May 1916), fresh disturbances having broken out, American marines occupied the capital and, during the following two months, most of the important towns. The Receiver took charge of the entire revenue and stopped all payments until the American interpretation of the 1907 treaty should be accepted. At last in November 1916 President Wilson having agreed 'with the deepest reluctance', Captain Knapp of the United States Navy proclaimed 'a state of Military Occupation... Military Government and...military law'. All the Ministers having abandoned their posts, American officers took charge of the Departments. Dominicans still held most of the subordinate civil posts, and had to work in unwonted fashion. Some of the dismissed sinecurists joined the bandits.

American officers trained an efficient native constabulary. Much was done for sanitation and health; a needful work for, as in Haiti, hygiene was a rare eccentricity: most of the people suffered from contagious diseases, and during a small-pox epidemic the clergy denounced vaccination. The reform of public finance—aided by the war boom and the high price of sugar—provided funds for schools, roads and other public works. This excellent work did not all go smoothly. For, since no Colonial Office or trained Colonial Service existed, the business was under the Navy Department, which from the early part of 1917 was absorbed in the work of the Great War. Owing to the needs of war, sergeants promoted to commissioned rank, men ignorant of the language and despising the mulatto population, undertook political and military tasks. Disarming the people, where all were armed, meant domiciliary visits. The marines occasionally adopted the *ley fuga*, and in dealing with suspected bandits they sometimes 'shot first and asked questions afterwards'. But injuries inflicted in the course of reform and constructive work were as nothing compared to those inflicted, both before and after, by contending native politicians. Press censorship and court-martials for critics of the administration damaged reputation: and the sarcastic indignation of all Spanish America was stirred up by a cartoon representing the New York statue of Liberty looking down on the figure of the Dominican poet Fiallo in convict dress. Fiallo, for a vehement newspaper attack on American rule, was condemned to three years' imprisonment, afterwards shortened to one year.

The military Government has been variously judged by American historians. Professor Melvin Knight finds the balance heavily against it, mentioning particularly the Tariff of 1919 which favoured manufacturers and was promptly abrogated after the American withdrawal. Jenks is critical but not so sweeping. The general character of the intervention and of Dominican conditions is illustrated by the informal and spontaneous reminiscences of the Australian, Mr W. P. Burke, who was equally intimate with Americans and Dominicans. He does not spare the former and tells some strange tales of violence, but he concludes: 'The American occupation was the best thing that ever happened to

Santo Domingo. Highways were built, sanitation was enforced disease was stamped out and the children were made to attend th newly erected Schools.'

From 1920 the Americans desired to escape from their invidiou position, but they still maintained the 1916 fiscal claims, which th Dominicans refused. Two years later these claims were modifiec and a Provisional Dominican Government was set up which fo two years shared responsibility with the military Government. I 1924 the occupation ended.

The Dominican politicians, left to themselves, returned to thei old ways. But a former sub-lieutenant of constabulary under the Americans, named Trujillo, made his way to the front, became general of the constabulary (which he kept and still keeps in the highest state of efficiency) and then head of the army. His upward progress, his methods of acquiring the sinews of political warfare and the election of 1930 are described by Mr Burke (pp. 197, etc.), who knew Trujillo intimately. The opposition abstained from voting and innumerable ballot papers were thrust into the urns for Trujillo. A fortnight after his installation a hurricane almost destroyed the capital, and 5000 people perished. Trujillo, who had been trained under American officers, burnt the bodies, organized rescue of the living and restored the capital: and Santo Domingo, the oldest European city in the New World, dropped the name given by Bartolomé Columbus and took that of its benefactor Trujillo. An excellent administrator and a hard worker, Trujillo suppressed the usual revolts, and he still preserves an autocratic peace, having entered upon a second term in 1934. In February 1937 he was decorated by the Pope with the Cross of St Gregory the Great for his services to the Church and to the Dominican people. Dominican exiles, like those from Cuba, find a hospitable asylum on Mexican soil.

HAITI

THE story of Haiti must now be resumed from 1844, where it was left on p. 399. Thenceforth the Government was a frequently changing dictatorship tempered by revolt. During seventy-two years (1843–1915) twenty-two autocrats (with one exception, generals) held office. Of these only two retired peaceably from office; eleven served for less than a year each; five died in office, one of them by poison; thirteen were deposed by revolt and two of them murdered: others escaped imminent death through the aid of foreign diplomatists or warships. Twelve of the twenty-two were pure black; six were 'griffe', that is to say almost black; four were mulatto. Six of these autocrats ruled for six years or longer, providing intervals of internal peace. But Soulouque, ruler for nearly twelve years (1847–59), was an ignorant stupid black, a follower of the magical and orgiastic Voodoo serpent-worship. He made two disastrous attempts to conquer Santo Domingo, executing some of the unsuccessful commanders. He permitted or encouraged a massacre of mulattoes, had himself crowned at huge expense as Emperor Faustin I and created fifty-nine dukes. Faced by a general revolt, Soulouque abdicated in 1859 and fled to the French Legation. He was rescued from a threatening mob by artillerymen landed from a passing British transport which conveyed the refugee ex-Emperor to Jamaica.

Some of the revolutions were not very serious affairs. But Sir Spencer St John, who was British Minister to Haiti for twelve years (1863–75) and knew the country for twenty years, describes tumultuous conditions, conspiracies, executions, two civil wars— in 1865 and 1867–9—and the occasional prevention of troubles by foreign warships and foreign troops. St John, a kindly observer, who speaks warmly of the attractive qualities and friendly good manners of the negro peasantry, gives convincing evidence of cannibalism sometimes accompanying the Voodoo orgies in the 'sixties and of occasional cannibalism even later. Polygamy he mentions incidentally. His account (which has been impugned without reason) fully justifies Froude's description of Haiti in 1888 as 'a caricature of civilization'. Froude adds: 'If the Americans forbid any other power to interfere, they will have to interfere themselves...the present order of things cannot last in an island so close under American shores.' Froude thus anticipates the 'Roosevelt corollary' with full approval, on general grounds, convinced that the abatement of a nuisance was incumbent on the United States.

After Soulouque the next longest reign was that of Salomon (1879–88), a cultivated man who had been Minister in Paris and had lived twenty years in Europe, yet described by Froude as 'a peremptory gentleman who made quick work with his political opponents'. And in 1883 St John wrote: 'Illegal military executions, murder and pillage, encouraged by the authorities, have been the principal episodes...of the last four years...dozens of those whom I well knew have been shot.' Every Haitian Government was anti-foreign and anti-white, so much so that foreign ownership of land was forbidden by law. This law, as usual in such cases, was sometimes evaded, particularly by German firms, on whose behalf some Haitian citizen held the land as ostensible owner.

In the present century a Haitian technique of 'election' was evolved. An aspirant for the presidency hired, by promises to pay after election and by permitting loot immediately, a force of Cacos (partly bandits but chiefly primitive mountain peasants) and occupied the town of Cap Haitien. He then marched south; and when he reached the town of St Marc, fifty miles from the capital, the reigning President, according to rule, was expected to vacate his office and the aspirant stepped in. There were no battles, but usually some street fighting, considerable pillage and some harmless people hurt or killed. The Cacos, professional king-makers, having received their reward, were now ready to assist the next candidate on the same terms. It is therefore hardly strange that in the course of six years and a half (December 1908–July 1915) seven Presidents rose and fell, of whom three, including Guillaume Sam, had been convicted by the tribunals of robbing the Treasury. But the plan did not always work smoothly, so that change of administration became costly and turbulent. Haitian disorder had brought visits of American warships twenty times, and in January 1914 British, French, German and American warships landed a few marines to protect foreign interests in the capital; in June 1914 French marines were landed for a few days at Cap Haitien.

Down to 1914 the interest on foreign loans had been paid, but only by reckless borrowing. That year brought general default and large issues of paper money. The army being unpaid, no Government was safe for a week. Administration was only carried on by dvances made against future receipts by the Banque Nationale, of which the shareholders were chiefly French, but some American. n August 1914 the Bank refused to advance more, and in December 1914 at the request of the Bank (which was working for American ntervention) unarmed American marines landed and conveyed 500,000 dollars in gold from the Bank to an American warship to be deposited in the safe custody of a New York Bank.

In March 1915 a negro politician, Guillaume Sam, headed a Caco revolution of the usual kind, but unusual in the fact that it was policed by Admiral Caperton of the United States Navy, who forbade fighting in towns. In every town between Cap Haitien and the capital, Sam and his puzzled Cacos found American officers awaiting them to notify this prohibition. Sam entered the capital as President: but his enemies, sheltered in the foreign legations, were conspiring against him at once, and a rival candidate was raising another Caco force in Cap Haitien. Sam imprisoned 167 political suspects in the capital. In July there was a rising in the city and the President fled to the French legation. On the same day officers faithful to Sam massacred the 167 prisoners. Early next morning a group of men forced their way into the French Legation, pulled Sam from under a bed and threw him to the mob outside, who tore him in pieces and dragged the dismembered trunk through the streets. At that moment Admiral Caperton's flagship was steaming into the harbour. That same afternoon, at the urgent request of the French, British and American Ministers and in obedience to telegraphic orders from Washington, the Admiral landed troops to 'protect American and foreign interests'. Intervention had begun.

A month later the Haitian Congress, in a supervised election, chose as President M. Dartiguenave, the candidate 'preferred by the United States': and in September 1915, martial law having been declared, the Haitian Cabinet accepted a treaty (afterwards ratified, under pressure, by the Haitian Congress) providing for fiscal control and a constabulary to be trained by Americans; the United States undertaking to aid the 'development of agricultural, mineral and commercial resources' and the 'establishment of the finances of Haiti on a firm and solid basis'. It was later agreed that

the arrangement should last for twenty years from the date o
ratification, until May 1936. In this respect it differed from the
Government set up in Santo Domingo in 1916 as an emergency
measure to be ended as soon as possible. There was another
difference. Santo Domingo in 1916–22 had no Government except
foreign military rule: in Haiti a Haitian President[1] and Council of
State ostensibly held authority throughout, co-operating with the
American authorities.

A Constitution, 'more in accordance with facts', was drafted.
Congress, consisting of the dispossessed and irate *élite* politicians,
refused to ratify it and was thereupon dissolved by decree, an
American officer of marines acting the part of Cromwell and
carrying the decree of dissolution into the Chamber (June 1917).
Then, through the form of a plebiscite, a Constitution was enacted
which by an ingenious clause enabled the President to dispense
with Parliament as long as he chose: and for twelve years (1918–30)
the President, with a nominated Council of State but no Congress,
shared authority with the American officials. In 1922 the Council
of State appointed Dartiguenave's successor, M. Borno, who was
re-elected President four years later by a Council of State nominated by himself.

Despite resistance from native sentiment, the Constitution of
1918 authorized the ownership of land by foreigners; the only
possible way, in American opinion, of improving agricultural
methods and developing the extensive waste lands.

Already the American authorities were at work: marines; constabulary officers; experts in finance, agriculture and engineering;
sanitary officials to impose hygiene and to combat the widespread
ills of hook-worm, malaria and syphilis. The Haitian army and
police were disbanded, to be replaced by an American-trained
constabulary. Concerning fiscal policy Millspaugh (Financial
Adviser-general Receiver of Haiti 1927–9) writes: 'While we have
in effect denied in Haiti that equality of economic opportunity
which we demanded in the mandated territories of Asia and Africa
and while we have encouraged American investments...we have

[1] Three Presidents were concerned: Dartiguenave, 1915–22; Borno, 1922–30;
Vincent, 1930, re-elected in 1936.

been for the most part scrupulously fair in economic matters to our unwilling wards'.[1]

Suppression of the Cacos and pacification, at the cost of some fighting and loss of life, seemed to be complete about the end of 1916. Two years later a serious uprising broke out in the mountains and spread over one-fourth of the country, partly provoked by revival of the obsolete law of *corvée*, forced and unpaid labour for a given number of days yearly, for the much-needed work of making or mending roads and paths: in itself perhaps not a grievous hardship, but oppressive when a man worked far from his hut or longer than the fixed time. Moreover some of the marines showed the southern contempt for negroes, and the Haitian constabulary recruits were slow to learn that a policeman need not be a rough bully. It was two years, 1918-20, before the revolt was crushed, with an estimated loss of 2250 Haitians killed in fight since 1915: a later American investigation put the number at 1500.

Reform followed: abolition of martial law and modification of the military character of government. From 1922 an American High Commissioner exercising civil functions—although a soldier held the post—controlled American activities and advised the Haitian President. The system was (in Millspaugh's phrase) a dual dictatorship; for President Borno (1922-30), an able man of character and experience, was not content to be a mere figurehead. Projects of law were referred to Washington; but questions were treated as matters of negotiation.

As the election of 1929 approached and Borno, accused of being pro-American, seemed to intend re-election, there was much anti-American agitation and some turbulence, partly due to economic depression. In consequence a Commission, appointed by President Hoover in February 1930, arranged that a fit person should become Provisional President (as eight years earlier in Santo Domingo) in order to hold a legal election. This was duly done and in November 1930 the Presidency for six years fell to M. Vincent, a leader of the agitation for American withdrawal but also a discreet and conciliatory negotiator upon delicate questions during the following months. The Commission also advised the 'increasingly rapid

[1] *Current History*, vol. XXXI, p. 919.

Haitianization of the services'; employment in Haiti of Americans 'free from strong racial antipathies'; gradual withdrawal of the marines; and replacement of the High Commissioner by a non-military Minister. Thenceforth the relations between the American and Haitian Governments were, in form at least, diplomatic. And after delicate negotiations the recommendations of the Commission were embodied in the Treaty of 1932, which provided that the constabulary should be completely commanded by Haitians before 31 December 1934; that the withdrawal of the marines should begin by that date and that fiscal control should then be modified by a new arrangement. These provisions were carried out before the stipulated date. The last marines were withdrawn in July–August 1934; and Haiti, a healthier and more settled country, was handed back to the Haitians. Limited fiscal control by Americans is to continue only till the retirement of certain outstanding bonds, probably about the year 1942. In 1936 President Vincent's presidency was extended by plebiscite for an additional five years.

The intervention had raised the standard of living and of health among the peasantry. But no magical transformation was possible. In 1923 the High Commissioner reported: 'Until the American intervention and for over 100 years, Haiti has been nothing more or less than a military oligarchy of the most severe type: 95 per cent. of its people are illiterate, and a large percentage unmoral. Under such conditions the word "democracy" has but an empty sound.' And in 1930 he wrote: 'The peasant of to-day has neither in character, intellect, education, in farming ability nor outlook greatly changed since 1804.' On the other hand Millspaugh writes: 'Their wants were mainly for the bare necessities of tropical and primitive existence...they were for the most part carefree and contented, and possessed everything in life that they had learned to want.' Whether or not the indolent negro peasant would be much happier for being educated into a citizen voter, obviously the élite needed a lesson. And here the American intervention has done much. The rapacious leaders of Caco revolutions have been replaced by estimable civilian Presidents: nor have violent shocks recurred during the four years since the American marines were withdrawn.

Whether or not it was wise policy on the part of the United States (a question outside the range of this volume) 'the temporary protectorate imposed on Haiti and Santo Domingo' (Bemis' words) was fully justified by the exceptional circumstances; and it was work done for the world. Mr Sumner Welles in his book on Santo Domingo, *Naboth's Vineyard*, finds 'The White Man's Burden' mawkish. Yet he commends the same sentiment expressed in prose, speaking of the United States as 'educator and civilizer'. But the enunciation of a general principle which might cover other cases is a different matter of grave concern to all Latin America: it may have been the best way of obtaining the assent of Congress in 1907. But this 'Roosevelt Corollary' was repudiated in a document, 'the Clark Memorandum', published by the State Department in 1930; also implicitly repudiated in a Convention concluded in that year after the Washington Conference of 1929 and again with explicit emphasis in the Peace Convention of December 1936.

But in 1912 a further definition (which might roughly be called the 'no-grant principle') had been added to the 'no-transfer principle'. In that year it was rumoured that a Japanese Fishing Company might acquire from an American Corporation a lease of extensive lands in Lower California, including Magdalena Bay, a valuable strategical point. The American Senate passed an unanimous resolution: 'when any harbor or other place in the American continents is so placed that the occupation thereof for naval or military purposes might threaten the communications or the safety of the United States, the Government of the United States could not see without grave concern the possession of such harbor or other place by any corporation or association which has such a relation to another Government, not American, as to give that Government political power of control for national purposes.' This resolution does not seem to have received explicit endorsement from the White House; but the unanimous vote of the Senate is a cogent matter.

NOTE. T. L. Stoddard, *The French Revolution in Santo Domingo* (New York, 1914); H. P. Davis, *Black Democracy** (New York, 1928); A. C. Millspaugh, *Haiti under American Control* (Boston, Mass., 1931);

S. St John, *Haiti or the Black Republic* (London, 1889); O. Shoenrich, *Santo Domingo** (New York, 1918); S. Welles, *Naboth's Vineyard; the Dominican Republic**, 2 vols. (New York, 1928); M. M. Knight, *The Americans in Santo Domingo* (New York, 1928); L. H. Jenks in *The Caribbean Area*, chs. VI and VII; D. G. Munro, *The United States and the Caribbean Area* (Boston, Mass., 1934); W. P. Burke, *Señor Burky* (London, 1935), pp. 123–246.

CHAPTER XXXII

LATIN AMERICA AND THE GREAT WAR

THE world-wide crisis of 1914–19 opened a new era for those countries, led them into intimate diplomatic relations with European powers, gave them a fuller national consciousness, assigned them their due place in the family of nations and brought general recognition of their weight in the volume of human affairs. For a generation past Latin America had claimed increasing attention from the outside world. Extension of steam navigation, building of railways, machinery applied to agriculture, influx of immigrants from southern Europe and of capital from northern Europe, growing demand in Europe for foodstuffs and raw materials—all these things favoured, particularly in the south temperate zone, a rapid economic development which may be roughly dated from the 'seventies. The outstanding fact in the recent history of Latin America and in her relation to the War is this creation of new wealth. The Pampa had become one of the chief granaries of the world; and Buenos Aires, the greatest city of the southern hemisphere, was the centre of a railway system almost equal in extent to that of the United Kingdom. Chile had been enriched by nitrate and copper, Brazil by rubber and coffee, and Mexico, somewhat later, by petroleum. The High Andes had become once more a treasure-house of mineral wealth: tropical hills, valleys and coastal plains had been made to yield the riches of their vegetable products.

Twenty years ago an American historian remarked that Europe and the United States had lately rediscovered Latin America. Early in the present century that rediscovery brought a closer approach—intellectual, social and political—on the part of the United States towards Latin America, through the teaching of Latin-American history in American Universities; scholarships in those Universities for Latin-American students; increasing study of the Spanish language; scientific and educational missions; the publication of books and magazines dealing with those lands. In 1906 the Comité France-Amérique was founded in France under the presidency of M. Gabriel Hanotaux in order to develop economic, intellectual and artistic relations between France and the nations of the New World.[1] Among its activities are the monthly review *France-Amérique* and the 'American Week', celebrated annually in some great French city. The same year, 1906, brought the foundation of the *Groupement des Universités et grandes Écoles de France pour les relations avec L'Amérique Latine*, an institution whose title indicates its aims.

Meantime, although, as a German author remarked, the British had made no cultural effort in Latin America, British intercourse with those lands had vastly increased and had contributed much to their economic growth and something to their habits of life. Germany too, and especially Hamburg, sedulously and successfully cultivated closer relations with them; and many Germans were employed in scientific institutions, in 'normal schools' (training-colleges for teachers) and in the training of troops. The Atlantic lands had received from Italy and from the Peninsula a great stream of immigration, and more recently a lesser stream from the Levant and from Central Europe.

A notable event was the invitation to the Latin-American republics to attend the second Peace Conference held at the Hague in 1907. Their representatives brought with them something of a revelation by their intellectual qualities, their grasp of the matters under discussion and their ready facility of expository speech, besides those social and conversational graces which find favour in diplomatic circles.

Thus the earlier attitude of uninformed and sometimes half-contemptuous indifference, widely prevalent in the outside world towards those countries, had already been modified when the Great War brought them within the orbit of international life.

Latin America, producing foodstuffs and raw materials, had hitherto acquiesced in economic dependence on Europe. European immigration (at least on the east coast), Government loans raised in Europe, provision of public utilities by European capital, importation of almost all manufactured articles from abroad: these

[1] These include all North America. But the Comité France-Amérique concerns itself mainly with Latin America and French Canada.

had been to most Latin Americans the accepted conditions of life. The outbreak of war was a sharp shock. The supply of European capital suddenly ceased: so also the stream of immigration. Scarcity of shipping and the diversion to war purposes of all European energies diminished the exportation from South America of all commodities not absolutely needed by the allies for the prosecution of the war. Imports from Europe fell. Germany, which had ranked third among outside nations trading with those lands, dropped out altogether, except for some devious and struggling efforts. What had seemed the natural order of things suddenly broke down. Those lands were thrown upon their own resources, obliged to provide their own labour, to furnish for themselves or do without things hitherto imported from Europe[1] and, until American capital was forthcoming, to manage their finances without foreign aid.

The first shock gave way gradually to a surprising economic recovery, not everywhere equal nor equally prompt in arrival. But in general, imports diminished, whereas the urgent demands of the allies for foodstuffs and raw materials produced in most of the States a great expansion in the value of exports, a favourable trade balance and a temporary increase of wealth. Hence arose, particularly in the A. B. C. countries,[2] an industrial effort to supply, by using home products and developing home manufactures, the needs hitherto supplied by imports. Moreover, while thus strengthening their own internal structure, these republics were also drawn closer together, and felt themselves more than ever to constitute a world in themselves. Owing to the interruption of the customary paths of commerce, the small existing trade between the Latin-American republics gained increase.

Upon the outbreak of the European War in August 1914 most of the Latin-American governments publicly announced neutrality, thereby showing consciousness of their influence in the world order; and some of them announced the rules, mainly based on the Hague Convention of 1907, which were to guide them as neutrals. But most educated people everywhere, except in Mexico,

---

[1] After a time, increasing imports from the United States in some degree provided a remedy.   [2] Argentina, Brazil, Chile.

favoured the allied cause, being moved by sympathy for France, which was revered, particularly in Brazil, as the pattern and guide of Latin civilization; and the entry of Italy into the War brought a fresh wave of pro-ally sentiment owing to the large population of Italian origin in the River Plate and in southern Brazil. Naturally there was everywhere a Germanophil minority, admirers of German science and education and of German thoroughness, method and order. In Chile, the country of stability and authority, the pro-German element was strong, particularly among the clergy (hostile to French anti-clericalism) and in the army (trained by Prussian officers) and was probably present in official circles among up-holders of authoritative order.

Chile, owing to the length of her coast-line, her many harbours and her possession of a coalfield on the Pacific coast, came into contact with German maritime activities in the South Pacific during the first six months of the War. The repeated violations of Chilian neutrality by German ships, and German evasions in reply to Chilian protests were damaging to the German cause. Yet the most open violation of Chilian neutrality was committed in March 1915 by two British warships which destroyed the German cruiser *Dresden*, anchored in a Chilian harbour.[1] A protest from Chile elicited a prompt admission of the offence and an apology from the British Foreign Office. Merchant-ships flying the flags of great European nations, most of them German but two of them British ships, were interned by the Chilian Government for violations of Chilian neutrality—a notable exercise of sovereignty.

Except for these incidents on the Pacific coast, these countries were remote from hostilities. But they were the objects of an anxious economic approach on the part of the belligerents and of assiduous courtship by Germany. The elaborate and costly German propaganda treated the favour of Latin America as one of the prizes of war.

But the German himself supplied a more potent counter-argu-

[1] The *Dresden* herself was violating Chilian neutrality by remaining at anchor for several days and refusing to leave when ordered to do so by the port authorities. She was in fact unable to leave for want of coal. Attacked at long range by British fire, the captain of the *Dresden* blew up his ship, to save her from falling into the hands of the enemy.

ment; that is to say the German submarine, the sinking of unarmed South American trading ships and the drowning of South American sailors. The official German announcement in January 1917 of unrestricted submarine warfare and of an extensive blockaded maritime zone brought to these countries unprecedented international problems, and unprecedented manifestations of national dignity. All the important maritime republics, except the pro-German governments of Mexico and of Venezuela, protested to the German Government against this breach of international law. Brazil declared that she would hold Germany responsible for any injury to the persons or property of Brazilians. The protests of Uruguay, Peru, Colombia and Guatemala were equally emphatic.

In February 1917 several republics sent sympathetic replies to the announcement by the United States of her severance of relations with Germany and again in April to her announcement that she had entered the War as a belligerent. In June Brazil revoked her decree of neutrality in the War between the United States and Germany, giving to her foreign policy 'a practical form of continental solidarity'. A few days later Uruguay issued a decree 'that no American country which in defence of its own rights should find itself in a state of war with nations of other continents will be treated as a belligerent'. In October, Brazil, provoked by the sinking of four unarmed Brazilian ships, entered the War as a belligerent, recognizing 'the state of war initiated by the German Government'. The Brazilian notification of this act to the neighbouring republics evoked cordial replies. In the same month Peru, impelled by the sinking of a Peruvian vessel and by unsatisfactory German explanations, severed relations. Bolivia had already severed relations, and a few months later (December 1917) Ecuador did the same, both these republics being moved to that action by maritime outrages and by nugatory German replies to their protests.

But more important than belligerent or political action was the economic aid furnished to the allies by those lands, including those which remained neutral. Exports from South America were a telling factor in the struggle. Nitrate and copper from the Pacific States supplied munitions. Corn, meat, and wool from the Pampa fed and clothed the allied armies. Brazil sent rubber and manganese, besides foodstuffs. This does not mean that neutral traders generally favoured one side. Had the path of commerce to Central Europe been open, neutrals would rightly have dealt with all belligerents: indeed during the War German firms bought much Argentine wool to await opportunity of transport to Europe. Yet the Argentine Government gave valuable economic aid to the allies: Uruguay, in severing diplomatic relations with the Central Powers, took the unusual course of severing commercial relations also; and both Uruguay and Peru, after severance of relations, aided the allies by granting to the United States the use of the German ships anchored in their ports.

Argentina demands special mention. In the first half of 1917 German submarines sank three Argentine ships. In response to protests, the German Government, rather than risk a rupture with the most powerful of the Spanish-American republics and the most important for German trade, made full apology, reparation and promises for the future—a German concession unexampled in the history of the War and a recognition by Germany of the high international status of the Republic.[1]

In September 1917 two dispatches from Count Luxburg, the German Minister in Buenos Aires, became known in which he had advised his Government to spare Argentine ships, or to 'sink them without trace'. Luxburg received his passports as a *persona non grata* to the Argentine Government; but there was no rupture. The German Government disavowed the actions of its Minister. Accordingly, in spite of popular mass meetings and resolutions of Congress demanding rupture of relations, the President (the person who really rules) maintained amicable relations with the Central Powers throughout. Irigoyen made two attempts to convene in Buenos Aires a conference of neutral Latin-American republics, attempts which led to nothing but the arrival of a Mexican mission in Buenos Aires. But Irigoyen was no pro-German. An American fleet visiting Buenos Aires in 1917 and a British diplomatic mission in 1918 received not only an enthusiastic popular ovation but also

[1] Professor P. A. Martin finds reason to think that, while Germany promised to spare Argentine ships, President Irigoyen made a secret promise to Germany that Argentine ships should not enter the zone barred by Germany. But ostensibly Irigoyen's diplomatic victory was complete.

warm official welcome. A more solid proof was the grant by the
Argentine Government of a large loan or credit to the British and
French Governments for the purchase of Argentine cereals and
other products. Uruguay also granted a large credit to the allied
powers for the purchase of her agricultural and pastoral products.
These grants were a notable episode in the Great War and a
damaging blow to Central Europe.

At the end of 1917 only five of the ten South American republics
maintained neutrality; but, except in the case of Venezuela, where
the Gómez Government was pro-German throughout, it was on
the whole a neutrality benevolent towards the allies—a concept
said to be novel in the history of international relations, but in this
case a very real one.

From October 1917 there was one South American belligerent,
Brazil. The first need was internal, to ensure the loyal citizenship
of the southern German-speaking population, estimated at 400,000
and possessing German schools, churches and newspapers. Imperial
German designs had held in view this possible transatlantic Deutsch-
thum; and the Brazilian Government now took decisive measures
that these people, most of them Brazilian-born, should adopt the
Portuguese language and be thoroughly Brazilian. The forty-six
German vessels anchored in Brazilian harbours were placed at the
disposal of the allies. The Brazilian navy was soon co-operating
with the United States squadron in patrolling the Atlantic coast
of South America. Early in 1918 Brazil accepted an invitation
from Great Britain to send a fleet of cruisers and destroyers to act
under the direction of the British admiralty. For nine months this
Brazilian fleet served off the coast of Africa. It was then transferred
to the Mediterranean but only reached Gibraltar on the eve of the
Armistice (10 November 1918).

The attitude of the Antillean and Caribbean republics evidently
depended on that of the United States. Panamá was in effect a
dependency of the United States: Cuba was under her tutelage:
American marines were keeping order in Nicaragua: Haiti from
1916 was 'a ward of the United States',[1] kept in order by American
magistrates and marines: and in the same year the United States

[1] The quotation is from P. A. Martin.

'assumed entire control'[1] of the Dominican Republic. In April 1917 Panamá and Cuba followed the United States into the War as belligerents. A year later Haiti and Nicaragua took the same course. Honduras followed, officially expressing conformity with United States policy. The Guatemala tyrant Cabrera severed relations, speaking of 'continental solidarity...and the bonds...existing between the United States and Guatemala', probably hoping to strengthen his Government by standing well with the United States, to secure himself against possible aggression from Mexico—always an uncomfortable neighbour—and to seize the extensive coffee estates which Germans had acquired by advancing money on mortgage to careless Guatemalan owners and then foreclosing. Lastly President Tinoco of Nicaragua, who had seized his post by a *coup d'état* in January 1917 and had not been recognized by the United States nor by any European Power except Germany, declared war against Germany in May 1918, hoping thereby to strengthen his Government and win recognition—a hope which was disappointed. Santo Domingo was in a peculiar position, having at the time no national government: but the country certainly had no relations with Germany, and the United States administration of Santo Domingo withdrew the *exequatur* of German consuls, thereby severing commercial relations.[2]

Thus of the Caribbean republics Salvador alone remained neutral, being more remote from the struggle than her four Central American neighbours and also more remote from contact with the United States: but to the United States' announcement of belligerency with Germany, Salvador replied with a message of sympathy to the Government and people of the United States and later promised 'friendly or benevolent neutrality' and offered the use of her harbours to the allies. Obviously four of the seven Caribbean belligerents entered the war as satellites of the United States and the other three as lying under her shadow. But it would be a mistake to regard these declarations as merely pygmaean bellicose

[1] The quotation is from P. A. Martin.

[2] The present writer in the summer of 1918 wrote to the Dominican Consul in London asking whether Santo Domingo was at war with Germany. The Consul, unable to reply, referred the question to the Dominican Consul-general in Paris. The latter official finally wrote that he did not know whether the Dominican Republic was at war or not.

gestures or as nothing more than (what in part they were) discreet acts of national self-assertion. Panamá, traversed by the Canal Zone, lay within the belligerent area and could not escape belligerent status. The adhesion of Cuba, with her long coast-line and her many excellent harbours, was valuable to the United States: the suppression of German spies or agents in the island and of communications with Germany was a blow to German efforts. Much more valuable were the gift to the United States of the German ships in Cuban harbours and the sale to the United States of the Cuban sugar crop on favourable terms. Cuba also gave generous aid to the Red Cross in France. A curious incident was the rupture of diplomatic relations with Cuba by Mexico in May 1918: evidently a clumsy pro-German and anti-United States move by President Carranza.

The other Central American and Antillean declarations of war, although they did not mean active hostilities, were in each case an economic blow to Germany and also a moral blow. For each declaration meant confidence in allied victory. These little governments would hardly have declared war but for certainty of being on the safe side.

The final position of the Latin-American States may thus be summarized.

Eight republics declared war with Germany: Brazil, Costa Rica, Cuba, Guatemala, Haiti, Honduras, Nicaragua, Panamá.

Uruguay declared that no American country defending itself against a nation of another continent would be treated as a belligerent, broke off diplomatic and commercial relations with Germany, offered the use of her ports to the warships of the allies and leased the German ships at Montevideo to the United States.

Peru broke off diplomatic relations with Germany, offered the use of her ports to the allies and handed over to the United States the German ships at Callao.

Bolivia and Ecuador severed relations with Germany. Relations between the Dominican Republic and Germany were also severed in peculiar circumstances, already explained.

Seven republics, Argentina, Chile, Colombia, Mexico, Paraguay,

Salvador, Venezuela, maintained their neutrality and their diplomatic relations with all the belligerents.

With the exception of Costa Rica, all the republics which had declared war or severed relations with Germany signed the Treaty of Versailles and thereby became members of the League of Nations. The States which had remained neutral were, with the exception of Mexico, invited to join the League and accepted the invitation.

NOTE. This chapter is mainly based on P. A. Martin, *Latin America and the War* (Baltimore, U.S.A., 1925); F. A. Kirkpatrick, *South America and the War* (Cambridge, 1918) was written before the Armistice; *The Times History of the War* is useful.

CHAPTER XXXIII

NORTH AND SOUTH

The States of America...a unit in world affairs, spiritual partners, standing together because thinking together, quick with common sympathies and common ideals.   WOODROW WILSON

Cultural incompatibility.   S. F. BEMIS

Two movements mentioned in the preceding chapters claim some exposition; *Americanismo*, a natural effort towards a family understanding between Latin Americans; and Pan-Americanism, a more artificial and more comprehensive system in which the United States hold the central seat.

Americanismo, a certain feeling of common patriotism, underlies the record of disputes, jealousies and needless geographical fissures. A Colombian and an Argentine, meeting abroad, although their homes are in effect more remote from one another than each from Europe, are not quite foreigners to one another, since both are *americanos*, speaking the same language, inheriting, in a broad sense, the same traditions and remembering united action in the War of Independence. The Peruvian Santos Chocano is the poet laureate of all Spanish America. Rubén Darío, Nicaraguan by birth, was at home in Chile and in Argentina—both of them sung by him in enthusiastic strains—and wherever men spoke the Castilian language. During the tyranny of Rosas, Argentine *émigrés* took part in the public life of Chile and practised at the Chilian bar. Sáenz Peña, President of Argentina (1910–13), was a general in the Peruvian army. Lesser incidents of this kind are so frequent as to escape notice. This Hispanic sentiment was fed by apprehensions concerning the 'Colossus of the North', by the Mexican War, by Walker's Nicaraguan adventure, by more recent American action in Panamá and in the Antilles, and by indignant sympathy over the well-meant but unwelcome attempt (now modified) to Americanize Puerto Rico, suppressing Hispanic culture in favour of alien ways and substituting English for the Castilian tongue.

The preceding chapter notes how the conditions of the Great War promoted this movement. Improved communications tend the same way. During the present century and particularly since 1914—notwithstanding one destructive war and recurrent jealousies between conterminous states—*Americanismo* has been not only a growing sentiment but something of a force.

Yet attempts to give tangible form to this force had little result. Bolívar tried it and failed, although his idea has never died. 'In 1831, 1838 and 1840 Mexico took the initiative in calling a new Congress; the countries which received the invitation accepted it with enthusiasm, but the meeting never took place.' So writes Alvarez in words which sound almost like a humorous comment on the whole movement. In 1847–8 the Peruvian Government, alarmed at Flores' Spanish designs, attempted to assemble a Congress at Lima. Envoys came from the five South American Pacific republics and drew up conventions—never ratified by their Governments. In 1856, after the Mexican War and the Nicaraguan filibustering, Chile, Peru and Ecuador signed at Santiago a Continental Treaty, 'disfigured by an obvious hostility towards the United States and Brazil'. The treaty was submitted to the other Spanish republics but was finally dropped. Yet 'all the governments, except that of Argentina, adhered to the central idea and expressed a lively enthusiasm for the formation of a permanent American League'.[1] Again in 1864, at the time of the Spanish occupation of Santo Domingo, the French adventure in Mexico and the recent seizure of the Chincha Islands, seven republics sent envoys to a conference at Lima, who signed conventions—never ratified. In 1877 a congress of jurists from five republics, afterwards joined by others, met at Lima, aiming at some juridical uniformity which might 'promote the South American Confederation': but the Chilian invasion ended the assembly and its conclusions were never ratified. In 1888 four republics sent envoys to a congress at Montevideo to arrange a treaty of private (Latin-American) international law: certain agreements were ratified by some States, but without much result. Thus these various partial assemblies produced nothing solid or permanent: yet they were

[1] Haring.

significant of a feeling for *América nuestra*. That feeling has sometimes shown itself—occasionally in disconcerting fashion—in Pan-
American Conferences and also in the League of Nations, where
the seat of the United States is vacant: and the proffered mediation
of the A. B. C. States in Mexico in 1914 shows that the troubles of
one Latin-American country, even the most remote, were felt to
be the concern of all. But the treaty of peace and alliance between
those three republics, signed in that same year, had the fate of
many earlier Latin-American pacts: it was never ratified by
Argentina. This proposed union between the three principal South
American countries was not welcomed by the smaller republics;
for obviously the *americano* sentiment rejects the predominance of
any State or group of States.

The story of Pan-Americanism demands a backward glance
at that rule or principle or tendency of United States policy
which, some time after Monroe's message, came to be known
as the Monroe Doctrine. To trace here its protean forms is impossible. Its bibliography is enormous: its latest historian, Professor
Dexter Perkins, has devoted three volumes to it, to be followed
by a fourth. Yet some salient points may be mentioned. When
Salvador in 1919 requested a definition of the Monroe Doctrine
(which had received a qualified and ambiguous recognition in the
Covenant of the League of Nations) Secretary Lansing, after some
delay, referred the applicant to President Wilson's address at the
second Pan-American Scientific Congress in 1916. That address
opens with the words: 'The Monroe Doctrine was proclaimed by
the United States on her own authority. It always has been
maintained and always will be maintained upon her own responsibility.... The Monroe Doctrine demanded merely that European
Governments should not attempt to extend their political systems
to this side of the Atlantic.'[1] Two years earlier Mr Elihu Root
said: 'Since the Monroe Doctrine is a declaration based upon this

---

[1] The rest of the speech, leaving the Monroe Doctrine intact, advocates union
to secure 'political independence and territorial integrity...international peace
...and domestic peace'; in fact a Pan-American scheme more comprehensive
than anything proposed later; since it seems to contemplate some method of
Pan-American interposition or pressure in the domestic affairs of an erring
member.

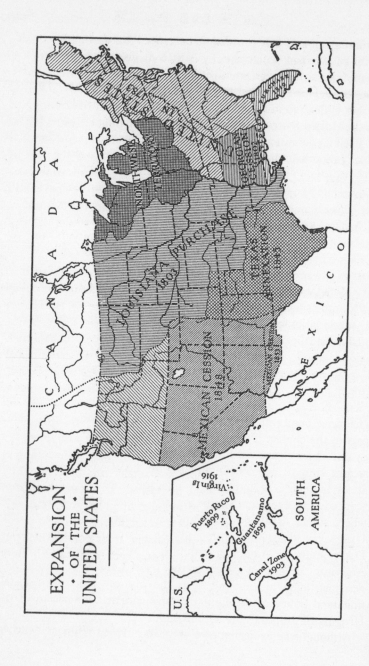

EXPANSION
· OF THE ·
UNITED STATES

CANADA

OREGON (JOINT OCCUPATION)

NORTHWEST TERRITORY

LOUISIANA PURCHASE
1803

TEXAS ANNEXATION
1845

MEXICAN CESSION
1848

MEXICAN CESSION 1853

MEXICO

U.S.

Virgin Is. 1916

Puerto Rico 1899

Guantanamo 1899

Canal Zone 1903

SOUTH AMERICA

nation's right of self-protection, it cannot be transmuted into a joint or common declaration by American states or any number of them.' In 1923 Secretary of State Hughes—now Chief Justice of the United States—declared in his centenary address: 'As the policy embodied in the Monroe Doctrine is distinctively the policy of the United States, the Government of the United States reserves to itself its definition, interpretation and application': words which clearly repudiate the strangely inaccurate description of the Monroe Doctrine as a 'regional understanding' in the League of Nations Covenant. 'It is a policy of self-defence', he continues, '...it still remains an assertion of the principle of national security.'

Monroe's message was (in Wilson's words) 'a hand held up in warning to Europe' in the discreet form of a domestic message to Congress. The position of the Latin-American republics in the matter has been purely passive, as is proved by the failure of their occasional endeavours to turn it into action. For within two years of Monroe's message Colombia, Brazil and Mexico severally applied to Washington for alliance or aid. The replies made it clear that no pledge had been given and that Congress alone could authorize action. And in 1826 Victoria, President of Mexico, told his Parliament that 'The memorable promise of President Monroe [there was no promise!]...is disclaimed by the present Government of the United States....We have no longer any sort of guarantee or promise, on the part of that Government, to take a part in the contest if a third power should become an auxiliary of Spain.' The bitter disillusionment of a Chilian emissary who sought support in Washington on the occasion of the Spanish attack in 1866 is perhaps hardly relevant, since the United States 'conceded to every nation the right to make peace or war'. But when at the Santiago Pan-American Conference of 1923 the Uruguayan delegation proposed the extension of the Monroe Doctrine to all American republics and the foundation of an American League of Nations, the United States representative was instructed to announce that the Monroe Doctrine was the unilateral policy of the United States and that discussion of the Uruguayan proposal was inadmissible.

Although the exclusion of European political influence and the

'Doctrine of the Two Spheres' have been guiding principles of American policy, nevertheless the United States, like every other nation—as a matter of common sense and expediency—have treated every question of foreign policy, as it arose, on its merits without excessive attention to abstract theory. To discuss whether each decision—a practical decision dictated by circumstances— conformed to a doctrine may seem to be merely unprofitable academic debate about the meaning of words. But this is not so; for the question affects the opinion of Latin Americans and even the disposition of governments towards the United States. Since American statesmen have been at pains to interpret their policy in terms of doctrinal orthodoxy, and since development of doctrine is a familiar concept, it is hardly strange that many Latin Americans —and many Yankees too, as Dr W. S. Robertson notes with regret —mistakenly regard the Monroe Doctrine as embracing the whole of American policy concerning the Western Hemisphere. Official opinion, being unasked, has usually been mute, except when silence might have been misinterpreted, or on the few occasions when the Monroe Doctrine has been invoked in Latin-American appeals to Washington. But the Brazilian Federal Senate-house significantly bears the name of Monroe, and the Brazilian delegates to the fourth Pan-American Conference at Buenos Aires in 1910 suggested to the Argentine and Chilian delegates that a unanimous expression of thanks from the Latin-American delegations (Bolivia being unrepresented) should be offered to the United States for the benefits conferred by the Monroe Doctrine. The Chilian delegation drew up a less precise and more non-committal resolu- tion, substituting for the words 'Monroe Doctrine' the phrase 'the declarations contained in the message of President Monroe'. But other delegations, being sounded in turn, suggested reservations and qualifications or talked of 'hegemony', and it was clear that neither that nor any form of words would win unanimity. Accord- ingly the proposal was not brought before the assembly. One must not exaggerate the significance of the natural and reasonable refusal by other delegations to endorse the all-embracing and unqualified approbation—proposed, perhaps indiscreetly, by Brazil—of every- thing that might be implied in the term 'Monroe Doctrine'. But the omission of those words in the substitute resolution, drafted by the Chilian delegation, is noticeable. And the whole incident, related by Alvarez, one of the Chilian delegates (p. 183), shows considerable differences of official opinion.

Semi-official and non-official Latin American judgments of the Monroe Doctrine have also varied. But the loudest opinion—perhaps because fault-finding is easy and assent or acquiescence is often silent—points to the map of North American expansion southward, and regards the Doctrine as a specious cover for aggression or hegemony. A recent semi-official history of Mexico declares that 'The Monroe Doctrine at birth was an act opposing European imperialism; but it even then rested on a foundation of American imperialism and of pride.' The chief contemporary spokesmen of this view are the Venezuelan Blanco-Fombona, the Mexican Carlos Pereyra and the Argentine Ugarte, whose book *The Destiny of the Continent* has been translated into English, with introductory comments, by Rippy.[1]

American historians have noted with some chagrin that the sensitive pride of Latin Americans and of their Governments has been hurt by other irritants; by patronizing, didactic and even admonitory tones sometimes emanating from Washington, simultaneous with warm professions of amity and esteem for 'sister republics' on a basis of complete equality; by partisan diplomatic appointments not always made with due regard to susceptibilities; by the occasional arrogance or indiscretion of American representatives and by unofficial incidents, noted by Haring in his book *Latin America looks at the United States*. In Uruguay and in Brazil—both always disposed to dissent from Argentine views—opinion, or at all events official opinion, has generally been friendly to the United States.

The 'no-transfer corollary' of the Doctrine, with its 'no-grant'

[1] A remark of Gil Fortoul (who treats the Monroe Doctrine with sarcastic scorn) may give pause to European critics of 'Monroism'. He observes that the United States and the European powers have one method of treating one another and other methods (respectively) of treating the peoples of Asia, those of Africa and those of Latin America. Thus he brands Europe and North America with the same stigma—with a good deal of truth. But it may be asked whether it would have been possible to give the same treatment (for example) to the Government of his countryman Castro, as to the Chanceries of Washington, or Paris, or London.

addition, has provoked singularly little observation, probably
because Latin Americans are not theoretical logicians and, since
the Spanish reoccupation of Santo Domingo, no concrete instance
has brought the rule into force. But it has not passed unnoticed.
The late Señor Pérez Triana, Colombian diplomatist and political
author—who recognized the benefits of the Pan-American Conferences and was by no means an indiscriminate Yankeephobe—
exclaimed with vehemence to the present writer: 'The Latin-
American Republics are not independent', explaining that they
were deprived of the sovereign right of ceding territory at their
own will. Root in 1914 states the case plainly, declaring that this
corollary asserts 'the same right of self-protection against the other
American states as well as against Europe': and Hughes in 1923
declared that the Doctrine 'embraces opposition to acquisition of
additional territory through transfer of dominion or sovereignty',
and he summarizes the Doctrine as being opposed (1) 'to any
non-American action encroaching upon the political independence
of American States under any guise, and (2) to the acquisition in
any manner of the control of additional territory in this hemisphere
by any non-American power'; although in the same address he
affirms 'the perfect equality of nations....It results from this
equality that no one can rightfully impose a rule upon another.'

The two vulnerable points of the Monroe Doctrine are that it is
announced by one power alone and that, although it has aimed at
protecting the American republics from European aggression, it
has not protected them from American aggression: it has not
defended Peru from Chile, nor Mexico and Colombia from the
United States. Pan-Americanism, especially in its most recent
phase, proposes to remedy the latter of these defects and possibly
(a more difficult matter) the former also.

'The prime motive' for the first inter-American Conference—
which met at Washington in 1889 and held sessions spread over
six months—'was the expansion of the commerce of the United
States...the achievements were most meagre.'[1] But the convening
of the assembly itself was a signal achievement: the United States

[1] S. F. Bemis, p. 738. The first six weeks were spent in a tour to industrial
centres in the United States.

had done at once a thing which Latin Americans had repeatedly essayed in vain; and a 'Bureau of American Republics' was set up at Washington. The succeeding conferences at Mexico in 1901, at Rio in 1906, at Buenos Aires in 1910 'accomplished very little of vital importance': but in 1910 the Bureau at Washington became the 'Pan-American Union', housed in a magnificent palace at Washington and providing continuity to the still incipient Pan-American movement.

Six years later, in 1916, the 'International High Commission' was created, a permanent body to carry on the commercial side of the movement. After the interruption of the Great War the fifth Pan-American Conference met at Santiago in 1923; three states, Mexico, Peru and Bolivia being unrepresented. An agreement, 'the Gondra Convention', was reached that future disputes between American states should be submitted, before any open breach, to a commission of enquiry, with limited powers. The sixth Conference at Havana in 1928—which was addressed by President Coolidge — showed uneasiness among the smaller States in regard to their big neighbour. Vital political questions were discreetly avoided: but relations became more cordial in the course of the sessions: it was agreed that Latin-American members should have a larger share in the work of the Union and that a Conference on Conciliation and Arbitration should be held. This Conference met at Washington in 1929 and drew up a scheme of compulsory arbitration (with certain limitations) which was later accepted by most of the republics: a definite and tangible result, for most of the resolutions of previous conferences had been rather recommendations to governments than positive conclusions.

In these Conferences the United States and Latin America were aiming at different things. Latin America, especially the smaller peoples, wanted security, whereas the aims of the United States were economic. They were sincerely anxious to promote peace among the republics, to promote their welfare and to further domestic peace within them severally. But concurrently with this benevolent amity, their national aim was economic.

The benefits of these assemblies are not to be measured merely by results that can be tabulated and catalogued. It was a great thing that men should be brought together from countries having much in common yet remote and almost unknown to one another— so remote that a Colombian diplomatist lecturing in London in 1917 remarked that, in the rare event of a Colombian having occasion to visit Buenos Aires, he would probably visit London on the way. As always in such cases, informal intercourse outside the council chamber counted for much. Moreover a multitude of non-political meetings for special purposes brought the American republics into consultation in various capital cities. Rippy counts nearly sixty such meetings before 1932; and several have followed since: conferences on sanitation, child welfare, the Red Cross, commerce, finance, education, journalism, scientific problems and various matters connected with communication and intercourse.

The seventh of the great Conferences, held at Montevideo in 1933, opens a new era in the relations between north and south. The end of interventions in the Caribbean area, the obvious sincerity of President Franklin Roosevelt's 'Good Neighbour' policy and the tactful cordiality of Mr Cordell Hull deeply impressed the Latin Americans, with whom personality counts for much: many resolutions were adopted of social, economic and cultural value, and something was done towards the organization of peace.

Still more remarkable was the special Peace Conference of all the twenty-one American republics held in Buenos Aires in December 1936, in response to personal letters addressed by President Franklin Roosevelt to all the Latin-American Presidents. President Roosevelt, after receiving an enthusiastic welcome and delivering his message of peace and goodwill in Rio and Montevideo, himself addressed the Buenos Aires assembly. After sessions lasting three weeks, three agreements were signed: the first two provide for the maintenance of peace by consultation and co-operation; the third, which forbids all intervention, was greeted by some of the delegates with the exclamation 'there is the end of the Monroe Doctrine'. Much more important than any concrete result was the moral effect, the conciliatory attitude of the United States, which made all the concessions, and the cordial faith in the sincerity of the 'Good Neighbour' policy.

President Justo in his original acceptance of Franklin Roosevelt's invitation declined to admit 'regional distinctions or separation of continents'; and in accepting the peace agreement the Argentine delegates, despite protests from Brazil but not from the Spanish republics, reserved Argentina's obligations to the League of Nations and refused any undertaking (possibly ruinous to Argentine pasture and agriculture) to withhold supplies from belligerents. Thus Argentina, representing a sentiment not merely Argentine, avoids accepting in its entirety the 'Doctrine of the Two Spheres'. Inevitably so, for Argentine contacts with Europe are immensely greater and more essential than with North or Central America. Indeed, the Two Spheres Doctrine does not mean the same thing to Latin America as to the United States. In the latter part of 1936 Brazil severed relations with the Government of Madrid on account of its supposed communist tendencies. The Mexican Government furnished munitions to the Madrid Government, while Guatemala, Nicaragua and Salvador recognized that of Burgos—later Salamanca. Mexico on joining the League of Nations in 1931 and Argentina on renewing active membership in 1932 declared that they did so without recognizing the Monroe Doctrine.

It is an interesting question whether these Pan-American agreements develop and enlarge the Monroe Doctrine, or supersede and abrogate it, or run parallel with it.

The Washington correspondent of *The Times* suggests that the Monroe Doctrine 'has been mutilated' (a thing declared impossible explicitly by Root and Lansing and implicitly by Wilson and Hughes) but that the Isthmian Doctrine—with reference to the Canal—remains. This seems much the same thing as saying that the Monroe Doctrine subsists, but can only find justifiable application in the Caribbean region (where, as Hughes remarks, 'The limited principles of the Monroe Doctrine are not enough'). This has often been said and was stated emphatically by the Argentine statesman Zeballos when ex-President Theodore Roosevelt visited Buenos Aires in 1913. On the other hand, the barring of intervention, 'direct or indirect', if literally interpreted, seems to abrogate the no-transfer and the no-grant corollaries, leaving every American nation free to cede territory to a non-American power or to make grants of any kind to a foreign corporation. It may be argued that, should such an unlikely difficulty occur, it can be solved by the amicable working of diplomacy between equal and sovereign nations. But such an argument condemns as unnecessary the two corollaries, which have been declared by the highest authority to be indispensable. Mr S. F. Bemis, writing before the 1936 Peace Conference but after the Montevideo Conference of 1933 (which almost reached the same conclusions), seems to favour the 'parallel' view, describing Pan-Americanism as a 'complement to the Monroe Doctrine' and quoting Blakeslee's remark that Pan-Americanism is a 'twin policy' to the Monroe Doctrine.

Professor Lockey, the historian of the Beginnings of Pan-Americanism, writing in the *Hispanic-American Historical Review* of August 1935, vigorously asserts the continued vitality of the Monroe Doctrine; just as in 1915 Secretary Lansing said, in agreement with Root and with Hughes: 'The Monroe Doctrine is a national policy of the United States; Pan-Americanism is an international policy of the Americas. Both do exist and, I trust, will ever exist, in all their vigor.' This conclusion—that the Monroe Doctrine is something distinct from Pan-Americanism—seems inevitable if the Monroe Doctrine is to subsist at all. For, whereas Pan-Americanism concerns the relations of American states with one another, the Monroe Doctrine concerns the attitude or policy of the United States towards European and other non-American States. Argentina, without protests from her Spanish-speaking neighbours, declines to commit herself to participate in that policy and reserves complete freedom in her relations with Europe. This does not detract from the notable achievement of the Pan-American movement in furthering peace and goodwill among the American peoples, an achievement to be greeted with unstinted cordiality.

The political or quasi-political Pan-American movement has accompanied and in some degree has aided a vast increase in economic intercourse, which has favoured closer social, intellectual and political intercourse. In the days of sailing-ships the voyage from New York to Pernambuco or Rio or Buenos Aires was longer than from Southampton or Cherbourg. To a steamship the distance

is about equal. But to-day 'Pan-American Airways' carry passengers in four days from New York to Buenos Aires and provide
'dawn to dusk' flights from the southern United States to northern
South America. Yet, though aeroplanes carry passengers and mails
(in itself a great matter) and also some merchandise, the ocean still
furnishes the main highways of commerce and of ordinary intercourse: and such intercourse for the most part still takes the road
to Europe from the River Plate and Southern Brazil. Mr Bemis
writes: 'Before the days of aerial navigation the nations of Hispanic
America, south of the Caribbean fringe, were quite as distinct from
the United States as from Europe. Indeed from the geophysical
point of view Asia and Africa are more closely connected to Europe
than is South America to North America.' Yet the remark, made
twenty years ago, that the two American continents face severally
towards Europe and not towards one another, needs modification
to-day. During the last third of the nineteenth century the United
States, from being mainly a producer of foodstuffs and raw materials,
was becoming an exporter of manufactured goods, seeking markets
to the south, as was made clear in the first Pan-American Conference of 1889. The movement grew during the present century; but
down to the outbreak of the Great War the economic contacts of
South America (apart from Mexico, Central America and the
Antilles) were vastly greater with Europe than with the United
States. The Director of the Pan-American Union pointed out with
some mortification how most of the American delegates to the
Buenos Aires Conference of 1910 found that the most convenient
route from the chief city of North America to the chief city of
South America lay through Europe.

War conditions brought a change. Martin writes: 'In 1913 not
a single vessel entered Buenos Aires flying the United States flag;
in 1919, 335 United States ships entered Argentine ports.' For
the sudden cessation in 1914 of European imports and of European
investment gave to the United States the opportunity which was
utilized to the full during the thirty-two months of American
neutrality. The movement continued: American capital poured
into Latin America and American trade vastly increased. Before
the war there were no American banks in South America; to-day

American banks have branches everywhere. Americans are creditors of Latin America to a huge extent and American corporations vie with those of Europe in developing the resources of these lands. Indeed the rapid growth of American investment and enterprise, although welcomed and sometimes solicited by the people concerned, has caused some disquietude, due partly to a feeling that American business has received more diplomatic support than is customary or desirable; and there has been talk of 'economic imperialism'; a subject which has been expounded by American writers in a series of volumes edited by Mr Harry E. Barnes and is mentioned by Haring (p. 215). The matter is not yet ripe for historical treatment. But the story of British investment in Argentina shows that foreign enterprise need not involve anything of the kind. No more sweeping concession to the foreigner can be quoted than the grant to the Argentine Central Railway Company of a strip of land six miles wide along the whole length of the line; whereby an extent of land greater than the Panamá Canal Zone was given in absolute ownership to a foreign corporation, to the great benefit of the donor and without the slightest derogation of national dignity: and the social influences accompanying British activities have been, on the whole, welcomed in Argentina.

Improved communications have aided the spread of North American commercial and industrial enterprise. The opening of the Panamá Canal in 1914 brought the west coast of North America within an easy voyage of New York and other Atlantic ports. To-day one may travel by an excellent motor road from New York to Mexico City; and before long it is hoped that a highway, overcoming great natural difficulties, may be continued to Panamá. Former projects of a future Pan-American railroad have given place to projects of a Pan-American highway. A plan for such a road—fully stating the immense difficulties and tracing a sea voyage between the two continents as part of the road—appeared in the *Bulletin of the Pan-American Union* for May 1935: and the recent opening of a motor road from Buenos Aires to Rosario, soon to be continued to Córdoba, was greeted as a link in the highway from Washington to Buenos Aires, although it may be questioned whether travellers by that road—or by rail or river—

from Buenos Aires to Rosario are fully aware that they are on the way to Washington.

FORM AND SUBSTANCE

It has become evident in recent times that representative government is not a panacea applicable to all parts of the earth's surface.   BERTRAND RUSSELL

Democracy is wrongly conceived when treated merely as a body of doctrine or simply a form of government. It is a stage of development. It is built up by slow habit. The English alone have approached popular institutions through habit. All other nations have rushed prematurely into them; through mere impatience with habit they have adopted democracy instead of cultivating it.
                                                                        WOODROW WILSON

President Franklin Roosevelt, in addressing the 1936 Conference at Buenos Aires, saluted his hearers as 'united in their common democratic faith'; and Mr Hull in his farewell address urged them to 'guard with a jealous eye democracy, their chosen form of government'. To inculcate virtue by treating its absence as inconceivable is a customary and laudable method of exhortation: but President Roosevelt, addressing his own people after his return home, declared that 'in a very real sense the Conference in Buenos Aires sent forth a message on behalf of all the democracies of the world to those nations who live otherwise'. This remark overlooks the fact that not one of the three Presidents who welcomed the speaker in Rio, Montevideo and Buenos Aires, held office through the normal working of constitutions: political arrests were filling Brazilian gaols under a dictatorship which was soon to throw off the thin disguise of a 'State of War': of the twenty Latin-American heads of State nine were generals, not counting the Cuban Colonel Batista; indeed the soldiers who ruled in Paraguay, Bolivia, Peru, Cuba and Santo Domingo, so far from offering a lesson to reactionary European leaders, seem to have taken a hint from Rome. A French writer recently remarked epigrammatically that Latin America has invented monarchy without a crown.

García Calderón in an article published in 1929, supplementary to his often-quoted book, notes two Latin-American tendencies in the present century; Indianism (active in Mexico but elsewhere rather to be sought in the realm of ideas or good intentions); and 'a clearly defined tendency towards dictatorship as a method of government'. Despite the Venezuelan change of administration, the passage of nine years since he wrote does not gainsay the observation, at all events in tropical America. But the words 'method of government' imply something different from the rule of the caudillos who once fought for power; the words suggest the acceptance of autocracy not as an accidental episode but as a system to facilitate legislation and administration and to ensure the progress and well-being which depends on discipline, peace and order; an intensely national system which owes much to recent European example but also recalls the nationalist and efficient rule of Francia and Rosas without (it is to be hoped) their exaggerations, caprices and needless cruelty. At all events Trujillo is better than Heureux, Benavides than Leguía and Batista than Machado. Throughout their history, both in Spanish days and later, Latin Americans, although they have seldom loved any government, have understood and esteemed strong personal rule unless intolerably oppressive.

Their methods, unless they outrage civilization (as formerly in Haiti and Santo Domingo), seem to be their own affair. Whether or not it be true that democracy of a certain type is universally applicable because intrinsically desirable, it seems much to expect of Latin Americans that they should adopt the ways of other people. And in fact President Franklin Roosevelt, by addressing personal letters to all Latin-American Presidents, without regard to the source of their authority, and by meeting their delegates at Buenos Aires, showed that Washington now observes the customary rule of amicable relations with all *de facto* governments which can fulfil the ordinary international obligations of a State.

In mentioning the relations of North and South, a word is due to the abundant and excellent work of United States Universities and scholars in the study and exposition of Latin-American history, work to which the present volume is indebted at every turn. The work is promoted by the foundation of many professorial chairs of Latin-American history, and by libraries—such as cannot be found in Europe or even in the Hispanic lands—devoted to Latin-American literature and history. In this way the academic and historical world of the United States renders a real service to their southern neighbours.

NOTE. A bewildering number of books might be mentioned. It seems best to refer the reader to the list on p. 98, and to add only three names: D. Perkins, *The Monroe Doctrine*, 1826–67 (Baltimore, U.S.A., 1933); *The Monroe Doctrine*, 1867–1907 (Baltimore, 1937) and S. F. Bemis, *A Diplomatic History of the United States* (New York, 1936). Wilgus, pp. 624–8, and Rippy, pp. 552–3, name many books concerning these matters.

CHAPTER XXXIV

THE LATIN AMERICANS

It is impossible to determine with exactitude to what human family we belong.
BOLÍVAR.

LATIN-AMERICAN writers in successive generations have acclaimed their immense cultural and intellectual debt to France. In the cities—hardly so in rural parts—the influence meets one everywhere: bookshops full of French works; a branch of the *Comité France-Amérique* in every capital; French professors exchanging chairs with Latin Americans; eminent French lecturers carrying the torch of French culture through a dozen lands. Paris always entertains a multitude of Latin-American visitors, besides many permanent residents. García Calderón, who lives in Paris and wrote his book in French, declares: 'These republics have lived by the light of French ideas.... France has effected a spiritual conquest of these democracies.' Yet he adds: 'The Spanish heredity survives, deep-rooted and secular. The democracies of South America, then, are Spanish, although the *élite* has always been inspired by French ideas.'

This deep-rooted Spanish character pervades life; in the unceasing watch on unmarried girls and the domestic seclusion of married women; in the Andalucian forms of courtship, amusing to a foreigner in their dilatory formalities; in the daily *tertulia* which turns every barber's and chemist's shop into a club; in easy indifference to punctuality or to hours of sleep and meals; in the patriarchal household, where servants often dwell as intimate friends through successive generations; in the clan-like agglomerations of relatives and in-laws, an esoteric world of common help and favour, more admirable socially than politically; as Madariaga says of Spain in his book *Englishmen, Frenchmen, Spaniards*: 'The family first, then friends, then the State.' Many of Keyserling's remarks on the Latin American and Madariaga's remarks on the Spaniard might almost be interchanged. From New Mexico to Chile, infants are lulled to sleep with the traditional airs and words of fifteenth-century ballads about the loves and wars of Christian and Moor. The Argentine gaucho improvising *décimas* to the guitar (or the concertina) in high falsetto tones, the Mexican Indian chanting in rude camp-fire rhymes the exploits of Villa or Zapata, are heirs of old Spain, whatever their parentage or complexion; and the prevalence of the Andalucian type of feminine beauty is remarkable.

The proverb 'Europe ends at the Pyrenees' sums up the most notable resemblance. The traveller from the north, on first entering the Peninsula or its daughter lands, breathes a novel atmosphere. There is something inconsequential in all that passes; cause and effect do not seem to work; motives do not seem to matter. Richard Ford remarked nearly a century ago: 'Everything in Spain happens by accident'; which means that action springs from impulse rather than from thought. The effect is a little disconcerting until familiarity brings understanding. Perhaps the Oriental tinge, which touches the Hispanic lands in both Hemispheres, is here discernible.

No one would impute to Latin Americans French logic or the precision and clarity of French prose. Latin Americans (like Peninsulares) delight in floods of sonorous and even incoherent oratory. Dr Coester, the historian of Spanish-American literature, puts it kindly: 'The rhythmic flow of their vocalic language excites in them an aesthetical emotion incomprehensible to people of other races.'

The Latin Americans who flock to *La Ville Lumière* would be bored by the true France of country town, hamlet and farm; the country where 'saving is almost a religious rite'. The Latin American delights in spending a fortune and, when all is gone, lives contentedly on his daily *puchero* and brings into the world a string of children with happy indifference about their future. A recent acute observer, after describing the material Americanization of Buenos Aires and the modern embellishments of Montevideo, remarks that private life in both countries is Spanish.[1] Cunninghame Graham, who knew Spain as well as most Spaniards and Uruguay better than most Uruguayans, declares: 'Montevideo is

[1] R. Forbes, *Eight Republics in Search of a Future* (London, 1933).

Spanish to the core.' This is the more remarkable in view of the large immigration into Uruguay of Italians and of French Basques in former days. The Spanish essence is predominant and pervasive. The Latin American—often bearing an Italian patronymic—who talks with humorous affection of Creole ways is unconsciously eulogizing his Spanish heritage. A Spanish naval officer once remarked to the present writer—not with any patriotic intent but in casual after-dinner talk at a Galician inn—what a pleasure it was to cruise among American (i.e. Latin American) ports, hearing everywhere his own language and finding himself everywhere at home. For the Spaniard, on stepping ashore, finds at once, in the streets, the cafés and the barbers' shops, that easy and familiar freemasonry which prevails wherever the Castilian tongue is spoken. And the student of Peninsular history in the nineteenth century is following no strange paths in tracing the history of the daughter lands. All this simply means that these countries of Hispanic origin possess and preserve a fundamental character of their own, admitting external influences but maintaining its native strength. This is not to deny the immense influence of France, so often gratefully acknowledged by Latin Americans. That influence must be heartily reaffirmed. But those countries are not Gallicized by learning much from France, just as they are not Americanized by copying the United States Constitution or Anglicized by football, golf and boy-scouting, or Germanized by German lessons in science, pedagogy and the art of war. Much more might be said of the influence of these three countries.

Candour compels brief mention of one topic: what Keyserling calls (with a touch of picturesque exaggeration) 'the extreme Don-Juanism of South American man'. The many illegitimate births—said to vary from 40 to 60 per cent. in different republics—need not in themselves imply excessive indulgence, since neglect of the marriage ceremony (often to avoid trouble and expense) does not preclude faithful lifelong unions. Besides, the figures include many semi-pagan tropical Indians. But, even so, the high proportion is significant. Those who read Spanish may find Latin-American sentiment and custom in such matters reflected in Latin-American novels, with allowance for novelistic exaggeration. Here also Spain supplies illustration: for example in the phases of Spanish life depicted by Pérez de Ayala in *Troteras y Danzaderas*.

The European sojourner in those lands—a more materialist world than that of his home—finds no basis for Latin-American talk of idealism, assumed to be something finer than supposed Yanqui' materialism and dollar-worship. The spiritual influence of the Roman Church is not widely conspicuous. 'Civilization' to the Latin American is apt to mean not the art of living in organized civic communities, but modern material conveniences borrowed from abroad. Nor from contact—largely monetary and commercial —with the Old World has Latin America always got the best that the Old World can give. Treasures of Peninsular, and generally of European, literature and art are found not among the palaces of Buenos Aires or Rio or Mexico City but among the 'Yanquis' in New York and California. Latin-American historians—usually with a local rather than an universal outlook—and Latin-American scholars have done and are doing admirable and disinterested work: but nothing even remotely comparable to the flow of scientific, historical and critical work from United States Universities. Literature would seem to be the vehicle of idealism, not merely in exhortations like that of the Uruguayan Rodó, but in the spirit and essence of poetry: and much of the most admired Latin-American poetry is versified rhetoric. If an ideal means not merely something fine to talk about but the best object of desire and action, possibly not fully attainable but kept in sight as a guide to conduct, then idealism is hardly a prominent Latin-American trait. Yet the fervent and even exaggerated cult of *La patria* supplies something impersonal, something resembling a religious sentiment. Moreover, the ideal of disinterested public service is commoner than it used to be and distinguishes, at least in some degree, present-day dictatorships from those of the past.

In one vital matter the Latin American is an enemy to materialism, that is to say in the happy unconscious philosophy which knows how to enjoy passively mere existence, is not wearied by idleness, does not worship success, prefers a kindly sociable leisure even to bodily comfort, and loves—even in official and commercial transactions— certain slow courtesies, sometimes tedious to the busy foreigner.

To generalize about Latin-American culture is impossible. The most polished and cultivated Latin Americans often belong to countries where the illiterate masses live in a totally different and sometimes unenviable world. But every capital contains a leisured aristocracy, well-groomed, pleasant in speech and manner, preferring to more active occupations the truly human recreations of conversation and informal intercourse. In every capital there is a prolific and usually well-written newspaper press, and also an output of literature which—even though little of it has a universal appeal—bespeaks considerable intellectual activity. The portraits which appear in the monthly *Bulletin of the Pan-American Union* and in the Parisian weekly *L'Amérique Latine* indicate that among the prominent men of the continental republics the European type prevails.

All this indicates a culture, urban in character, even in countries which live by pasture and agriculture. Passing mention is due to the modern conveniences of life in most of the great cities: fine theatres and official buildings, efficient hygienic public services, model hospitals, well-equipped medical schools and sometimes model prisons. These world-wide things are not distinctively Latin American. In those countries they have been largely learnt from foreigners and constructed under foreign direction. And Latin-American cities have had the advantage of adopting them—sometimes slowly enough in respect of the less conspicuous but more essential matters—after they had been developed by experience elsewhere: and there are still strange contrasts between the great cities and some smaller places, even important provincial capitals. Indeed, until the general spread of the motor-car, road-making was strangely neglected: and a generation ago, in stepping off the pavement of great and flourishing cities, one stepped back a century or two into a rural world where primitive conditions, devoid of most of the graces of life, were regarded as the natural and even desirable state of things. In recent years, with improved communications and largely owing to the example of foreigners settled in those lands, country-house life and rural ways have followed a pleasanter and more civilized pattern.

One point demands emphasis. While western Europe laments

declining population, in Latin America population is increasing almost everywhere, not only through immigration but by natural growth in countries where immigrants are few but room abounds. Improved education and hygiene, unless they teach birth control, should further that increase; and in time these many millions should count for much. Those peoples are not wanting in intelligence or physical vigour. They believe in the future of their stock, and comparison of present conditions with those of fifty years ago justifies their confidence.

APPENDIX

Some recent incidents suggest an additional page concerning (1) dictatorships, and (2) inter-American relations.[1]

In Bolivia and Paraguay exhausting war led to autocracy: in both countries 'return to normality' is officially promised or begun. In Santo Domingo the *generalísimo* Trujillo, dictator since 1930, declined re-election as President in 1938, but accepted office as Minister for Foreign Affairs. It has been already hinted that many see, in the recent revival of autocracy, not so much military encroachment on civil functions as a movement of reform, the replacement of the semi-hereditary ring of placemen and place-hunters by the only men who have power to do it; that is to say soldiers, but citizen-soldiers, men of superior education, moved by a real desire to serve or save the State.

Opinions naturally vary about the probable results of the 1936 Peace Conference. Some say 'Just another Peace Pact. What will come after Roosevelt?' But more hopeful views are justified. Argentina, which in the Conference baulked much of the North American programme, and Peru, the most undisguised autocracy in Latin America, have both proposed Mr Cordell Hull for the Nobel Peace Prize. President Roosevelt is the candidate proposed by Cuba, where Batista commands 138 votes in a House of 162 Deputies.

The recent massacre of some hundreds of Haitian labourers on Dominican soil, followed by reprisals, must have had serious consequences, but for the discretion of the respective Governments. President Vincent of Haiti asked and obtained the good offices of Venezuela and of the United States in adjusting the matter. Again, the United States, Costa Rica and Venezuela recently offered their friendly aid in a Honduran-Nicaraguan frontier dispute. One of the powers which in one case accepted, and in the other case, offered, an amicable task, was the United States. These episodes indicate a community of action, hitherto rare, among American republics; and a cordiality which has little to do with forms of government or even with international engagements. Latin-American amity towards Europe is no less cordial. In these respects, the note of optimism, which concludes the last chapter, may here be repeated.

[1] The expropriation of Mexican oil-fields is too recent for historical treatment.

INDEX